UW Library BOOK SALE

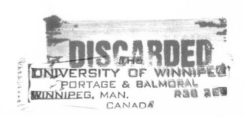

THE
ECOLOGICAL
APPROACH TO
VISUAL PERCEPTION

THE
ECOLOGICAL
APPROACH TO
VISUAL PERCEPTION

James J. Gibson
CORNELL UNIVERSITY

HOUGHTON MIFFLIN COMPANY   BOSTON

DALLAS   GENEVA, ILLINOIS   HOPEWELL, NEW JERSEY   PALO ALTO   LONDON

Printed in the U.S.A.

Library of Congress Catalog Card Number: 78–69585

ISBN: 0–395–27049–9

To my son and daughter
with pride
and to Eli, Michael, and Elizabeth
with love

CONTENTS

꘡

CONTENTS

PREFACE

Vision is a strange and wonderful business. I have been puzzling over its perplexities for 50 years. I used to suppose that the way to understand it was to learn what is accepted as true about the physics of light and the retinal image, to master the anatomy and physiology of the eye and the brain, and then to put it together into a theory of perception that could be tested by experiments. But the more I learned about physics, optics, anatomy, and visual physiology, the deeper the puzzles got. The experts in these sciences seemed confident that they could clear up the mysteries of vision eventually but only, I decided, because they had no real grasp of the perplexities.

Optical scientists, it appeared, knew about light as radiation but not about light considered as illumination. Anatomists knew about the eye as an organ but not about what it can do. Physiologists knew about the nerve cells in the retina and how they work but not how the visual system works. What they knew did not seem to be relevant. They could create holograms, prescribe spectacles, and cure diseases of the eye, and these are splendid accomplishments, but they could not explain vision.

Physics, optics, anatomy, and physiology describe facts, but not facts at a level appropriate for the study of perception. In this book I attempt a new level of description. It will be unfamiliar, and it is not fully developed, but it provides a fresh approach where the old perplexities do not block the way.

What are its antecedents? I am aware of my debt to the Gestalt psychologists, especially to Kurt Koffka. I have extended many of his ideas. I owe a great deal to the functionalists in American psychology, William James and E. B. Holt, for example. I was influenced in the thirties by Edward Tolman on the one hand, and by Leonard Troland on the other. The doctrine of stimuli and responses seems to me false, but I do not on that account reject behaviorism. Its influence is on the wane, no doubt, but a regression to mentalism would be worse. Why must we seek explanation in *either* Body or Mind? It is a false dichotomy. As for introspection, so-called, it can be done in the style of David Katz or Albert Michotte without falling into the error of elementarism.

I have learned a great deal from my contemporaries, Robert MacLeod, Ulric Neisser, Julian Hochberg, Ivo Kohler, Fabio Metelli, Hans Wallach, Ernst Gombrich, and especially Gunnar Johansson. My students, too, are my teachers, and since the listing in my last book, the principal influences are from James Farber, Thomas Lombardo, Harold Sedgewick, and Anthony Barrand. I also had a very early student who has become a contemporary as the years pass, Mary Henle. I thank all of them from the bottom of my heart.

There are several friends and colleagues who are pushing ahead with the ecological approach to psychology without having been my students. It would seem that they believe in it without persuasion. Robert Shaw, William Mace, Michael Turvey, and David Lee are scrambling through the underbrush along with me, and I am grateful for their company. So are Edward Reed and Rebecca Jones, who compiled the index.

This book has been written and revised in pieces over a period of ten years. So many helpful persons have read and criticized these pieces that I can only thank them as a group. But I am especially indebted to William Mace, Trinity College, Jacob Beck, University of Oregon, and Michael Turvey, University of Connecticut, for their criticisms of the final manuscript.

Above all there is the Susan Linn Sage Professor of Psychology at Cornell who worked very hard on this book, even if she did not write it. She is married to me, and we share responsibility for important decisions. Any errors in this book that remain are her fault as much as mine.

J.J.G.

THE
ECOLOGICAL
APPROACH TO
VISUAL PERCEPTION

INTRODUCTION

This is a book about how we see. How do we see the environment around us? How do we see its surfaces, their layout, and their colors and textures? How do we see where we are in the environment? How do we see whether or not we are moving and, if we are, where we are going? How do we see what things are good for? How do we see how to do things, to thread a needle or drive an automobile? Why do things look as they do?

This book is a sequel to *The Perception of the Visual World*, which came out in 1950. It is rather different, however, because my explanation of vision was then based on the retinal image, whereas it is now based on what I call the ambient optic array. I now believe we must take an ecological approach to the problems of perception.

We are told that vision depends on the eye, which is connected to the brain. I shall suggest that natural vision depends on the eyes in the head on a body supported by the ground, the brain being only the central organ of a complete visual system.

When no constraints are put on the visual system, we look around, walk up to something interesting and move around it so as to see it from all sides, and go from one vista to another. That is natural vision, and that is what this book is about.

The textbooks and handbooks assume that vision is simplest when the eye is held still, as a camera has to be, so that a picture is formed that can be transmitted to the brain. Vision is studied by first requiring the subject to fixate a point and then exposing momentarily a stimulus or a pattern of stimuli around the fixation point. I call this *snapshot vision*. If the exposure period is made longer, the eye will scan the pattern to which it is exposed, fixating the parts in succession, unless the subject is prohibited from doing so. I call this *aperture vision*, for it is a little like looking at the environment through a knothole in a fence. The investigator assumes that each fixation of the eye is analogous to an exposure of the film in a camera, so that what the brain gets is something like a sequence of snapshots.

The headrest of the laboratory prevents the observer from turning his head and looking around, which provides what I will call *ambient vision*. It also, of course, prevents him from getting up and walking around, which provides *ambulatory vision*. Are these forms of vision? I suggest they are; in fact, they are the kind of vision we need in life, not just pictorial depth perception. We need to see all the way around at a given point of observation and to take different points of observation. The crux of the matter is whether or not natural vision is compounded of units like the snapshot. I very much doubt that vision is simplest when the experimenter tries to make the eye work as if it were a photographic camera, even the kind that takes pictures in rapid succession.

Looking around and getting around do not fit into the standard idea of what visual perception is. But note that if an animal has eyes at all it swivels its head around and it goes from place to place. The single, frozen field of view provides only impoverished information about the world. The visual system did not evolve for this. The evidence suggests that visual awareness is in fact panoramic and does in fact persist during long acts of locomotion.

Part I of this book is about the environment to be perceived. Part II is about the information for perception. Part III is about the activity of perception. Finally, Part IV is about pictures and the special kinds of awareness that go with looking at them. Picture vision comes last because it can be understood only after we are clear about ambient vision and ambulatory vision.

First, the environment must be described, since what there is to be perceived has to be stipulated before one can even talk about perceiving it. This is not the world of physics but the world at the level of ecology. Second, the information available for perception in an illuminated medium must be described. This is not just light for stimulating receptors but the information in the light that can activate the system. Ecological optics is required instead of classical optics. Third (and only here do we come to what is called psychology proper), the process of perception must be described. This is not the processing of sensory inputs, however, but the extracting of invariants from the stimulus flux. The old idea that sensory inputs are converted into perceptions by operations of the mind is rejected. A radically new way of thinking about perception is proposed.

The ecological approach to perception was adopted in my book *The Senses Considered as Perceptual Systems*, which came out in 1966. Actually, it is a new approach to the whole field of psychology, for it involves rejecting the stimulus-response formula. This notion, borrowed from the so-called hard science of physiology, helped to get rid of the doctrine of the soul in psychology, but it never really worked. Neither mentalism on the one hand nor conditioned-response behaviorism on the other is good enough. What psychology needs is the kind of thinking that is beginning to be attempted in what is loosely called systems theory.

Environmentalism is a powerful movement nowadays, but in psychology it has generated more enthusiasm than discipline. There is no central core of theoretical concepts on which to base it. The right conceptual level has not yet been found. This book makes an effort to find the right level. A few psychologists, such as E. Brunswik

(1956) and R. G. Barker (1968), have moved in this direction, but none has ended with the sort of theory being put forward here.

The great virtue of the headrest, the bite-board, the exposure device, the tachistoscope, the darkroom with its points of light, and the laboratory with its carefully drawn pictorial stimuli was that they made it possible to study vision *experimentally*. The only way to be sure an observer sees what he says he does is to set up an experimental situation and check him out. Experimental verification can be trusted. These controls, however, made it seem as if snapshot vision and aperture vision were the whole of it, or at least the only vision that could be studied. But, on the contrary, natural vision *can* be studied experimentally. The experiments to be reported in Part III on perception involve the providing of optical information instead of the imposing of optical stimulation. It is not true that "the laboratory can never be like life." The laboratory *must* be like life!

It has to be admitted that the controlled displaying of information is vastly more difficult than the controlled applying of stimulation. Experimenters are just beginning to learn how to display information in a few scattered laboratories, at Cornell, Uppsala, the University of Connecticut, and Edinburgh. The experiments I will report in Part III are mostly my own, and the evidence, therefore, is scanty. Other students of information-based perception are at work, but the facts have not yet been accumulated. The vast quantity of experimental research in the textbooks and handbooks is concerned with snapshot vision, fixed-eye vision, or aperture vision, and it is not relevant. I do assure my readers that I know this body of research. I have even contributed to it. But they will have to take my word for it.

I am also asking the reader to suppose that the concept of space has nothing to do with perception. Geometrical space is a pure abstraction. Outer space can be visualized but cannot be seen. The cues for depth refer only to paintings, nothing more. The visual third dimension is a misapplication of Descartes's notion of three axes for a coordinate system.

The doctrine that we could not perceive the world around us unless we already had the concept of space is nonsense. It is quite the other way around: We could not conceive of empty space unless we could see the ground under our feet and the sky above. Space is a myth, a ghost, a fiction for geometers. All that sounds very strange, no doubt, but I urge the reader to entertain the hypothesis. For if you agree to abandon the dogma that "percepts without concepts are blind," as Kant put it, a deep theoretical mess, a genuine quagmire, will dry up. This is one of the main themes of the chapters that follow.

A whole set of interesting facts about retinal photographic vision will not be described in this book—facts about vision with a fixed eye or vision with a shutter; such facts as the blind spot, the entoptic phenomena, the gaps in the visual field (scotomas), the afterimages of prolonged fixation, the tests for so-called acuity, the examining of the retina with an ophthalmoscope, the symptoms of eye disease, and the prescribing of corrective spectacles. These are the facts of ophthalmology and optometry and the psychophysiology of vision at the level of cells.

These facts all depend on the subject's being willing to hold his eye fixed like a camera. They are perfectly good facts, and they have their place. They are much better known than the facts with which this book is concerned, and their scientific status is such that those persons who specialize in them assume with confidence that physical and physiological optics provide the only basis for visual perception. But those persons have no conception of the perplexities to which their assumption leads. And there is a better basis for visual perception, as I shall try to show.

ONE

THE ENVIRONMENT TO BE PERCEIVED

ONE

THE ANIMAL
AND
THE ENVIRONMENT

In this book, *environment* will refer to the surroundings of those organisms that perceive and behave, that is to say, animals. The environment of plants, organisms that lack sense organs and muscles, is not relevant in the study of perception and behavior. We shall treat the vegetation of the world as animals do, as if it were lumped together with the inorganic minerals of the world, with the physical, chemical, and geological environment. Plants in general are not animate; they do not move about, they do not behave, they lack a nervous system, and they do not have sensations. In these respects they are like the objects of physics, chemistry, and geology.

The world can be described at different levels, and one can choose which level to begin with. Biology begins with the division between the nonliving and the living. But psychology begins with the division between the inanimate and the animate, and this is where we choose to begin. The animals themselves can be divided in different ways. Zoology classifies them by heredity and anatomy, by phylum, class, order, genus, and species, but psychology can classify them by their way of life, as predatory or preyed upon, terrestrial or aquatic, crawling or walking, flying or nonflying, and arboreal or ground-living. We are more interested in ways of life than in heredity.

The environment consists of the *surroundings* of animals. Let us observe that in one sense the surroundings of a single animal are the same as the surroundings of all animals but that in another sense the surroundings of a single animal are different from those of any other animal. These two senses of the term can be troublesome and may cause confusion. The apparent contradiction can be resolved, but let us defer the problem until later. (The solution lies in the fact that animals are mobile.) For the present it is enough to note that the surroundings of *any* animal include other animals as well as the plants and the nonliving things. The former are just as much parts of its environment as the inanimate parts. For any animal needs to distinguish not only the substances and objects of its material environment but also the other animals and the differences between them. It cannot afford to confuse prey with predator, own-species with another species, or male with female.

THE MUTUALITY OF ANIMAL
AND ENVIRONMENT

The fact is worth remembering because it is often neglected that the words *animal* and *environment* make an inseparable pair. Each term implies the other. No animal could exist without an environment surrounding it. Equally, although not so obvious, an environment implies an animal (or at least an organism) to be surrounded. This means that the surface of the earth, millions of years ago before life developed on it, was not an environment, properly speaking. The earth was a physical reality, a part of the universe, and the subject matter of geology. It was a potential environment, prerequisite to the evolution of life on this planet. We might agree to call it a world, but it was not an environment.

The mutuality of animal and environment is not implied by physics and the physical sciences. The basic concepts of space, time, matter, and energy do not lead naturally to the organism-environment concept or to the concept of a species and its habitat. Instead, they seem to lead to the idea of an animal as an extremely complex object of the physical world. The animal is thought of as a highly organized *part* of the physical world but still a part and still an object. This way of thinking neglects the fact that the animal-object is surrounded in a special way, that an environment is ambient for a living object in a different way from the way that a set of objects is ambient for a physical object. The term *physical environment* is, therefore, apt to get us mixed up, and it will usually be avoided in this book.

Every animal is, in some degree at least, a perceiver and a behaver. It is sentient and animate, to use old-fashioned terms. It is a perceiver *of* the environment and a behaver *in* the environment. But this is not to say that it perceives the world of physics and behaves in the space and time of physics.

THE DIFFERENCE BETWEEN
THE ANIMAL ENVIRONMENT AND
THE PHYSICAL WORLD

The world of physics encompasses everything from atoms through terrestrial objects to galaxies. These things exist at different levels of size that go to almost unimaginable extremes. The physical world of atoms and their ultimate particles is measured at the level of millionths of a millimeter and less. The astronomical world of stars and galaxies is measured at the level of light-years and more. Neither of these extremes is an environment. The size-level at which the environment exists is the intermediate one that is measured in millimeters and meters. The ordinary familiar things of the earth are of this size—actually a narrow band of sizes relative to the far extremes. The sizes of animals, similarly, are limited to the intermediate terrestrial scale. The size of the smallest animal is an appreciable fraction of a millimeter, and that of the largest is only a few meters.

The masses of animals, likewise, are measured within the range of milligrams to kilograms, not at the extremes of the scale, and for good physiological reasons. A cell must have a minimum of substances in order to permit biochemical reactions; living animals cannot exceed a maximum mass of cells if they are all to be nourished and if they are to be mobile. In short, the sizes and masses of things in the environment are comparable with those of the animals.

UNITS OF THE ENVIRONMENT

Physical reality has structure at all levels of metric size from atoms to galaxies. Within the intermediate band of terrestrial sizes, the environment of animals and men is itself structured at various levels of size. At the level of kilometers, the earth is shaped by mountains and hills. At the level of meters, it is formed by boulders and cliffs and canyons, and also by trees. It is still more finely structured at the level of millimeters by pebbles and crystals and particles of soil, and also by leaves and grass blades and plant cells. All these things are structural units of the terrestrial environment, what we loosely call the forms or shapes of our familiar world.

Now, with respect to these units, an essential point of theory must be emphasized. The smaller units are embedded in the larger units by what I will call *nesting*. For example, canyons are nested within mountains; trees are nested within canyons; leaves are nested within trees; and cells are nested within leaves. There are forms within forms both up and down the scale of size. Units are nested within larger units. Things are components of other things. They would constitute a hierarchy except that this hierarchy is not categorical but full of transitions and overlaps. Hence, for the terrestrial environment, there is no special proper unit in terms of which it can be analyzed once and for all. There are no atomic units of the world considered as an environment. Instead, there are subordinate and superordinate units. The unit you choose for describing the environment depends on the level of the environment you choose to describe.

The size-levels of the world emphasized by modern physics, the atomic and the cosmic, are inappropriate for the psychologist. We are concerned here with things at the ecological level, with the habitat of animals and men, because we all behave with respect to things we can look at and feel, or smell and taste, and events we can listen to. The sense organs of animals, the perceptual systems (Gibson, 1966b), are not capable of detecting atoms or galaxies. Within their limits, however, these perceptual systems are still capable of detecting a certain range of things and events. One can see a mountain if it is far enough away and a grain of sand if it is close enough. That fact is sufficiently wonderful in itself to deserve study, and it is one of the facts that this book will try to explain.

The explanation of how we human observers, at least some of us, can *visualize* an atom or a galaxy even if we cannot *see* one will not be attempted at this stage of the inquiry. It is not so much a problem of perception as it is of thinking, and there will be more about this later. We must first consider how we can perceive the environment—how we apprehend the same things that our human ancestors did before they learned about atoms and galaxies. We are concerned with direct perception, not so much with the indirect perception got by using microscopes and telescopes or by photographs and pictures, and still less with the kind of apprehension got by speech and writing. These higher-order modes of apprehension will only be considered in Part IV of this book, at the end.

UNITS OF THE GROUND SURFACE

The literal *basis* of the terrestrial environment is the ground, the underlying surface of support that tends to be on the average flat—that is to say, a plane—and also level, or perpendicular to gravity. And the ground itself is structured at various levels of metric size, these units being nested within one another. The fact to be noted now, since it is important for the theory of perspective in Part II, is that these units tend to be repeated over the whole surface of the earth. Grains of sand tend to be of the same size everywhere, and so do pebbles and rocks. Blades of grass are all more or less similar to one another, and so are clumps of grass and bushes. These natural units are not, of course, perfectly uniform like the man-made tiles of a pavement. Nevertheless, even if their repetition is not metrically regular, it is stochastically regular, that is to say, regular in a probabilistic way. In short, the component units of the ground do not get smaller as one goes north, for instance. They tend to be evenly spaced; and if they are scattered, they tend to be evenly scattered.

THE TIME SCALE OF THE ENVIRONMENT: EVENTS

Another difference between the environment to be described and the world of physics is in the temporal scale of the process and events we choose to consider. The duration of processes at the level of the universe may be measured in millions of years, and the duration of processes at the level of the atom may be measured in millionths of a second. But the duration of processes in the environment is measured only in years and seconds. The various life spans of the animals themselves fall within this range. The changes that are perceived, those on which acts of behavior depend, are neither

Figure 1.1
The structure of the terrestrial earth as seen from above.
In this aerial photograph only the large-scale features of the terrain are shown. (Photo by Grant Heilman)

extremely slow nor extremely rapid. Human observers cannot perceive the erosion of a mountain, but they can detect the fall of a rock. They can notice the displacement of a chair in a room but not the shift of an electron in an atom.

The same thing holds for frequencies as for durations. The very slow cycles of the world are imperceptible, and so are the very rapid cycles. But at the level of a mechanical clock, each motion of the pendulum can be seen and each click of the escapement can be heard. The rate of change, the transition, is within the limits of perceptibility.

In this book, emphasis will be placed on events, cycles, and changes at the terrestrial level of the physical world. The changes we shall study are those that occur in the environment. I shall talk about changes, events, and sequences of events but not about time as such. The flow of abstract empty time, however useful this concept may be to the physicist, has no reality for an animal. We perceive not time but processes, changes, sequences, or so I shall assume. The human awareness of clock-time, socialized time, is another matter.

Just as physical reality has structure at all levels of metric size, so it has structure at all levels of metric duration. Terrestrial processes occur at the intermediate level of duration. They are the natural units of sequential structure. And once more it is important to realize that smaller units are nested within larger units. There are events within events, as there are forms within forms, up to the yearly shift of the path of the sun across the sky and down to the breaking of a twig. And hence there are no elementary units of temporal structure. You can describe the events of the environment at various levels.

The acts of animals themselves, like the events of the environment they perceive, can be described at various levels, as subordinate and superordinate acts. And the duration of animal acts is comparable to the duration of environmental events. There are no elementary atomic responses.

The natural units of the terrestrial environment and the natural units of terrestrial events should not be confused with the *metrical* units of space and time. The latter are arbitrary and conventional. The former are unitary in one sense of the term, and the latter are unitary in a quite different sense. A single whole is not the same as a standard of measurement.

PERMANENCE AND CHANGE OF THE LAYOUT

Space and time will not often be referred to in this book, but a great deal will be said about permanence and change. Consider the shape of the terrestrial environment, or what may be called its *layout*. It will be assumed that the layout of the environment is both permanent in some respects and changing in some other respects. A living room, for example, is relatively permanent with respect to the layout of floor, walls, and ceiling, but every now and then the arrangement of the furniture in the room is changed. The shape of a growing child is relatively permanent for some features and changing for others. An observer can recognize the same room on different occasions while perceiving the change of arrangement, or the same child at different ages while noticing her growth. The permanence underlies the change.

Permanence is relative, of course; that is, it depends on whether you mean persistence over a day, a year, or a millennium. Almost nothing is forever permanent; nothing is either immutable or mutable. So it is better to speak of *persistence* under change. The "permanent objects" of the world, which are of so much concern to psychologists and philosophers, are actually only objects that persist for a very long time.

The abstract notion of invariance and variance in mathematics is related to what is meant by persistence and change in the environment. There are variants and invariants in any transformation, constants and variables. Some properties are conserved and others not conserved. The same words are not used by all writers (for example, Piaget, 1969), but there is a common core of meaning in all such pairs of terms. The point to be noted is that for persistence and change, for invariant and variant, each term of the pair is reciprocal to the other.

PERSISTENCE IN THE ENVIRONMENT

The persistence of the geometrical layout of the environment depends in part on the kind of substance composing it and its rigidity or resistance to deformation. A solid substance is not readily changed in shape. A semisolid substance is more easily changed in shape. A liquid substance takes on whatever may be the shape of its solid container. The upper surface of a liquid substance tends to the ideal shape of a plane perpendicular to gravity, but this is easily disturbed, as when waves form. When we speak of the permanent layout of the environment, therefore, we refer mainly to the solid substances. The liquids of the world, the streams and oceans, are shaped by the solids, and as for the gaseous matter of the world, the air, it is not shaped at all. I will argue that the air is actually a *medium* for terrestrial animals.

When a solid substance with a constant shape melts, as a block of ice melts, we say that the object has ceased to exist. This way of speaking is ecological, not physical, for there is physical conservation of matter and mass despite the change from solid to liquid. The same would be true if a shaped object disintegrated, changing from solid to granular. The object does not persist, but the matter does. Ecology calls this a *nonpersistence*, a destruction of the object, whereas physics calls it a mere *change of state.* Both assertions are correct, but the former is more relevant to the behavior of animals and children. Physics has sometimes been taken to imply that when a liquid mass has evaporated and the substance has been wholly dispersed in the air, or when an object has been consumed by fire, *nothing* has really gone out of existence. But this is an error. Even if terrestrial matter cannot be annihilated, a resistant light-reflecting surface can, and this is what counts for perception.

Going out of existence, cessation or destruction, is a kind of environmental event and one that is extremely important to perceive. When something is burned up, or dissolved, or shattered, it *disappears.* But it disappears in special ways that have recently been investigated at Cornell (Gibson, 1968*a*). It does not disappear in the way that a thing does when it becomes hidden or goes around a corner. Instead, the form of the object may be optically dispersed or dissipated, in the manner of smoke. The visual basis of this kind of perception will be further considered in Part II on ecological optics.

The environment normally manifests some things that persist and some that do not, some features that are invariant and some that are variant. A wholly invariant environment, unchanging in all parts and motionless, would be completely rigid and obviously would no longer be an environment. In fact, there would be neither animals nor plants. At the other extreme, an environment that was changing in all parts and was wholly variant, consisting only of swirling clouds of matter, would also not be an environment. In both extreme cases there would be space, time, matter, and energy, but there would be no habitat.

The fact of an environment that is mainly rigid but partly nonrigid, mainly motionless but partly movable, a world that is both changeless in many respects and changeable in others but is neither dead at one extreme nor chaotic at the other, is of great importance for our inquiry. This fact will become evident later when we talk about the geometry of the environment and its transformations.

On Persistence and Change

Our failure to understand the concurrence of persistence and change at the ecological level is probably connected with an old idea—the *atomic theory of persistence and change,* which asserts that what persists in the world are atoms and what changes in the world are the positions of atoms, or their arrangement. This is still an influential assumption in modern physics and chemistry, although it goes back to Democritus and the Greek thinkers who followed him. There will be more about the atomistic assumption in Chapter 6 on events and how they are perceived.

MOTION IN THE ENVIRONMENT

The motions of things in the environment are of a different order from the motions of bodies in space. The fundamental laws of motion hold for celestial mechanics, but events on earth do not have the elegant simplicity of the motions of planets. Events on earth begin and end abruptly instead of being continuous. Pure velocity and acceleration, either linear or angular, are rarely observable except in machines. And there are very few ideal elastic bodies except for billiard balls. The terrestrial world is mostly made of surfaces, not of bodies in space. And these surfaces often flow or undergo stretching, squeezing, bending, and breaking in ways of enormous mechanical complexity.

So different, in fact, are environmental motions from those studied by Isaac Newton that it is best to think of them as changes of structure rather than changes of position of elementary bodies, changes of form rather than of point locations, or changes in the layout rather than motions in the usual meaning of the term.

SUMMARY

The environment of animals and men is what they perceive. The environment is not the same as the physical world, if one means by that the world described by physics.

The observer and his environment are complementary. So are the set of observers and their common environment.

The components and events of the environment fall into natural units. These units are nested. They should not be confused with the metric units of space and time.

The environment persists in some respects and changes in other respects. The most radical change is going out of existence or coming into existence.

TWO

MEDIUM, SUBSTANCES, SURFACES

According to classical physics, the universe consists of bodies in space. We are tempted to assume, therefore, that we live in a physical world consisting of bodies in space and that what we *perceive* consists of objects in space. But this is very dubious. The terrestrial environment is better described in terms of a *medium, substances,* and the *surfaces* that separate them.

THE MEDIUM

Let us begin by noting that our planet consists mainly of earth, water, and air—a solid, a liquid, and a gas. The earth forms a substratum; the water is formed by the substratum into oceans, lakes, and streams; and the formless gases of the air make a layer of atmosphere above the earth and the water. The interface between any two of these three states of matter—solid, liquid, and gas—constitutes a surface. The earth-water interface at the bottom of a lake is one such, the water-air interface at the top is another, and the earth-air interface is a third—the most important of all surfaces for terrestrial animals. This is the *ground.* It is the ground of their perception and behavior, both literally and figuratively. It is their surface of support.

One characteristic of a gas or a liquid as contrasted with a solid is the fact that a detached solid body can move through it without resistance. Air is "insubstantial" and so is water, more or less. It thus affords locomotion to an animate body. A gas or a liquid, then, is a *medium* for animal locomotion. Air is a better medium for locomotion than water because it offers less resistance. It does not require the streamlined anatomy needed by a fish for rapid movements.

Another characteristic of a gas or liquid medium is that it is generally transparent, transmitting light, whereas a solid is generally opaque, absorbing or reflecting light. A homogeneous medium thus affords vision. The way in which it does so will be described in Part II. For the present it is sufficient to observe that a terrestrial medium is a region in which light not only is transmitted but also *reverberates,* that is, bounces

16

back and forth between surfaces at enormous velocity and reaches a sort of steady state. The light has to be continually replenished from a source of illumination because some of it is absorbed by the substances of the environment, but the reverberating flux of light brings about the condition we call *illumination*. Illumination "fills" the medium in the sense that there is *ambient* light at any point, that is, light coming to the point from all directions. Ambient light, as we shall see, is not to be confused with radiant light.

A third characteristic of air or water is that it transmits vibrations or pressure waves outward from a mechanical event, a source of sound waves. It thus makes possible hearing what we call the sound; more exactly, it permits listening to the vibratory event. (The solid earth also transmits pressure waves, to be sure, but we do not ordinarily call them sound waves unless we are thinking in terms of physics. In physics a medium is any substance, including solids, that transmits waves.)

A fourth characteristic is the fact that a medium of air or water allows rapid chemical diffusion whereas the earth does not. Specifically, it permits molecules of a foreign substance to diffuse or dissolve outward from a source whenever it is volatile or soluble. In this way, the medium affords "smelling" of the source, by which I mean detecting of the substance at a distance.

Let us next observe that animal locomotion is not usually aimless but is guided or controlled—by light if the animal can see, by sound if the animal can hear, and by odor if the animal can smell. Because of illumination the animal can see things; because of sound it can hear things; because of diffusion it can smell things. The medium thus contains information about things that reflect light, vibrate, or are volatile. By detecting this information, the animal guides and controls locomotion.

If we understand the notion of medium, I suggest, we come to an entirely new way of thinking about perception and behavior. The medium in which animals can move about (and in which objects can *be* moved about) is at the same time the medium for light, sound, and odor coming from sources in the environment. An enclosed medium can be "filled" with light, with sound, and even with odor. Any point in the medium is a possible point of observation for any observer who can look, listen, or sniff. And these points of observation are continuously connected to one another by paths of possible locomotion. Instead of geometrical points and lines, then, we have points of observation and lines of locomotion. As the observer moves from point to point, the optical information, the acoustic information, and the chemical information change accordingly. Each potential point of observation in the medium is unique in this respect. The notion of a medium, therefore, is not the same as the concept of space inasmuch as the points in space are not unique but equivalent to one another.

All these facts about moving bodies and about the transmission of light, sound, and odor in a medium are *consistent* with physics, mechanics, optics, acoustics, and chemistry, but they are facts of higher order that have never been made explicit by those sciences and have gone unrecognized. The science of the environment has its own facts.

Another important characteristic of a medium, it should now be noted, is that it contains oxygen and permits breathing. The principles of respiration are the same in the water as in the air; oxygen is absorbed and carbon dioxide is emitted after the burning of fuel in the tissues. This ceaseless chemical exchange of substance is truly the "flame of life." The animal must breathe, whether by gills or by lungs. It must breathe all the time and everywhere it goes. Thus, the medium needs to be relatively constant and relatively homogeneous.

Both the air and the water do afford breathing. The amount of oxygen in the air has not departed much from 21 percent in countless ages. The amount of dissolved oxygen in the water, although variable, tends to be sufficient. Animals have been able to rely on oxygen, and this is why evolution could proceed. Similarly, both the air and the water tend to be homogeneous, although fresh water differs from salt water. From place to place, the composition of air changes very little and the composition of water changes very gradually, for the temporary gradients that arise are dissipated by winds and currents. There are no sharp *transitions* in a medium, no boundaries between one volume and another, that is to say, no surfaces. This homogeneity is crucial. It is what permits light waves and sound waves to travel outward from a source in spherical wave fronts. Indeed, it is what makes a chemical emanation from a source foreign to the medium itself, and thus capable of being smelled.

Finally, a sixth characteristic of a medium for animal life is that it has an intrinsic polarity of up and down. Gravity pulls downward, not upward. Radiant light comes from above, not below, from the sky, not the substratum, and this is as true in the water as in the atmosphere. Because of gravity, water pressure and air pressure increase downward and decrease upward. The medium is not isotropic, as the physicist says, along this dimension. Hence it is that a medium has an *absolute* axis of reference, the vertical axis. Even the two horizontal axes of reference are not wholly arbitrary, for they depend on sunrise and sunset. This fact reveals another difference between medium and space, for in space the three reference axes are arbitrary and can be chosen at will.

THE PROPERTIES OF THE ATMOSPHERE

To sum up, the characteristics of an environmental medium are that it affords respiration or breathing; it permits locomotion; it can be filled with illumination so as to permit vision; it allows detection of vibrations and detection of diffusing emanations; it is homogeneous; and finally, it has an absolute axis of reference, up and down. All these offerings of nature, these possibilities or opportunities, these *affordances* as I will call them, are invariant. They have been strikingly constant throughout the whole evolution of animal life.

EVENTS IN THE ATMOSPHERE

The atmospheric medium, unlike the underwater medium, is subject to certain kinds of change that we call weather. Sometimes there are drops or droplets of water in the air, rain or fog. Annually, in some latitudes of the earth, the air becomes cold and the water turns to ice. Occasionally the air currents flow strongly, as in storms and hurricanes. Rain, wind, snow, and cold, the latter increasing toward the poles of the earth, prevent the air from being perfectly homogeneous, uniform, and unchanging. The changes are rarely so extreme as to kill off the animals, but they do necessitate various kinds of adaptation and all sorts of behavioral adjustments, such as hibernation, migration, shelter-building, and clothes-wearing.

SUBSTANCES

Consider next the portion of the environment that does *not* freely transmit light or odor and that does *not* permit the motion of bodies and the locomotion of animals. Matter in the solid or semisolid state is said to be *substantial*, whereas matter in the gaseous state is *insubstantial*, and matter in the liquid state is in between these extremes. Substances in this meaning of the term are more or less rigid. That is, they are more or less resistant to deformation, more or less impenetrable by solid bodies, and more or less permanent in shape. They are usually opaque to light. And the substantial portion of the environment is heterogeneous unlike the medium, which tends to be homogeneous.

The substances of the environment differ in chemical composition. As everybody knows, there is a limited set of chemical elements, ninety or a hundred, and a much larger set of chemical compounds. More important for our purposes is the fact that there is an unlimited set of *mixtures* of elements and compounds, some being homogeneous mixtures and some not. The latter, the heterogeneous mixtures, may be called *aggregates*. The air is a homogeneous mixture of oxygen and nitrogen with carbon dioxide; the water is a homogeneous mixture of H_2O with dissolved oxygen and salts. But the earth, together with the "furniture" of the earth, is a heterogeneous aggregate of different substances.

Rock, soil, sand, mud, clay, oil, tar, wood, minerals, metal, and above all, the various tissues of plants and animals are examples of environmental substances. Each of these has a more or less specific composition, but almost none is a chemical compound, a pure chemical of the sort that is found on the shelves of chemistry laboratories. A few substances such as clay are amorphous, that is, lacking in structural components, but most of them are geometrical aggregates, that is, they are made of crystals and clumps, of cells and organs, of structures within structures. These substances rather than chemicals are important for animals, for they must distinguish these in order to live.

What a substance is composed of can be analyzed at various levels. There is the compounding of chemical elements, but there are also the mixing of compounds and the complex aggregating of mixtures. When we talk about the composition of a substance, what it is made of, we must keep in mind the level of analysis that is appropriate to the problem being considered.

Why animals need to distinguish among the different substances of the environment is obvious. The substances have different biochemical, physiological, and behavioral effects on the animal. Some are nutritive, some are nonnutritive, and some are toxic. And it is very useful for a hungry animal to be able to distinguish the edible from the inedible substances at a distance, by vision or smell, rather than relying only on contact sensitivity, taste or touch.

Substances differ in all sorts of ways. They differ in *hardness* or rigidity. They differ in *viscosity*, which is technically defined as resistance to flow. They differ in *density*, defined as mass per unit volume. They differ in *cohesiveness* or strength, that is, resistance to breaking. They differ in *elasticity*, the tendency to regain the previous shape after deformation. They differ in *plasticity*, the tendency to hold the subsequent shape after deformation. Presumably all these properties of substances are explainable by the microphysical forces of attraction among molecules, but they do not have to be analyzed at this level in order to be facts. Flint and clay were distinguishable substances for our primitive, tool-making ancestors long before men understood chemistry. So were wood, bone, and fiber.

Substances considered as compounds differ in their susceptibility to chemical reactions, in their degree of solubility in water, in their degree of volatility in air, and thus in their chemical stability or resistance to chemical transformation. And they also differ, as will be emphasized later, in the degree to which they absorb light; a substance such as coal absorbs most of the light falling on it, whereas chalk, for example, absorbs very little of the light falling on it.

The substances of the environment change, of course, both structurally and chemically. Some solids dissolve, and their surfaces cease to exist. Leaves shrivel, and plants decompose. Animals decay and return their substances to the environment. Metal rusts, and even the hardest rock eventually disintegrates into soil. The cycles of such changes are studied in ecology. Their causes at the molecular level of analysis are chemical and physical; they are governed by microphysical forces and by chemical reactions of the sort that chemists isolate and control in test tubes. But these changes also occur at a *molar* level of analysis as contrasted with the molecular level, and then they are environmental events, not simply physicochemical events. Large-scale chemical reactions are visible. The event we call *combustion* or fire is large-scale rapid oxidation. This is of enormous importance to animals, and they look out for it. But other forms of oxidation are too slow to be easily observed, the rusting of iron, for example.

A great many substances of the environment, of course, do *not* change either structurally or chemically, and the nonchange is even more important than the change. It is chiefly on this account that the environment is persistent. But also, even when substances change, they are often restored by processes of growth, compensation, and restitution so that an equilibrium or steady state arises and there is invariance despite change—an invariance of higher order than mere physicochemical persistence.

THE STATUS OF WATER: MEDIUM
OR SUBSTANCE?

We must decide how we are to consider water. It is the medium for aquatic animals, not a substance, but it is a substance for terrestrial animals, not the medium. It is insubstantial when taken with reference to the aquatic environment but substantial when taken with reference to the terrestrial environment. This difficulty, however, does not invalidate the distinction but only makes it depend on the kind of animal being considered. The animal and its environment, remember, are reciprocal terms. The mediums of water and air have much in common, but they are sufficiently different to make it necessary hereafter to concentrate on the environment of terrestrial animals like ourselves. For us, water falls into the category of substances, not medium.

The underwater medium is bounded both above and below, by a surface of water-to-air and a surface of water-to-mud. The atmospheric medium is bounded only below, by a surface of air-to-earth (or air-to-water), and it has no definite upper boundary. The fish is buoyed up by its medium and needs no surface of support. Our kind of animal must hold itself up off the ground with effort, working to maintain posture and equilibrium. The fish is cradled in the water and is never in any danger of falling down or falling off. We are always in such danger. The fish need never make contact with the bottom. But we cannot for long avoid contact with the earth, and only upon the earth can we come to rest. All animals—in the water, on the ground, or in the air—must orient to gravity in order to behave, that is, they must keep right side up (Gibson, 1966b, Ch. 4), but this basic orienting activity is different in the fish, the quadruped, and the bird.

Some animals, to be sure, can get about in both water and air: the amphibians.

They live an interesting life, and how they can perceive in either environment is a problem very much worth study. The interface between air and water is not the barrier for them that it is for us. Humans can temporarily wear aqualungs, but not for long. We are terrestrial animals. Hereafter, I will concentrate on the terrestrial environment of animals like ourselves.

We will also leave out of account very small animals that live in the soil. Earthworms and microorganisms actually get about in the spaces between solid particles that contain both air and water, so they do not constitute exceptions to the general rule relating medium and substances.

CONCLUSIONS ABOUT SUBSTANCES

To summarize what has been said about substances, they differ in both chemical and physical composition. They are compounded and aggregated in extremely complicated ways and thus do not tend toward homogeneity, as the medium does. They are structured in a hierarchy of nested units. And these different components have very different possibilities for the behavior of animals, for eating, for resisting locomotion, for manipulation, and for manufacture.

SURFACES AND THE ECOLOGICAL LAWS OF SURFACES

For describing the environment, we have now established the triad of medium, substances, and surfaces, allowing for both persistence and change. The medium is separated from the substances of the environment by *surfaces*. Insofar as substances persist, their surfaces persist. All surfaces have a certain *layout*, as I will call it, and the layout also tends to persist. The persistence of the layout depends on the resistance of the substance to change. If a substance is changed into the gaseous state, it is no longer substantial and the surface together with its layout ceases to exist. These statements provide a new way of describing the environment.

For our purposes, this description is superior to the accepted description in terms of space, time, matter and material bodies, the forms of these bodies, and their motions. It is novel, but only in the sense that it has never been explicitly stated. Everything in the above paragraph has long been known implicitly by practical men—the surveyors of the earth, the builders, and the designers of the environment. It is *tacit* knowledge (Polanyi, 1966). This description is superior because it is appropriate to the study of the perception and behavior of animals and men as a function of what the environment affords, that is, to psychology.

The above description, to be complete, should include the reverberating flux of light in the medium. The way in which light is absorbed and reflected at surfaces and the way this action depends on the composition of the substances should also be considered. At the ecological level of size, surfaces soak up or throw back the illumination falling upon them, although at the atomic level of size, matter and light energy are said to *interact*. Substances are substantial with respect to light as much as they are substantial with respect to force. They resist the penetration of light as they resist the penetration of a moving body. And substances differ among themselves in the former respect as much as they do in the latter.

In our concern with surfaces and their purely geometrical layout, we must not forget that the air is filled with sunlight during the day and that some illumination always remains, even during the night. This fact, too, is an invariant of nature. Light comes from the sky and becomes ambient in the air. This is what makes persisting surfaces potentially visible as well as potentially tangible. How they are actually seen by animals with eyes is the problem of this book (although admittedly we are arriving at the problem only by slow stages). A *potentially visible surface* is one that could be looked at from some place in the medium where an animal *might* be. Nothing is implied about the actual stimulation of an eye, not yet. And no slightest reference is made to sensations of vision.

No mention has yet been made of luminous surfaces such as very hot bodies that emit light, or of flat surfaces of transparent substances such as glass that transmit light with refraction, or of polished flat surfaces such as mirrors that reflect light "regularly." Emission, absorption, transmission, refraction, and diffraction refer to abstract laws of physical and geometrical optics. It may be possible to combine them in complex ways to explain the gross facts of illuminated terrestrial surfaces, but that possibility is something to be considered later.

Why, in the triad of medium, substances, and surfaces, are surfaces so important? The surface is where most of the action is. The surface is where light is reflected or absorbed, not the interior of the substance. The surface is what touches the animal, not the interior. The surface is where chemical reaction mostly takes place. The surface is where vaporization or diffusion of substances into the medium occurs. And the surface is where vibrations of the substances are transmitted into the medium.

A formulation of what might be called the *ecological laws of surfaces* would be useful. The following laws are proposed, without any claim of completeness. The list will serve, however, to focus the discussion, and it also provides an outline of what is to follow. The laws are not independent of one another and must be considered in combination.

1. All persisting substances have surfaces, and all surfaces have a layout.
2. Any surface has resistance to deformation, depending on the *viscosity* of the substance.

3. Any surface has resistance to disintegration, depending on the *cohesion* of the substance.
4. Any surface has a characteristic texture, depending on the *composition* of the substance. It generally has both a layout texture and a pigment texture.
5. Any surface has a characteristic shape, or large-scale layout.
6. A surface may be strongly or weakly illuminated, in light or in shade.
7. An illuminated surface may absorb either much or little of the illumination falling on it.
8. A surface has a characteristic reflectance, depending on the substance.
9. A surface has a characteristic distribution of the reflectance ratios of the different wavelengths of the light, depending on the substance. This property is what I will call its color, in the sense that different distributions constitute different colors.

SUBSTANCE, SURFACE, LAYOUT, AND PERSISTENCE

The first law above merely summarizes what has been emphasized repeatedly about the substantial persisting surfaces of the environment. Combined with the second law, it explains why the level terrestrial surface, the ground, offers support for animals. They can crawl on the earth as a lizard or a human infant does, or they can walk or run on it because it is solid. But the law of layout also applies to surfaces like walls and obstacles that are barriers to locomotion—surfaces with which they will collide unless they stop short. A surface can be laid out parallel to gravity as well as perpendicular to it, so that surfaces can surround them as well as support them. A surface can even be held up by walls so as to be above them, that is, there can be a roof over their heads as well as a floor under their feet. A medium can be more or less enclosed by surfaces, and a cave, or a burrow, or a house is such an enclosure.

RESISTANCE TO DEFORMATION

The second law allows for variation in the solidity of surfaces. It says that substances vary in the degree to which they resist deformation, from rigid to plastic to semisolid to liquid. When measured in terms of resistance to *flow*, this variable is called *viscosity*. The more fluid or flowing the substance, the more penetrable the surface, and the more changeable (less permanent) the layout. This law implies that the bog or swamp offers practically no support for standing or walking to heavy animals, and that the pond or lake offers no support. There will be more about the perception of a surface of support by terrestrial animals in Chapter 9.

With respect to obstacles, the second law implies that the surfaces of flexible substances are yielding or can be pushed aside, whereas the surfaces of rigid substances cannot. With respect to fluid substances, this law implies that fluid surfaces are polymorphic in the extreme; they can be poured, spilled, and splashed, and they can be smeared, painted, and dabbled in. The human infant explores these possibilities with great zest; the adult artisan has learned to perceive and take advantage of them.

RESISTANCE TO DISINTEGRATION

The third law allows for variation in the degree to which surfaces are breakable or go to pieces. The surface of a viscoelastic substance will stretch and remain continuous under the application of a force, whereas the surface of a rigid substance may be disrupted and become discontinuous. This distinction, incidentally, is fundamental to *topology*, the branch of mathematics sometimes called "rubber sheet geometry," in which it is assumed that a plane (actually a surface) can be bent or curved or stretched or compressed but cannot be torn.

The second and third laws explain why clay can be pressed into the shape of a pot, whereas flint has to be chipped into the shape of an axe. And they explain why the pot and the axe become useless when broken. These laws imply that a house of glass is a poor place to live and the person who lives in one should certainly not throw stones.

CHARACTERISTIC TEXTURE

The fourth law concerns what I call *texture*, which might be thought of as the structure of a surface, as distinguished from the structure of the substance underlying the surface. We are talking about the relatively fine structure of the environment at the size-level around centimeters and millimeters. Surfaces of rock, or of plowed soil, or of grass are aggregated of different units—crystals, clumps, and grass blades, respectively—but these units are nested within larger units.

The texture of a surface arises from two main facts: first, a natural substance is seldom *homogeneous* but is more or less aggregated of different homogeneous substances; and second, it is seldom *amorphous* but is more or less aggregated of crystals and chunks and pieces of the same stuff. Hence, the surface of a natural substance is also neither homogeneous nor amorphous but has both a chemical and a physical texture; it is generally both conglomerated and corrugated. It has what I will call a *pigment texture* and a *layout texture*. It is generally both speckled and rough.

This says that a perfectly homogeneous and perfectly smooth surface is an abstract

Figure 2.1
The characteristic textures of the surfaces of various substances.

Grass, cloth, pebbles, water, clouds, and wood grain are shown. Can you identify them? (Photos by Phil Brodatz, "Textures" and "Wood and Woodgrains")

MEDIUM, SUBSTANCES, SURFACES

limiting case. A polished surface of glass approximates to it, but it has to be manufactured. Mirrors are rare in nature (although the still surface of the pool into which Narcissus gazed is a natural mirror).

When the chemical and geometrical units of a surface are relatively small, the texture is *fine*; when they are relatively large, the texture is *coarse*. If the units are sufficiently distinct to be counted, the *density* of the texture can be measured as the number of units in an arbitrary unit of area, a square centimeter or meter. But this is often very hard to do because units of texture are generally nested within one another at different levels of size. The texture of commercial sandpapaer can be graded from fine to coarse, but the textures of vegetation cannot. Moreover, the units of texture vary in form, and there are forms within forms, so that the "form" of a texture escapes measurement. The ideal pigment texture of a checkerboard and the ideal layout texture of a tessellated surface are rare.

The law says that rock, shale, soil, and humus have different textures and that mud, clay, sand, ice, and snow have different textures. It says that the bark and the leaf and the fruit of a tree are differently textured and that the surfaces of animals are differently textured, by fur, feathers, or skin. The surfaces of the substances from which primitive men fashioned tools have different textures—flint, clay, wood, bone, and fiber. The surfaces of the artificial environment—plywood, paper, fabric, plaster, brick—have different textures. The surfaces with which man is beginning almost to carpet the earth are differently textured—the pavements of concrete, asphalt, and other aggregates. The texture in each case specifies what the substance is, what the surface is made of, its composition. And that, as noted above, is something of great importance. The relations between the layout texture of a surface, the pigment texture, and the shadow texture are complex; they will be considered below and in Chapter 5.

It is important to understand the determinants of surface texture, so that we will later be able to understand what I call *optical texture* when this notion is introduced in Part II. The two are not at all the same thing. It is enough to observe now that surfaces are homogeneous only as a limiting case—for example, the plaster wall behind a stage setting that looks like the sky from a distance—and that surfaces are smooth only as a limiting case, such as a sheet of plate glass and a mirror. Under certain conditions a homogeneous, very smooth, flat, large surface is not visible to a person or animal with ordinary eyesight.

CHARACTERISTIC SHAPE

The fifth law has to do with the layout of the environment on a scale that is relatively *large*—its coarse structure or macrostructure. A surface can often be analyzed into facets, and a layout can often be analyzed into faces. This terminology refers to *facing*, that is, facing or not facing the source of illumination and facing or not facing the point of observation. For the present, let us take a surface to mean a flat surface, a face, and a layout of adjoining surfaces to mean a set of faces meeting at dihedral angles, that is, edges and corners. These terms will be defined later.

The law has to do with surface layout at the size-level of environmental *enclosures* and environmental *objects*. It asserts that enclosures and objects have characteristic shapes. Enclosures differ in shape as, for example, a cave, a tunnel, and a room differ. Objects differ in shape as, for example, the polyhedrons of solid geometry differ (the tetrahedron, pyramid, cube, octahedron, and so on) and in all the ways that the irregular polyhedrons differ. These geometrical solids, so-called, progress toward enormous complexity, but they can all be analyzed in terms of three components called *faces*, *edges*, and *vertices*. These components have meaning for environmental objects because, for example, the edge is characteristic of a cutting tool and the vertex is characteristic of a piercing tool.

Obviously, differently shaped enclosures afford different possibilities of inhabiting them. And differently shaped solids afford different possibilities for behavior and manipulation. Man, the great manipulator, exploits these latter possibilities to the utmost degree.

HIGH AND LOW ILLUMINATION

The sixth law says that the light falling on a surface, the incident light, may be high or low, intense or dim, but that generally there is some illumination even at night. The completely dark room of the vision laboratory, like the deep interior of a cave, is a limiting case.

The amount of sunlight falling on a terrestrial surface depends on the condition of the atmosphere, clear or cloudy; but it also depends on two other factors that combine: the position of the sun in the sky and the orientation of the surface relative to the sky. It should be remembered that light comes from the whole sky as well as from the sun, and from other reflecting surfaces as well. Light reverberates between the sky and the earth and between surfaces. Direct illumination from a source is always mixed with indirect illumination. The incident light is never unidirectional, as it would be in empty space, but more or less omnidirectional. Nevertheless, there is always a "prevailing" illumination, a direction at which the incident light is strongest.

A surface facing the prevailing illumination will be more highly illuminated than a surface not facing it. This seems to be a general principle relating illumination to surface layout. This principle means that the different adjacent faces of the environment will be differently illuminated at any given time of day. But it also means that the faces under high illumination early in the day will be under low illumination late in the day and vice versa because of the motion of the sun across the sky. This daily exchange between the lighted state and the shaded state of a given surface is an important but little noted fact about the environment. It will be further elaborated in Chapter 5.

HIGH AND LOW ABSORPTION OF LIGHT

The seventh law says that, of the illumination falling on a surface, more or less will be absorbed by it depending on the chemical composition of the substance. Certain substances like pure carbon absorb much, and others like chalk absorb little. This is why carbon is black and chalk is white.

In optics there are two alternatives to the absorption of light by a surface, transmission and reflection. For present purposes, only reflection will be emphasized, because most surfaces are not transparent like optical glass and pure water but are opaque. And in any case *no* substance is perfectly transmitting. Only the medium itself ever approximates to perfect transmission. A surface that transmitted all the light falling on it would not be a surface but would be the mere ghost of a surface, like the insubstantial fiction of a geometrical plane. Sheets of polished glass and surfaces of still water only transmit enough of the incident light to be called transparent.

CHARACTERISTIC REFLECTANCE

The eighth law is a corollary of the seventh. It says that the amount of light bounced back into the medium, instead of being soaked up by the surface, is a characteristic of the substance. That is, the ratio of light reflected to light incident is a constant for any given compound or any homogeneous mixture. This ratio is the *reflectance* of a surface.

Coal has a low reflectance (about 5 percent), and snow has a high reflectance (about 80 percent). When substances of this sort are conglomerated, the surface will have what I called a pigment texture; it will be speckled. Granite and marble are substances whose surfaces are mottled or variegated in this way.

CHARACTERISTIC SPECTRAL REFLECTANCE

The ninth law of ecological surfaces asserts that a surface has a characteristic distribution of the reflectance ratios of the different wavelengths of the incident light and that these different distributions constitute different colors. The word *color* here means *hue*, or chromatic color as distinguished from achromatic color, the variation of black, gray, and white.

For animals and humans, the colors of surfaces as defined above are more important than the colors of sunsets, rainbows, and flames. They specify the ripeness or unripeness of fruit and distinguish the leaf from the flower. Along with the textures of those surfaces, the colors help to distinguish feathers and fur and skin. Surface color is inseparably connected with surface texture, for colors often go with textures, and colored objects are apt to be particolored. The color and texture of a surface together specify the *composition* of the substance, what it is made of, and this is important, as noted above.

THE QUALITIES OF SUBSTANTIAL SURFACES

A tentative classification of surfaces is now possible. First, there are *luminous* surfaces as distinguished from *illuminated* surfaces, those that emit light and those that do not. Second, there are *more illuminated* and *less illuminated* surfaces, those we call lighted and shaded. Third, there are the surfaces of *volumes* as distinguished from the surfaces of *sheets* and *films*. Fourth, there are *opaque* surfaces as distinguished from *semitransparent* and *translucent* surfaces; these forms of nonopaqueness will be further analyzed in Part II. Fifth, there are *smooth* surfaces and *rough* surfaces, the former being of two kinds, *glossy* and *matte*, and the latter having a great variety of forms of roughness. The distinction between smooth and rough is not as simple as it sounds but, in general, implies the mirror-reflecting of light at one extreme and the scatter-reflecting of light at the other. Sixth, there are *homogeneous* and *conglomerated* surfaces, the former being monocolored and the latter particolored; the "color" of a surface or of any bit of a surface refers to both its *overall reflectance* (black, gray, or white) and its *spectral reflectance* (hue). Finally, seventh, there are *hard, intermediate,* and *soft* surfaces, depending on the substance that underlies the surface.

These seven modes or qualities take the place of the so-called modes of appearance of color (Beck, 1972). And, when surface layout is also considered, they take the place of the so-called qualities of objects, color on the one hand and "form, size, position, solidity, duration, and motion" on the other. These latter are John Locke's "primary" qualities, those that were supposed to be "in the objects" instead of merely "in us." This distinction between primary and secondary qualities is quite unnecessary and is wholly rejected in the above description.

SUMMARY

We live in an environment consisting of substances that are more or less substantial; of a medium, the gaseous atmosphere; and of the surfaces that separate the substances from the medium. We do not live in "space."

The medium permits unimpeded locomotion from place to place, and it also permits the seeing, smelling, and hearing of the substances at all places. Locomotion and behavior are continually controlled by the activities of seeing, smelling, and hearing, together with touching.

The substances of the environment need to be distinguished. A powerful way of doing so is by seeing their surfaces.

A surface has characteristic properties that can persist or change, such as its layout, its texture, the property of being lighted or shaded, and the property of reflecting a certain fraction of the illumination falling on it.

THREE

THE MEANINGFUL
ENVIRONMENT

The world of physical reality does not consist of meaningful things. The world of ecological reality, as I have been trying to describe it, does. If what we perceived were the entities of physics and mathematics, meanings would have to be imposed on them. But if what we perceive are the entities of environmental science, their meanings can be *discovered*.

A NOMENCLATURE FOR SURFACE LAYOUT

Consider first the difference between the terms used in describing what I have called the layout of a habitat and the terms used in geometry. *Surfaces* and *the medium* are ecological terms; *planes* and *space* are the nearest equivalent geometrical terms, but note the differences. Planes are colorless; surfaces are colored. Planes are transparent ghosts; surfaces are generally opaque and substantial. The intersection of two planes, a line, is not the same as the junction of two flat surfaces, an edge or corner. I will try to define the ecological terms explicitly. The following terminology is a first attempt at a theory of surface layout, a sort of applied geometry that is appropriate for the study of perception and behavior.

The *ground* refers, of course, to the surface of the earth. It is, on the average, level, that is to say, perpendicular to the force of gravity. It is the reference surface for all other surfaces. It is also said to be horizontal, and this word refers to the horizon of the earth, the margin between earth and sky, a fact of ecological optics that has not yet been considered. Note that both gravity and the sky are implied by the ground. A special case of the ground is a floor.

An *open environment* is a layout consisting of the surface of the earth alone. It is a limiting case, only realized in a perfectly level desert. The surface of the earth is usually more or less "wrinkled" by convexities and concavities. It is also more or less "cluttered"; that is, it is not open but partly enclosed. There will be much more of this in Part II.

An *enclosure* is a layout of surfaces that surrounds the medium in some degree. A wholly enclosed medium is a limiting case, at the other extreme from an open environment. It is only realized in a windowless cell that does not afford entry or exit. The surfaces of an enclosure all face inward. An egg or cocoon, to be sure, is a wholly enclosed environment for an embryo or a pupa, but eventually it has to be broken.

A *detached object* refers to a layout of surfaces completely surrounded *by* the medium. It is the inverse of a complete enclosure. The surfaces of a detached object all face outward, not inward. This is not a limiting case, for it is realized in objects that are moving or are movable. Animate bodies, animals, are detached objects in this sense, however much they may otherwise differ from inanimate bodies. The criterion is that the detached object can be moved without breaking or rupturing the continuity of any surface.

An *attached object* refers to a layout of surfaces less than completely surrounded by the medium. The substance of the object is continuous with the substance of another surface, often the ground. The surface layout of the object is not topologically closed as it is for the detached object and as it also is for the complete enclosure. An attached object may be merely a *convexity*.

It may be noted that objects are *denumerable*, they can be counted, whereas a substance is not denumerable and neither is the ground. Note also, parenthetically, that an organism such as a tree is an attached object in the environment of animals since it is rooted in the ground like a house with foundations, but it is a detached object, a whole organism, when considered as a plant with roots between soil particles.

A *partial enclosure* is a layout of surfaces that only partly encloses the medium. It may be only a *concavity*. But a cave or a hole is often a shelter.

A *hollow object* is an object that is also an enclosure. It is an object from the outside but an enclosure from the inside, part of the total surface layout facing outward and the other part inward. A snail shell and a hut are hollow objects.

A *place* is a location in the environment as contrasted with a point in space, a more or less extended surface, or layout. Whereas a point must be located with reference to a coordinate system, a place can be located by its inclusion in a larger place (for example, the fireplace in the cabin by the bend of the river in the Great Plains). Places can be named, but they need not have sharp boundaries. The habitat of an animal is made up of places.

A *sheet* is an object consisting of two parallel surfaces enclosing a substance, the surfaces being close together relative to their dimensions. A sheet should not be confused with a geometrical plane. A sheet may have flat surfaces or curved surfaces, and it may be flexible or freely changeable in shape. A membrane of the sort found in living bodies, permeable or impermeable, is an example of a sheet.

A *fissure* is a layout consisting of two parallel surfaces enclosing the medium that are very close together relative to their size. The surfaces of rigid solids often have fissures (cracks).

A *stick* is an elongated object.

A *fiber* is an elongated object of small diameter, such as a wire or thread. A fiber should not be confused with a geometrical line.

A *dihedral,* in this terminology, refers to the junction of two flat surfaces and should not be confused with the intersection of two planes in abstract geometry. A *convex dihedral* is one that tends to enclose a substance and to make an *edge*; a *concave dihedral* is one that tends to enclose the medium and to make a *corner.* You cannot bark your shin on the intersection of two limitless planes or on the apex of an abstract dihedral angle. Neither can you do so on a corner; you can only do so on an edge. A *sharp edge* is an acute convex dihedral. The termination of a sheet will be called a *cut edge.*

Parenthetically, it may be noted that the last five entities, fissure, stick, fiber, and the two kinds of dihedral, convex and concave, are all embodiments of a *line* in geometry and that all of them are to be distinguished from a *margin* or *border.* A line is a sort of ghost of these different entities.

A *curved convexity* is a curved surface tending to enclose a substance.

A *curved concavity* is a curved surface tending to enclose the medium.

The foregoing terms apply to *surface geometry* as distinguished from *abstract geometry.* What are the differences between these two? A surface is substantial; a plane is not. A surface is textured; a plane is not. A surface is never perfectly transparent; a plane is. A surface can be seen; a plane can only be visualized.

Moreover, a surface has only one side; a plane has two. A geometrical plane, that is, must be conceived as a very thin sheet in space, not as an interface or boundary between a medium and a substance. A surface may be either convex or concave, but a plane that is convex on one side is necessarily concave on the other. In surface geometry the junction of two flat surfaces is either an edge or a corner; in abstract geometry the intersection of two planes is a line. A surface has the property of facing a source of illumination or a point of observation; a plane does not have this property. In surface geometry an object and an enclosure can be distinguished; in abstract geometry they cannot.

Finally, in abstract analytic geometry the position of a body is specified by coordinates on three chosen axes or dimensions in isotropic space; in surface geometry the position of an object is specified relative to gravity and the ground in a medium having an intrinsic polarity of up and down. Similarly, the *motion* of a body in abstract geometry is a change of position along one or more of the dimensions of space, or a rotation of the body (spin) on one or more of these axes. But the motion of an object in surface geometry is always a *change in the overall surface layout,* a change in the shape of the environment in some sense. And since environmental substances are often not rigid, their surfaces often undergo deformation, and these motions—stretching, squeezing, bending, twisting, flowing, and the like—are not the motions of abstract bodies.

WHAT THE ENVIRONMENT AFFORDS
THE ANIMAL

The environment of any animal (and of all animals) contains substances, surfaces and their layout, enclosures, objects, places, events, and the other animals. This description is very general; it holds true for insects, birds, mammals, and men. Let us now attempt a more particular description, selecting those surfaces, layouts, objects, and events that are of special concern to animals that behave more or less as we do. The total environment is too vast for description even by the ecologist, and we should select those features of it that are perceptible by animals like ourselves. A further treatment of what the environment affords will be given later, in Chapter 8.

TERRAIN FEATURES

The level ground is only rarely an open environment, as noted a few pages back. It is usually cluttered. An open environment affords locomotion in any direction over the ground, whereas a cluttered environment affords locomotion only at *openings*. These rules refer, of course, to pedestrian animals, not flying animals or climbing animals. The human animal is a pedestrian, although he is descended from arboreal primates and has some climbing ability. The general capacity to go through an opening without colliding with the edges is not limited to pedestrians, however. It is a characteristic of all visually controlled locomotion (Gibson, 1958).

A *path* affords pedestrian locomotion from one place to another, between the terrain features that prevent locomotion. The preventers of locomotion consist of *obstacles, barriers, water margins,* and *brinks* (the edges of cliffs). A path must afford *footing*; it must be relatively free of rigid foot-sized obstacles.

An *obstacle* can be defined as an animal-sized object that affords collision and possible injury. A *barrier* is a more general case; it may be the face of a cliff, a wall, or a man-made fence. Note parenthetically that a barrier usually prevents looking-through as well as going-through but not always; a sheet of glass and a wire fence are barriers, but they can be seen through. A cloud, on the other hand, may prevent looking-through but not going-through. These special cases will be treated later.

A *water margin* (a margin is not to be confused with an edge in this terminology) prevents pedestrian locomotion; it permits other kinds, but let us postpone consideration of the various affordances of water.

A *brink*, the edge of a cliff, is a very significant terrain feature. It is a falling-off place. It affords injury and therefore needs to be perceived by a pedestrian animal. The edge is dangerous, but the near surface is safe. Thus, there is a principle for the control of locomotion that involves what I will call the *edge* of danger and a *gradient* of danger, that is, the closer to the brink the greater the danger. This principle is very general.

A *step*, or stepping-off place, differs from a brink in size, relative to the size of the animal. It thus affords pedestrian locomotion. A stairway, a layout of adjacent steps, affords both descent and ascent. Note that a stairway consists of convex edges and concave corners alternating, in the nomenclature here employed.

A *slope* is a terrain feature that may or may not afford pedestrian locomotion depending on its angle from the surface of the level ground and its texture. A ramp with low inclination can be negotiated; a cliff face with high inclination cannot.

Humans have been altering the natural features of the terrain for thousands of years, constructing paths, roads, stairways, and bridges over gorges and streams. Paths, roads, stairways, and bridges facilitate human locomotion and obviate climbing. Humans have also been constructing obstacles and barriers to *prevent* locomotion by enemies, human or animal. Humans have built walls, moats, and fences to prevent access to an enclosure, that is, to their camps and fortresses. And then, of course, they had to build doors in the walls, drawbridges over the moats, and gates in the fences to permit their own entry and exit.

SHELTERS

The atmospheric medium, it will be remembered, is neither *entirely* homogeneous nor *wholly* invariant. Sometimes there is rain in the air, or hail, or snow. Sometimes the wind blows, and in certain latitudes of the earth the air periodically becomes too cold for warm-blooded animals, who will die if they lose more heat to the medium than they gain by oxidizing food. For such reasons, many animals and all human beings must have shelters. They often take shelter in caves or holes or burrows, which are animal-sized partial enclosures. But some animals and all humans of recent times *build* shelters, constructing them in various ways and of various materials. These are generally what I called hollow objects, not simply cavities in the earth. Birds and wasps build nests, for example, especially for sheltering their young. Human animals build what I will call *huts*—a generic term for simple human artificial shelters.

A hut has a site on the ground, and it is an attached object from the outside. But it also has an inside. Its usual features are, first, a *roof* that is "get-underneath-able" and thus affords protection from rain and snow and direct sunlight; second, *walls*, which afford protection from wind and prevent the escape of heat; and third, a *doorway* to afford entry and exit, that is, an *opening*. A hut can be built of sticks, clay, thatch, stones, brick, or many other more sophisticated substances.

WATER

The margin between land and water stops the pedestrian. But animals can wade if the water is shallow, float if their specific gravity is not too high, or skitter over the surface if they are insects. Some terrestrial animals can swim on the surface of water, as the human animal can after a fashion, and dive under the surface for a short time. But water does not afford respiration to terrestrial animals with lungs, and they are always in danger of drowning.

Considered as a substance instead of a surface or a medium, water is a necessity for terrestrial life, not a danger. Animal tissue consists mainly of solutions in water, and the fluids of the body have to be replenished. Animals must drink. Only the intake of fresh water prevents death by dessication, or what we call thirst. So they need to recognize water when they meet with it.

Water causes the wetting of dry surfaces. It affords bathing and washing, to elephants as well as to humans. Streams of water can be dammed, by beavers as well as by children and hydraulic engineers. Ditches can be dug and aqueducts built. Pots can be made to contain water, and then it affords pouring and spilling. Water, in short, has many kinds of meaning.

FIRE

Fire was the fourth of the "elements" that constituted the world, in the belief of the Greek thinkers. They were the first analyzers of the environment, although their analysis depended on direct observation. They observed earth, air, water, and then fire. In our chemical sophistication, we now know that fire is merely a rapid chemical reaction of oxidation, but nevertheless we still perceive a fire as such. It is hardly an object, not a substance, and it has a very unusual surface. A fire is a terrestrial *event*, with a beginning and an end, giving off heat and consuming fuel. Natural fires in the forests or plains were and still are awesome to animals, but our ancestors learned very early how to control fire—how to begin it (with a fire drill, for example), how to make it persist (by feeding it fuel), how to conserve it (with a slow match), and how to quench it. The controlling of fire is a unique human habit. Our primitive hunting ancestors became very skilled at it. And as they watched the fire, they could see a prime example of persistence with change, of invariance under transformation.

A fire affords warmth even in the open but especially in a shelter. It provides illumination and, in the form of a torch, can be carried about, even into the depths of a cave. But a fire also affords injury to the skin. Like the brink of a cliff, one cannot get too close. There is a gradient of danger and a limit at which warmth becomes injury. So the controlling of fire entails the control of motor approach to fire and the detecting of the limit.

Once this control is learned by the adult and the child, fire affords many benefits besides warmth and illumination. It allows the cooking of food substances and the boiling of water in pots. It permits the glazing of clay and the reduction of minerals to metals. Fire, like water, has many kinds of meaning, many uses, many values.

OBJECTS

The term *object* as used in philosophy and psychology is so inclusive as to be almost undefinable. But as I have defined it above, it refers only to a persisting substance with a closed or nearly closed surface and can be either detached or attached. I always refer to a "concrete" object, not an "abstract" one. In this restricted sense, the surface of an object has a definite texture, reflectance, color, and layout, the surface layout being its shape. These are some of the distinguishing features of an object in relation to other objects.

An *attached* object of the appropriate size permits a primate to grasp it, as a monkey grasps a tree branch. (A bird can grasp with its claws in the same way.) Such an object is something to hold on to and permits climbing. A *detached* object of the appropriate size to be grasped is even more interesting. It affords carrying, that is, it is portable. If the substance has an appropriate mass-to-volume ratio (density), it affords throwing, that is, it is a missile.

A hollow object such as a pot can be used to contain water or wine or grain and to store these substances. An object with a level surface knee-high from the ground

---

THE DETECTING OF A LIMIT AND
THE MARGIN OF SAFETY

The mathematical concept of a variable, an asymptote, and a limit is an intellectual achievement of great complexity. But the perceiving of a limit of action is quite simple. Terrestrial animals perceive a brink as a limit of approach, and the mathematical complexity is not a problem for the visual system. The observer, even a child, sees the distance between himself and the brink, the so-called *margin of safety*.

THE MEANINGFUL ENVIRONMENT

can be used to sit on. An elongated object, a stick, if the substance is elastic and flexible, affords bending and thus can be made into a bow for launching arrows. A rigid, straight stick, not bent or curved, can be rotated on its long axis without wobbling; it can be used as a fire drill or as an axle for a wheel. The list of examples could go on without end.

TOOLS

Tools are detached objects of a very special sort. They are graspable, portable, manipulatable, and usually rigid. The purposive use of such objects is not entirely confined to the human animal, for other animals and other primates take advantage of thorns and rocks and sticks in their behavior, but humans are probably the only animals who *make* tools and are surely the only animals who walk on two feet in order to keep the hands free.

The missile that can be thrown is perhaps the earliest of tools. When combined with a launching device, it can become very versatile. The discovery of missiles was surely one of the factors that made the human animal a formidable hunter as compared to the animals with teeth and claws. Soon after that discovery, presumably, came the invention of striking tools, edged tools, and pointed tools.

An elongated object, especially if weighted at one end and graspable at the other, affords hitting or hammering (a club). A graspable object with a rigid sharp edge affords cutting and scraping (a knife, a hand axe, or a chopper). A pointed object affords piercing (a spear, an arrow, an awl, or a needle). These tools may be combined in

Figure 3.1
A tool is a sort of extension of the hand.
This object in use affords a special kind of cutting, and one can actually feel the cutting action of the blades.

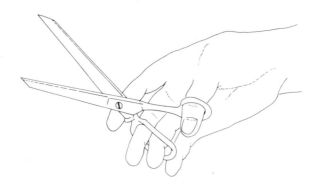

various ways to make other tools. Once again it may be noted that users of such tools must keep within certain limits of manipulation, since they themselves may be struck or cut or pierced.

When in use, a tool is a sort of extension of the hand, almost an attachment to it or a part of the user's own body, and thus is no longer a part of the environment of the user. But when not in use, the tool is simply a detached object of the environment, graspable and portable, to be sure, but nevertheless external to the observer. This *capacity to attach something to the body* suggests that the boundary between the animal and the environment is not fixed at the surface of the skin but can shift. More generally it suggests that the absolute duality of "objective" and "subjective" is false. When we consider the affordances of things, we escape this philosophical dichotomy.

When being worn, clothing, even more than a tool, is a part of the wearer's body instead of a part of the environment. Apart from the utility of modulating heat loss, clothing permits the individual to change the texture and color of his surface, to put on a second skin, as it were. When not being worn, a body covering is simply a detached object of the environment made of fabric or the skin of a dead animal—a complex, flexible, curved sheet in our terminology. But the article objectively affords wearing, as a tool affords using. And when it is worn it becomes attached to the body and is no longer a part of the environment.

Much more could be said about tools, but this will serve as an introduction. Note that the discussion has been limited to relatively small or portable tools. Technological man has made larger tools, machines, for cutting, boring, pounding, and crushing, and also for earth-moving and for construction and also, of course, for locomotion.

OTHER ANIMALS

Animate objects differ from inanimate objects in a variety of ways but notably in the fact that they move spontaneously. Like all detached objects, animate objects can be pushed and displaced by external forces, they can fall when pulled by the force of gravity—in short, they can be passively moved—but they also can move actively under the influence of *internal* forces. They are partly composed of viscoelastic substances as well as rigid skeletons, and their movements are always deformations of the surface. Moreover the style of movement, the mode of deformation, is unique for each animal. These special objects differ in size, shape, texture, color, odor, and in the sounds they emit, but above all they differ in the way they move. Their postures change in specific modes while their underlying invariants of shape remain constant. That is to say, animals have characteristic behaviors as well as characteristic anatomies.

Animals are thus by far the most complex objects of perception that the environment presents to an observer. Another animal may be prey or predator, potential mate or rival, adult or young, one's own young or another's young. Moreover, it may be temporarily asleep or awake, receptive or unreceptive, hungry or satiated. What the other animal affords is specified by its permanent features and its temporary state, and it can afford eating or being eaten, copulation or fighting, nurturing or nurturance.

What the other animal affords the observer is not only behavior but also social interaction. As one moves so does the other, the one sequence of action being suited to the other in a kind of behavioral loop. All social interaction is of this sort—sexual, maternal, competitive, cooperative—or it may be social grooming, play, and even human conversation.

This brief description does not even begin to do justice to the power of the notion of affordances in social psychology. The old notions of social stimuli and social responses, of biological drives and social instincts are hopelessly inadequate. An understanding of life with one's fellow creatures depends on an adequate description of what these creatures offer and then on an analysis of how these offerings are perceived.

HUMAN DISPLAYS

Finally, we come to a very special class of artificial objects—or perhaps *devices* is a better term—that display optical information. I refer to solid images of several types, pictures of many sorts, and all the surfaces of the environment that bear writing. Some twenty or thirty thousand years ago sculptures and pictures were first made, and some four or five thousand years ago writing was developed and records began to be kept. By now images and records are everywhere. A *display*, to employ a useful generic term, is a surface that has been shaped or processed so as to exhibit information for more than just the surface itself (Gibson, 1966*b*, pp. 26–28, 224–244). For example, a surface of clay is only clay, but it may be molded in the shape of a cow or scratched or painted with the profile of a cow or incised with the cuneiform characters that stand for a cow, and then it is more than just a surface of clay.

There will be more about displays in Part IV, after we have considered the information for visual perception in Part II and the activity of visual perception in Part III. It can be suggested in a preliminary way, however, that images, pictures, and written-on surfaces afford a special kind of knowledge that I call *mediated* or *indirect*, knowledge at second hand. Moreover, images, pictures, and writing, insofar as the substances shaped and the surfaces treated are permanent, permit the storage of information and the accumulation of information in storehouses, in short, civilization.

THE ENVIRONMENT OF ONE OBSERVER AND
THE ENVIRONMENT OF ALL OBSERVERS

The essence of an environment is that it *surrounds* an individual. I argued in Chapter 1 that the way in which a physical object is surrounded by the remainder of the physical world is not at all the same as the way in which a living animal is surrounded by an environment. The latter surrounds or encloses or is ambient in special ways that I have tried to describe.

The term *surroundings* is nevertheless vague, and this vagueness has encouraged confusion of thought. One such is the question of how the surroundings of a single animal can also be the surroundings of all animals. If it is assumed that no two observers can be at the same place at the same time, then no two observers ever have the same surroundings. Hence, the environment of each observer is "private," that is, unique. This seems to be a philosophical puzzle, but it is a false puzzle. Let us resolve it. One may consider the layout of surrounding surfaces with reference to a stationary point of observation, a center where an individual is standing motionless, as if the environment were a set of frozen concentric spheres. Or one may consider the layout of surrounding surfaces with reference to a *moving* point of observation along a path that any individual can travel. This is much the more useful way of considering the surroundings, and it recognizes the fact that animals do in fact move about. The animal that does not move is asleep—or dead.

The available paths of locomotion in a medium constitute the set of all possible points of observation. In the course of time, each animal moves through the same paths of its habitat as do other animals of its kind. Although it is true that no two individuals can be at the same place at the same time, any individual can stand in all places, and all individuals can stand in the same place at different times. Insofar as the habitat has a persisting substantial layout, therefore, all its inhabitants have an equal opportunity to explore it. In this sense the environment surrounds all observers in the same way that it surrounds a single observer.

The old idea that each observer stands at the center of his or her private world and that each environment is therefore unique gets its main support from a narrow conception of optics and a mistaken theory of visual perception. A broader conception of optics will be given in Part II, and a better theory of visual perception will be presented in Part III. The fact of a moving point of observation is central for the ecological approach to visual perception, and its implications, as we shall see, are far-reaching.

꩜

SUMMARY

Formal plane geometry has been contrasted with an unformalized and quite unfamiliar geometry of surfaces. But the latter is more appropriate for describing the environment in which we perceive and behave, because a surface can be seen whereas a plane cannot. The differences between a plane and a surface have been pointed out.

A tentative list of the main features of surface layout has been proposed. The definitions are subject to revision, but terms of this sort are needed in ecology, architecture, design, the biology of behavior, and the social sciences instead of the planes, forms, lines, and points of geometry. The term *object*, especially, has been defined so as to give it a strictly limited application unlike the general meaning it has in philosophy and psychology.

The fundamental ways in which surfaces are laid out have an intrinsic meaning for behavior unlike the abstract, formal, intellectual concepts of mathematical space.

TWO

THE INFORMATION
FOR VISUAL
PERCEPTION

FOUR

THE RELATIONSHIP BETWEEN STIMULATION AND STIMULUS INFORMATION

Having described the environment, I shall now describe the information available to observers for perceiving the environment. Only then will we be prepared to consider how they perceive, what the activity of perception consists of, and how they can control behavior in the environment.

For visual perception, the information is obviously in light. But the term *light* means different things in different sciences, and we shall have to sort out the different meanings to avoid confusion. Most of us are confused, including the scientists themselves. The science of light is called *optics*. But the science of vision is also called optics, and the textbooks are not at all clear about the difference. Let us try to distinguish light as physical energy, light as a stimulus for vision, and light as information for perception.

What I call *ecological optics* is concerned with the available information for perception and differs from physical optics, from geometrical optics, and also from physiological optics. Ecological optics cuts across the boundaries of these existing disciplines, borrowing from all but going beyond them.

Ecological optics rests on several distinctions that are not basic in physical optics: the distinction between luminous bodies and nonluminous bodies; the difference between light as radiation and light as illumination; and the difference between radiant light, propagating outward from a source, and ambient light, coming to a point in a medium where an eye might be stationed. Since these differences are fundamental, they should be stated at the beginning. Why they are so important will become clear.

THE DISTINCTION BETWEEN LUMINOUS
AND ILLUMINATED BODIES

Some material bodies emit light, and others do not. Light comes from sources such as the sun in the sky and from other sources close at hand such as fires or lamps on the earth. They "give" light, as we say, whereas ordinary objects do not. Nonluminous objects only reflect some part of the light that falls on them from a source. And yet we can see the nonluminous bodies along with the luminous ones. In fact, most of the things that need to be seen are nonluminous; they are only seen "by the light of" the source. The question is, *how* are they seen? For they do not *stimulate* the eye with light in the same way that luminous bodies do. The intermediate case of luminescent bodies is exceptional.

A terrestrial surface that gives light is usually, although not always, distinguishable from one that does not; it is visibly luminous, as distinct from being visibly illuminated. In physical optics, the case of reflected light is reduced to the re-emission of light by the atoms of the reflecting surface. But in ecological optics, the difference between a luminous and an illuminated surface is crucial. Where a reflecting surface in physical optics is treated as if it were a dense set of tiny luminous bodies, in ecological optics a reflecting surface is treated as if it were a true surface having a texture. There will be more of this later.

THE DISTINCTION BETWEEN RADIATION AND ILLUMINATION

Radiant energy as studied in physics is propagated through empty space at enormous velocity. Such energy can be treated either as particles or as waves (and this is a great puzzle, even to physicists), but it travels in straight lines, or rays. The paths of photons are straight lines, and the perpendiculars to the wave fronts are straight lines. Moreover, light comes from atoms and returns to atoms. They give off and take in energy in quantal units. Matter and energy interact. There are elegant laws of this radiation, both at the size-level of atoms and on the grand scale of the universe. But at the ecological level of substances, surfaces, and the medium, we need be concerned only with some of these laws, chiefly scattering, reflection, and absorption.

WHY ECOLOGICAL OPTICS?

The term *ecological optics* first appeared in print in an article with that title in *Vision Research* (Gibson, 1961). It seemed to me that the study of light, over the centuries, had not produced a coherent discipline. The science of radiant energy in physics, the science of optical instruments, and the science of the eye were quite different. The textbooks and journals of optics gave the impression of monolithic authority, but there were deep contradictions between the assumptions of the various branches of optics. When I discovered that even an occasional physicist recognized these cracks in the foundations of the optical establishment (Ronchi, 1957), I ventured to suggest that optics at the level appropriate for perception should have a new name.

In daylight, part of the radiant light of the sun reaches the earth in parallel rays, but another part is scattered by being transmitted through an atmosphere that is never perfectly transparent. This light is even more thoroughly scattered when it strikes the textured ground, by what can be called *scatter reflection*. (This is not to be confused with *mirror reflection*, which is governed by the simple law of equal angles of the incident ray and the reflected ray. Mirror reflection seldom happens, for there are no mirrors on the ground, and even water surfaces, which could act as mirrors, are usually rippled.) The scatter-reflected light is in turn reflected back from the sky. Each new reflection further disperses the incident rays. The light thus finds its way into shelters that are not open to the sun, or even to the sky. In semienclosed spaces the light continues to bounce back and forth at 186,000 miles per second. It finds its way through

Figure 4.1

The steady state of reverberating light in an illuminated medium under the sky.

Although at any point in the air the illumination comes from all directions, the *prevailing* illumination is from the left in this diagram because the direct radiation from the sun comes from the left.

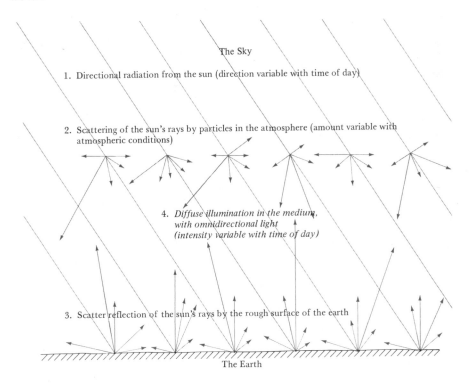

STIMULATION AND STIMULUS INFORMATION

chinks and crevices and into caverns, until the energy is finally absorbed. This light can hardly be thought of as radiation now; it is illumination.

Illumination is a fact of higher order than radiation. In physical optics, experimenters try to avoid what they call stray light in the dark room. But in ecological optics, this light that has gone astray is just what interests us. The opticist works with rays of light, rays that diverge in all directions from their source and never converge to a point unless they are focused by a lens. But an organism has to work with light that converges from all directions and, moreover, has different intensities in different directions.

Many-times reflected light in a medium has a number of consequences that, although important for vision, have not been recognized by students of optics. Chief among them is the fact of ambient light, that is, light that surrounds a point, any point, in the space where an observer could be stationed.

THE DISTINCTION BETWEEN RADIANT LIGHT
AND AMBIENT LIGHT

Radiation becomes illumination by *reverberating* between the earth and the sky and between surfaces that face one another. But that term, referring as it does to sound, does not do justice to the unimaginable quickness of the flux or to the uncountable multiplicity of the reflections back and forth or to their unlimited scattering. If the illumination is conceived as a manifold of rays, one can imagine every point on every surface of any environment as radiating rays outward from that point, as physicists do. Every such radiating pencil is completely "dense." One could think of the rays as completely filling the air and think of each point in the air as a point of intersection of

Figure 4.2
Radiant light from a point source and ambient light to a point in the medium.
A creature with eyes is shown at the point in the air, but it need not be occupied.

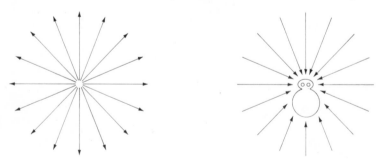

rays coming from all directions. It would follow that light is ambient at every point. Light would come to every point; it would surround every point; it would be environing at every point. This is one way of conceiving ambient light.

Such an omnidirectional flux of light could not exist in empty space but only in an environment of reflecting surfaces. In any ordinary terrestrial space, the illumination reaches an equilibrium, that is, it achieves what is called a *steady state*. The input of energy from the sun is just balanced by the absorption of energy at the surfaces. With any change in the source, a new steady state is immediately reached, as when the sun goes down or is hidden by a cloud. No matter how abrupt the rise or fall of intensity of the light coming from a lamp, the rise or fall of illumination in the room is just as abrupt. The system is said to be open rather than closed inasmuch as addition of energy to the airspace and subtraction of energy from it are going on all the time, but the *structure* of the reverberation remains the same and does not change. What could this structure be? It is possible to conceive a nested set of solid angles at each point in the medium, as distinguished from a dense set of intersecting lines. The set of solid angles would be the same whatever the intensity of illumination might be (there will be more about this later). They are angles of intercept, based on the environment. The flow of energy is relevant to the stimulation of a retina, but the set of solid angles considered as projections is more relevant to stimulus information.

Consider the differences between radiant light and ambient light that have so far been stated or implied. Radiant light causes illumination; ambient light is the result of illumination. Radiant light diverges from an energy source; ambient light converges to a point of observation. Radiant light must consist of an infinitely dense set of rays; ambient light can be thought of as a set of solid angles having a common apex. Radiant light from a point source is not different in different directions; ambient light at a point is different in different directions. Radiant light has no structure; ambient light has structure. Radiant light is propagated; ambient light is not, it is simply there. Radiant light comes from atoms and returns to atoms; ambient light depends upon an environment of surfaces. Radiant light is energy; ambient light can be information.

THE STRUCTURING OF AMBIENT LIGHT

Only insofar as ambient light has *structure* does it specify the environment. I mean by this that the light at the point of observation has to be different in different directions (or there have to be *differences* in different directions) in order for it to contain any information. The differences are principally differences of intensity. The term that will be used to describe ambient light with structure is an *ambient optic array*. This implies an arrangement of some sort, that is, a pattern, a texture, or a configuration. The array has to have parts. The ambient light cannot be homogeneous or blank. (See the illustrations in Chapter 5.)

What would be the limiting case of ambient light *without* structure? It would arise if the air were filled with such a dense fog that the light could not reverberate between surfaces but only between the droplets or particles in the medium. The air would then be translucent but not transparent. Multiple reflection would occur only between closely packed microsurfaces, yielding a sort of microillumination of things too small to see. At any point of observation there would be radiation, but without differences in different directions, without transitions or gradations of intensity, there would be no structure and no array. Similarly, homogeneous ambient light would occur inside a translucent shell of some strongly diffusing substance that was illuminated from outside. The shell would transmit light but not structure.

In the case of unstructured ambient light, an environment is not specified and no information *about* an environment is available. Since the light is undifferentiated, it cannot be discriminated, and there is no information in *any* meaning of that term. The ambient light in this respect is no different from ambient darkness. An environment could exist behind the fog or the darkness, or nothing could exist; either alternative is possible. In the case of ambient light that is unstructured in one part and structured in an adjacent part, such as the blue sky above the horizon and the textured region below it, the former specifies a void and the latter a surface. Similarly, the homogeneous area between clouds specifies emptiness, and the heterogeneous areas specify clouds.

The structuring of ambient light by surfaces, especially by their pigmentation and their layout, will be described in the next chapter. Chiefly, it is the opaque surfaces of the world that reflect light, but we must also consider the luminous surfaces that emit light and the semitransparent surfaces that transmit light. As far as the evidence goes, we will describe how the light specifies these surfaces, their composition, texture, color, and layout, their gross properties, not their atomic properties. And this specifying of them is useful information about them.

STIMULATION AND STIMULUS INFORMATION

In order to stimulate a photoreceptor, that is, to excite it and make it "fire," light energy must be absorbed by it, and this energy must exceed a certain characteristic amount known as the *threshold* of the receptor. Energy must be *transduced,* as the physiologist likes to put it, from one form to another. The rule is supposed to hold for each of a whole bank of photoreceptors, such as is found in the retina. Hence, if an eye were to be stationed at some point where there is ambient light, part of the light would enter the pupil, be absorbed, and act as stimulation. If *no* eye or any other body that absorbs light is stationed at that point, the flying photons in the air (or the wave fronts) would simply pass through the point without interfering with one another. Only *potential* stimulation exists at such a point. *Actual* stimulation depends on the presence of photoreceptors.

Consider an observer with an eye at a point in a fog-filled medium. The receptors in the retina would be stimulated, and there would consequently be impulses in the fibers of the optic nerve. But the light entering the pupil of the eye would not be different in different directions; it would be unfocusable, and no image could be formed on the retina. There could be no retinal image because the light on the retina would be just as homogeneous as the ambient light outside the eye. The possessor of the eye could not *fix* it on anything, and the eye would drift aimlessly. He could not look from one item to another, for no items would be present. If he turned the eye, the experience would be just what it was before. If he moved the eye forward in space, nothing in the field of view would change. Nothing he could do would make any difference in what he could experience, with this single exception: if he closed the eye, an experience that he might call brightness would give way to one he might call darkness. He could distinguish between stimulation of his photoreceptors and nonstimulation of them. But as far as perceiving goes, his eye would be just as blind when light entered it as it would be when light did not.

This hypothetical case demonstrates the difference between the retina and the eye, that is, the difference bewween receptors and a perceptual organ. Receptors are *stimulated,* whereas an organ is *activated.* There can be stimulation of a retina by light without any activation of the eye by stimulus information. Actually, the eye is part of a dual organ, one of a pair of mobile eyes, and they are set in a head that can turn, attached to a body that can move from place to place. These organs make a hierarchy and constitute what I have called a *perceptual system* (Gibson, 1966*b*, Ch. 3). Such a system is never simply stimulated but instead can go into activity in the presence of stimulus information. The characteristic activities of the visual system will be described in Chapter 12 of this book.

The distinction between stimulation for receptors and stimulus information for the visual system is crucial for what is to follow. Receptors are passive, elementary, anatomical components of an eye that, in turn, is only an organ of the complete system (Gibson, 1966*b*, Ch. 2). The traditional conception of a sense is almost wholly abandoned in this new approach. Stimulation by light and corresponding sensations of brightness are traditionally supposed to be the *basis* of visual perception. The inputs of the nerves are supposed to be the data on which the perceptual processes in the brain operate. But I make a quite different assumption, because the evidence suggests that stimuli as such contain no information, that brightness sensations are not elements of perception, and that inputs of the retina are not sensory elements on which the brain operates.

Visual perception can fail not only for lack of stimulation but also for lack of stimulus information. In homogeneous ambient darkness, vision fails for lack of stimulation. In homogeneous ambient light, vision fails for lack of information, even with adequate stimulation and corresponding sensations.

DO WE EVER SEE LIGHT AS SUCH?

The difference between stimulation and stimulus information can be shown in another way, by considering two contradictory assertions: (1) nothing can be seen, properly speaking, but light; and (2) light, properly speaking, can never be seen. At least one of these assertions must be wrong.

Classical optics, comparing the eye to a camera, has taught that nothing can possibly get into the eye but light in the form of rays or wave fronts. The only alternative to this doctrine seemed to be the naive theory that little copies of objects got into the eye. If all that can ever reach the retina is light in this form, then it would follow that all we can ever *see* is this light. Sensations of light are the fundamental basis of visual perception, the data, or what is *given*. This line of reasoning has seemed unassailable up to the present. It leads to what I have called the sensation-based theories of perception (Gibson, 1966b). We cannot see surfaces or objects or the environment directly; we only see them indirectly. All we ever see directly is what stimulates the eye, light. The verb *to see*, properly used, means *to have one or more sensations of light*.

What about the opposite assertion that we *never* see light? It may at first sound unreasonable, or perhaps false, but let us examine the statement carefully. Of all the possible things that can be seen, is light one of them?

A single point of light in an otherwise dark field is not "light"; it specifies either a very distant source of light or a very small source, a luminous object. A single instant or "flash" of such a point specifies a brief event at the source, that is, the *on* and the *off*. A fire with coals or flames, a lamp with a wick or filament, a sun or a moon—all these are quite specific objects and are so specified; no one sees merely light. What about a luminous *field*, such as the sky? To me it seems that I see the sky, not the luminosity as such. What about a *beam* of light in the air? But this is not seeing light, because the beam is only visible if there are illuminated particles in the medium. The same is true of the shafts of sunlight seen in clouds under certain conditions.

One can perceive a rainbow, to be sure, a spectrum, but even so that is not the seeing of light. Halos, highlights on water, and scintillations of various kinds are all manifestations of light, not light as such. The only way we see illumination, I believe, is by way of that which is illuminated, the surface on which the beam falls, the cloud, or the particles that are lighted. We do not see the light that is *in* the air, or that *fills* the air. If all this is correct, it becomes quite reasonable to assert that all we ever see is the environment or facts about the environment, never photons or waves or radiant energy.

What about the sensation of being dazzled by looking at the sun, or the sensation of glare that one gets from looking at glossy surfaces that reflect an intense source? Are these not sensations of light as such, and do we not then see pure physical energy? Even in this case, I would argue that the answer is no; we are perceiving a state of the eye akin to pain, arising from excessive stimulation. We perceive a fact about the body as distinguished from a fact about the world, the fact of overstimulation but not the light that caused it. And the experiencing of facts about the body is not the basis of experiencing facts about the world.

If light in the exact sense of the term is never seen as such, it follows that seeing the environment cannot be *based on* seeing light as such. The stimulation of the receptors in the retina cannot be seen, paradoxical as this may sound. The supposed sensations resulting from this stimulation are not the data for perception. Stimulation may be a necessary condition for seeing, but it is not sufficient. There has to be stimulus information available to the perceptual system, not just stimulation of the receptors.

In ordinary speech we say that vision depends on light, and we do not need to know physics to be able to say it with confidence. All of us, including every child, know what it is like to be "in the dark." We cannot see anything, not even our own bodies. Approaching dangers and collisions ahead cannot be foreseen, and this is, with some reason, alarming. But what we mean when we say that vision depends on light is that it depends on illumination and on sources of illumination. We do not necessarily mean that we have to see light or have sensations of light in order to see anything else.

Just as the stimulation of the receptors in the retina cannot be seen, so the mechanical stimulation of the receptors in the skin cannot be felt, and the stimulation of the hair cells in the inner ear cannot be heard. So also the chemical stimulation of the receptors in the tongue cannot be tasted, and the stimulation of the receptors in the nasal membrane cannot be smelled. We do not perceive stimuli.

THE CONCEPT OF THE STIMULUS AS
AN APPLICATION OF ENERGY

The explicit assumption that only the receptors of observers are stimulated and that their sense organs are not stimulated but activated is in disagreement with what most psychologists take for granted. They blithely use the verb *stimulate* and the noun *stimulus* in various ways not consistent with one another. It is convenient and easy to do so, but if the words are slippery and if we allow ourselves to slide from one meaning to another unawares, we are confused without knowing it. I once examined the writings of modern psychology and found eight separate ways in which the use of the term *stimulus* was equivocal (Gibson, 1960*a*).

The concept of the stimulus comes from physiology, where it first meant whatever application of energy fires a nerve cell or touches off a receptor or excites a reflex response. It was taken over by psychology, because it seemed that a stimulus explained not only the arousal of a sensation but the arousal of a response, including responses much more elaborate than reflexes. If all behavior consisted of responses to stimuli, it looked as if a truly scientific psychology could be founded. This was the stimulus-response formula. It was indeed promising. Both stimuli and responses could be measured. But a great variety of environmental facts had to be called stimuli because a variety of things can be responded to. If anything in the world can be called a stimulus, the concept has got out of hand and its original meaning has been lost. I suggest that we go back to its meaning in physiology. In this book I shall use the term strictly. For I now wish to make the clearest possible contrast between stimulus energy and stimulus information.

Note that a stimulus, strictly speaking in the physiologist's sense, is *anything* that touches off a receptor or causes a response; it is the *effective* stimulus, and whatever application of energy touches off the receptor is effective. The photoreceptors in the eye are usually triggered by light but not necessarily; they are also triggered by mechanical or electrical energy. The mechanoreceptors of the skin and the chemoreceptors of the mouth and nose are more or less specialized for mechanical and chemical energy respectively but not completely so; they are just especially "sensitive" to those kinds of energy. A stimulus in this strict meaning carries no information about its source in the world; that is, it does not specify its source. Only stimulation that comes in a structured array and that changes over time specifies its external source.

Note also that a stimulus, strictly speaking, is temporary. There is nothing lasting about it, as there is about a persisting object of the environment. A stimulus must begin and end. If it persists, the response of the receptor tapers off and ceases; the term for this is *sensory adaptation*. Hence, a permanent object cannot possibly be specified by a stimulus. The stimulus information for an object would have to reside in something persisting during an otherwise changing flow of stimulation. And note above all that an object cannot *be* a stimulus, although current thinking carelessly takes for granted that it is one.

An application of stimulus energy exceeding the threshold can be said to *cause* a response of the sensory mechanism, and the response is an *effect*. But the presence of stimulus information cannot be said to cause perception. Perception is not a response to a stimulus but an act of information pickup. Perception may or may not occur in the presence of information. Perceptual awareness, unlike sensory awareness, does not have any discoverable stimulus threshold. It depends on the age of the perceiver, how well he has learned to perceive, and how strongly he is motivated to perceive. If perceptions are based on sensations and sensations have thresholds, then perceptions should have thresholds. But they do not, and the reason for this, I believe, is that perceptions are not based on sensations. There are magnitudes for applied stimuli above which sensations occur and below which they do not. But there is no magnitude of information above which perceiving occurs and below which it does not.

When stimulus energy is transformed into nervous impulses, they are said to be *transmitted* to the brain. But stimulus information is not anything that could possibly be sent up a nerve bundle and delivered to the brain, inasmuch as it has to be isolated and extracted from the ambient energy. Information as here conceived is not transmitted or conveyed, does not consist of signals or messages, and does not entail a sender and a receiver. This will be elaborated later.

When a small packet of stimulus energy is absorbed by a receptor, what is lost to the environment is gained by the living cells. The amount of energy may be as low as a few quanta, but nevertheless energy is conserved. In contrast to this fact, stimulus information is not lost from the environment when it is gained by the observer. There is no such thing as conservation of information. It is not limited in amount. The available information in ambient light, vibration, contact, and chemical action is inexhaustible.

A stimulus, then, carries some of the meaning that the word had in Latin, a goad stuck into the skin of an ox. It is a brief and discrete application of energy to a sensitive surface. As such, it specifies little beyond itself; it contains no information. But a flowing array of stimulation is a different matter entirely.

AMBIENT ENERGY AS AVAILABLE STIMULATION

The environment of an observer was said to consist of substances, the medium, and surfaces. Gravity, heat, light, sound, and volatile substances fill the medium. Chemical and mechanical contacts and vibrations impinge on the observer's body. The observer is immersed as it were in a sea of physical energy. It is a flowing sea, for it changes and undergoes cycles of change, especially of temperature and illumination. The observer, being an organism, exchanges energy with the environment by respiration, food consumption, and behavior. A very small fraction of this ambient sea of energy constitutes stimulation and provides information. The fraction is small, for only the ambient odor entering the nose is effective for smelling, only the train of air vibrations impinging on the eardrums is effective for hearing, and only the ambient light at the entrance pupil of an eye is effective for vision. But this tiny portion of the sea of energy is crucial for survival, because it contains information for things at a distance.

It should be obvious by now that this minute inflow of stimulus energy does not consist of discrete inputs—that stimulation does not consist of stimuli. The flow is continuous. There are, of course, episodes in the flow, but these are nested within one another and cannot be cut up into elementary units. Stimulation is not momentary.

Radiant energy of all wavelengths falls on an individual, that is, impinges on the skin. The infrared radiation will give warmth, and the ultraviolet will cause sunburn, but the narrow band of radiation in between, light, is the only kind that will excite the photoreceptors in the eye after entering the pupil. An eye, or at least a vertebrate chambered eye as distinguished from the faceted eye of an insect, usually takes in something less than a hemisphere of the ambient light, according to G. L. Walls (1942). A pair of eyes like those of a rabbit, pointing in opposite directions, takes in nearly the whole of the ambient light at the same time. Ambient light is structured, as we have seen. And the purpose of a dual ocular system is to register this structure or, more exactly, the invariants of its changing structure. Ambient light is usually very rich in what we call pattern and change. The retinal images register both. And a retinal image involves stimulation of its receptive surface but not, as often supposed, a set or a sequence of stimuli.

THE ORTHODOX THEORY OF
THE RETINAL IMAGE

The generally accepted theory of the eye does not acknowledge that it registers the invariant structure of ambient light but asserts that it forms *an image of an object* on the back of the eye. The object, of course, is in the outer world, and the back of the eye is a photoreceptive surface attached to a nerve bundle. What is the difference between these theories?

The theory of image formation in a dark chamber like the eye goes back more than 350 years to Johannes Kepler. The germ of the theory as stated by him was that everything visible radiates, more particularly that every point on a body can emit rays in all directions. An opaque reflecting surface, to be sure, receives radiation from a source and then re-emits it, but in effect it becomes a collection of radiating point sources. If an eye is present, a small cone of diverging rays enters the pupil from each point source and is caused by the lens to converge to another point on the retina. The diverging and converging rays make what is called a *focused pencil* of rays. The dense set of focus points on the retina constitutes the retinal image. There is a one-to-one projective correspondence between radiating points and focus points.

A focused pencil of rays consists of two parts, the diverging cone of radiant light and the converging cone of rays refracted by the lens, one cone with its vertex on the object and the other with its vertex in the image. This pencil is then repeated for every point on the object. Thus, there is a limitless set of rays in each pencil and a limitless set of pencils for each object. The history of optics suggests that Kepler was mainly responsible for this extraordinary intellectual invention. It involved difficult ideas, but it was and still is the unchallenged foundation of the theory of image formation. The notion of an object composed of points has proved over the centuries to be sympathetic to physicists, because most of them assume that an object really consists of its atoms. And later, in the nineteenth century, the notion of a retinal image consisting of sharp points of focused light did not seem strange to physiologists because they were familiar with punctate stimuli, for example, on the skin.

This theory of point-to-point correspondence between an object and its image lends itself to mathematical analysis. It can be abstracted to the concepts of projective

Figure 4.3

A focused pencil of rays connecting a radiating point on a surface with a focus point in the retinal image.

The rays in the pencil are supposed to be infinitely dense. Note that only the rays that enter the pupil are effective for vision. (From *The Perception of the Visual World* by James Jerome Gibson and used with the agreement of the reprint publisher, Greenwood Press, Inc.)

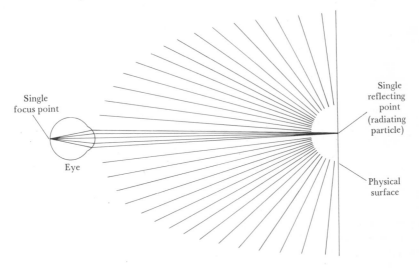

geometry and can be applied with great success to the design of cameras and projectors, that is, to the making of pictures with light, photography. The theory permits lenses to be made with smaller "aberrations," that is, with finer points in the point-to-point correspondence. It works beautifully, in short, for the images that fall on screens or surfaces and that are intended to be looked at. But this success makes it tempting to believe that the image on the retina falls on a kind of screen and is itself something intended to be looked at, that is, a picture. It leads to one of the most seductive fallacies in the history of psychology—that the retinal image is something to be seen. I call this the "little man in the brain" theory of the retinal image (Gibson, 1966*b*, p. 226), which conceives the eye as a camera at the end of a nerve cable that transmits the image to the brain. Then there has to be a little man, a homunculus, seated in the brain who looks at this physiological image. The little man would have to have an eye to see it with, of course, a *little* eye with a *little* retinal image connected to a *little* brain, and so we have explained nothing by this theory. We are in fact worse off than before, since we are confronted with the paradox of an infinite series of little men, each within the other and each looking at the brain of the next bigger man.

If the retinal image is not transmitted to the brain as a whole, the only alternative has seemed to be that it is transmitted to the brain element by element, that is, by signals in the fibers of the optic nerve. There would then be an element-to-element correspondence between image and brain analogous to the point-to-point correspondence between object and image. This seems to avoid the fallacy of the little man in the brain who looks at an image, but it entails all the difficulties of what I have called the

---

JAMES MILL ON VISUAL SENSATION, 1829

"When I lift my eyes from the paper on which I am writing, I see from my window trees and meadows, and horses and oxen, and distant hills. I see each of its proper size, of its proper form, and at its proper distance; and these particulars appear as *immediate* informations of the eye as the colors which I see by means of it. Yet philosophy has ascertained that we derive nothing from the eye whatever but sensations of color. . . . How then, is it that we receive accurate information by the eye of size and shape and distance? By association merely" (Mill, *Analysis of the Phenomena of the Human Mind*, 1829).

How is it indeed! Mill answered, *by association.* But others answered, *by innate ideas of space* or *by rational inference from the sensations* or *by interpretation of the data.* Still others have said, *by spontaneous organization of sensory inputs to the brain.* The current fashionable answer is, *by computerlike activities of the brain on neural signals.* We have empiricism, nativism, rationalism, Gestalt theory, and now information-processing theory. Their adherents would go on debating forever if we did not make a fresh start. *Has* philosophy ascertained that "we derive nothing from the eye whatever but sensations of color"? *No.* "Sensations of color" meant *dabs* or *spots* of color, as if in a painting. Perception does not begin that way.

sensation-based theories of perception. The correspondence between the spots of light on the retina and the spots of sensation in the brain can only be a correspondence of intensity to brightness and of wavelength to color. If so, the brain is faced with the tremendous task of constructing a phenomenal environment out of spots differing in brightness and color. If these are what is seen directly, what is given for perception, if these are the data of sense, then the fact of perception is almost miraculous.

Even the more sophisticated theory that the retinal image is transmitted as signals in the fibers of the optic nerve has the lurking implication of a little man in the brain. For these signals must be in code and therefore have to be decoded; signals are messages, and messages have to be interpreted. In both theories the eye sends, the nerve transmits, and a mind or spirit receives. Both theories carry the implication of a mind that is separate from a body.

It is not necessary to assume that *anything whatever* is transmitted along the optic nerve in the activity of perception. We need not believe that *either* an inverted picture or a set of messages is delivered to the brain. We can think of vision as a perceptual system, the brain being simply part of the system. The eye is also part of the system, since retinal inputs lead to ocular adjustments and then to altered retinal inputs, and so on. The process is circular, not a one-way transmission. The eye-head-brain-body system registers the invariants in the structure of ambient light. The eye is not a camera that forms and delivers an image, nor is the retina simply a keyboard that can be struck by fingers of light.

A DEMONSTRATION THAT THE RETINAL IMAGE
IS NOT NECESSARY FOR VISION

We are apt to forget that an eye is not necessarily a dark chamber, on the back surface of which an inverted image is formed by a lens in the manner described by Kepler. Although the eyes of vertebrates and mollusks are of this sort, the eyes of arthropods are not. They have what is called a *compound eye*, with no chamber, no lens, and no sensory surface but with a closely packed set of receptive tubes called *ommatidia*. Each tube points in a different direction from every other tube, and presumably the organ can thus register differences of intensity in different directions. It is therefore part of a system that registers the structure of ambient light.

In a chapter on the evolutionary development of visual systems (Gibson, 1966*b*, Ch. 9), I described the chambered eye and the compound eye as two different ways of accepting an array of light coming from an environment (pp. 163 ff.). The camera eye has a concave mosaic of photoreceptors, a retina. The compound eye has a convex packet of photoreceptive light tubes. The former accepts an infinite number of pencils of light, each focused to a point and combining to make a continuous image. The latter accepts a finite number of samples of ambient light, without focusing them and without forming an optical image. But if several thousand tubes are packed together, as in the eye of a dragonfly, visual perception is quite good. There is nothing behind a dragonfly's eye that could possibly be seen by you, no image on a surface, no picture. But nevertheless the dragonfly sees its environment.

Zoologists who study insect vision are so respectful of optics as taught in physics textbooks that they are constrained to think of a sort of *upright* image as being formed in the insect eye. But this notion is both vague and self-contradictory. There is no screen on which an image could be formed. The concept of an ambient optic array, even if not recognized in optics, is a better foundation for the understanding of vision in general than the concept of the retinal image. The registering of differences of intensity in different directions is *necessary* for visual perception; the formation of a retinal image is not.

THE CONCEPT OF OPTICAL INFORMATION

The concept of information with which we are most familiar is derived from our experiences of communicating with other people and being communicated with, not from our experience of perceiving the environment directly. We tend to think of information primarily as being sent and received, and we assume that some intermediate kind of transmission has to occur, a "medium" of communication or a "channel" along which the information is said to flow. Information in this sense consists of messages, signs, and signals. In early times messages, which could be oral, written, or pictorial, had to be sent by runner or by horseman. Then the semaphore system was

---

The Fallacy of the Image in the Eye

Ever since someone peeled off the back of the excised eye of a slaughtered ox and, holding it up in front of a scene, observed a tiny, colored, inverted image of the scene on the transparent retina, we have been tempted to draw a false conclusion. We think of the image as *something to be seen*, a picture on a screen. You can see it if you take out the ox's eye, so why shouldn't the ox see it? The fallacy ought to be evident.

The question of how we can see the world as upright when the retinal image is inverted arises because of this false conclusion. All the experiments on this famous question have come to nothing. The reginal image is not anything that can be seen. The famous experiment of G. M. Stratton (1897) on reinverting the retinal image gave unintelligible results because it was misconceived.

invented, and then the electrical telegraph, wireless telegraphy, the telephone, television, and so on at an accelerated rate of development.

We also communicate with others by making a picture on a surface (clay tablet, papyrus, paper, wall, canvas, or screen) and by making a sculpture, a model, or a solid image. In the history of image-making, the chief technological revolution was brought about by the invention of photography, that is, of a photosensitive surface that could be placed at the back of a darkened chamber with a lens in front. This kind of communication, which we call graphic or plastic, does not consist of signs or signals and is not so obviously a message from one person to another. It is not so obviously transmitted or conveyed. Pictures and sculptures are apt to be displayed, and thus they *contain* information and make it available for anyone who looks. They nevertheless are, like the spoken and written words of language, *man-made*. They provide information that, like the information conveyed by words, is mediated by the perception of the first observer. They do not permit firsthand experience—only experience at second hand.

The ambient stimulus information available in the sea of energy around us is quite different. The information for perception is not transmitted, does not consist of signals, and does not entail a sender and a receiver. The environment does not communicate with the observers who inhabit it. Why should the world speak to us? The concept of stimuli as signals to be interpreted implies some such nonsense as a world-soul trying to get through to us. The world is *specified* in the structure of the light that reaches us, but it is entirely up to us to perceive it. The secrets of nature are not to be understood by the breaking of its code.

Optical information, the information that can be extracted from a flowing optic array, is a concept with which we are not at all familiar. Being intellectually lazy, we try to understand perception in the same way we understand communication, in terms of the familiar. There is a vast literature nowadays of speculation about the media of communication. Much of it is undisciplined and vague. The concept of information most of us have comes from that literature. But this is not the concept that will be adopted in this book. For we cannot explain perception in terms of communication; it is quite the other way around. We cannot convey information about the world to others unless we have perceived the world. And the available information for our perception is radically different from the information we convey.

SUMMARY

Ecological optics is concerned with many-times-reflected light in the medium, that is, *illumination.* Physical optics is concerned with electromagnetic energy, that is, *radiation.*

Ambient light coming to a point in the air is profoundly different from radiant light leaving a point source. The ambient light has structure, whereas the radiant light does not. Hence, ambient light makes available information about reflecting surfaces, whereas radiant light can at most transmit information about the atoms from which it comes.

If the ambient light were unstructured or undifferentiated, it would provide no information about an environment, although it would stimulate the photoreceptors of an eye. Thus, there is a clear distinction between stimulus information and stimulation. We do not have sensations of light triggered by stimuli under normal conditions. The doctrine of discrete stimuli does not apply to ordinary vision.

The orthodox theory of the formation of an image on a screen, based on the correspondence between radiating points and focus points, is rejected as the basis for an explanation of ecological vision. This theory applies to the design of optical instruments and cameras, but it is a seductive fallacy to conceive the ocular system in this way. One of the worst results of the fallacy is the inference that the retinal image is transmitted to the brain.

The information that can be extracted from ambient light is not the kind of information that is transmitted over a channel. There is no sender outside the head and no receiver inside the head.

FIVE

THE AMBIENT OPTIC ARRAY

The central concept of ecological optics is the ambient optic array at a point of observation. To be an *array* means to have an arrangement, and to be *ambient at a point* means to surround a position in the environment that could be occupied by an observer. The position may or may not be occupied; for the present, let us treat it as if it were not.

What is implied more specifically by an *arrangement*? So far I have suggested only that it has *structure*, which is not very explicit. The *absence of structure* is easier to describe. This would be a homogeneous field with no differences of intensity in different parts. An array cannot be homogeneous; it must be heterogeneous. That is, it cannot be undifferentiated, it must be differentiated; it cannot be empty, it must be filled; it cannot be formless, it must be formed. These contrasting terms are still unsatisfactory, however. It is difficult to define the notion of structure. In the effort to clarify it, a radical proposal will be made having to do with *invariant* structure.

What is implied by *ambient at a point*? The answer to this question is not so difficult. To be ambient, an array must surround the point completely. It must be environing. The field must be closed, in the geometrical sense of that term, the sense in which the surface of a sphere returns upon itself. More precisely, the field is unbounded. Note that the field provided by a picture on a plane surface does not satisfy this criterion. No picture can be ambient, and even a picture said to be panoramic is never a completely closed sphere. Note also that the temporary field of view of an observer does not satisfy the criterion, for it also has boundaries. This fact is obviously of the greatest importance, and we shall return to it in Chapter 7 and again in Chapter 12.

Finally, what is implied by the term *point* in the phrase *point of observation*? Instead of a geometrical point in abstract space, I mean a position in ecological space, in a medium instead of in a void. It is a place where an observer *might* be and from which an act of observation *could* be made. Whereas abstract space consists of points, ecological space consists of places—locations or positions.

A sharp distinction will be made between the ambient array at an unoccupied point of observation and the array at a point that is occupied by an observer, human or other. When the position becomes occupied, something very interesting happens to the ambient array: it contains information about the body of the observer. This modification of the array will be given due consideration later.

The point of observation in ecological optics might seem to be the equivalent of the station point in perspective geometry, the kind of perspective used in the making of a representative painting. The station point is the point of projection for the picture plane on which the scene is projected. But the terms are not at all equivalent and should not be confused, as we shall see. A station point has to be stationary. It cannot move relative to the world, and it must not move relative to the picture plane. But a point of observation is never stationary, except as a limiting case. Observers move about in the environment, and observation is typically made from a moving position.

HOW IS AMBIENT LIGHT STRUCTURED? PRELIMINARY CONSIDERATIONS

If we reject the assumption that the environment consists of atoms in space and that, hence, the light coming to a point in space consists of rays from these atoms, what do we accept? It is tempting to assume that the environment consists of *objects* in space and that, hence, the ambient array consists of *closed-contour forms* in an otherwise empty field, or "figures on a ground." For each object in space, there would correspond a form in the optic array. But this assumption is not close to being good enough and must also be rejected. A form in the array could not correspond to each object in space, because some objects are hidden behind others. And in any case, to put it radically, the environment does not consist of objects. The environment consists of the earth and the sky with objects *on* the earth and *in* the sky, of mountains and clouds, fires and sunsets, pebbles and stars. Not all of these are segregated objects, and some of them are nested within one another, and some move, and some are animate. But the environment is all these various things—places, surfaces, layouts, motions, events, animals, people, and artifacts that structure the light at points of observation. The array at a point does not consist of forms in a field. The figure-ground phenomenon does not apply to the world in general. The notion of a closed contour, an outline, comes from the art of drawing an object, and the phenomenon comes from the experiment of presenting an observer with a drawing to find out what she perceives. But this is not the only way, or even the best way, to investigate perception.

We obtain a better notion of the structure of ambient light when we think of it as divided and subdivided into component parts. For the terrestrial environment, the sky-earth contrast divides the unbounded spherical field into two hemispheres, the upper being brighter than the lower. Then both are further subdivided, the lower

Figure 5.1

The ambient optic array from a wrinkled earth outdoors under the sky.

In this illustration it is assumed that illumination has reached a steady state. The earth is shown as wrinkled or humped, but not as cluttered. The dashed lines in this drawing depict the envelopes of visual solid angles, not rays of light. The nesting of these solid angles has not been shown. The contrasts in this diagram are caused by differential illumination of the humps of the earth. Compare this with the photograph of hills and valleys in Figure 5.9. This is an optic array at a single fixed point of observation. It illustrates the main invariants of natural perspective: the separation of the two hemispheres of the ambient array at the horizon, and the increasing density of the optical texture toward its maximum at the horizon. These are invariant even when the array flows, as it does when the point of observation moves.

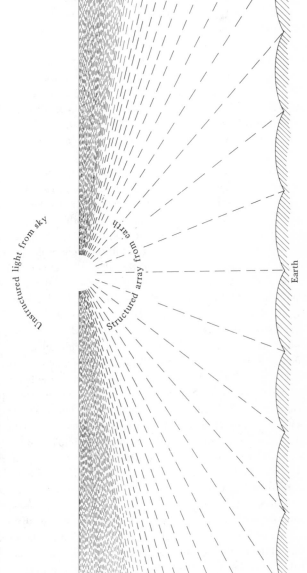

Unstructured light from sky

Structured array from earth

Earth

much more elaborately than the upper and in quite a different way. The components of the earth, as I suggested in Chapter 1, are nested at different levels of size—for example, mountains, canyons, trees, leaves, and cells. The components of the *array* from the earth also fall into a hierarchy of subordinate levels of size, but the components of the array are quite different, of course, from the components of the earth. The components of the array are the *visual angles* from the mountains, canyons, trees, and leaves (actually, what are called *solid angles* in geometry), and they are conventionally measured in degrees, minutes, and seconds instead of kilometers, meters, and millimeters. They are *intercept angles*, as we shall see. All these optical components of the array, whatever their size, become vanishingly small at the margin between earth and sky, the horizon; moreover, they change in size whenever the point of observation moves. The substantial components of the earth, on the other hand, do not change in size.

There are several advantages in conceiving the optic array in this way, as a nested hierarchy of solid angles all having a common apex instead of as a set of rays intersecting at a point. Every solid angle, no matter how small, has form in the sense that its cross-section has a form, and a solid angle is quite unlike a ray in this respect. Each solid angle is unique, whereas a ray is not unique and can only be identified arbitrarily, by a pair of coordinates. Solid angles can fill up a sphere in the way that sectors fill up a circle, but it must be remembered that there are angles within angles, so that their sum does not *add* up to a sphere. The surface of the sphere whose center is the common apex of all the solid angles can be thought of as a kind of transparent film or shell, but it should not be thought of as a picture.

The structure of an optic array, so conceived, is without gaps. It does not consist of points or spots that are discrete. It is completely filled. Every component is found to consist of smaller components. Within the boundaries of any form, however small, there are always other forms. This means that the array is more like a hierarchy than like a matrix and that it should not be analyzed into a set of spots of light, each with a locus and each with a determinate intensity and frequency. In an ambient hierarchical structure, loci are not defined by pairs of coordinates, for the relation of location is not given by degrees of azimuth and elevation (for example) but by the relation of inclusion.

The difference between the relation of *metric location* and the relation of *inclusion* can be illustrated by the following fact. The stars in the sky can be located conveniently by degrees to the right of north and degrees up from the horizon. But each star can also be located by its inclusion in one of the constellations and by the superordinate pattern of the whole sky. Similarly, the optical structures that correspond to the leaves and trees and hills of the earth are each included in the next larger structure. The texture of the earth, of course, is dense compared to the constellations of discrete stars and thus even less dependent than they are on a coordinate system. If this is so, the perception of the direction of some particular item on the earth, its direction-from-here, is not a problem in its own right. The perceiving of the environment does not consist of perceptions of the differing directions of the items of the environment.

THE LAWS OF NATURAL PERSPECTIVE:
THE INTERCEPT ANGLE

The notion of a visual angle with its apex at the eye and its base at an object in the world is very old. It goes back to Euclid who postulated what he called a "visual cone" for each object in space. The term is not exact, for the object need not be circular and the figure does not have to be a cone. Ptolemy spoke of the "visual pyramid," which implied that the object was rectangular. Actually, we should refer to the *face* of an object, which can have any shape whatever, and to a corresponding *solid angle*, having an envelope. A cross-section of this envelope is what we call the *outline of the object*. We can now note that the solid angle shrinks as the distance of the object from the apex increases, and it is laterally squeezed as the face of the object is slanted or turned. These are the two main laws of perspective for objects. Euclid and Ptolemy and their

Figure 5.2
The ambient optic array from a room with a window.

This drawing shows a cluttered environment where some surfaces are projected at the point of observation and the remainder are not, that is, where some are unhidden and the others are hidden. The hidden surfaces are indicated by dotted lines. Only the faces of the layout of surfaces are shown, not the facets of their surfaces, that is, their textures.

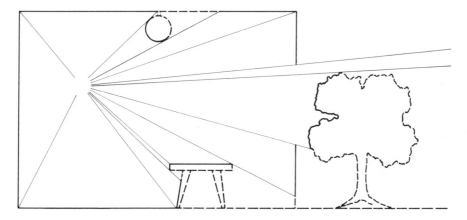

successors for many centuries never doubted that objects were seen by means of these solid angles, whether conical, pyramidal, or otherwise. They were the basis of ancient optics. Nothing was then known of inverted retinal images, and the comparison of the eye with a camera would not be made for a thousand years. The ancients did not understand the eye, they were puzzled by light, they had no conception of the modern doctrine that nothing gets into the eye but light, but they were clear about visual angles.

The conception of the ambient optic array as a set of solid angles corresponding to objects is thus a continuation of ancient and medieval optics. Instead of only free-standing objects present to an eye, however, I postulate an environment of illuminated surfaces. And instead of a group of solid angles, I postulate a nested complex of them. The large solid angles in the array come from the *faces* of this layout, from the facades of detached objects, and from the interspaces or holes that we call background or sky (which Euclid and Ptolemy seem never to have thought of). The small solid angles in the array come from what might be called the *facets* of the layout as distinguished from the faces, the textures of the surfaces as distinguished from their forms. As already has been emphasized, however, the distinction between these size-levels is arbitrary.

Natural perspective, as I conceive it, is the study of an ambient array of solid angles that correspond to certain distinct geometrical parts of a terrestrial environment, those that are separated by edges and corners. There are elegant trigonometric relations between the angles and the environmental parts. There are gradients of size and density of the angles along meridians of the lower half of the array, the earth, with sizes vanishing and density becoming infinite at the horizon. These relations contain a great amount of information about the parts of the earth. No one who understood them would think of questioning their validity. It is a perfectly clear and straightforward discipline, although neglected and undeveloped. But the environment does not *wholly* consist of sharply differentiated geometrical parts or forms. Natural perspective does not apply to shadows with penumbras and patches of light. It does not apply to sunlit surfaces with varying degrees of illumination. It geometrizes the environment and thus oversimplifies it. The most serious limitation, however, is that natural perspective omits motion from consideration. The ambient optic array is treated as if its structure were frozen in time and as if the point of observation were motionless.

Although I have called this discipline *natural perspective*, the ancients called it *perspectiva*, the Latin word for what we now call *optics*. In modern times, the term *perspective* has come to mean a technique—the technique of picture-making. A picture is a surface, whether it be painted by hand or processed by photography, and per-spective is the art of "representing" the geometrical relationships of natural objects on that surface. When the Renaissance painters discovered the procedures for perspective representation, they very properly called the method *artificial perspective*. They understood that this had to be distinguished from the natural perspective that governed the ordinary perception of the environment. Since that time we have become so picture-minded, so dominated by pictorial thinking, that we have ceased to make the distinction. But to confuse pictorial perspective with natural perspective is to misconceive the problem of visual perception at the outset. The so-called cues for depth in a picture are not at all the same as the information for surface layout in a frozen ambient array, although pictorial thinking about perception tempts us to assume that they are the same. Pictures are artificial displays of information frozen in time, and this fact will be evident when the special kind of visual perception that is mediated by such displays is treated in detail in Part IV.

Natural perspective, as well as artificial perspective, is restricted in scope, being concerned only with a frozen optical structure. This restriction will be removed in what follows.

Figure 5.3
The same ambient array with the point of observation occupied by a person.
When an observer is present at a point of observation, the visual system begins to function.

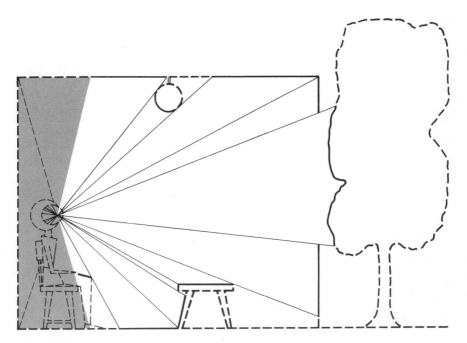

OPTICAL STRUCTURE WITH A MOVING POINT
OF OBSERVATION

A point of observation at rest is only the limiting case of a point of observation in motion, the null case. Observation implies movement, that is, locomotion with reference to the rigid environment, because all observers are animals and all animals are mobile. Plants do not observe but animals do, and plants do not move about but animals do. Hence, the structure of an optic array at a stationary point of observation is only a special case of the structure of an optic array at a moving point of observation. The point of observation normally proceeds along a path of locomotion, and the "forms" of the array change as locomotion proceeds. More particularly, every solid angle

Figure 5.4
The change of the optic array brought about by a locomotor movement of the observer.
The thin solid lines indicate the ambient optic array for the seated observer, and the thin dashed lines the altered optic array after standing up and moving forward. The difference between the two arrays is specific to the difference between the points of observation, that is, to the path of locomotion. Note that the whole ambient array is changed, including the portion behind the head. And note that what was previously hidden becomes unhidden.

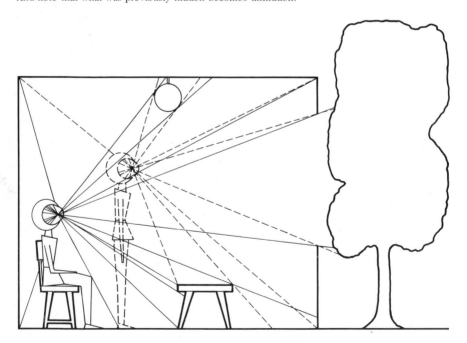

included within the array, large or small, is enlarged or reduced or compressed or, in some cases, wiped out. It is wiped out, of course, when its surface goes out of sight.

The optic array *changes*, of course, as the point of observation moves. But it also does *not* change, not completely. Some features of the array do not persist and some do. The changes come from the locomotion, and the nonchanges come from the rigid layout of the environmental surfaces. Hence, the nonchanges specify the layout and count as information about it; the changes specify locomotion and count as another kind of information, about the locomotion itself. We have to distinguish between two kinds of structure in a normal ambient array, and I shall call them the *perspective structure* and the *invariant structure*.

PERSPECTIVE STRUCTURE AND INVARIANT STRUCTURE

The term *structure* is vague, as we have seen. Let us suppose that a kind of essential structure underlies the superficial structure of an array when the point of observation moves. This essential structure consists of what is invariant despite the change. What is invariant does not emerge unequivocally except with a flux. The essentials become evident in the context of changing nonessentials.

Consider the paradox in the following piece of folk wisdom: "The more it changes, the more it is the same thing." Wherein is it true and wherein false? If *change* means *to become different but not to be converted into something else*, the assertion is true, and the saying emphasizes the fact that whatever is invariant is more evident with change than it would be without change. If *change* means *to become different by being converted into something else*, the assertion is self-contradictory, and the paradox arises. But this is not what the word ordinarily means. And assuredly it is not what change in the ambient array means. One arrangement does not become a wholly different arrangement by a displacement of viewpoint. There is no jump from one to another, only a variation of structure that serves to reveal the nonvariation of structure. The pattern of the array does not ordinarily scintillate; the forms of the array do not go from triangular to quadrangular, for example.

There are many invariants of structure, and some of them persist for long paths of locomotion while some persist only for short paths. But what I am calling the *perspective structure* changes with every displacement of the point of observation—the shorter the displacement the smaller the change, and the longer the displacement the greater the change. Assuming that the environment is never reduplicated from place to place, the arrested perspective is unique at each stationary point of observation, that is, for each point of observation there is one and only one arrested perspective. On the other hand, invariants of structure are common to all points of observation—some for all points in the whole terrestrial environment, some only for points within the boundaries of certain locales, and some only for points of observation within (say) a single room. But to repeat, the invariant structure separates off best when the frozen perspective structure begins to flow.

Consider, for example, the age-old question of how a rectangular surface like a tabletop can be given to sight when presumably all that an eye can see is a large number of forms that are trapezoids and only one form that is rectangular, that one being seen only when the eye is positioned on a line perpendicular to the center of the surface. The question has never been answered, but it can be reformulated to ask, What are the invariants underlying the transforming perspectives in the array from the tabletop? What specifies the shape of this rigid surface as projected to a moving point of observation? Although the changing angles and proportions of the set of trapezoidal projections are a fact, the unchanging relations among the four angles and the invariant proportions over the set are another fact, equally important, and they uniquely specify the rectangular surface. There will be experimental evidence about optical transformations as information in Chapter 9.

We tend to think of each member of the set of trapezoidal projections from a rectangular object as being a form in space. A change is then a transition from one form to another, a transformation. But this habit of thought is misleading. Optical change is not a transition from one form to another but a reversible process. The superficial form becomes different, but the underlying form remains the same. The structure changes in some respects and does not change in others. More exactly, it is variant in some respects and invariant in others.

The geometrical habit of separating space from time and imagining sets of frozen forms in space is very strong. One can think of each point of observation in the medium as stationary and distinct. To each such point there would correspond a unique optic array. The set of all points is the space of the medium, and the corresponding set of all optic arrays is the whole of the available information about layout. The set of all line segments in the space specifies all the possible displacements of points of observation in the medium, and the corresponding set of transformation families gives the information that specifies all the possible paths. This is an elegant and abstract way of thinking, modeled on projective geometry. But it does not allow for the complexities

---

REDUPLICATION

It is easy to make copies or duplicates of a picture but the world is never exactly the same in one place as it is in another. Nor is one organism ever exactly the same as another. One cubic yard of empty abstract space is exactly the same as another, but that is a different matter.

of optical change and does not do justice to the fact that the optic array *flows in time* instead of going from one structure to another. What we need for the formulation of ecological optics are not the traditional notions of space and time but the concepts of variance and invariance considered as reciprocal to one another. The notion of a *set* of stationary points of observation in the medium is appropriate for the problem of a whole crowd of observers standing in different positions, each of them perceiving the environment from his own point of view. But even so, the fact that all observers can perceive the same environment depends on the fact that each point of view can move to any other point of view.

THE SIGNIFICANCE OF CHANGING PERSPECTIVE IN THE AMBIENT ARRAY

When the moving point of observation is understood as the general case, the stationary point of observation is more intelligible. It no longer is conceived as a single geometrical point in space but as a pause in locomotion, as a temporarily fixed position relative to the environment. Accordingly, an arrested perspective structure in the ambient array specifies to an observer such a fixed position, that is, rest; and a flowing perspective structure specifies an unfixed position, that is, locomotion. The optical information for distinguishing locomotion from nonlocomotion is available, and this is extremely valuable for all observers, human or animal. In physics the motion of an observer in space is "relative," inasmuch as what we call motion with reference to one chosen frame of reference may be nonmotion with reference to another frame of reference. In ecology this does not hold, and the locomotion of an observer in the environment is absolute. The environment is simply that with respect to which either locomotion or a state of rest occurs, and the problem of relativity does not arise.

Locomotion and rest go with flowing and frozen perspective structure in the ambient array; they are what the flow and the nonflow *mean*. They contain information about the potential observer, not information about the environment, as the invariants do. But note that information about a world that surrounds a point of observation implies information about the point of observation that is surrounded by a world. Each kind of information implies the other. Later, in discussing the occupied point of observation, I shall call the former *exterospecific information* and the latter *propriospecific information*.

Not only does flowing perspective structure specify locomotion, but the particular instance of flow specifies the particular path of locomotion. That is, the difference of perspective between the beginning and the end of the optical change is specific to the difference of position between the beginning and the end of the locomotor displacement. But more than that, the *course* of the optical flow is specific to the *route* the path of locomotion takes through the environment. Between one place and another there are many different routes. The two places are specified by their different arrested perspectives, but the different routes between them are in correspondence with different optical sequences between the two perspectives. There will be more of this later. It is enough now to point out that the visual control of locomotion by an observer, purposive locomotion such as homing, migrating, finding one's way, getting from place to place, and being oriented, depends on just the kind of sequential optical information described.

It is important to realize that the flowing perspective structure and the underlying invariant structure are concurrent. They exist at the same time. Although they specify different things, locomotion through a rigid world in the first instance and the layout of that rigid world in the second instance, they are like the two sides of a coin, for each implies the other. This hypothesis, that optical change can seemingly specify two things at the same time, sounds very strange, as if one cause were having two effects or as if one stimulus were arousing two sensations. But there is nothing illogical about the idea of concurrent specification of two reciprocal things. Such an idea is much needed in psychology.

THE CHANGE BETWEEN HIDDEN
AND UNHIDDEN SURFACES: COVERING EDGES

We are now prepared to face a fact that has seemed deeply puzzling, a fact that poses the greatest difficulty for all theories of visual perception based on sensations. The layout of the environment includes unprojected (hidden) surfaces at a point of observation as well as projected surfaces, but observers perceive the layout, not just the projected surfaces. Things are seen *in the round* and one thing is seen *in front* of another. How can this be? Information must be available for the whole layout, not just for its facades, for the covered surfaces as well as the covering surfaces. What is this information? Presumably it becomes evident over time, with changes of the array. I will argue that the information is implicit in the *edges that separate* the surfaces or, rather, in the optical specification of these edges. I am suggesting that if covering edges are specified, both the covered and the covering surfaces are also specified.

To suggest that an observer can see surfaces that are unseen is, of course, a paradox. I do not mean that. I am not saying that one can see the unseen, and I am suspicious of visionaries who claim that they can. A vast amount of mystification in the history of human thought has arisen from this paradox. The suggestion is that one can perceive surfaces that are temporarily *out of sight,* and what it is to be out of sight will be carefully defined. The important fact is that they come into sight and go out of sight as the observer moves, first in one direction and then in the opposite direction. If locomotion is reversible, as it is, whatever goes out of sight as the observer travels comes into sight as the observer returns and conversely. The generality of this principle has never been realized; it applies to the shortest locomotions, in centimeters, as well as to the longest, in kilometers. But it has not been elaborated. I will call it the *principle of reversible occlusion*. The theory of the cues for depth perception includes one cue called "movement parallax" and another called "superposition," both related to the above principle, but these terms are vague and do not even begin to explain what needs to be explained. What we see is not depth as such but *one thing behind another*. The new principle can be made explicit. I will attempt to do so, at some length.

Figure 5.5
Objects seen in the round and behind other objects.
Do you perceive covered surfaces as well as covering surfaces in this photograph? (Photo by Jim Scherer.)

PROJECTED AND UNPROJECTED SURFACES

There are many commonsense words that refer to the fact of covered and uncovered things. Objects and surfaces are said to be hidden or unhidden, screened or unscreened, concealed or revealed, undisclosed or disclosed. We might borrow a technical word in astronomy, *occultation*, but it means primarily the shutting off of the light from a celestial source, as in an eclipse. We need a word for the cutting off of a visual solid angle, not of light rays. I have chosen the word *occlusion* for it. An occluded surface is one that is out of sight or hidden from view. An occluding edge is the edge of an occluding surface. The term was first introduced in a paper by J. J. Gibson, G. A. Kaplan, H. N. Reynolds, and K. Wheeler (1969) on the various ways in which a thing can pass between the state of being visible and the state of being invisible. The experiment will be described in Chapter 11.

Occlusion arises because of two facts about the environment, both described in Chapter 2. First, surfaces are generally opaque; and second, the basic environment, the earth, is generally cluttered. As to the first, if surfaces were as transparent as air, they would not reflect light at all and there would be no use for vision. Most substances are nontransmitting (they reflect and absorb instead), and therefore light is reflected back from the surface. A few substances are partially transmitting or "translucent," and hence a sheet of such a substance will transmit part of the radiant light but will not transmit the structure of the ambient array; it will let through photons but not visual solid angles. There can be an obstructing of the *view* without obstructing of the *light*, although an obstructing of the light will of course also obstruct the view. If we add the fact that surfaces are also generally textured, the facts of opaque surfaces as contrasted with the surfaces of semitransparent and translucent substances become intelligible.

The second fact is that the environment is generally cluttered. What I called an open environment is seldom or never realized, although it is the only case in which all surfaces are projected and none are unprojected. An open environment has what we call an unobstructed view. But the flat and level earth receding unbroken to a pure linear horizon in a great circle, with a cloudless sky, would be a desolate environment indeed. Perhaps it would not be quite as lifeless as geometrical space, but almost. The *furniture* of the earth, like the furnishings of a room, is what makes it livable. The earth as such affords only standing and walking; the furniture of the earth affords all the rest of behavior. The main items of the clutter (following the terminology adopted in Chapter 3) are *objects*, both attached and detached, *enclosures*, *convexities* such as hills, *concavities* such as holes, and *apertures* such as windows. These features of surface layout give rise to occluding surfaces or, more exactly, to the *separation* of occluding and occluded surfaces.

A surface is *projected* at a point of observation if it has a visual solid angle in the ambient optic array; it is *unprojected* if it does not. A projected surface may become unprojected in at least three ways—if its solid angle is diminished to a point, if the solid angle is compressed to a line, or if the solid angle is wiped out. In the first case we say that the surface is too far away, in the second that it is turned so as not to face the point of observation, in the third that the view is obstructed. The second case, that of facing toward or away, is instructive. A wall or a sheet of paper has two "faces" but only one can *face* a fixed point. The relation between the occluding and occluded surfaces is given by the relation of each to the point; the relation is not merely geometrical but also optical. The relation is designated when we distinguish between the *near* side and the *far* side of an object. (It is not, however, well expressed by the terms *front* and *back*, since they are ambiguous. They can refer to such surfaces as the front and the back of a house or the front and the back of a head. Terms can be borrowed from ordinary language only with discretion!)

GOING OUT OF AND COMING INTO SIGHT

A point of observation is to be thought of as moving through the medium to and fro, back and forth, often along old paths but sometimes along new ones. Displacements of this position are reversible and are reversed as its occupier comes and goes, even as she slightly shifts her posture. Any face or facet, any surface of the layout, that is progressively hidden during a displacement is progressively unhidden during its reversal. Going out of sight is the inverse of coming into sight. Hence, occluding and occluded surfaces interchange. The occluding ones *change into* the occluded ones and vice versa, not by changing from one entity to another but by a special transition.

The terms *disappearance* and its opposite, *appearance*, should not be used for this transition. They have slippery meanings, like *visible* and *invisible*. For a surface may disappear by going out of existence as well as by going out of sight, and the two cases are profoundly different. A surface that disappears because it is no longer projected to *any* point of observation, because it has evaporated, for example, should not be confused with a surface that disappears because it is no longer projected to a fixed point of observation. The latter can be seen from another position; the former cannot be seen from any position. Failure to distinguish these meanings of *disappear* is common; it encourages careless observation and vague beliefs in ghosts, or in the reality of the "unseen." To *disappear* can also refer to a surface that continues to exist but is no longer projected to any point of observation because of darkness. Or we might speak of something disappearing "in the distance," referring to a surface barely projected to a point of observation because its visual solid angle has diminished to a limit. These modes of so-called disappearance are quite radically different. The differences between (1) a surface that ceases to exist, (2) a surface that is no longer illuminated, (3) a surface that lies on the horizon, and (4) a surface that is occluded are described in a paper by

Gibson, Kaplan, Reynolds, and Wheeler (1969) and are illustrated in a motion picture film (Gibson, 1968a). An experimental study of the perception of occlusion using motion picture displays has been reported by Kaplan (1969).

THE LOCI OF OCCLUSION: OCCLUDING EDGES

We must now distinguish an edge that is simply the junction of two surfaces from an edge that causes one surface to hide another, an *occluding edge*. In the proposed terminology of layout in Chapter 3, I defined an *edge* as the apex of a convex dihedral (as distinguished from a *corner*, which is the apex of a concave dihedral). But an occluding edge is a dihedral where only one of the surfaces is projected to the point of observation—an *apical* occluding edge. I also defined a *curved convexity* (as distinguished from a *curved concavity*), and another kind of occluding edge is the *brow* of this convexity, that is, the line of tangency of the envelope of the visual solid angle—a *curved* occluding edge. The apical occluding edge is "sharp," and the curved occluding edge is "rounded." The two are illustrated in Figure 5.6. The latter slides along the surface as the point of observation moves, but the former does not. Note that an occluding edge always requires a convexity of some sort, a protrusion of the substance into the medium.

These two kinds of occluding edges are found in the ells of corridors, the brinks of cliffs, the brows of hills, and the near sides of holes in the ground. One face or facet or part of the layout hides another to which it may be connected and which it may adjoin. This is different from what I called a detached object, by which I mean the movable or moving object having a topologically closed surface with substance inside and medium outside. The detached object produces a visual solid angle in the optic array, as noted by Euclid and Ptolemy, and yields a closed-contour figure in the visual

Figure 5.6

The sharp occluding edge and the rounded occluding edge at a fixed point of observation.

The hidden portions of the surface layout are indicated by dotted lines.

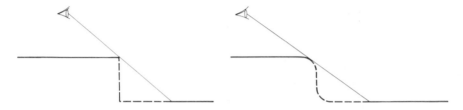

field, as described by Edgar Rubin and celebrated by the gestalt psychologists under the name of the "figure-ground phenomenon." Occluding edges are a special case, because not only does the near side of the object hide the far side but the object covers a sector of the surface behind it, the ground, for example. The occluding edges may be apical, as when the object is a polyhedron, or the locus of the tangent of the envelope of the solid angle to the surface, as when the object is curved. These are illustrated in Figure 5.7, where both the hiding of the far side and the covering of the background are shown. The object is itself rounded or solid, and it is superposed on the ground, which is also continuous behind the object. These two kinds of occlusion may be treated separately.

SELF-OCCLUSION AND SUPERPOSITION

An object, in the present terminology, is both voluminous and superposed. It exists in volume and it may lie in front of another surface, or another object. In short, an object always occludes itself and generally also occludes something else. The effect of a moving point of observation is different in the two cases.

Projected and unprojected surfaces interchange as the point of observation moves, but the interchange between parts of the object is not like that between parts of the background. There is an interchange between *opposite faces* of the object but an interchange of *adjacent areas* of the surface behind the object. For the object, the near side turns into the far side and vice versa, whereas for the background an uncovered

Figure 5.7
Both the far side of an object and the background of the object are hidden by its occluding edges.
Two detached objects are shown, one with sharp occluding edges and the other with rounded occluding edges.

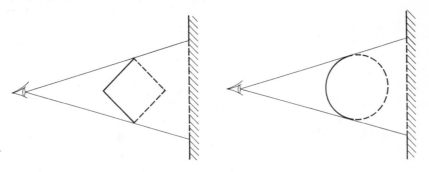

area becomes covered and vice versa. The change of optical structure in the former case is by way of perspective transformation, whereas the disturbance of optical structure in the latter case is more radical, a "kinetic disruption" being involved.

In Figure 5.7, as the point of observation moves each face of the facade of the polyhedron undergoes transformation, for example, from trapezoid to square to trapezoid. Ultimately, when the face is maximally foreshortened, it is what we call "edge on," that is, it becomes an occluding edge. The near face turns into a far face by way of the edge. While this is happening at one edge, the other edge is revealing a previously hidden face. A far face turns into a near face. The two occluding edges in the diagram are perfectly reciprocal; while one is converting near into far, the other is converting far into near. The width of the polyhedron goes into depth, and the depth comes back into width. Width and depth are thus interchangeable.

Similarly, one could describe the transformation of each facet of the textured surface of the curved object. If the object is a sphere, the circular occluding edge (the *outline*, in pictorial terminology) does not transform, but the optical structure within it does. At one edge the texture is progressively turning from projected into unprojected, from near into far, while at the other edge the texture is progressively turning from unprojected into projected, from far into near. The transition occurs at the limit of the slant transformation, the ultimate of perspective foreshortening, but actually the optical texture reaches and goes beyond this purported limit. It has to go beyond it because it comes from beyond that limit at the other occluding edge.

SUPERPOSITION

Now consider the separated background behind the objects in Figure 5.7, the fact of superposition as distinguished from the fact of solidity. As the point of observation moves, the envelope of the visual solid angle sweeps across the surface. The leading edge progressively covers the texture of the surface, while the trailing edge progressively uncovers it. I have suggested metaphorically that the texture is "wiped out" and "unwiped" at the lateral borders of the figure (Gibson, 1966b, pp. 199 ff.). This was inspired by the metaphors used by A. Michotte in describing experiments on what he called the "tunnel effect" (Michotte, Thinès, and Crabbé, 1964). A somewhat more exact description of this optical change will be given below. But note that if the texture that is progressively covered has the same structure as the texture that is progressively uncovered the unity of the surface is well specified.

The metaphor of "wiping" is inexact. A better description of the optical transition was given by Gibson, Kaplan, Reynolds, and Wheeler (1969), and it was also described by Kaplan (1969) as a "kinetic disruption." There is a disturbance of the structure of the array that is not a transformation, not even a transformation that passes through its vanishing limit, but a breaking of its adjacent order. More exactly, there is either a progressive decrementing of components of structure, called *deletion,* or its opposite, a progressive incrementing of components of structure, called *accretion.* An edge that is covering the background deletes from the array; an edge that is uncovering the background accretes to it. There is no such disruption for the surface that is covering or uncovering, only for the surface that is being covered or uncovered. And nondisruption, I suggest, is a kind of invariance.

THE INFORMATION TO SPECIFY THE
CONTINUATION OF SURFACES

A surface always "bends under" an occluding edge, and another surface generally "extends behind" it. These surfaces are connected or continuous. Is there information in a changing optic array to specify the connnectedness or continuity?

Here is a tentative hypothesis for the continuous object surface:

Whenever a perspective transformation of form or texture in the optic array goes to its limit and when a series of forms or textures are progressively foreshortened to this limit, a continuation of the surface of an object is specified at an occluding edge. This is the formula for going out of sight; the formula is reversed for coming into sight.

Here is a tentative hypothesis for the continuous background surface:

Whenever there occurs a regular disturbance of the persistence of forms and textures in the optic array such that they are progressively deleted at a contour, the continuation of the surface of a ground is specified at an occluding edge. This is for going out of sight; substituting accretion for deletion gives the formula for coming into sight.

These two hypotheses make no assertions about perception, only about the information that is normally available for perception. They do not refer to *space*, or to the *third dimension*, or to *depth*, or to *distance*. Nothing is said about forms or patterns in two dimensions. But they suggest a radically new basis for explaining the perception of solid superposed objects, a new theory based not on cues or clues or signs but on the direct pickup of solidity and superposition. An object is in fact voluminous; a background is in fact continuous. A picture or an image of an object is irrelevant to the question of how it is perceived.

The assumption for centuries has been that the sensory basis for the perception of an object is the outline form of its image on the retina. Object perception can only be based on form perception. First the silhouette is detected and then the depth is added, presumably because of past experiences with the cues for depth. But the fact is that the progressive foreshortening of the face of an object is perceived as the turning of the object, which is precisely what the transformation specifies, and is never perceived as a change of form, which ought to be seen if the traditional assumption is correct—that the silhouette is detected and then the depth is added.

The two hypotheses stated above depend on a changing optic aray, and so far the only cause of such change that has been considered is the moving point of observation. The reader will have noted that a moving *object* will also bring about the same kinds of disturbance in the structure of the array that have been described above. A moving object in the world is an event, however, not a form of locomotion, and the information for the perception of events will be treated in Chapter 6.

THE CASE OF VERY DISTANT SURFACES

It is interesting to compare the occluding edges of objects and other convexities on the surface of the earth with the *horizon* of the earth, the great circle dividing the ambient array into two hemispheres. It is the limit of perspective minification for terrestrial surfaces, just as the edge-on line is the limit of perspective compression (foreshortening) for a terrestrial surface. Objects such as railroad trains on the Great Plains and ships on the ocean are said to vanish in the distance as they move away from a fixed point of observation. The line of the horizon in the technology of pictorial perspective is said to be the locus of vanishing points for the size of earth-forms and for the convergence of parallel edges on the earth. The railroad train "vanishes" at the same optical point

Figure 5.8
Cartoon. (Drawing by S. Harris; © 1975 The New Yorker Magazine, Inc.)

where the railroad tracks "meet" in the distance. The horizon is therefore analogous to an occluding edge in being one of the loci at which things go out of and come into sight. But going out of sight in the distance is very different from going out of sight at a sharp or a rounded edge nearby. The horizon of the earth, therefore, is not an occluding edge for any terrestrial object or earth-form. It does not in fact *look* like an occluding edge. It could only be visualized as an occluding edge for the lands and seas beyond the horizon if the seemingly flat earth were conceived as curved and if the environment were thought of as a globe too vast to see.

It has long been a puzzle to human observers, however, that the horizon is in fact visibly an occluding edge for *celestial* objects such as the sun and the moon. Such objects undergo progressive deletion at a contour, as at sunset, and undergo progressive accretion at the same contour, as at moonrise. This is in accordance with the second hypothesis above. The object is obviously beyond the horizon, more distant than the visible limit of earthly distance, and yet there is some information for its being a solid surface. This conflicting information explains, I think, the apparently enormous size of the sun and the moon at the horizon. It also explains many of the ideas of pre-Copernican astronomy about heavenly bodies. We should realize that the terrestrial environment was the only environment that people could be *sure* of before Copernicus—the only environment that could be perceived directly. Terrestrial objects and surfaces had affordances for behavior, but celestial objects did not. More will be said about the perception of objects on earth as distinguished from objects in the sky in Part III.

SUMMARY: THE OPTICS OF OCCLUSION

1. In the ideal case of a terrestrial earth without clutter, all parts of the surface are projected to all points of observation. But such an open environment would hardly afford life.

2. In the case of an earth with furniture, with a layout of opaque surfaces on a substratum, some parts of the layout are projected to any given fixed point of observation and the remaining parts are unprojected to that point.

3. The optically uncovered surface of an object is always *separated* from the optically covered surface at the occluding edge. At the same time, it is always *connected* with the optically covered surface at the occluding edge.

4. The continuation of the far side with the near side is specified by the *reversibility* of occlusion.

5. Any surface of the layout that is hidden at a given fixed point of observation will be unhidden at some other fixed point.

6. Hidden and unhidden surfaces *interchange*. Whatever is revealed by a given movement is concealed by the reverse of that movement. This principle of reversible occlusion holds true for both movements of the point of observation and motions of detached objects.

7. We can now observe that the *separation* between hidden and unhidden surfaces at occluding edges is best specified by the *perspective* structure of an array, whereas the *connection* between hidden and unhidden surfaces at edges is specified by the underlying *invariant* structure. Hence, probably, a pause in locomotion calls attention to the difference between the hidden and the unhidden, whereas locomotion makes evident the continuousness between the hidden and the unhidden.

The seeming paradox of the perceiving or apprehending of hidden surfaces will be treated further in Chapter 11.

HOW IS AMBIENT LIGHT STRUCTURED?
A THEORY

Let us return to the question of how ambient light is given its invariant structure, the question asked at the beginning of this chapter but not answered except in a preliminary way. Ambient light can only be structured by something that surrounds the point of observation, that is, by an environment. It is not structured by an empty medium of air or by a fog-filled medium. There have to be surfaces—both those that emit light and those that reflect light. Only because ambient light is structured by the substantial environment can it contain information about it.

So far it has been emphasized that ambient light is made to constitute an array by a single feature of these surfaces, their layout. But just *how* does the layout structure the light? The answer is not simple. It involves the puzzling complexities of light and shade. Moreover, the layout of surfaces is not the only cause of the structuring of light; the *conglomeration* of surfaces makes a contribution, that is, the fact that the environment is multicolored. The different surfaces of the layout are made of different substances with different reflectances. Both lighted or shaded surfaces and black or white surfaces make their separate contributions to the invariant structure of ambient light. And how light-or-shade can be perceived separately from black-or-white has long been a puzzling problem for any theory of visual sense perception.

I tried to formulate a theory of the structuring of ambient light in my last book (Gibson, 1966*b*), asserting that three causes existed, the layout of surfaces, the pigmentation of surfaces, and the shadowing of surfaces (pp. 208–216). But the third of these causes is not cognate with the other two, and the interaction between them was

not clearly explained. The theory was static. Here, I shall formulate
sources of *invariant* optical structure in relation to the sources of *vari*
structure. What is clear to me now that was not clear before is that structure as such,
frozen structure, is a myth, or at least a limiting case. Invariants of structure do not
exist except in relation to variants.

THE SOURCES OF INVARIANT OPTICAL STRUCTURE

The main invariants of the terrestrial environment, its persisting features, are the layout
of its surfaces and the reflectances of these surfaces. The layout tends to persist because
most of the substances are sufficiently solid that their surfaces are rigid and resist
deformation. The reflectances tend to persist because most of the substances are
chemically inert at their interfaces with the air, and their surfaces keep the same
composition, that is, the same colors, both achromatic and chromatic. Actually, at the
level of microlayout (texture) and microcomposition (conglomeration), layout and reflectances merge. Or, to put it differently, the layout texture and the pigment texture
become inseparable.

Note once more that an emphasis on the geometry of surfaces is abstract and
oversimplified. The faces of the world are *not* made of some amorphous, colorless,
ghostly substance, as geometry would lead us to believe, but are made of mud or sand,
wood or metal, fur or feathers, skin or fabric. The faces of the world are colorful as well
as geometrical. And what they afford depends on their substance as well as their shape.

THE SOURCES OF VARIANT OPTICAL STRUCTURE

There are two regular and recurrent sources of changing structure in the ambient light
(apart from local events, which will be considered in the next chapter). First, there are
the changes caused by a moving point of observation, and second, there are the changes
caused by a moving source of illumination, usually the sun. Many pages have been
devoted to the former, and we must now consider the latter. The motion of the sun
across the sky from sunrise to sunset has been for countless millions of years a basic
regularity of nature. It is a fact of ecological optics and a condition of the evolution of
eyes in terrestrial animals. But its importance for the theory of vision has not been
fully recognized.

The puzzling complexities of light and shade cannot be understood without taking
into account the fact of a *moving* source of illumination. For whenever the source of
light moves, the direction of the light falling on the surfaces of the world is altered and
the shadows themselves move. The layout and coloration of surfaces persist, but the

lightedness and shadedness of these surfaces do not. It is not just that the optic array is different at noon with high illumination from what it is at twilight with low illumination; it is that the optic array has a different structure in the afternoon than it has in the morning.

VARIANTS AND INVARIANTS WITH A MOVING SOURCE OF ILLUMINATION

Just how does pure layout structure the ambient light? It is easy to understand how a mosaic of black and white substances would structure the ambient light but not how a pure layout would do so. For in this case the structuring would have to be achieved wholly by differential illumination, by light and shade. There are two principles of light and shade under natural conditions that seem to be clear: the direction of the prevailing illumination and the progressive weakening of illumination with multiple reflection.

The illumination on a surface comes from the sun, the sky, and other surfaces that face the surface in question. A surface that faces the sun is illuminated "directly," a surface that faces away from the sun but still faces the sky is illuminated less directly, and a surface within a semienclosure that faces only other surfaces is illuminated still less directly. The more the light has reverberated, the more of it is absorbed and the dimmer it becomes. Hence it is that surfaces far from the mouth of a cave are more weakly illuminated than those near the mouth. But within any airspace, any concavity of the terrain or any semienclosure, there is a direction of the *prevailing* illumination, that is, a direction from which more light comes than from any other.

The illumination of any face of the layout relative to adjacent faces depends on its inclination to the prevailing illumination. Crudely speaking, the surface that "faces the light" gets more than its neighbor. More exactly, a surface perpendicular to the prevailing illumination gets the most, a surface inclined to it gets less, a surface parallel to it gets still less, and a surface inclined *away* from it gets the least. The pairs of terms *lighted* and *shadowed* or *in light* and *in shadow* should not be taken as dichotomies, for there are all gradations of relative light and shade. These two principles of the direction and the amount of illumination are an attempt to distill a certain ecological simplicity from the enormous complexities of analytical physical optics and the muddled practice of illumination engineering.

A wrinkled surface of the same substance evidently structures the ambient light by virtue of two facts: there is always a prevailing direction of illumination, and consequently the slopes facing in this direction throw back more energy than the slopes not facing in this direction. A *flat* surface of *different* substances structures the ambient light by virtue of the simple fact that the parts of high reflectance throw back more energy than the parts of low reflectance.

Figure 5.9 shows an array from a wrinkled layout of terrestrial surfaces, actually an aerial photograph of barren hills and valleys. The bare earth of this desert has everywhere the same reflectance. The top of the photograph is to the north of the terrain. The picture was taken in the morning, and the sun is in the east. Some of the slopes face east, and some face west; the former are lighted and the latter shaded. It can be observed that various inclinations of these surfaces to the direction of the prevailing illumination determine various relative intensities in the array; the more a surface departs from the perpendicular to this direction, the darker is the corresponding patch in the optic array.

Now consider what happens as the sun moves across the sky. All those surfaces that were lighted in the morning will be shaded in the afternoon, and all those that were shaded in the morning will be lighted in the afternoon. There is a continual, if slow, process of change from lighted to shaded on certain slopes of the layout and the reverse change on certain other slopes. These slopes are related by orientation. Two faces of any convexity are related in this way, as are two faces of any concavity. A ridge can be said to consist of two opposite slopes, and so can a valley. The reciprocity of light and shade on such surfaces might be described by saying that the lightness and the shadedness *exchange places*. The underlying surfaces do not interchange of course, and their colors, if any, do not interchange. They are persistent, but the illumination is variable in this special reciprocal way.

In the optic array, presumably, there is an underlying invariant structure to specify the edges and corners of the layout and the colors of the surfaces, and at the same time there is a changing structure to specify the temporary direction of the prevailing illumination. Some components of the array never exchange places—that is, they are never permuted—whereas other components of the array do. The former specify a solid surface; the latter specify insubstantial shadows only. The surface and its color are described as opaque; the shadow is described as transparent.

The decreasing of illumination on one slope and the increasing of illumination on an adjacent slope as the sun moves are analogous to the foreshortening of one slope along with the inverse foreshortening of an adjacent slope as the point of observation moves. I suggest that the true relative colors of the adjacent surfaces emerge as the lighting changes, just as the true relative shapes of the adjacent surfaces emerge as the perspective changes. The perspectives of the convexities and concavities of Figure 5.9 are variant with locomotion; the shadows of these convexities and concavities are variant with time of day; the constant properties of these surfaces underlie the changing perspectives and the changing shadows and are specified by invariants in the optic array.

Figure 5.9
Hills and valleys on the surface of the barren earth.

The hills in this aerial photograph, the convexities or protuberances, can be compared to the "humps" shown in Figure 5.1

It is true that the travel of the sun across the sky is very slow and that the correlated interchange of the light and the shade on surfaces is a very gradual fluctuation. Neither is as obvious as the motion perspective caused by locomotion. But the fact is that shifting shadows and a moving sun are regularities of ecological optics whether or not they are ever noticed by any animal. They have set the conditions for the perception of the terrain by terrestrial animals since life emerged from the sea. They make certain optical information available. And, although shifting shadows and a moving sun are too slow to be noticed in daylight, a moving source of illumination and the resultant shadows become more obvious at night. One has only to carry a light from place to place in a cluttered environment in order to notice the radical shifts in the pattern of the optic array caused by visibly moving shadows. And yet, of course, the layout of surfaces and their relative coloration is visible underneath the moving shadows.

How the differential colors of surfaces are specified in the optic array separately from the differential illumination of surfaces is, of course, a great puzzle. The difference between black and white is never confused with the difference between lighted and shadowed, at least not in a natural environment as distinguished from a controlled laboratory display. There are many theories of this so-called constancy of colors in perception, but none of them is convincing. A new approach to the problem is suggested by the above considerations.

From an ecological point of view, the color of a surface is relative to the colors of adjacent surfaces; it is not an absolute color. Its reflectance ratio is specified only in relation to other reflectance ratios of the layout. For the natural environment is an *aggregate* of substances. Even a surface is sometimes a *conglomerate* of substances. This means that a range of black, gray, and white surfaces and a range of chromatically colored surfaces will be projected as solid angles in a normal optic array. The colors are not seen separately, as stimuli, but together, as an arrangement. And this range of colors provides an invariant structure that underlies *both* the changing shadow structure with a moving sun and the changing perspective structure with a moving observer. The edges and corners, the convexities and concavities, are thus specified as multicolored surfaces, not as mere slopes; as speckled or grained or piebald or whatever, not as ghostly gray shapes.

The experimental discoveries of E. H. Land (1959) concerning color perception with what he calls a "complete image" as distinguished from color perception with controlled patches of radiation in a laboratory are to be understood in the above way, I believe.

RIPPLES AND WAVES ON WATER:
A SPECIAL CASE

It is interesting and revealing to compare the optical information for a solid wrinkled surface as shown in Figure 5.9 and the information for a liquid wavy surface, which the reader will have to visualize. Both consist of convexities and concavities, but they are motionless on the solid surface and moving on the liquid surface. In both cases the convexities are lighted on one slope and shadowed on the other. In both cases the surface is all of the same color or reflectance. The difference between the two arrays is to be found chiefly in the two *forms of fluctuation* of light and shade. In the terrestrial array, light and shade exchange places slowly in one direction; they do not oscillate. In the aquatic array, light and shade interchange rapidly in both directions; they oscillate. In fact, when the sun is out and the ripples act as mirrors, the reflection of the sun can be said to flicker or flash on and off. This specific form of fluctuation is characteristic of a water surface.

SUMMARY

When ambient light at a point of observation is structured it is an ambient optic array. The point of observation may be stationary or moving, relative to the persisting environment. The point of observation may be unoccupied or occupied by an observer.

The structure of an ambient array can be described in terms of visual solid angles with a common apex at the point of observation. They are angles of intercept, that is, they are determined by the persisting environment. And they are nested, like the components of the environment itself.

The concept of the visual solid angle comes from natural perspective, which is the same as ancient optics. No two such visual angles are identical. The solid angles of an array change as the point of observation moves, that is, the perspective structure changes. Underlying the perspective structure, however, is an invariant structure that does *not* change. Similarly, the solid angles of an array change as the sun in the sky moves, that is, the shadow structure changes. But there are also invariants that underlie the changing shadows.

The moving observer and the moving sun are conditions under which terrestrial vision has evolved for millions of years. But the invariant principle of reversible occlusion holds for the moving observer, and a similar principle of reversible illumination holds for the moving sun. Whatever goes out of sight will come into sight, and whatever is lighted will be shaded.

SIX

EVENTS AND THE
INFORMATION
FOR PERCEIVING EVENTS

So far, little has been said about change in the environment. The point of observation could change and the source of illumination could change, but the streams did not flow, the pebbles did not roll, the leaves did not fall, and the animals did not scurry about. The environment has been described as shaped and textured and colored, as well as illuminated by a moving sun, but as if frozen. Let us now bring the environment to life. We need to consider a world in which events can happen.

Ecological events, as distinguished from microphysical and astronomical events, occur at the level of substances and the surfaces that separate them from the medium. Substances differ in rigidity and thus in the degree to which their surfaces resist deformation. Between the surfaces of clouds at one extreme and of solid rock at the other are liquids, viscous substances, viscoelastic substances, and granular substances whose surfaces are intermediate between these extremes in their resistance to deformation. The reshaping of a surface requires force, the amount of force depending on the substance.

It will also be remembered that substances differ in chemical inertness, or the degree to which they resist reactions with agents like oxygen in the medium. The more inert a substance is, the more its surface and its composition will tend to persist. Substances also differ in their readiness to evaporate or sublimate, and this too affects the persistence of their surfaces.

The distinction between objects that are attached to the ground and those that are not should also be remembered in connection with ecological events. The detached object can be moved without breaking the continuity of its surface with another surface, but the attached object cannot. Note that an object can be resting on a surface of support, in contact with it, without being *attached* to it. These distinctions will be used in discussing motions as ecological events.

The laws of motion for bodies in space as formulated by Isaac Newton apply only to idealized detached objects. The falling apple that, according to legend, hit Newton on the head and led him to conceive the law of universal gravity was only an incident in a sequence of ecological events: as the seasons changed, the apple had to grow and ripen before it could fall, collide, and finally decay.

The surface of a substance is where a mechanical action like collision is located, where chemical reactions take place, where vaporization occurs, or solution, or diffusion into the medium. All these are ecological events.

Just what are we to mean by an *ecological event*? Is it possible to define and classify events? It ought to be attempted. For only if we know what we mean by an event can we describe the change in the ambient optic array that specifies it, and only then can we begin to study the perceiving of it. A good many psychologists have tried to experiment with the perception of what they vaguely call motion. A few, including the writer, have begun to do experiments on the perception of what they call events, but none has yet made a systematic ecological approach to the problem. Most of the existing experiments have been based on the assumption that the perception of motion depends on the motion of a spot of light across the retina, a sensation of motion, and the experimenters are preoccupied with the deep contradictions to which this assumption gives rise (Gibson, 1968b).

A CLASSIFICATION OF TERRESTRIAL EVENTS

The events we are concerned with are "external," so a displacement of the point of observation will be excluded, because it refers to the locomotion of a potential observer, not to the motion of a surface. The change of occlusion that usually goes with a displacement of the point of observation is a very peculiar optical event, because it has both objective reference and subjective reference at the same time. That is, the revealing and concealing of a surface depend on both the location of the surface and the location of the point of observation.

The events we are concerned with are mainly terrestrial, so the motion of the sun across the sky will be put aside, together with the peculiar motions of shadows that depend on it. We are now interested in events that occur quite independently of where the observer is and where the sun is.

What kinds of events can be said to occur, after these exclusions? Tentatively, it would seem that they can be divided into three main varieties: change in the layout of surfaces, change in the color and texture of surfaces, and change in the existence of surfaces. Change of layout is caused by forces; change of color and texture is caused by change in the composition of the substance; and change in the existence of a surface is caused by a change in the state of the substance. Consider them one by one.

꙳

CHANGE OF LAYOUT DUE TO COMPLEX FORCES

A change of layout due to complex forces refers to any alteration of the shape of the surfaces of the environment, including the repositioning of detached objects by displacement. Among all the entities that make up the furniture of the earth, some are mobile and some are not. What we are most inclined to call *motions* are translations and rotations of detached objects—the falling weight, the spinning top, the rolling ball, and the hurled missile. We learn about these from studying mechanics. But there are many other changes in the layout of surfaces that are even more significant: the flexible deformations of the surface of another animal, the rippling and pouring of water, the elastic and plastic changes of rubber and clay, and the breaking or rupturing of a surface. We are somewhat less inclined to call these changes motions, but they are nonetheless mechanical events caused by forces. They do not have the elegant simplicity of the motions of celestial bodies under the influence of the force of gravity, but they are lawful and they have a kind of higher-order simplicity at their proper level of analysis.

CHANGES OF LAYOUT

Rigid Translations and Rotations of an Object
Displacements (falling body, flying arrow)
Turns (opening door)
Combinations (rolling ball)

Collisions of an Object
With rebound and without

Nonrigid Deformations of an Object
Inanimate (drops of fluid, lumps of clay)
Animate (change of posture of animal)

Surface Deformations
Waves
Flow
Elastic or plastic changes

Surface Disruptions
Rupturing, cracking
Disintegration
Explosion

The above tabulation, although incomplete, is suggestive. It has to do with what might be called *ecological mechanics*, which is rather different from either celestial mechanics on the one hand or particle mechanics on the other, including thermodynamics. Carpenters and builders are familiar with this branch of physics, although it is not taught in school. The displacements and turns of detached objects can be classed as changes of layout because they are rearrangements of the furniture of the earth, not pure translations and rotations along and around the three axes of Cartesian coordinate space. The earth is the background of these motions. The terrestrial substratum is an absolute frame of reference for them, since it is itself never displaced or turned. The world does not move, not at this level of analysis. On this account the contemporaries of Copernicus were quite justifiably shocked when he tried to convince them that the world did move.

At this level of analysis, the deformations and disruptions of a surface are not reduced to the motions of elementary particles of matter, either. Stretching-relaxing, for example, is an event in its own right, not a set of events; it is not reduced to a set of interrelated displacements of the elements of a surface.

The subvarieties of events in the above table may, of course, occur in combination; animal locomotion, for example, consists of displacements and turns relative to the ground, but it is accomplished by deformations of the animal-object, such as the flexing and extending of its parts. A collision may occur between two elastic objects or between an elastic object and the ground, so that one displacement is immediately followed by another and a *train* of events arises. Or, in the case of a machine with moving parts, a configuration of *concurrent* events is established. Man has invented a great number of mechanical moving parts, each with its characteristic motion—the wheel, roller, crank, and gear; the lever, rocker, pendulum, and hinge; the piston, slide, pinion, escapement, and screw. Thus, when a complex machine is running there is a sort of hierarchy of concurrent events. But note that a machine is assembled from such parts, each of which is a detached object in present terminology. A living organism, in contrast, is not assembled from parts, and its members, although they move, constitute a different sort of hierarchy.

Note that displacements and turns and deformations, even wave motions and the flow of a stream, may occur without breaking the continuity of any surface. Rupture

---

The Substratum

The earth considered as a substratum is not only that with respect to which anything moves, it is also that with respect to which anything is right side up, or tilted, or inverted. That is to say, it extends from horizon to horizon; it is horizontal. Gravity is absolute, not relative, at the ecological level.

The puzzling psychological problems of the uprightness of a picture relative to its frame, of a pattern relative to a page, and of an image relative to a retina are not primary problems but derivative.

occurs when the continuity fails, and this is a highly significant ecological event. For the cracked ground, as in an earthquake, cannot be walked upon, and a torn roof does not afford shelter. The broken pot no longer holds water, and the broken skin of the animal constitutes an injury. The maximum of disruption can be thought of as disintegration. The surface "falls to pieces," as we say, which means a complete failure of continuity. In that case, the event passes from a change in layout to a change in existence; the surface ceases to exist because the substance has changed its "state."

Finally, let us note another very interesting fact about these events: some are *reversible in time* and some are not. Displacements and turns, together with locomotions, can go backward as well as forward. Locomotion, as I emphasized earlier, entails both going and coming, and this is why hidden surfaces become unhidden and unhidden surfaces become hidden. Similarly, lighted surfaces become shadowed and shadowed surfaces become lighted. Any rigid motion of a body in physical mechanics has an equivalent motion in the opposite direction. This reversibility holds for certain nonrigid deformations, although not all, but it does *not* hold for the disruption of a surface. More exactly, the change from integral to broken is not the reverse of the change from broken to integral; the process of going to pieces is not the opposite of the process of repairing. At the extreme case, when a surface disintegrates, it is not reciprocal to the aggregating and connecting of parts so as to yield a whole surface. The difference between the two processes can be observed by making a motion picture sequence of a surface being broken, or a fabric being torn, and then comparing the film run forward with the film run backward (Gibson and Kaushall, 1973).

CHANGE OF COLOR AND TEXTURE DUE TO
CHANGE IN COMPOSITION

Theoretically, a surface can change color without changing shape and change shape without changing color. These are often supposed to be independent "qualities" of an object, and much has been made of the supposed difference between the "secondary" qualities of an object and its "primary" qualities. Actually, color and shape are oversimplified qualities, for texture merges with color and yet is a kind of shape at the level of small-scale layout. We shall here speak of color and texture in combination, since they are specific to the composition of the substance. When the substance is altered by a chemical reaction, the surface is altered. It changes in achromatic color and in chromatic color, and it also usually changes texture, inasmuch as the fine structure goes from, say, crystalline to amorphous. Animals need to perceive the affordances of substances, their chemical values or utilities, in advance of making contact with their surfaces, as I have pointed out before (Gibson, 1966b, Ch. 8) and will return to again in this book. A change in affordance is thus signified by the natural chemical changes of greening, ripening, flowering, and fading. They are important ecological events, as are the physiological reactions of animals that bring about alterations of plumage or fur or skin.

CHANGES OF COLOR AND TEXTURE

Plant Surfaces
Greening (increase in chlorophyll)
Fading (decrease in chlorophyll)
Ripening (increase in sugar)
Flowering (presence of nectar)

Animal Surfaces
Coloration of skin (sexual receptivity, as in the baboon)
Change of plumage (maturity)
Change of fur (onset of winter)

Terrestrial Surfaces
Weathering of rock (oxidation)
Blackening of wood (fire)
Reddening of iron (rusting)

The tabulation above presents a few examples of significant surface changes that do not involve gross changes of layout or shape. Commonly, of course, these changes are correlated. Leaves wither and fall as well as turn color when winter approaches. The several varieties of environmental events combine to yield a multiple guarantee of information. A fire with flames, considered as an ecological event instead of an abstract chemical event, consists of complex motions and deformations, fluctuating luminous surfaces, reddening and blackening of the opaque surfaces, billowing smoke, and finally a disappearance of the solid surfaces. A fire is even specified to the skin, the ears, and the nose as well as to the eyes.

Chemical events at the ecological level involve colored and textured surfaces, whereas chemical events at the molecular and atomic level do not. Molecules and atoms are not colored, and this is an old puzzle for color perception. There is no information in an optic array about radiating atoms, but there is good information about the composition of the substance relative to other substances.

Chemical reactions considered as molecular conversions in test tubes are very often reversible, and this fact can be expressed in chemical equations with double arrows pointing in both directions. But let us note that chemical changes at the ecological level are not reversible in time. Ripening, rusting, and burning do not go backward. There are balanced *cycles* of ecological change, to be sure, as, for example, the carbon dioxide cycle, but they are progressive in time, I think, not reversible.

WAXING AND WANING OF A SURFACE DUE TO CHANGE IN THE STATE OF MATTER

A surface is the interface between a substance and the medium. Substances, however complex, can be classed as solid, viscous, viscoelastic, liquid, and particulate. A gas is not a substance although it is, of course, matter. When a substance goes into the gaseous state it becomes merely a compnent of the medium, and its surface ceases to exist. It has not been *dematerialized*, but it has been *desubstantialized*. It no longer reflects light, and it is therefore not specified in any ambient array at any point of observation. It has not merely gone out of sight; it has *gone out of existence* (Chapter 5). Some of the ways in which surfaces are nullified or destroyed or demolished are listed in the left-hand column of the table below.

Surfaces also, of course, *come into* existence from the gaseous state, or change from liquid to solid, and examples of these events are given in the right-hand column.

Changes of Surface Existence

Liquid to gas (evaporating, boiling)	Gas to liquid (condensation, rain)
Solid to gas (sublimation)	Gas to solid?
Cloud to gas (dissipation)	Gas to cloud (formation)
Solid to liquid (melting)	Liquid to solid (freezing)
Solid into solution (dissolving)	Solution into solid (crystallization, precipitation)
Disintegration	Aggregation
Biological decay	Biological growth
Destruction	Construction

When ice or snow melts, a surface is so radically altered that it can be considered to be destroyed, and when a puddle of water evaporates, the surface is certainly destroyed. When the reflecting surface of a cloud dissipates, it is annihilated although it was semitransparent and barely substantial to begin with, being nothing but a mass

---

Surface Theory and Atomic Theory

The fact that surfaces go out of and come into existence is little recognized in physics, as noted in Chapter 1. The atomic theory is emphasized instead. Beginning with Parmenides and Democritus, the theory asserts that nothing is ever created or destroyed; only the atoms, themselves unchanging, are rearranged. Aristotle disagreed. He insisted that there was an actual genesis of things in the world and a passing away of them. At the ecological level Aristotle was quite right. And it is at this level, the level of *surfaces*, that we *perceive* the world. At the level of atoms we do not (Randall, 1960).

of droplets. When a surface disintegrates or an organism dies, the substances are scattered and the surface ceases. Ecological surface destruction is fairly obvious, but ecological surface creation is not, except for the slow growth of animals and plants.

In the above table I have tried to show the best possible case for the opposition of these processes, but it seems clear that they are not reversible in time. Evaporation and condensation are opposite at a certain level, but a water surface is not created as the reverse of the process by which it is destroyed. In none of these event pairs, I think, is the one simply a *going backward* of the other, such that if a film of one event were reversed, it would represent the other, as I noted above (Gibson and Kaushall, 1973).

SUMMARY: WHAT SHALL WE TAKE AS AN EVENT?

The foregoing classification is a kind of preliminary survey only. Ecological events are various and difficult to formalize. But when we attempt to reduce them to elementary physical events, they become impossibly complex, and physical complexity then blinds us to ecological simplicity. For there *are* regularities to be found at the higher level, regularities that cannot now be encompassed by the simple equations of mechanics and physics. The movements of animals, for example, are lawful in ways that cannot yet be derived from the laws of orthodox mechanics, and perhaps never can be. A too strict adherence to mechanics has hampered the study of terrestrial events.

Events as Primary Realities   In the first place, the flow of ecological events is distinct from the abstract passage of time assumed in physics. The stream of events is heterogeneous and differentiated into parts, whereas the passage of time is supposed to be homogeneous and linear. Isaac Newton asserted that "absolute, true, and mathematical time, of itself and from its own nature, flows equably without relation to anything external." But this is a convenient myth. It assumes that events occur "in" time and that time is empty unless "filled." This habitual way of thinking puts the cart before the horse. We should begin thinking of events as the primary realities and of time as an abstraction from them—a concept derived mainly from regular repeating events, such as the ticking of clocks. Events are perceived, but time is not (Gibson, 1975).

It is the same with space as with time. Objects do not *fill* space, for there was no such thing as empty space to begin with. The persisting surfaces of the environment are what provide the framework of reality. The world was never a void. As for the medium, the region in which motion and locomotion can occur, where light can reverberate and surfaces can be illuminated, this might be called *room* but it is not *space*. Surfaces and their layout are perceived, but space is not, as I have long been arguing (Gibson, 1950).

It might be said, without going as far as I have done above, that time *consists* of the events filling it and that space *consists* of the objects filling it. But I will argue that this formula still perpetuates the fallacy. The metaphor of *filling* is wrong. Time and space are not empty receptacles to be filled; instead, they are simply the ghosts of events and surfaces.

Time is not another dimension of space, a fourth dimension, as modern physics assumes for reasons of mathematical convenience. The reality underlying the dimension of time is the sequential order of events, and the reality underlying the dimensions of space is the adjacent order of objects or surface parts. Sequential order is not comparable to adjacent order; it is not even *analogous* to adjacent order. For the order of events cannot be permuted, whereas the order of parts can. You can reshuffle the parts but not the events, as you can rearrange the furniture in a room but not the happenings that occur in it.

Recurrence and Nonrecurrence   There is always some degree of recurrence and some degree of nonrecurrence in the flow of ecological events. That is, there are cases of pure repetition, such as the stepping motions of the escapement of a clock and the rotations of its hands, and cases of nonrepetition or novelty, such as cloud formations and the shifting sandbars of a river. Each new sunrise is like the previous one and yet unlike it, and so is each new day. An organism, similarly, is never quite the same as it was before, although it has rhythms. This rule for events is consistent with the general formula of nonchange underlying change.

Reversible and Nonreversible Events   Some ecological events are reversible sequences, whereas others are nonreversible. Change of position can go backward, but change of state cannot. More exactly, the sequential order of the short events that make up a long event, beginning to end, cannot be turned around, end to beginning, without violating certain laws of ecological physics. Breaking is not reciprocal to mending, and when it is made to seem so the event is magical. This fact is in contrast to events governed by the formal laws of physics where, except for thermodynamics, events could as well go backward as forward. The variable of time in these equations "has no arrow." This suggests then that the so-called irreversibility of time is actually the irreversibility of some, but not all, ecological events. It is simply not true that the only way of specifying the direction of time is by increase of entropy.

The Nesting of Events   The flow of ecological events consists of natural units that are nested within one another—episodes within episodes, subordinate ones and superordinate ones. What we take to be a unitary episode is therefore a matter of choice and depends on the beginning and the end that are appropriate, not on the units of measurement. The number of espisodes in a sequence cannot be counted unless the unit episode has been decided upon. Episodes, like surfaces, are structured at various levels. Years and days are natural units of sequential structure; hours, minutes, and seconds are arbitrary and artificial units. Some of the best examples of a nested hierarchy of sequential events are found in the behavior of animals, and most obviously in the human production of events such as speech, music, and the theater. If we can understand these nested sequences, it may be possible to understand how it could be that in some cases the *outcome* of an event sequence is implicit at the *outset*—how the end is present at the beginning—so that it is possible to *foresee* the end when an observer *sees* the beginning.

The Affordances of Events　　Finally, it should be emphasized that some natural events demand or invite appropriate behaviors. Some have what I called *affordances* for animals, just as do places, objects, and other animals, and others involve a *change* in the affordance of the place, object, or other animal. A fire affords warmth on a cold night; it also affords being burnt. An approaching object affords either contact without collision or contact with collision; a tossed apple is one thing, but a missile is another. For one of our early ancestors, an approaching rabbit afforded eating whereas an approaching tiger afforded being eaten. These events are not stimuli, and it is preposterous for psychologists to call them that. The question is: what information is available in the light by means of which these events can be perceived?

THE OPTICAL INFORMATION FOR
PERCEIVING EVENTS

We can now ask what happens in the ambient optic array when there is an event in the environment. What specifies the event? In general terms, the answer must be that there is a disturbance in the invariant structure of the array. Presumably there are different kinds of disturbances for different kinds of events.

Once again, let us remind ourselves that events in the world should not be confused with the information in light corresponding to them. Just as there are no material objects in an array but only the invariants to specify objects, so there are no material events in an array but only the information to specify events. No object in the world is literally replicated in ambient light by a copy or simulacrum. And as for what *happens* in the world, it could not possibly be replicated or copied in the light. We ought to realize this, but nevertheless there has been a strong temptation to assume that the *motions* of bodies in the world are copied by motions of elements in the light, or at least that motions in two dimensions are copied, although not motions in depth. But I shall try to show that this assumption is quite mistaken since the two kinds of "motion," physical and optical, have nothing in common and probably should not even have the same term applied to them. The beginning and the end of the disturbance in the light correspond to the beginning and the end of the event in the world, but that is about as far as the correspondence goes.

MECHANICAL EVENTS

With respect to mechanical events, consider first the case of a rigid translation where the distance of the object from the point of observation remains constant. As the object is displaced relative to the environment, you might think that the corresponding visual solid angle would simply be displaced relative to the sphere of ambient light. The visual form would not change; the "figure" would simply move over the "ground." But this is wrong, however plausible it sounds. The visual solid angle for the object is only one of an array of solid angles. The array is filled; it is mathematically dense. A given patch cannot move in the way that a body can move in space, for it has no space to move in. What happens is nothing simpler than a disturbance of structure. At one border of the visual solid angle, progressive deletion occurs, while at the opposite border progressive accretion occurs. The former corresponds to the leading edge of the object and the latter to the trailing edge. Or, if the background of the translating object is not textured, as happens with an object moving in a large, empty gap such as the sky, then the *interspaces* between the edges of the object and the nearest edges constitute patches that are decremented and incremented. This decrementing and incrementing is similar to the deletion and accretion of textural units. What I am saying is that even a motion in the sky is a change in the sky-form, that even a displacement within the frame of a window is a change of structure and not simply a motion.

The above case of rigid translation is special; the object neither approaches nor recedes from the point of observation, and no change occurs within the contour corresponding to the object. Normally there is magnification or minification of the contour. Magnification is accompanied by progressive deletion of the optical structure outside the contour and minification by its opposite, progressive accretion. This says that an object hides more and more of the environment as it comes closer to the point of observation, and less and less as it goes farther away. *Magnification* of a form in the array means the approach of something, and *minification* means the recession of something. When a visual solid angle of the ambient array approaches a hemisphere, the ultimate limit that a solid angle can reach, an angle 180° in width, an event of great significance is specified, that is, *an object in contact with the point of observation*. This is a general law of natural perspective. The actual pickup of this information by an animal having eyes is a psychological problem of great interest. The behavior of animals when an impending contact or collision is specified by this "looming" of the form has been studied by W. Schiff (1965). What happens when the observer approaches an object or an aperture is different and will be described in Chapter 12.

These optical disturbances are clearly not *copies* of the corresponding motions of objects, as everyone would agree. But what about the case of the pure rotation of an object on its axis, a Newtonian spin? There need be little or no progressive incrementing and decrementing of the background in this case. If the object is a sphere, disk, or wheel that rotates on an axis that is on the line of sight to the point of observation, you might say that the rotation of the circular form in the array is a copy of the rotation of the circular object in the world, point for point. But this would be a misconception, even for this special case. What happens optically is a sort of *shearing* or *slippage* of the texture at the contour as the object rotates in front of its background, although nothing is taken from or added to the array. This is a disturbance in the continuity of the array. Another way of putting it is to say that the alignments of textural units, the radii of the circle, for instance, are shifted at the contour. Apart from this special case, all other rotations of objects, and all noncircular objects, will cause progressive loss and gain of optical texture by foreshortening to the limit at one border and inverse fore-shortening from the limit at the other border; that is to say, faces of the object will go out of and come into sight. In short, objects in general cannot rotate without causing a change of occlusion.

What happens in the array when a surface in the world is *deformed*? It is plausible in that case to suppose that the deformation of the optical texture is a copy of the deformation of the substantial texture, since the optical units are projections of the substantial units, by natural perspective, and are in one-to-one correspondence with them. It would seem that the uneven flow of the surface of water in a river—the bubbles and flecks of the surface—has a corresponding flow of the optical texture in the array. But this does not hold for the ripples or waves over the surface, because the ripples do not move in the same way the textured surface does. The fluctuation of light and shade does not correspond to the surface. And, of course, if the crests of the waves are high they will begin to hide the troughs, and the occluding edges will spoil the projective correspondence.

What happens in the array when a surface is ruptured or broken? The mathematical continuity of the surface texture fails, and so does the mathematical continuity of the optical texture. As the crack in the surface becomes a gap, occluding edges appear where there were none previously. As the gap widens, a new surface is revealed. A different optical texture fills the gap and is added to the array. This emergence of new structure in the gap is perhaps the crucial information. A precise decription is needed, but this may prove to be difficult. Mathematicians do not seem to have been successful with the problem of discontinuity.

With respect to mechanical events of all sorts, then, it is a serious mistake to assume that "an optical motion is a projection in two dimensions of a physical motion in three dimensions" (Gibson, 1957, p. 289), as I myself once wrote in a paper on what I called "optical motions and transformations." The notion of point-to-point correspondence in projective geometry, simple and powerful as it is, does not apply to the optics of events any more than it applies to the optics of opaque surfaces. For it leaves occlusion out of account. The fallacy lies deep in our conception of empty space, especially the so-called third dimension of space. Whatever the perception of space may be, if there is any such thing, it is *not* simply the perception of the dimension of depth.

CHEMICAL EVENTS

What happens in the optic array when the composition of a surface in the multicolored layout of surfaces is altered? The green plant flowers, and the green fruit ripens; the rock weathers, and the wood blackens. The change in composition is almost always specified by a change in reflectance, both unselective and selective, both achromatic and chromatic. A substance is necessarily a *colorant* in the general sense of the term, if not a pigment.

The reflectances of surfaces tend to persist insofar as the substances are chemically inert, as I pointed out, and this persistence is a source of invariant structure in the ambient optical array. But they do *not* persist when the substances are *not* inert, and the surfaces of organisms especially are chemically active. Plants and animals change their color and texture with the seasons of the year.

But, unhappily, we do not know what happens in the optic array when one of the surfaces of the environment changes color. There is a "disturbance," no doubt, of the underlying invariant structure, but that is vague. The difficulty is that we do not know what invariant in an array specifies a *persistent* surface color in the world, let alone a changing surface color. We do not know what specifies *composition*. We do not know how black and white are specified separately from shaded and lighted. I suggested that the moving source of illumination was basic to the problem, but I have not developed the theory.

It is easier to say what happens in the optic array when one of the surfaces of the environment changes texture. The pigment texture of a flat, conglomerate surface is projected in the array, and the quality, density, and regularity of the pigment texture are specified in the optical texture despite all kinds of perspective transformations. These "forms" of texture are also invariant under changing direction of illumination and changing amount of illumination. Perhaps the composition of the substance is given in this way and, since that is what counts for animals, the pure abstract reflectance of the surface is of lesser importance than we are apt to suppose.

DESTRUCTION AND CREATION OF SURFACES

Finally, we ask what information is in an optic array for the coming into and going out of existence of surfaces caused by changes in the state of matter. The reader will recall that whenever ambient light is structured in one part and unstructured in an adjacent part a surface is specified in the former and a void in the latter. Thus, the textured region below the horizon specifies the solid earth, and the homogeneous region above it specifies the empty sky. Similarly, the heterogeneous areas in the sky specify surfaces, even if only clouds, and the homogeneous areas between clouds specify the absence of a surface. The leafy canopy in a forest provides an overhead texture; the holes in the canopy are textureless, and it is into these holes that the birds fly. So long as any visual solid angle in the array remains unstructured it specifies a hole; it can be magnified to the hemispherical limit, and the bird will not collide with any surface but will fly through the hole.

In the upper hemisphere of the ambient array, cloud surfaces dissipate, and we say they *vanish*. The optical texture is supplanted by the absence of texture. Cloud surfaces also form in the sky, and we say that they have *materialized*. The absence of texture is supplanted by texture. In the lower hemisphere of the array, the optical transitions are more complex, for there is always a background texture. With evaporation of a liquid surface, or the sublimation of a solid surface, or the dissolving of it, the optical texture is supplanted by that of whatever lay behind it. As one structure is nullified, another takes its place. Sometimes the substance of the object becomes transparent during the transition, which means that one surface is specified behind another. This information is displayed in what the motion picture technician calls a dissolve, whereby one layout goes out of sight as another comes into sight in precisely the same place. There is a "fade-out" and a "fade-in," both of which occur at the same time.

THE THEORY OF SPIRITS

These our actors
Are melted into air, into thin air:
And, like the baseless fabric of this vision,
The cloud-capped towers, the gorgeous palaces,
The solemn temples, the great globe itself
Yea, all which it inherit, shall dissolve
And, like this insubstantial pageant faded,
Leave not a rack behind.
Shakespeare, The Tempest

THE INFORMATION FOR VISUAL PERCEPTION

The optical transitions that specify dissipation, evaporation, sublimation, dissolution, disintegration, and decay seem to be complex variants of the substitution of one texture for another. No systematic study of them has ever been made. But children notice them, are fascinated, and look closely at the regions of the optic array where such substitutions occur. Presumably they learn to distinguish among these substitutions and to perceive what they mean.

The difference between the loss of optical texture from an array by progressive substitution and the loss of optical texture from an array by progressive deletion on one side of a contour has been illustrated in preliminary fashion by a motion picture film (Gibson, 1968a). The loss by substitution should specify a surface that goes out of existence. The loss by deletion should specify a surface that goes out of sight at an occluding edge, as described in the last section. These radically different happenings are, in fact, seen, or so people say when they watch the film.

THE KINDS OF DISTURBANCE OF OPTICAL STRUCTUCE

I said that the most general term for what happens in the optic array when something happens in the world is *a disturbance of its structure*. There is no existing terminology for describing optical changes (or physical changes, for that matter), so one has to grope for the best terms. I have spoken of optical *transformations* and of *permutations*. I talked about *fluctuations* in connection with changing light and shade. I have referred to optical *transitions*. I argued that one should not speak of *motions* in the array. The best general term seems to be *disturbances*. Consider the kinds that have been described:

1. Progressive deletion and accretion of units on one side of a contour (displacement of an object against a background)
2. Progressive decrementing and incrementing of gaps (displacement of an object against the sky)
3. Shearing or slippage of optical texture at a contour (rotation of a disk)
4. Perspective transformation by foreshortening and its opposite (turning of the face of an object)
5. Magnification to the limit and minification (approach and recession of an object)
6. Deformation (fluid, viscous, and elastic events)
7. Emergence of new structure (rupturing)
8. Nullification of texture (dissipation in the sky)
9. Substitution of new texture for old (dissipation on earth)
10. Change of "color structure" (chemical events)

What a strange list of phenomena! They are not easy to describe or to understand. Yet these optical happenings or something like them occur all the time in the array of light to the eye. Even if no one sees them as such, they carry the information about events in the environment. In the changing array from a motion picture screen, an array that is saturated with meaning, these must be the "motions" of the motion picture that convey the meaning. They are surely lawful, and they deserve to be studied in their own right, from a fresh point of view, and without the accumulated prejudices that the theory of light stimuli has fostered.

Can these disturbances of structure be treated mathematically? They surely cannot all be treated with the same mathematical method, for some of them do not conform to the assumptions of the theory of sets. Some of the above changes do not preserve a one-to-one mapping of units over time, inasmuch as the array gains or loses units in time. Accretion or deletion of texture during occlusion is one such case. Foreshortening or compression of texture preserves one-to-one mapping only until it reaches its limit, after which texture is lost. The emergence of new texture with rupturing of a surface, the nullification of texture with dissipation of a surface, and the substitution of new texture for old are still other cases of the failure of one-to-one mapping, or projective correspondence. In all of these cases it is not the fact that each unit of the ambient array at one time goes into a corresponding unit of the array at a later time. The case of an optic array that undergoes "flashing" or scintillation of its units is another example, and so is what I called fluctuation in connection with changing light and shade.

On the other hand, some of these optical disturbances do seem to preserve one-to-one correspondence of units over time, namely, the perspective transformations, the deformations or topological transformations, and even the shearing or slippage of optical texture at a contour. In the case of a partial permutation of a spot-texture, or a radical permutation such as the random displacements called Brownian movement, there is still a persistence of units without gain or loss. The invariants under transformation, the ratios and proportions and relations among units, are richest for the disturbances at the beginning of the above list and poorest for the permutations at the end, but invariants are discoverable throughout. A disturbance of connectedness or adjacent order is more serious than a mere disturbance of form. A complete scrambling of the

---

THE OPTICAL MAGNIFICATION OF NESTED FORMS

If a surface is composed of units nested within larger units, its optic array is composed of solid angles nested within larger solid angles. As a point of observation approaches a surface, all angles are magnified toward the limit of a whole angle (180°), even those whose units were too small to see at a distance. The closer a surface, the more its subordinate units become visible. Does this progress have an end?

adjacent order of units is still more serious. But a mathematical theory of invariants may be possible for all these disturbances of structure with persistence. What is lacking is a theory of the invariants that are preserved under disturbances with *nonpersistence* of units.

These disturbances in the optic array are not *similar* to the events in the environment that they specify. The superficial likenesses are misleading. Even if the optical disturbances could be reduced to the motions of spots, they would not be like the motions of bodies or particles in space. Optical spots have no mass and no inertia, they cannot collide, and in fact, because they are usually not spots at all but forms nested within one another, they cannot even move. This is why I suggested that a so-called optical motion had so little in common with a physical motion that it should not even be *called* a motion.

In what way, if any, does an optical disturbance correspond to the event in the environment that it specifies? It corresponds in sequential order. The beginning and the end of the disturbance in the array are concurrent with the beginning and the end of the event in the environment, and there is no latency or delay. If events are simultaneous, the disturbances are simultaneous. If an event consists of subordinate events, then the disturbance will consist of subordinate disturbances, as when a ball rolls downstairs in a sequence of bounces. If an event is gradual, the disturbance is gradual (a balloon being blow up), and if an event is abrupt, the disturbance is abrupt (the balloon bursting). If an event is unitary (a ball rolling behind a screen and then out again), the disturbance is unitary—deletion and then accretion at the occluding edges. Or so, at least, I suggested.

If a series of repeated events occurs in the environment, a series of repeated disturbances occurs in the ambient optic array. When the events are mechanical, these optical disturbances are usually accompanied by sounds, as in the colliding of objects and the rupturing or cracking of surfaces. The chains of optical and acoustical disturbances run in parallel. And the sequential order of this information flow cannot be tampered with. Unlike the adjacent order of a series of objects, the sequential order of a series of events cannot be rearranged. Some of the *individual* events that compose the grand sequence of a day can go backward, displacements for example, but the sequential order of their occurrence is immutable. This is why "time" is said to have an "arrow," I believe, and this is why "time travel" is a myth.

THE CAUSATION OF EVENTS

A special kind of mechanical event involving two detached objects and two successive displacements is a *collision*, in which the first displacement *causes* the second. It is a superordinate event with two subordinate events. The "bumping" of one elastic object by another is perhaps the most obvious example of a causal sequence that we have.

For an inanimate object, collision may cause breaking, bending, chipping, deformation, and so on, as well as displacement. For the animate object, it may cause injury and all sorts of complex reactions. Philosophers and psychologists since Hume have been debating the question of whether or not such causation could be perceived. Hume asserted that although the motions of the two objects could be sensed, one after the other, it was quite impossible to see the one motion *causing* the other. Only succession can be perceived, not causation, he believed.

A. Michotte (1963) has attempted to refute Hume. In Chapter 10 we shall consider his evidence. Can one truly perceive a dynamic event as such? Is there information to specify it? Recent experiments at Uppsala suggest there is (Runeson, 1977).

SUMMARY

A preliminary classification of ecological events was attempted. Only if we have decided what to take as an event can we describe the change in the optic array that results from it. And only after that can we begin to do experiments on the perception of an event. The assumption that a motion in the world brings about a motion in the optic array is quite wrong, although it is often taken for granted.

Three varieties of events were distinguished: changes of surface layout, changes of surface color or texture, and changes in the existence of a surface. Examples of the first variety are translations and rotations of an object, collisions, deformations, and disruptions. Examples of the second are the often nameless but significant alterations of the surfaces of plants and animals. Examples of the third are the transitions of evaporation, dissipation, melting, dissolving, and decay. Although some of these events are reversible, many are not.

Ecological events, it was concluded, are nested within longer events, are sometimes recurrent and sometimes novel, are meaningful, and do not flow evenly in the manner of Newton's "absolute mathematical time."

The optical information for distinguishing the various events can only be various disturbances of the local structure of the optic array. A very tentative description was given of certain types of optical disturbance: deletion-accretion, shearing, transformation, magnification-minification, deformation, nullification, and substitution. These disturbances have only begun to be studied, and the mathematical analysis of them has scarcely been attempted. Nevertheless, strange to say, they are what we are visually most sensitive to, all of us, animals, babies, men, women, and moviegoers.

SEVEN

THE OPTICAL INFORMATION FOR SELF-PERCEPTION

It has frequently been assumed in previous chapters that the point of observation for an ambient optic array is not occupied. The point has been thought of as a position at which observation *could* be made, a position that *could* be occupied but need not be. Such a position could just as well be occupied by *another* observer and, since all positions can be occupied by any observer, the invariants of the array under locomotion can be shared by all observers. It was important to establish this principle that the point of observation is public, not private, but now we must consider the other side of the coin. When a point of observation is occupied, there is also optical information to specify the observer himself, and this information *cannot* be shared by other observers. For the body of the animal who is observing temporarily conceals some portion of the environment in a way that is unique to that animal. I call this information *propriospecific* as distinguished from *exterospecific*, meaning that it specifies the self as distinguished from the environment.

THE SPECIFYING OF THE SELF BY THE FIELD OF VIEW

The *field of view* of an animal, as I will use the term, is the solid angle of the ambient light that can be registered by its ocular system. The field of view, unlike the ambient array, is bounded; it is a sort of *sample* of the whole sphere. The angular scope of the field of view depends on the placement of the eyes in the head, some animals having lateral eyes and a nearly panoramic field of view and others having frontal eyes and a roughly hemispherical field of view (Walls, 1942, Ch. 10). Horses belong to the first group and humans to the second. In both ocular systems, the separate fields of view of the two eyes overlap in front, but the amount of overlap is very much greater in humans than it is in animals with semipanoramic vision. By the field of view, I mean the combined fields of view of the two eyes.

An attempt is made in Figure 7.1 to show a cross-section of the field of view of the left orbit of a human observer. If the reader will put his or her left eye close to the page, one gets an approximation of the sample of the ambient light that the illustrator could see with his head still and his right eye closed. The illustrator was reclining, with his feet up, facing the corner of a room. His nose, lips, and cheek and part of his left arm are represented. The drawing is an updating of one made by Ernst Mach in the 1880s that he entitled "The Visual Ego." What is being illustrated here is the stationary field of view of an eye socket with the head fixed and the eye mobile, not the shifting field of view with a fixed eye and a turning head; the latter is different and will be described later. For this drawing, the artist had to turn his eye in order to see clearly the peripheral details in the field of view.

A field of view is a large visual solid angle, with an envelope. The important fact about a field of view is its boundaries, vague and indefinite boundaries, to be sure, but still boundaries. They are in some ways like occluding edges, the occluding edges of a window. The edges of the field of view hide the environment behind them, as those of a window do, and when the field moves there is an accretion of optical structure at the leading edge with deletion of structure at the trailing edge, as in the cabin of a steam shovel with a wide front window and controls that enable the operator to turn the cabin to the right or the left. But the edges of the field of view are *unlike* the edges of a window inasmuch as, for the window, a *foreground* hides the background whereas, for the field of view, the *head of the observer* hides the background. Ask yourself what it is that you see hiding the surroundings as you look out upon the world—not darkness surely, not air, not nothing, but the ego! The illustration of course is misleading in this respect.

Whenever a point of observation is occupied by a human, about half of the surrounding world is revealed to the eyes and the remainder is concealed by the head. What is concealed is occluded not by a surface, a projected surface of the sort described when the laws of occluding and occluded surfaces were formulated, but by a unique entity. It is not a part of the world, but it does conform to the principle of reversible occlusion, by which those surfaces that go out of sight with one movement come back into sight with the opposite movement. The head turns, and whatever was in back of the head at one time will be in front of the head at another and vice versa. This fact is fundamental for the theory of perception to be proposed. The purpose of vision, I shall argue, is to be aware of the surroundings, the ambient environment, not merely

Figure 7.1
The ego as seen by the left eye. The temporary field of view of the left orbit of an observer.
(From *The Perception of the Visual World* by James Jerome Gibson and used with the agreement of the reprint publisher, Greenwood Press, Inc.)

of the field in front of the eyes. The ambient information is always available to any observer who turns his or her head. Visual perception is panoramic and, over time, the panorama is registered.

There are other remarkable features of the field of view besides its oval boundaries. Still other occluding edges appear within it, those of the nose, the body, the limbs, and the extremities, some of which can be seen in the drawing. The edges of the eye socket, the eyebrows, the nose and cheek bones are only the nearest; the edges of the arms, legs, hands, and feet are more distant, but they still occlude the surfaces of the "outer" environment. The hands and feet behave more like the occluding edges of an object than like the occluding edges of a window; they are actually protrusions into the field of view from below. They are therefore attached objects in the present terminology, but they are attached to the observer, not to the ground, and they are elastic. When these semiobjects move, there is deletion of optical structure at the leading edge and accretion at the trailing edge, just as with objects in the world.

Information exists in a normal ambient array, therefore, to specify the nearness of the parts of the self to the point of observation—first the head, then the body, the limbs, and the extremities. The experience of a central self in the head and a peripheral self in the body is not therefore a mysterious intuition or a philosophical abstraction but has a basis in optical information.

I have described this information for perceiving the self in terms applicable to a human observer, but the description could be applied to an animal without too much change. In all bilaterally symmetrical animals, the eyes are in the head, the head is

---

The Distinction Between the Field of View and the Visual Field

The field of view being described here should not be confused with the visual field. As I used the term, the *visual field* means a kind of introspective experience ccontrasted with the naive experience of the *visual world* (Gibson, 1950*b*, Ch. 3). It is the momentary patchwork of visual sensations. But the field of view is a fact of ecological optics.

Actually, there are always *two* fields of view available to any animal with two eyes. That is, there are two ambient optic arrays at two different points of observation, each of which is sampled by one eye. Since the points of observation are separated by the interocular distance, the optic arrays are different. I term this difference *disparity*, by analogy with the *retinal disparity* studied so intensively by physiological image optics.

The difference between the disparity of two array samples and the disparity of two retinal images is considerable. The difference between a theory of disparity as information and the traditional theory of the "fusion" of disparate images is radical. There will be more of this later, especially in Chapters 11 and 12.

attached to a body, and (for terrestrial animals) the body is supported by the ground. But the horse and the human look out upon the world in different ways. They have radically different fields of view; their noses are different, and their legs are different, entering and leaving the field of view in different ways. Each species sees a different self from every other. Each *individual* sees a different self. Each person gets information about his or her body that differs from that obtained by any other person.

NONVISUAL INFORMATION
ABOUT THE SELF

It is obvious, of course, that perceptual systems other than the visual system are active and that the body is a source of stimulus information for these other so-called senses as well as for vision. Proprioception is either taken to be one of the senses by sensory physiologists or taken to be several related senses, as conceived by Sir Charles Sherrington. A deep theoretical muddle is connected with proprioception. I tried to clear it up in my book on the perceptual systems (Gibson, 1966*b*) by reformulating the whole meaning of the term *sense*. In my view, proprioception can be understood as egoreception, as sensitivity to the self, not as one special channel of sensations or as several of them. I maintain that all the perceptual systems are propriosensitive as well as exterosensitive, for they all provide information in their various ways about the observer's activities. The observer's movements usually produce sights and sounds and impressions on the skin along with stimulation of the muscles, the joints, and the inner ear. Accordingly, information that is specific to the self is picked up as such, no matter what sensory nerve is delivering impulses to the brain. The point I wish to make is that information about the self is multiple and that all kinds are picked up concurrently. An individual not only sees himself, he hears his footsteps and his voice, he touches the floor and his tools, and when he touches his own skin he feels both his hand and his skin at the same time. He feels his head turning, his muscles flexing, and his joints bending. He has his own aches, the pressures of his own clothing, the look of his own eyeglasses—in fact, he lives within his own skin.

This theory of information for self-perception, it should be noted, contradicts one of the most deep-seated assumptions of traditional sensory physiology—the doctrine that a neural input can be specific only to the receptor that initiated it, that is, the doctrine of the specific qualities of the nerves, or specific "nerve energies" as Johannes Müller called them. According to this doctrine, proprioception is ascribed to specialized proprioceptors. But I have rejected this theory of specificity and substituted another that is quite radically different.

EGORECEPTION AND EXTEROCEPTION
ARE INSEPARABLE

The optical information to specify the self, including the head, body, arms, and hands, *accompanies* the optical information to specify the environment. The two sources of information coexist. The one could not exist without the other. When a man sees the world, he sees his nose at the same time; or rather, the world and his nose are both specified and his awareness can shift. Which of the two he notices depends on his attitude; what needs emphasis now is that information is available for both.

The supposedly separate realms of the subjective and the objective are actually only poles of attention. The dualism of observer and environment is unnecessary. The information for the perception of "here" is of the same kind as the information for the perception of "there," and a continuous layout of surfaces extends from one to the other. This fact can be noted in Figure 7.1. What I called *gradients* in 1950, the gradients of increasing density of texture, of increasing binocular disparity, and of decreasing motility that specify increasing distance all the way from the observer's nose out to the horizon, are actually variables between two limits, implying just this complementarity of proprioception and exteroception in perception. Self-perception and environment perception go together.

What Happens When the Head Is Tilted?

In a chapter entitled "The Problem of the Stable and Boundless Visual World" (Gibson, 1950), I put the question of why, when one tilts the head, the world does not appear to tilt but remains visibly upright. Is it now clear that the question was misconceived? It has long been a puzzle for theories of visual perception based on the input from the retina. No satisfactory answer has been agreed upon. (Psychology is plagued with efforts to find answers to the wrong questions!)

What happens when your head is tilted is simply that you are aware of it. The change of retinal stimulation is exactly concomitant with changes in the stimulation coming from muscles and joints and from the inner ear, and these all specify the same fact. The tilt of the retina behind the normal retinal image is observed, whereas the tilt of a hypothetical pattern of input *relative to the receptor mosaic* is not noticed. Why should it be? Curious anomalies will arise, to be sure, if the information got by the visual system is *discrepant* with that obtained by the muscle-joint system, or the vestibular system, for then the observer is uncertain what to mean by the word *tilt*; he is confused, and the results of the experiment are open to many interpretations.

Efforts to answer the question of why the world looks upright, stable, and unbounded despite all the vicissitudes of the retinal input are still going on. Up-to-date knowledge of this research can be obtained by reading *Stability and Constancy in Visual Perception* (Epstein, 1977). This is an admirable book if you accept its premises.

THE INFORMATION FOR THE PERCEIVING
OF DISTANCE

The problem of how distance can be perceived is very old. If it is taken to be the distance of an object in space, then it is "a line endwise to the eye," as Bishop Berkeley pointed out in 1709, and it projects only one point on the retina. Hence, distance *of itself* is invisible and, if so, a whole set of perplexities arise that have never been resolved. Distance may be thought of, however, as extending along the ground instead of through the air, and then it is *not* invisible. It is projected as a *gradient* of the decreasing optical size and increasing optical density of the features of the ground, as I argued in 1950. But this gradient of forms getting smaller and finer and more closely packed together has a limit at the horizon of the earth where, according to the laws of natural perspective, all visual solid angles shrink to zero. The gradient is also anchored at another limit, by the forms projected from the nose, body, and limbs. The nose projects at the maximum of nearness just as the horizon projects at the maximum of farness.

Distance therefore is *not* a line endwise to the eye as Bishop Berkeley thought. To think so is to confuse abstract geometrical space with the living space of the environment. It is to confuse the Z-axis of a Cartesian coordinate system with the number of paces along the ground to a fixed object.

The nose is *here*. It projects the largest possible visual solid angle in the optic array. Not only that, it provides the maximum of crossed double imagery or crossed disparity in the dual array, for it is the farthest possible edge to the right in the left eye's field of view and the farthest possible edge to the left in the right eye's field of view. This also says that to look at the nose one must converge the two eyes maximally. Finally, the so-called motion parallax of the nose is an absolute maximum, which is to say that, of all the occluding edges in the world, the edge of the nose sweeps across the surfaces behind it at the greatest rate whenever the observer moves or turns his head. For each of the three kinds of optical gradient that I proposed as "stimuli" for seeing depth in *The Perception of the Visual World* (Gibson, 1950*b*)—size perspective, disparity perspective, and motion perspective—the nose provides an absolute base line, the absolute zero of distance-from-here.

THE SPECIFYING OF HEAD TURNING

The head can be turned as well as displaced. Turning the head is looking around; displacing it is locomotion. The head can be turned on a vertical axis as in looking from side to side, on a horizontal axis as in looking up and down, and even on a sagittal axis as in tilting the head. The sky will always enter the field in looking up, and the ground will always enter the field in looking down. Three pairs of semicircular canals in the vestibule of the inner ear, set in place relative to the three axes, register these turns and specify the degree of head rotation. This fact is well known and has been widely studied. What is not so familiar is the fact that these turns of the head are also registered by vision. They are specified by what I have called the *sweeping* of the field of view over the ambient array during head turns and the *wheeling* of the field over the array during head tilts. The sweeping and wheeling of this window with its special private occluding edges are not simply "motions" but deletions and accretions of optical structure. To say only that the field of view "moves" over the world as the head moves is inexact and insufficient; the world is revealed and concealed as the head moves, in ways that specify exactly how the head moves. Whatever goes out of sight as the head turns right comes into sight as the head turns left; whatever goes out of sight as the head is lifted comes into sight as the head is lowered. The optical texture that is deleted

Figure 7.2
A sequence of overlapping fields of view obtained by turning the head to the right.
This is the same room and the same man as in Figure 7.1, except that his feet are now lined up with the window instead of with the corner of the room. The head turns through an angle of about 90°. His nose is always at the right-hand edge of the field. The field of view is a *sliding sample* of the ambient array.

OPTICAL INFORMATION FOR SELF-PERCEPTION

is subsequently accreted. It is invariant under this reversible optical change. It conforms to the principle of reversible occlusion.

The temporary field of view of an eye socket is a *sample* of the ambient optic array, and the head is continually sampling the array. Each sample is a segment that overlaps with earlier and later segments. Moreover, it is a changing segment with elements being progressively included and excluded at the margins. And in a sufficiently long sequence of these segments, the whole structure of the array is specified.

The combined field of view of two eye sockets (and all higher animals have two eyes) consists of two samples of the ambient array. They overlap more or less, more in humans than in horses, and thus the same structure is included in both segments. But it is not *quite* the same structure, because the two points of observation are slightly separated and there is a resulting *disparity* of the two structures. This disparity, or mismatch, is at a maximum for the contour projected from the edge of the animal's nose, as I pointed out above. The edge of the nose is the left-hand edge of what the right eye sees but the right-hand edge of what the left eye sees, and this maximum mismatch constitutes information for the zero of distance, that is, for the awareness of oneself at the center of a layout of surfaces receding from here. The minimum of mismatch is at the horizon. There will be more about disparity later.

THE SPECIFYING OF LIMB MOVEMENTS

Consider in more detail the protrusions into the field of view of those complex shapes with deforming outlines that are the projections of the limbs and extremities of the observer's body. They normally enter and leave the field at its lower edge, or else the field sweeps down to reveal them. They are almost never at rest. They specify objects in some ways, but of course they are only semiobjects. I am tempted to call them *subjective objects,* and this paradox would emphasize the fact that no line can be drawn between the subjective and the objective. In the primate and the human, the five-pronged shapes that specify the hands are especially meaningful. Their deforming contours and the underlying invariants make possible what psychologists have called, very inadequately, eye-hand coordination. More exactly, they are the basis of the visual control of manipulation. And when an object grasped by the hand is used as a tool, it becomes a sort of extension of the hand, almost a part of the body.

Infants, both monkey and human, practice looking at their hands for hours, as well they should, for the disturbances of optical structure that specify the niceties of pre-hension have to be distinguished. All manipulations, from the crudest act of grasping by the infant to the finest act of assembly by the watchmaker, must be guided by optical disturbances if they are to be successful. Some kinds of transformations and occlusions were listed in the last chapter.

The optical minification of the squirming silhouette of the hand specifies extension of the arm, reaching out, while optical magnification specifies flection of the arm, pulling in. A hand occludes progressively less of the environment as it recedes and progressively more of the environment as it approaches. A certain nonsymmetrical magnification of the hand will bring it to the mouth, as every baby learns. A symmetrical magnification of the hand will cause it to cover the eyes so that nothing can be seen. But then, of course, one can peek through the fingers, which is not only pleasurable but a lesson in practical optics.

The visual solid angle of the hand cannot be reduced below a certain minimum; the visual solid angle of a detached object like a ball can be made very small by throwing it. These ranges of magnification and minification between limits link up the extremes of *here* and *out there*, the body and the world, and constitute another bridge between the subjective and the objective.

You might think that contact of the hand or foot with a surface during extension of the limb is specified by a mechanical impression on the skin, by touch, and that there would be no use for an optical specification as well. Nevertheless, there is such optical specification. When the decreasing occlusion of the surface by the extremity ceases, and when there is no accretion or deletion of surface texture by the occluding edges of the hand or foot, then the extremity is in contact with the surface and not sliding over it. This specifies, for example, that the foot is on the ground. Terrestrial animals are accustomed to have their feet on the ground and to have both cutaneous and optical information for this state of affairs. This explains why an invisible glass floor high above the real floor supplies mechanical support but not optical support, and why it is that human infants and other terrestrial animals show distress, flinching and behaving as if falling, when placed on such a transparent floor (Chapter 9).

These are a few examples of the rules that make visual egoreception so useful. The surfaces of the hands, of the tools held by the hands, and the working surfaces that they alter are all given as a changing layout of the nearby environment, the information for which is contained in the changing structure of the optic arrays at the two eyes.

THE SPECIFYING OF LOCOMOTION

At a moving point of observation no less than a stationary point of observation, the ambient array is sampled by the observer, who can look around the world while moving as well as while stationary. The edges of the observer's field of view will sweep over the flowing ambient array in the same way that they sweep over the frozen ambient array. A person can face backward while riding in a vehicle, or walk backward for that matter, and observe how the array flows inward, instead of outward as it does when one faces forward.

If we consider for the present an open environment, one that is not cluttered, locomotion is specified by flow of the array and rest by nonflow. The flow is a change in perspective structure, a change in the perspectives of the ground if outdoors and of the floor, walls, and ceiling if indoors. There is not only a static perspective of the array but also a *motion perspective*, as I once called it (Gibson, Olum, and Rosenblatt, 1955). This will be described, along with experiments, in Chapter 9. The main law of flowing perspective is that it is centrifugal in half the array and centripetal in the other half, but these two hemispheres are not invariant. They shift around and thus are not to be confused with the permanent hemispheres of earth and sky. More particularly, a focus of centrifugal outflow is always accompanied by another focus of centripetal inflow at the opposite pole of the sphere. This axis is the line of the displacement of the observer. Hence, the focus of expansion is the direction in which one is going, and the focus of contraction is the direction from which one is coming. This direction may change during locomotion, of course, relative to the permanent environment of earth and sky, and the two foci of inflow and outflow may change correspondingly relative to other *invariants* of the ambient array.

I have distinguished between invariant structure and perspective structure in Chapter 5. The invariant structure of the array that specifies the persisting world *underlies* the changing perspective structure. The pattern of outflow and inflow is *superposed*, as it were, on the nonchanging features of the array. One of these nonchanging features is the earth-sky contrast at the horizon, and another is the texture of the earth. The flow pattern *shifts* as the observer changes direction, now in one direction and then another, and reverses when the direction is reversed, but the invariants of structure and texture never shift. They specify the unmoving terrain, whereas the flow pattern specifies the observer's locomotion with reference to the terrain.

How do we see where we are going? We guide or steer our locomotion, when we are in control of it, by locating those invariant features of the array that specify a destination, whatever it may be, and then keeping the focus of optical outflow centered on that item. In short, we magnify the form that specifies the goal. A child runs to his mother by enlarging her image to the limit, that is, to the largest possible solid angle; a bee flies to a flower by precisely the same rule. The rule is related to the principle of what I have called the "symmetricalizing" of stimulation (Gibson, 1966*b*, pp. 72 ff.). We shall return to this problem in Part III, where we will also consider the control of locomotion to a *hidden* destination.

The centrifugal outflow of the array that specifies locomotion does not interfere with the information that specifies surface layout; the invariants are all the better for the transformation. The moving self and the unmoving world are reciprocal aspects of the same perception. To say that one perceives an outflow of the world ahead and an inflow of the world behind as one moves forward in the environment would be quite false. One experiences a rigid world and a flowing array. The optical flow of the ambient array is almost never perceived as motion; it is simply *experienced as kinesthesis,* that is *egolocomotion* (Warren, 1976).

Consider, finally, an environment with hidden surfaces. An open environment projects a continuous flow pattern to the eye of a moving observer, but a cluttered environment does not. The existence of occluding edges brings about the revealing and

Figure 7.3
The flow of the optic array during locomotion parallel to the ground.
A bird is flying over the wrinkled earth. The texture of the lower hemisphere of the optic array flows in the manner shown here. The vectors in this diagram represent angular velocities of the optical elements. The flow velocities are plotted exactly in Figure 13.1.

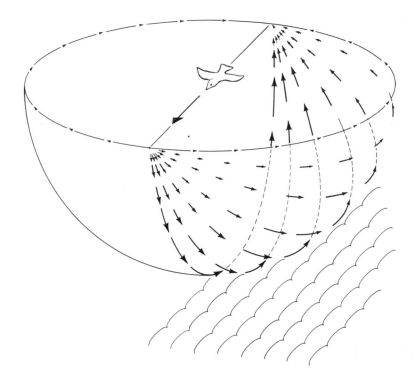

Figure 7.4
The outflow of the optic array from the focus of expansion on the horizon.
This is what a human flier would see looking ahead in the direction of locomotion. There is a gradient of increasing rate of flow downward from the horizon. (From *The Perception of the Visual World* by James Jerome Gibson and used with the agreement of the reprint publisher, Greenwood Press, Inc.)

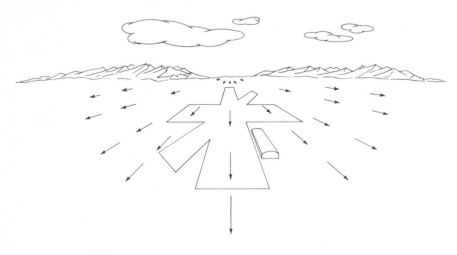

Figure 7.5
The flow of the optic array to the right of the direction of locomotion.
This is what the flier would see if he looked 90° to the right, that is, if he sampled the ambient array to the right. (From *The Perception of the Visual World* by James Jerome Gibson and used with the agreement of the reprint publisher, Greenwood Press, Inc.)

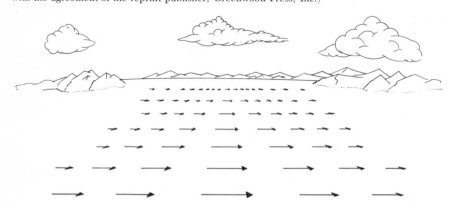

THE INFORMATION FOR VISUAL PERCEPTION

Figure 7.6
The outflow of the optic array in a landing glide.
This is what the flier would see if he aimed down at the landing field. In these three drawings
(Figures 7.4–7.6) the shapes are supposed to depict the underlying invariant structure of the optic
array, and the vectors are supposed to depict the changing perspective structure of the array.
Note that all flow vanishes at two limits: the horizon and the point of aim. (From *The Perception
of the Visual World* by James Jerome Gibson and used with the agreement of the reprint publisher,
Greenwood Press, Inc.)

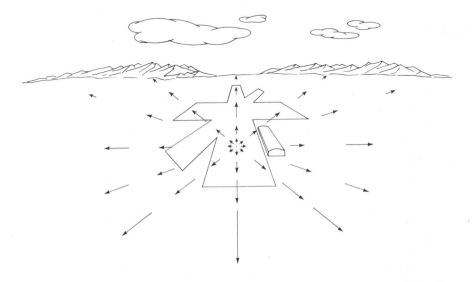

concealing of surfaces and the incrementing and decrementing of the corresponding
optical textures. This kind of change is not a flow or a transformation, because the units
of the array, some of them, do not map from preceding to succeeding arrays. The
invariants that specify the layout of the real environment, then, are not simply invariants
under projective transformations. There will be more of this in Part III.

How is this optical flow related to classical kinesthesis, which is supposed to be
the sense of movement? A person who walks or runs or rides a bicycle does get
sensations from the muscles and joints that specify movement. All I propose is that
visual kinesthesis should be recognized along with muscle-joint kinesthesis. The latter
does not function during passive locomotion in a vehicle. Visual kinesthesis yields the
only reliable information about displacement. The classical sense of movement is not
trustworthy, for a fish in a stream and a bird in a wind have to exercise their muscles
and joints strenuously merely to stay in the same place. The animal is moving in one

meaning but not in another. Locomotion with respect to the earth, active or passive, is registered by vision (this will be elaborated in Chapter 10), but supplementary information about the movement of a limb relative to the body is picked up by the haptic system (Gibson, 1966b, Ch. 4).

SUMMARY

Information about the self accompanies information about the environment, and the two are inseparable. Egoreception accompanies exteroception, like the other side of a coin. Perception has two poles, the subjective and the objective, and information is available to specify both. One perceives the environment and coperceives oneself.

The edges of the field of view occlude the outer environment, and, as the head turns, the occlusion changes, revealing what was concealed and concealing what was revealed. The same thing happens with locomotion as with head turning. The rule is, whatever goes out of sight comes into sight, and whatever comes into sight goes out of sight. Thus it is that a stationary and permanent environment is specified along with a moving observer, one who looks around, moves about, and does things with his hands and feet.

Three types of movement have been distinguished—head turning relative to the body, limb movement relative to the body, and locomotion relative to the environment. Each has a unique type of optical information to specify it: the sweeping of the field of view over the ambient array in the case of head turning; the protrusion of special shapes into the field of view in the case of limb movement (especially manipulation); and the flow of the ambient array in the case of locomotion. The pickup of this information, I propose, should in all cases be called *visual kinesthesis*.

EIGHT

THE THEORY OF AFFORDANCES

I have described the environment as the surfaces that separate substances from the medium in which the animals live. But I have also described what the environment *affords* animals, mentioning the terrain, shelters, water, fire, objects, tools, other animals, and human displays. How do we go from surfaces to affordances? And if there is information in light for the perception of surfaces, is there information for the perception of what they afford? Perhaps the composition and layout of surfaces *constitute* what they afford. If so, to perceive them is to perceive what they afford. This is a radical hypothesis, for it implies that the "values" and "meanings" of things in the environment can be directly perceived. Moreover, it would explain the sense in which values and meanings are external to the perceiver.

The *affordances* of the environment are what it *offers* the animal, what it *provides* or *furnishes*, either for good or ill. The verb *to afford* is found in the dictionary, but the noun *affordance* is not. I have made it up. I mean by it something that refers to both the environment and the animal in a way that no existing term does. It implies the complementarity of the animal and the environment. The antecedents of the term and the history of the concept will be treated later; for the present, let us consider examples of an affordance.

If a terrestrial surface is nearly horizontal (instead of slanted), nearly flat (instead of convex or concave), and sufficiently extended (relative to the size of the animal) and if its substance is rigid (relative to the weight of the animal), then the surface *affords support*. It is a surface of support, and we call it a substratum, ground, or floor. It is stand-on-able, permitting an upright posture for quadrupeds and bipeds. It is therefore walk-on-able and run-over-able. It is not sink-into-able like a surface of water or a swamp, that is, not for heavy terrestrial animals. Support for water bugs is different.

Note that the four properties listed—horizontal, flat, extended, and rigid—would be *physical* properties of a surface if they were measured with the scales and standard units used in physics. As an affordance of support for a species of animal, however, they have to be measured *relative to the animal*. They are unique for that animal. They are not just abstract physical properties. They have unity relative to the posture and behavior of the animal being considered. So an affordance cannot be measured as we measure in physics.

Terrestrial surfaces, of course, are also climb-on-able or fall-off-able or get-underneath-able or bump-into-able relative to the animal. Different layouts afford different behaviors for different animals, and different mechanical encounters. The human species in some cultures has the habit of sitting as distinguished from kneeling or squatting. If a surface of support with the four properties is also knee-high above the ground, it affords sitting on. We call it a *seat* in general, or a stool, bench, chair, and so on, in particular. It may be natural like a ledge or artificial like a couch. It may have various shapes, as long as its functional layout is that of a seat. The color and texture of the surface are irrelevant. Knee-high for a child is not the same as knee-high for an adult, so the affordance is relative to the size of the individual. But if a surface is horizontal, flat, extended, rigid, and knee-high relative to a perceiver, it can in fact be sat upon. If it can be discriminated as having just these properties, it should *look* sit-on-able. If it does, the affordance is perceived visually. If the surface properties are seen relative to the body surfaces, the self, they constitute a seat and have meaning.

There could be other examples. The different substances of the environment have different affordances for nutrition and for manufacture. The different objects of the environment have different affordances for manipulation. The other animals afford, above all, a rich and complex set of interactions, sexual, predatory, nurturing, fighting, playing, cooperating, and communicating. What other persons afford, comprises the whole realm of social significance for human beings. We pay the closest attention to the optical and acoustic information that specifies what the other person is, invites, threatens, and does.

THE NICHES OF THE ENVIRONMENT

Ecologists have the concept of a *niche*. A species of animal is said to utilize or occupy a certain niche in the environment. This is not quite the same as the *habitat* of the species; a niche refers more to *how* an animal lives than to *where* it lives. I suggest that a niche is a set of affordances.

The natural environment offers many ways of life, and different animals have different ways of life. The niche implies a kind of animal, and the animal implies a kind of niche. Note the complementarity of the two. But note also that the environment as a whole with its unlimited possibilities existed prior to animals. The physical, chemical, meteorological, and geological conditions of the surface of the earth and the pre-existence of plant life are what make animal life possible. They had to be invariant for animals to evolve.

There are all kinds of nutrients in the world and all sorts of ways of getting food; all sorts of shelters or hiding places, such as holes, crevices, and caves; all sorts of materials for *making* shelters, nests, mounds, huts; all kinds of locomotion that the environment makes possible, such as swimming, crawling, walking, climbing, flying. These offerings have been taken advantage of; the niches have been occupied. But, for all we know, there may be many offerings of the environment that have *not* been taken advantage of, that is, niches not yet occupied.

In architecture a niche is a place that is suitable for a piece of statuary, a place into which the object fits. In ecology a niche is a setting of environmental features that are suitable for an animal, into which it fits metaphorically.

An important fact about the affordances of the environment is that they are in a sense objective, real, and physical, unlike values and meanings, which are often supposed to be subjective, phenomenal, and mental. But, actually, an affordance is neither an objective property nor a subjective property; or it is both if you like. An affordance cuts across the dichotomy of subjective-objective and helps us to understand its inadequacy. It is equally a fact of the environment and a fact of behavior. It is both physical and psychical, yet neither. An affordance points both ways, to the environment and to the observer.

The niche for a certain species should not be confused with what some animal psychologists have called the *phenomenal environment* of the species. This can be taken erroneously to be the "private world" in which the species is supposed to live, the "subjective world," or the world of "consciousness." The behavior of observers depends on their perception of the environment, surely enough, but this does not mean that their behavior depends on a so-called private or subjective or conscious environment. The organism depends on its environment for its life, but the environment does not depend on the organism for its existence.

MAN'S ALTERATION OF THE
NATURAL ENVIRONMENT

In the last few thousand years, as everybody now realizes, the very face of the earth has been modified by man. The layout of surfaces has been changed, by cutting, clearing, leveling, paving, and building. Natural deserts and mountains, swamps and rivers, forests and plains still exist, but they are being encroached upon and reshaped by man-made layouts. Moreover, the *substances* of the environment have been partly converted from the natural materials of the earth into various kinds of artificial materials such as bronze, iron, concrete, and bread. Even the *medium* of the environment—the air for us and the water for fish—is becoming slowly altered despite the restorative cycles that yielded a steady state for millions of years prior to man.

Why has man changed the shapes and substances of his environment? To change what it affords him. He has made more available what benefits him and less pressing what injures him. In making life easier for himself, of course, he has made life harder for most of the other animals. Over the millennia, he has made it easier for himself to get food, easier to keep warm, easier to see at night, easier to get about, and easier to train his offspring.

This is not a *new* environment—an artificial environment distinct from the natural environment—but the same old environment modified by man. It is a mistake to separate the natural from the artificial as if there were two environments; artifacts have to be manufactured from natural substances. It is also a mistake to separate the cultural environment from the natural environment, as if there were a world of mental products distinct from the world of material products. There is only one world, however diverse, and all animals live in it, although we human animals have altered it to suit ourselves. We have done so wastefully, thoughtlessly, and, if we do not mend our ways, fatally.

The fundamentals of the environment—the substances, the medium, and the surfaces—are the same for all animals. No matter how powerful men become they are not going to alter the fact of earth, air, and water—the lithosphere, the atmosphere, and the hydrosphere, together with the interfaces that separate them. For terrestrial animals like us, the earth and the sky are a basic structure on which all lesser structures depend. We cannot change it. We all fit into the substructures of the environment in our various ways, for we were all, in fact, formed by them. We were created by the world we live in.

SOME AFFORDANCES OF THE TERRESTRIAL ENVIRONMENT

Let us consider the affordances of the medium, of substances, of surfaces and their layout, of objects, of animals and persons, and finally a case of special interest for ecological optics, the affording of concealmeant by the occluding edges of the environment (Chapter 5).

THE MEDIUM

Air affords breathing, more exactly, respiration. It also affords unimpeded locomotion relative to the ground, which affords support. When illuminated and fog-free, it affords visual perception. It also affords the perception of vibratory events by means of sound fields and the perception of volatile sources by means of odor fields. The airspaces between obstacles and objects are the paths and the places where behavior occurs.

The optical information to specify air when it is clear and transparent is not obvious. The problem came up in Chapter 4, and the experimental evidence about the seeing of "nothing" will be described in the next chapter.

THE SUBSTANCES

Water is more substantial than air and always has a surface with air. It does not afford respiration for us. It affords drinking. Being fluid, it affords pouring from a container. Being a solvent, it affords washing and bathing. Its surface does not afford support for large animals with dense tissues. The optical information for water is well specified by the characteristics of its surface, especially the unique fluctuations caused by rippling (Chapter 5).

Solid substances, more substantial than water, have characteristic surfaces (Chapter 2). Depending on the animal species, some afford nutrition and some do not. A few are toxic. Fruits and berries, for example, have more food value when they are ripe, and this is specified by the color of the surface. But the food values of substances are often misperceived.

Solids also afford various kinds of manufacture, depending on the kind of solid state. Some, such as flint, can be chipped; others, such as clay, can be molded; still others recover their original shape after deformation; and some resist deformation strongly. Note that manufacture, as the term implies, was originally a form of manual behavior like manipulation. Things were fabricated *by hand*. To identify the substance in such cases is to perceive what can be done with it, what it is good for, its utility; and the hands are involved.

THE SURFACES AND THEIR LAYOUTS

I have already said that a horizontal, flat, extended, rigid surface affords support. It permits equilibrium and the maintaining of a posture with respect to gravity, this being a force perpendicular to the surface. The animal does not fall or slide as it would on a steep hillside. Equilibrium and posture are prerequisite to other behaviors, such as locomotion and manipulation. There will be more about this in Chapter 12, and more evidence about the perception of the ground in Chapter 9. The ground is quite literally the *basis* of the behavior of land animals. And it is also the basis of their visual perception, their so-called space perception. Geometry began with the study of the earth as abstracted by Euclid, not with the study of the axes of empty space as abstracted by Descartes. The affording of support and the geometry of a horizontal plane are therefore not in different realms of discourse; they are not as separate as we have supposed.

The flat earth, of course, lies *beneath* the attached and detached objects on it. The earth has "furniture," or as I have said, it is cluttered. The solid, level, flat surface extends behind the clutter and, in fact, extends all the way out to the horizon. This is not, of course, the earth of Copernicus; it is the earth at the scale of the human animal, and on that scale it is flat, not round. Wherever one goes, the earth is separated from the sky by a horizon that, although it may be hidden by the clutter, is always there. There will be evidence to show that the horizon can always be seen, in the sense that it can be visualized, and that it can always be felt, in the sense that any surface one touches is experienced in relation to the horizontal plane.

Of course, a horizontal, flat, extended surface that is *nonrigid*, a stream or lake, does not afford support for standing, or for walking and running. There is no footing, as we say. It may afford floating or swimming, but you have to be equipped for that, by nature or by learning.

A *vertical*, flat, extended, and rigid surface such as a wall or a cliff face is a barrier to pedestrian locomotion. Slopes between vertical and horizontal afford walking, if easy, but only climbing, if steep, and in the latter case the surface cannot be flat; there must be "holds" for the hands and feet. Similarly, a slope downward affords falling if steep; the brink of a cliff is a falling-off place. It is dangerous and looks dangerous. The affordance of a certain layout is perceived if the layout is perceived.

Civilized people have altered the steep slopes of their habitat by building stairways so as to afford ascent and descent. What we call the steps afford stepping, up or down, relative to the size of the person's legs. We are still capable of getting around in an arboreal layout of surfaces, tree branches, and we have ladders that afford this kind of locomotion, but most of us leave that to our children.

A cliff face, a wall, a chasm, and a stream are barriers; they do not afford pedestrian locomotion unless there is a door, a gate, or a bridge. A tree or a rock is an obstacle. Ordinarily, there are paths between obstacles, and these openings are visible. The progress of locomotion is guided by the perception of barriers and obstacles, that is, by the act of steering into the openings and away from the surfaces that afford injury. I have tried to describe the optical information for the control of locomotion (Gibson, 1958), and it will be further elaborated in Chapter 13. The *imminence* of collision with a surface during locomotion is specified in a particularly simple way, by an explosive rate of magnification of the optical texture. This has been called *looming* (e.g., Schiff, 1965). It should not be confused, however, with the magnification of an opening between obstacles, the opening up of a *vista* such as occurs in the approach to a doorway.

THE OBJECTS

The affordances of what we loosely call *objects* are extremely various. It will be recalled that my use of the terms is restricted and that I distinguish between *attached* objects and *detached* objects. We are not dealing with Newtonian objects in space, all of which are detached, but with the furniture of the earth, some items of which are attached to it and cannot be moved without breakage.

Detached objects must be comparable in size to the animal under consideration if they are to afford behavior. But those that are comparable afford an astonishing variety of behaviors, especially to animals with hands. Objects can be manufactured and manipulated. Some are portable in that they afford lifting and carrying, while others are not. Some are graspable and other not. To be graspable, an object must have opposite surfaces separated by a distance less than the span of the hand. A five-inch cube can be grasped, but a ten-inch cube cannot (Gibson, 1966b, p. 119). A large object needs a "handle" to afford grasping. Note that the size of an object that constitutes a graspable size is specified in the optic array. If this is true, it is *not* true that a tactual sensation of size has to become associated with the visual sensation of size in order for the affordance to be perceived.

Sheets, sticks, fibers, containers, clothing, and tools are detached objects that afford manipulation (Chapter 3). Additional examples are given below.

1. An elongated object of moderate size and weight affords wielding. If used to hit or strike, it is a *club* or *hammer*. If used by a chimpanzee behind bars to pull in a banana beyond its reach, it is a sort of *rake*. In either case, it is an extension of the arm. A rigid staff also affords leverage and in that use is a *lever*. A pointed elongated object affords piercing—if large it is is a *spear*, if small a *needle* or *awl*.

2. A rigid object with a sharp dihedral angle, an edge, affords cutting and scraping; it is a *knife*. It may be designed for both striking and cutting, and then it is an *axe*.

3. A graspable rigid object of moderate size and weight affords throwing. It may be a *missile* or only an object for play, a *ball*. The launching of missiles by supplementary tools other than the hands alone—the sling, the bow, the catapult, the gun, and so on—is one of the behaviors that makes the human animal a nasty, dangerous species.

4. An elongated elastic object, such as a *fiber*, *thread*, *thong*, or *rope*, affords knotting, binding, lashing, knitting, and weaving. These are kinds of behavior where manipulation leads to manufacture.

5. A hand-held tool of enormous importance is one that, when applied to a surface, leaves traces and thus affords *trace-making*. The tool may be a *stylus, brush, crayon, pen,* or *pencil,* but if it marks the surface it can be used to depict and to write, to represent scenes and to specify words.

We have thousands of names for such objects, and we classify them in many ways: pliers and wrenches are tools; pots and pans are utensils; swords and pistols are weapons. They can all be said to have properties or qualities: color, texture, composition, size, shape and features of shape, mass, elasticity, rigidity, and mobility. Orthodox psychology asserts that *we perceive these objects insofar as we discriminate their properties or qualities.* Psychologists carry out elegant experiments in the laboratory to find out how and how well these qualities are discriminated. The psychologists assume that objects are *composed* of their qualities. But I now suggest that what we perceive when we look at objects are their affordances, not their qualities. We can discriminate the dimensions of difference if required to do so in an experiment, but what the object affords us is what we normally pay attention to. The special combination of qualities into which an object can be analyzed is ordinarily not noticed.

If this is true for the adult, what about the young child? There is much evidence to show that the infant does not begin by first discriminating the qualities of objects and then learning the combinations of qualities that specify them. Phenomenal objects are *not* built up of qualities; it is the other way around. The affordance of an object is what the infant begins by noticing. The meaning is observed before the substance and surface, the color and form, are seen as such. An affordance is an invariant combination of variables, and one might guess that it is easier to perceive such an invariant unit

---

To Perceive an Affordance Is Not to Classify an Object

The fact that a stone is a missile does not imply that it cannot be other things as well. It can be a paperweight, a bookend, a hammer, or a pendulum bob. It can be piled on another rock to make a cairn or a stone wall. These affordances are all consistent with one another. The differences between them are not clear-cut, and the arbitrary names by which they are called do not count for perception. If you know what can be done with a graspable detached object, what it can be used for, you can call it whatever you please.

The theory of affordances rescues us from the philosophical muddle of assuming fixed classes of objects, each defined by its common features and then given a name. As Ludwig Wittgenstein knew, you *cannot* specify the necessary and sufficient features of the class of things to which a name is given. They have only a "family resemblance." But this does not mean you cannot learn how to use things and perceive their uses. You do not have to classify and label things in order to perceive what they afford.

than it is to perceive all the variables separately. It is never necessary to distinguish *all* the features of an object and, in fact, it would be impossible to do so. Perception is economical. "Those features of a thing are noticed which distinguish it from other things that it is not—but not *all* the features that distinguish it from *everything* that it is not" (Gibson, 1966*b*, p. 286).

OTHER PERSONS AND ANIMALS

The richest and most elaborate affordances of the environment are provided by other animals and, for us, other people. These are, of course, detached objects with topologically closed surfaces, but they change the shape of their surfaces while yet retaining the same fundamental shape. They move from place to place, changing the postures of their bodies, ingesting and emitting certain substances, and doing all this spontaneously, initiating their own movements, which is to say that their movements are *animate*. These bodies are subject to the laws of mechanics and yet *not* subject to the laws of mechanics, for they are not *governed* by these laws. They are so different from ordinary objects that infants learn almost immediately to distinguish them from plants and nonliving things. When touched they touch back, when struck they strike back; in short, they *interact* with the observer and with one another. Behavior affords behavior, and the whole subject matter of psychology and of the social sciences can be thought of as an elaboration of this basic fact. Sexual behavior, nurturing behavior, fighting behavior, cooperative behavior, economic behavior, political behavior—all depend on the perceiving of what another person or other persons afford, or sometimes on the misperceiving of it.

What the male affords the female is reciprocal to what the female affords the male; what the infant affords the mother is reciprocal to what the mother affords the infant; what the prey affords the predator goes along with what the predator affords the prey; what the buyer affords the seller cannot be separated from what the seller affords the buyer, and so on. The perceiving of these mutual affordances is enormously complex, but it is nonetheless lawful, and it is based on the pickup of the information in touch, sound, odor, taste, and ambient light. It is just as much based on stimulus information as is the simpler perception of the support that is offered by the ground under one's feet. For other animals and other persons can only give off information about themselves insofar as they are tangible, audible, odorous, tastable, or visible.

The other person, the generalized *other*, the *alter* as opposed to the *ego*, is an ecological object with a skin, even if clothed. It is an object, although it is not *merely* an object, and we do right to speak of *he* or *she* instead of *it*. But the other person has a surface that reflects light, and the information to specify what he or she is, invites, promises, threatens, or does can be found in the light.

PLACES AND HIDING PLACES

The habitat of a given animal contains *places*. A place is not an object with definite boundaries but a region (Chapter 3). The different places of a habitat may have different affordances. Some are places where food is usually found and others where it is not. There are places of danger, such as the brink of a cliff and the regions where predators lurk. There are places of refuge from predators. Among these is the place where mate and young are, the home, which is usually a partial enclosure. Animals are skilled at what the psychologist calls place-learning. They can find their way to significant places.

An important kind of place, made intelligible by the ecological approach to visual perception, is a place that affords concealment, a *hiding place*. Note that it involves social perception and raises questions of epistemology. The concealing of oneself from other observers and the hiding of a detached object from other observers have different kinds of motivation. As every child discovers, a good hiding place for one's body is not necessarily a good hiding place for a treasure. A detached object can be concealed both from other observers and from the observer himself. The observer's body can be concealed from other observers but *not* from himself, as the last chapter emphasized. Animals as well as children hide themselves and also hide objects such as food.

One of the laws of the ambient optic array (Chapter 5) is that at any fixed point of observation some parts of the environment are revealed and the remaining parts are concealed. The reciprocal of this law is that the observer himself, his body considered as part of the environment, is revealed at some fixed points of observation and concealed at the remaining points. An observer can perceive not only that other observers are unhidden or hidden from him but also that he is hidden or unhidden from other observers. Surely, babies playing peek-a-boo and children playing hide-and-seek are practicing this kind of apprehension. To *hide* is to position one's body at a place that is concealed at the points of observation of other observers. A "good" hiding place is one that is concealed at nearly all points of observation.

All of these facts and many more depend on the principle of occluding edges at a point of observation, the law of reversible occlusion, and the facts of opaque and nonopaque substances. What we call privacy in the design of housing, for example, is the providing of opaque enclosures. A high degree of concealment is afforded by an enclosure, and complete concealment is afforded by a complete enclosure. But note that there are peepholes and screens that permit seeing without being seen. A transparent sheet of glass in a window transmits both illumination and information, whereas a *translucent* sheet transmits illumination but not information. There will be more of this in Chapter 11.

Note also that a glass wall affords seeing through but not walking through, whereas a cloth curtain affords going through but not seeing through. Architects and designers know such facts, but they lack a theory of affordances to encompass them in a system.

SUMMARY: POSITIVE AND NEGATIVE AFFORDANCES

The foregoing examples of the affordances of the environment are enough to show how general and powerful the concept is. Substances have biochemical offerings and afford manufacture. Surfaces afford posture, locomotion, collision, manipulation, and in general behavior. Special forms of layout afford shelter and concealment. Fires afford warming and burning. Detached objects—tools, utensils, weapons—afford special types of behavior to primates and humans. The other animal and the other person provide mutual and reciprocal affordances at extremely high levels of behavioral complexity. At the highest level, when vocalization becomes speech and manufactured displays become images, pictures, and writing, the affordances of human behavior are staggering. No more of that will be considered at this stage except to point out that speech, pictures, and writing still have to be perceived.

At all these levels, we can now observe that some offerings of the environment are beneficial and some are injurious. These are slippery terms that should only be used with great care, but if their meanings are pinned down to biological and behavioral facts the danger of confusion can be minimized. First, consider substances that afford ingestion. Some afford nutrition for a given animal, some afford poisoning, and some are neutral. As I pointed out before, these facts are quite distinct from the affording of pleasure and displeasure in eating, for the experiences do not necessarily correlate with the biological effects. Second, consider the brink of a cliff. On the one side it affords walking along, locomotion, whereas on the other it affords falling off, injury. Third, consider a detached object with a sharp edge, a knife. It affords cutting if manipulated in one manner, but it affords being cut if manipulated in another manner. Similarly, but at a different level of complexity, a middle-sized metallic object affords grasping, but if charged with current it affords electric shock. And fourth, consider the other person. The animate object can give caresses or blows, contact comfort or contact injury, reward or punishment, and it is not always easy to perceive which will be provided. Note that all these benefits and injuries, these safeties and dangers, these positive and negative affordances are properties of things *taken with reference to an observer* but not properties of the *experiences of the observer*. They are not subjective values; they are not feelings of pleasure or pain added to neutral perceptions.

There has been endless debate among philosophers and psychologists as to whether values are physical or phenomenal, in the world of matter or only in the world of mind. For affordances as distinguished from values, the debate does not apply. Affordances are neither in the one world or the other inasmuch as the theory of two worlds is rejected. There is only one environment, although it contains many observers with limitless opportunities for them to live in it.

THE ORIGIN OF THE CONCEPT OF AFFORDANCES: A RECENT HISTORY

The gestalt psychologists recognized that the meaning or the value of a thing seems to be perceived just as immediately as its color. The value is clear *on the face of it*, as we say, and thus it has a *physiognomic* quality in the way that the emotions of a man appear *on his face*. To quote from the *Principles of Gestalt Psychology* (Koffka, 1935), "Each thing says what it is. . . . a fruit says 'Eat me'; water says 'Drink me'; thunder says 'Fear me'; and woman says 'Love me' " (p. 7). These values are vivid and essential features of the experience itself. Koffka did not believe that a meaning of this sort could be explained as a pale context of memory images or an unconscious set of response tendencies. The postbox "invites" the mailing of a letter, the handle "wants to be grasped," and things "tell us what to do with them" (p. 353). Hence, they have what Koffka called "demand character."

Kurt Lewin coined the term *Aufforderungscharakter*, which has been translated as *invitation character* (by J. F. Brown in 1929) and as *valence* (by D. K. Adams in 1931; cf. Marrow, 1969, p. 56, for the history of these translations). The latter term came into general use. *Valences* for Lewin had corresponding *vectors*, which could be represented as arrows pushing the observer toward or away from the object. What explanation could be given for these valences, the characters of objects that invited or demanded behavior? No one, not even the gestalt theorists, could think of them as physical and, indeed, they do not fall within the province of ordinary physics. They must therefore be phenomenal, given the assumption of dualism. If there were *two* objects, and if the valence could not belong to the physical object, it must belong to the phenomenal object—to what Koffka called the "behavioral" object but not to the "geographical" object. The valence of an object was bestowed upon it in experience, and bestowed by a need of the observer. Thus, Koffka argued that the postbox has a demand character only when the observer needs to mail a letter. He is attracted to it when he has a letter to post, not otherwise. The value of something was assumed to change as the need of the observer changed.

The concept of affordance is derived from these concepts of valence, invitation, and demand but with a crucial difference. The affordance of something does *not change* as the need of the observer changes. The observer may or may not perceive or attend to the affordance, according to his needs, but the affordance, being invariant, is always there to be perceived. An affordance is not bestowed upon an object by a need of an observer and his act of perceiving it. The object offers what it does because it is what it is. To be sure, we define *what it is* in terms of ecological physics instead of physical physics, and it therefore possesses meaning and value to begin with. But this is meaning and value of a new sort.

For Koffka it was the *phenomenal* postbox that invited letter-mailing, not the *physical* postbox. But this duality is pernicious. I prefer to say that the real postbox (the *only* one) affords letter-mailing to a letter-writing human in a community with a postal system. This fact is perceived when the postbox is identified as such, and it is apprehended whether the postbox is in sight or out of sight. To feel a special attraction to it when one has a letter to mail is not surprising, but the main fact is that it is perceived as part of the environment—as an item of the neighborhood in which we live. Everyone above the age of six knows what it is for and where the nearest one is. The perception of its affordance should therefore not be confused with the temporary special attraction it may have.

The gestalt psychologists explained the directness and immediacy of the experience of valences by postulating that the ego is an object in experience and that a "tension" may arise between a phenomenal object and the phenomenal ego. When the object is in "a dynamic relation with the ego" said Koffka, it has a demand character. Note that the "tension," the "relation," or the "vector" must arise in the "field," that is, in the field of phenomenal experience. Although many psychologists find this theory intelligible, I do not. There is an easier way of explaining why the values of things seem to

Figure 8.1

The changing perspective structure of a postbox during approach by an observer.

As one reduces the distance to the object to one-third, the visual solid angle of the object increases three times. Actually this is only a detail near the center of an outflowing optic array. (From *The Perception of the Visual World* by James Jerome Gibson and used with the agreement of the reprint publisher, Greenwood Press, Inc.)

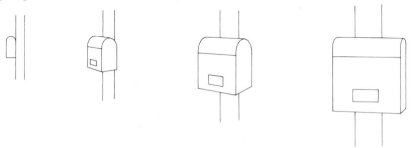

be perceived immediately and directly. It is because the affordances of things for an observer are specified in stimulus information. They *seem* to be perceived directly because they *are* perceived directly.

The accepted theories of perception, to which the gestalt theorists were objecting, implied that *no* experiences were direct except sensations and that sensations mediated all other kinds of experience. Bare sensations had to be clothed with meaning. The seeming directness of meaningful perception was therefore an embarrassment to the orthodox theories, and the Gestaltists did right to emphasize it. They began to undermine the sensation-based theories. But their own explanations of why it is that a fruit says "Eat me" and a woman says "Love me" are strained. The gestalt psychologists objected to the accepted theories of perception, but they never managed to go beyond them.

THE OPTICAL INFORMATION FOR
PERCEIVING AFFORDANCES

The theory of affordances is a radical departure from existing theories of value and meaning. It begins with a new definition of what value and meaning *are*. The perceiving of an affordance is not a process of perceiving a value-free physical object to which meaning is somehow added in a way that no one has been able to agree upon; it is a process of perceiving a value-rich ecological object. Any substance, any surface, any layout has some affordance for benefit or injury to someone. Physics may be value-free, but ecology is not.

The central question for the theory of affordances is not whether they exist and are real but whether information is available in ambient light for perceiving them. The skeptic may now be convinced that there is information in light for some properties of a surface but not for such a property as being good to eat. The taste of a thing, he will say, is not specified in light; you can see its form and color and texture but not its palatability; you have to *taste* it for that. The skeptic understands the stimulus variables that specify the dimensions of visual sensation; he knows from psychophysics that brightness corresponds to intensity and color to wavelength of light. He may concede the invariants of structured stimulation that specify surfaces and how they are laid out and what they are made of. But he may boggle at invariant combinations of invariants that specify the affordances of the environment for an observer. The skeptic familiar with the experimental control of stimulus variables has enough trouble understanding the invariant variables I have been proposing without being asked to accept invariants of invariants.

Nevertheless, a unique combination of invariants, a *compound* invariant, is just another invariant. It is a unit, and the components do not *have* to be combined or associated. Only if percepts were combinations of sensations would they have to be associated. Even in the classical terminology, it could be argued that when a number of stimuli are completely covariant, when they *always* go together, they constitute a single "stimulus." If the visual system is capable of extracting invariants from a changing optic array, there is no reason why it should not extract invariants that seem to us highly complex.

The trouble with the assumption that high-order optical invariants specify high-order affordances is that experimenters, accustomed to working in the laboratory with low-order stimulus variables, cannot think of a way to *measure* them. How can they hope to isolate and control an invariant of optical structure so as to apply it to an observer if they cannot quantify it? The answer comes in two parts, I think. First, they should not hope to *apply* an invariant to an observer, only to make it available, for it is not a stimulus. And, second, they do not have to quantify an invariant, to apply numbers to it, but only to give it an exact mathematical description so that other experimenters can make it available to *their* observers. The virtue of the psychophysical experiment is simply that it is disciplined, not that it relates the psychical to the physical by a metric formula.

An affordance, as I said, points two ways, to the environment and to the observer. So does the information to specify an affordance. But this does not in the least imply separate realms of consciousness and matter, a psychophysical dualism. It says only that the information to specify the utilities of the environment is accompanied by information to specify the observer himself, his body, legs, hands, and mouth. This is only to reemphasize that exteroception is accompanied by proprioception—that to perceive the world is to coperceive oneself. This is wholly inconsistent with dualism in any form, either mind-matter dualism or mind-body dualism. The awareness of the world and of one's complementary relations to the world are not separable.

The child begins, no doubt, by perceiving the affordances of things for her, for her own personal behavior. She walks and sits and grasps relative to her own legs and body and hands. But she must learn to perceive the affordances of things for other observers as well as for herself. An affordance is often valid for all the animals of a species, as when it is part of a niche. I have described the invariants that enable a child to perceive the same solid shape at different points of observation and that likewise enable two or more children to perceive the same shape at different points of observation. These are the invariants that enable two children to perceive the common *affordance* of the solid shape despite the different perspectives, the affordance of a toy, for example. Only when each child perceives the values of things for others as well as for herself does she begin to be socialized.

MISINFORMATION FOR AFFORDANCES

If there is information in the ambient light for the affordances of things, can there also be misinformation? According to the thoery being developed, if information is picked up perception results; if misinformation is picked up misperception results.

The brink of a cliff affords falling off; it is in fact dangerous and it looks dangerous to us. It seems to look dangerous to many other terrestrial animals besides ourselves, including infant animals. Experimental studies have been made of this fact. If a sturdy sheet of plate glass is extended out over the edge it no longer affords falling and in fact is not dangerous, but it may still *look* dangerous. The optical information to specify depth-downward-at-an-edge is still present in the ambient light; for this reason the device was called a *visual cliff* by E. J. Gibson and R. D. Walk (1960). Haptic information was available to specify an adequate surface of support, but this was contradictory to the optical information. When human infants at the crawling stage of locomotion were tested with this apparatus, many of them would pat the glass with their hands but would not venture out on the surface. The babies misperceived the affordance of a transparent surface for support, and this result is not surprising.

Similarly, an adult can misperceive the affordance of a sheet of glass by mistaking a closed glass door for an open doorway and attempting to walk through it. He then crashes into the barrier and is injured. The affordance of collision was not specified by the outflow of optical texture in the array, or it was insufficiently specified. He mistook glass for air. The occluding edges of the doorway were specified and the empty visual solid angle opened up symmetrically in the normal manner as he approached, so his behavior was properly controlled, but the imminence of collision was not noticed. A little dirt on the surface, or highlights, would have saved him.

These two cases are instructive. In the first a surface of support was mistaken for air because the optic array specified air. In the second case a *barrier* was mistaken for air for the same reason. Air downward affords falling and is dangerous. Air forward affords passage and is safe. The mistaken perceptions led to inappropriate actions.

Errors in the perception of the surface of support are serious for a terrestrial animal. If quicksand is mistaken for sand, the perceiver is in deep trouble. If a covered pitfall is taken for solid ground, the animal is trapped. A danger is sometimes hidden—

Things That Look like What They Are

If the affordances of a thing are perceived correctly, we say that it looks like what it *is*. But we must, of course, *learn* to see what things really are—for example, that the innocent-looking leaf is really a nettle or that the helpful-sounding politician is really a demagogue. And this can be very difficult.

the shark under the calm water and the electric shock in the radio cabinet. In the natural environment, poison ivy is frequently mistaken for ivy. In the artificial environment, acid can be mistaken for water.

A wildcat may be hard to distinguish from a cat, and a thief may look like an honest person. When Koffka asserted that "each thing says what it is," he failed to mention that it may lie. More exactly, a thing may not look like what it is.

Nevertheless, however true all this may be, the basic affordances of the environment are perceivable and are usually perceivable directly, without an excessive amount of learning. The basic properties of the environment that make an affordance are specified in the structure of ambient light, and hence the affordance itself is specified in ambient light. Moreover, an invariant variable *that is commensurate with the body of the observer himself* is more easily picked up than one not commensurate with his body.

SUMMARY

The medium, substances, surfaces, objects, places, and other animals have affordances for a given animal. They offer benefit or injury, life or death. This is why they need to be perceived.

The possibilities of the environment and the way of life of the animal go together inseparably. The environment constrains what the animal can do, and the concept of a niche in ecology reflects this fact. Within limits, the human animal can alter the affordances of the environment but is still the creature of his or her situation.

There is information in stimulation for the physical properties of things, and presumably there is information for the environmental properties. The doctrine that says we must distinguish among the variables of things before we can learn their meanings is questionable. Affordances are properties taken with reference to the observer. They are neither physical nor phenomenal.

The hypothesis of information in ambient light to specify affordances is the culmination of ecological optics. The notion of invariants that are related at one extreme to the motives and needs of an observer and at the other extreme to the substances and surfaces of a world provides a new approach to psychology.

THREE

VISUAL PERCEPTION

NINE

EXPERIMENTAL EVIDENCE FOR DIRECT PERCEPTION: PERSISTING LAYOUT

Direct perception is what one gets from seeing Niagara Falls, say, as distinguished from seeing a picture of it. The latter kind of perception is *mediated*. So when I assert that perception of the environment is direct, I mean that it is not mediated by *retinal* pictures, *neural* pictures, or *mental* pictures. *Direct perception* is the activity of getting information from the ambient array of light. I call this a process of *information pickup* that involves the exploratory activity of looking around, getting around, and looking at things. This is quite different from the supposed activity of getting information from the inputs of the optic nerves, whatever they may prove to be.

The evidence for direct visual perception has accumulated slowly, over many years. The very idea had to be developed, the results of old experiments had to be reinterpreted, and new experiments had to be carried out. The next two chapters are devoted to the experimental evidence.

The experiments will be considered under three main headings: first, the direct perception of surface layout; second, the direct perception of *changing* surface layout; and third, the direct perception of the movements of the self. This chapter is devoted to the direct perception of surface layout.

EVIDENCE FOR THE DIRECT PERCEPTION OF SURFACE LAYOUT

Some thirty years ago, during World War II, psychologists were trying to apply the theory of depth perception to the problems of aviation, especially the problem of how a flier lands an airplane. Pilots were given tests for depth perception, and there was controversy as to whether depth perception was learned or innate. The same tests are still being given, and the same disagreement continues.

The theory of depth perception assumes that the third dimension of space is lost in the two-dimensional retinal image. Perception must begin with form perception, the flat patchwork of colors in the visual field. But there are supposedly *cues* for depth, which, if they are utilized, will add a third dimension to the flat visual field. A list of the cues for depth is given in most psychology textbooks: linear perspective, apparent size, superposition, light and shade, relative motion, aerial perspective, accommodation (the monocular cues), along with binocular disparity and convergence (the binocular cues). You might suppose that adequate tests could be made of a prospective flier's ability to use these cues and that experiments could be devised to find out whether or not they were learned.

The trouble was that none of the tests based on the cues for depth predicted the success or failure of a student pilot, and none of the proposals for improving depth perception by training made it any easier to learn to fly. I was deeply puzzled by this fact. The accepted theory of depth perception did not work. It did not apply to problems where one might expect it to apply. I began to suspect that the traditional list of cues for depth was inadequate. And in the end I came to believe that the whole theory of depth perception was false.

I suggested a new theory in a book on what I called the *visual world* (Gibson, 1950*b*). I considered "the possibility that there is literally no such thing as a perception of space without the perception of a continuous background surface" (p. 6). I called this a *ground theory* of space perception to distinguish it from the *air theory* that seemed to underlie the old approach. The idea was that the world consisted of a basic surface with adjoining surfaces, not of bodies in empty air. The character of the visual world was given not by objects but by the background of the objects. Even the space of the airplane pilot, I said, was determined by the ground and the horizon of the earth, not by the air through which he flies. The notion of space of three dimensions with three axes for Cartesian coordinates was a great convenience for mathematics, I suggested, but an abstraction that had very little to do with actual perception.

I would now describe the ground theory as a theory of the *layout* of surfaces. By *layout*, I mean the relations of surfaces to the ground and to one another, their arrangement. The layout includes both places and objects, together with other features. The theory asserts that the perception of surface layout is direct. This means that perception does not begin with two-dimensional form perception. Hence, there is no special kind of perception called depth perception, and the third dimension is not lost in the retinal image since it was never in the environment to begin with. It is a loose term. If *depth* means the dimension of an object that goes with height and width, there is nothing special about it. Height becomes depth when the object is seen from the top, and width becomes depth when the object is seen from the side. If depth means distance from *here*, then it involves self-perception and is continually changing as the observer moves about. The theory of depth perception is based on confusion and perpetuated by the fallacy of the retinal picture.

I now say that there is information in ambient light for the perception of the layout of surfaces but not that there are cues or clues for the perception of depth. The traditional list of cues is worthless if perception does not begin with a flat picture. I tried to reformulate the list in 1950 as "gradients and steps of retinal stimulation" (Gibson, 1950*b*, pp. 137 ff.). The hypothesis of gradients was a good beginning, but the reformulation failed. It had the great handicap of being based on physiological optics and the retinal image instead of ecological optics and the ambient array.

Such is the hypothesis of the direct perception of surface layout. What is the evidence to support it? Some experiments had been carried out even before 1950, outdoor experiments in the open air instead of laboratory experiments with spots of light in a darkroom, but they were only a beginning (Gibson, 1947). Much more experimental evidence has accumulated in the last twenty-five years.

THE PSYCHOPHYSICS OF SPACE AND
FORM PERCEPTION

The studies to be described were thought of as psychophysical experiments at the time they were performed. There was to be a new psychophysics of perception as well as the old psychophysics of sensation. For I thought I had discovered that there were stimuli for perceptions in much the same way that there were known to be stimuli for sensations. This now seems to me a mistake. I failed to distinguish between stimulation proper and stimulus information, between what happens at passive receptors and what is available to active perceptual systems. Traditional psychophysics is a laboratory discipline in which physical stimuli are applied to an observer. He is prodded with controlled and systematically varied bits of energy so as to discover how his experience varies correspondingly. This procedure makes it difficult or impossible for the observer to extract invariants over time. Stimulus prods do not ordinarily carry information about the environment.

What I had in mind by a psychophysics of perception was simply the emphasis on perception as direct instead of indirect. I wanted to exclude an extra process of inference or construction. I meant (or should have meant) that animals and people *sense* the environment, not in the meaning of having sensations but in the meaning of *detecting*. When I asserted that a gradient in the retinal image was a *stimulus* for perception, I meant only that it was sensed as a unit; it was not a collection of points whose separate sensations had to be put together in the brain. But the concept of the stimulus was not clear to me. I should have asserted that a gradient is stimulus *information*. For it is first of all an invariant property of an optic array. I should not have implied that a percept was an automatic response to a stimulus, as a sense impression is supposed to be. For even then I realized that perceiving is an act, not a response, an act of attention, not a triggered impression, an achievement, not a reflex.

So what I should have meant by a "psychophysical" theory of perception in 1950 and by perception as a "function of stimulation" in the essay I wrote in 1959 (Gibson, 1959) was the hypothesis of a one-stage process for the perception of surface layout instead of a two-stage process of first perceiving flat forms and then interpreting the cues for depth.

I now believe that there is no such thing as flat-form perception, just as there is no such thing as depth perception. (There are drawings and pictures, to be sure, but these are not "forms," as I will explain in Part IV. The theory of form perception in psychology is no less confused than the theory of depth perception.) But this was not clear when I wrote my book in 1950, where I promised not only a psychophysics of space perception in Chapter 5 but also a psychophysical approach to form perception in Chapter 10. This sounded promising and progressive. Visual outline forms, I suggested, are not unique entities. "They could be arranged in a systematic way such that each form would differ only gradually and continuously from all others" (Gibson, 1950b, p. 193). What counts is not the form as such but the dimensions of variation of form. And psychophysical experiments could be carried out if these dimensions were isolated.

Here was the germ of the modern hypothesis of the distinctive features of graphic symbols. It also carries the faint suggestion of a much more radical hypothesis, that what the eye picks up is a sequential transformation, not a form. The study of form discrimination by psychophysical methods has flourished in the last thirty years. W. R. Garner, Julian Hochberg, Fred Attneave, and others have achieved the systematic variation of outline forms and patterns in elegant ways (e.g., Garner, 1974). My objection to this research is that it tells us nothing about perceiving the environment. It still assumes that vision is simplest when there is a form on the retina that copies a form on a surface facing the retina. It perpetuates the fallacy that form perception is basic. It holds back the study of invariants in a changing array. But the hypothesis that forms are directly perceived does not upset the orthodoxies of visual theory as does the hypothesis that invariants are directly perceived, and hence it is widely accepted.

The psychophysical approach to surface perception is much more radical than the psychophysical approach to form perception, and it has *not* been widely accepted over the last twenty-five years. Has its promise been fulfilled? Some experiments can be summarized, and the evidence should be pulled together.

EXPERIMENTS ON THE PERCEPTION OF A SURFACE
AS DISTINGUISHED FROM NOTHING

Metzger's Experiment   Is tridimensional space perception based on bidimensional sensations to which the third dimension is added, or is it based on surface perception? The first experiment bearing on this issue is that of W. Metzger in 1930. He faced the eyes of his observer with a large, dimly lighted plaster wall, which rendered the light coming to the visual system unfocusable. Neither eye could accommodate, and probably the eyes could not converge. The total field (*Ganzfeld*) was, as he put it, *homogeneous*. Under high illumination, the observer simply perceived the wall, and the outcome was so obvious as to be uninteresting. But under low illumination, the fine-grained texture of the surface was no longer registered by a human eye, and the observer reported seeing what he called a fog or haze or mist of light. He certainly did not see a surface in two dimensions, and therefore Metzger was tempted to conclude that he saw something in three dimensions; that is, he was perceiving "space."

But I did not see depth in the "mist of light." Another way to get a homogeneous field is to confront the eyes with a hemisphere of diffusing glass highly illuminated from the outside (Gibson and Dibble, 1952). A better way is to cover each eye with a fitted cap of strongly diffusing translucent material worn like a pair of goggles (Gibson and Waddell, 1952). The structure of the entering light, the optical texture, can thus be eliminated at any level of intensity. What my observers and I saw under these conditions could better be described as "nothing" in the sense of "no thing." It was like looking at the sky. There was no surface and no object at any distance. Depth was not present in the experience but missing from it. What the observer saw, as I would now put it, was an empty *medium*.

The essence of Metzger's experiment and its subsequent repetitions is not the plaster wall or the panoramic surface or the diffusing glass globe or the eye-caps. The experiment *provides* discontinuities in the light to an eye at one extreme and *eliminates* them at the other. The purpose of the experiment is to control and vary the projective capacity of light. This must be isolated from the stimulating capacity of light. Metzger's experiment points to the distinction between an optic array with structure and a nonarray without structure. To the extent that the array has structure it specifies an environment.

A number of experiments using a panoramic surface under low illumination have been carried out, although the experimenters did not always realize what they were doing. But all the experiments involved more or less faint discontinuities in the light to the eye. What the observers said they saw is complex and hard to describe. One attempt was made by W. Cohen in 1957, and the other experiments have been surveyed by L. L. Avant (1965). It is fair to say that there are intermediate perceptions between seeing *nothing* and seeing *something* as the discontinuities become stronger. These are the polar opposites of perception that are implied by Metzger's experiment, not the false opposites of seeing in two dimensions and seeing in three dimensions.

The confusion over whether there is or is not "depth" in Metzger's luminous fog is what led me to think that the whole theory of depth, distance, the third dimension, and space is misconceived. The important result is the neglected one that a surface is seen when the array has structure, that is, differences in different directions. A perfectly flat surface in front of the eyes is still a layout, that is, a wall. And that is all that "seeing in two dimensions" can possibly mean.

The Experiment with Translucent Eye-Caps   Eliminating optical texture from the light entering the eye by means of translucent diffusing goggles is an experiment that has been repeated many times. The observer is blind, not to light, for the photoreceptors are still stimulated, but to the environment, for the ocular system is inactivated; its adjustments are frustrated. The observer cannot *look at* or *look around,* and I shall devote a chapter to this activity later. The eye-caps have also been adapted for experiments on the development of vision in young animals. It was known that when diurnal animals such as primates were reared from birth in complete darkness they were blind by certain criteria when brought into an illuminated environment (although this was not true of nocturnal animals whose ancestors were used to getting around in the dark). Now it was discovered that animals deprived of optical structure but not of optical stimulation were also partly blind when the eye-caps were removed. Crudely speaking, they could not *use* their eyes properly. Anatomical degeneration of the photoreceptors had not occurred, as with the animals reared in the dark, but the exploratory adjustments of the visual system had not developed normally. The experiments are described in Chapter 12 of *Perceptual Learning and Development* by Eleanor J. Gibson (1969).

Experiments with a Sheet of Glass   It is fairly well known that a clean sheet of plate glass that projects no reflections or highlights to the observer's eye is, as we say, invisible. This fact is not self-explanatory, but it is very interesting. It means that one perceives air where a material surface exists, because air is specified by the optic array. I have seen people try to walk through plate-glass doors to their great discomfiture and deer try to jump through plate-glass windows with fatal results.

A perfectly clear sheet of glass transmits both light considered as energy and an *array* of light considered as information. A frosted or pebbled sheet of glass transmits optical energy but *not* optical information. The clear sheet can be seen through, as we say, but the frosted sheet cannot. The latter can be seen, but the former cannot. An imperceptible sheet of glass can be made increasingly perceptible by letting dust or powder fall on it or by spattering it. Even the faintest specks can specify the surface. In this intermediate case, the sheet transmits both the array from the layout behind the glass and the array from the glass itself. We say that we see the farther surface *through* the glass surface. The optical structure of one is *mixed* or *interspersed* with the optical structure of the other. The transparency of the near surface, more properly its semitransparency, is then perceived (Gibson, 1976). One sees two surfaces, separated in depth, in the same direction from here or, better, within the same visual solid angle of the ambient array. At least one sees them separated if the interspersed structures are different, or if the elements of one move relative to the elements of the other (E. J. Gibson, Gibson, Smith, and Flock, 1959).

Many of the above assertions are based on informal experiments that have not been published. But the reader can check them for himself with little trouble. I conclude that a surface is experienced when the structural information to specify it is picked up.

Experiments with a Pseudotunnel   In the case of a sheet of glass, a surface may exist and go unperceived if it is not specified. In the next experiment, a surface may be nonexistent but may be perceived if it is specified. The pseudosurface in this case was not flat and frontal but was a semienclosure, a cylindrical tunnel viewed from one end. I called it an *optical tunnel* to suggest that the surface was not material or substantial but was produced by the light to the eye. Another way of describing it would be to say that it was a *virtual* but not a *real* tunnel.

The purpose of the experiment was to provide information for the perception of the inside surface of a cylinder without the ordinary source of this information, the inside surface of a cylinder. I would now call this a *display*. The fact that the perception was illusory is incidental. I wanted to elicit a synthetic perception, and I, therefore,

Figure 9.1
The optic array coming to the eye from the optical tunnel.
There are nine contrasts in this cross-section of the array, that is, nine transitions of luminous intensity. The next figure shows a longitudinal section. The point of observation for the figure on the left is centered with the tunnel, whereas the point of observation for the figure on the right is to the right of center. (From J. J. Gibson, J. Purdy, and L. Lawrence: "A Method of Controlling Stimulation for the Study of Space Perception: The Optical Tunnel," *Journal of Experimental Psychology*, 1955, 50, 1–14. Copyright 1955 by the American Psychological Association. Reprinted by permission.)

had to synthesize the information. It was an experiment in perceptual psychophysics, more exactly, psycho-optics. The observers were fooled, to be sure, but that was irrelevant. There was no information in the array to specify that it *was* a display. This situation, I shall argue, is very rare.

My collaborators and I (Gibson, Purdy, and Lawrence, 1955) generated a visual solid angle of about 30° at the point of observation. This array consisted of alternating dark and light rings nested within one another, separated by abrupt circular contours. The number of rings and contours from the periphery to the center of the array could be varied. At one extreme there were thirty-six contours, and at the other seven.

Thus the *mean density* of the contrasts in the array was varied from fine to coarse. The *gradient* of this density could also be varied; normally the density increased from the periphery toward the center.

The source of this display, the apparatus, was a set of large, very thin, plastic sheets, each hiding the next, with a one-foot hole cut in the center of each. They were indirectly illuminated from above or below. The contours in the array were caused by the edges of the sheets. The texture of the plastic was so fine as to be invisible. Black and white sheets could be hung in alternation one behind another, or, as a control, all-black or all-white surfaces could be displayed. The observers looked into these holes

Figure 9.2
A longitudinal section of the optical tunnel shown in Figure 9.1.

Nine plastic sheets are shown, black and white alternating, with the cut edges of the nine holes aligned. The increase in the density of the contrasts from the periphery to the center of the array is evident. (From J. J. Gibson, J. Purdy, and L. Lawrence: "A Method of Controlling Stimulation for the Study of Space Perception: The Optical Tunnel," *Journal of Experimental Psychology*, 1955, 50, 1–14. Copyright 1955 by the American Psychological Association. Reprinted by permission.)

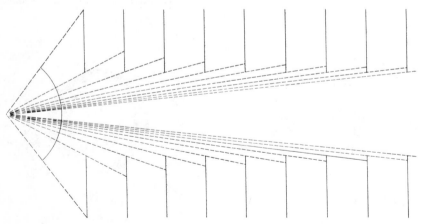

from a booth, and extreme precautions were taken to prevent them from having any preconception of what they would see.

The principal result was as follows. When all-black or all-white surfaces were used, the observers saw nothing; the area within the first hole was described as a hazy or misty fog, a dark or light film, without obvious depth. At the other extreme, when thirty-six dark and light rings were displayed, all observers saw a continuous striped cylindrical surface, a solid tunnel. No edges were seen, and "a ball could be rolled from the far end to the entrance."

When nineteen contrasts were displayed, two-thirds of the observers described a solid tunnel. When thirteen contrasts were displayed, half did so; and when seven contrasts were displayed, only one-third did so. In each case, the remainder said they saw either segments of surface with air in between or a series of circular edges (which was, of course, correct). With fewer contrasts, the experience became progressively less continuous and substantial. The proximity of these contours had proved to be crucial. *Surfaciness* depended on their mean density in the array.

What about the cylindrical shape of the surface, the receding layout of the tunnel? This could be altered in a striking way and the tunnel converted into a flat surface like an archery target with rings around a bull's-eye simply by rearranging the sheets in the

Figure 9.3
An arrangement that provides an array with a constant density of contrasts from periphery to center.

Only the first seven apertures are shown. The observer does not see a tunnel with this display but a flat surface with concentric rings, something like an archery target, so long as the head is immobile and one eye is covered. (From J. J. Gibson, J. Purdy, and L. Lawrence: "A Method of Controlling Stimulation for the Study of Space Perception: The Optical Tunnel," *Journal of Experimental Psychology*, 1955, 50, 1–14. Copyright 1955 by the American Psychological Association. Reprinted by permission.)

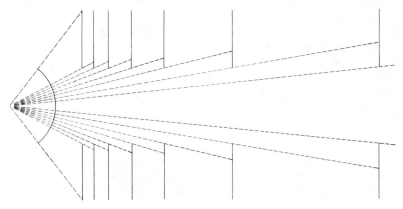

way illustrated. The *gradient* of increasing proximity toward the center of the array gives way to an equal proximity. But the target surface instead of the tunnel surface appeared only if the observer's head was fixed and one eye was covered, that is, if the array was frozen and single. If the head was moved or the other eye used, the tunnel shape was again seen. The frozen array specified a flat target, but the dual or transforming array specified a receding tunnel. This is only one of many experiments in which perception with monocular fixed vision is exceptional.

Conclusion   These experiments with a dimly lighted wall, with translucent eye-caps, with a sheet of glass, and with a pseudotunnel seem to show that the perception of *surfaciness* depends on the proximity to one another of discontinuities in the optic array. A surface is the interface between matter in the gaseous state and matter in the liquid or solid state. A surface comes to exist as the matter on one side of the interface becomes more *substantial* (Chapter 2). The medium is insubstantial. Mists, clouds, water, and solids are increasingly substantial. These substances are also increasingly *opaque*, except for a substance like glass, which is rare in nature. What these experiments have done is to vary systematically the optical information for the perception of substantiality and opacity. (But see the next chapter on the perception of *coherence*.)

The experiment with the pseudotunnel also seems to show that the perception of a surface as such entails the perception of its layout, such as the front-facing layout of a wall or the slanting layout of a tunnel. Both are kinds of layout, and the traditional distinction between two-dimensional and three-dimensional vision is a myth.

EXPERIMENTS ON THE PERCEPTION OF THE SURFACE OF SUPPORT

The ground outdoors or the floor indoors is the main surface of support. Animals have to be supported against gravity. If the layout of surfaces is to be substituted for space in the theory of perception, this *fundamental* surface should get first consideration. How is it perceived? Animals like us can always *feel* the surface of support except when falling freely. But we can also *see* the surface of support under our feet if we are, in fact, supported. The ground is always specified in the lower portion of the ambient array. The standing infant can always see it and can always see her feet hiding parts of it. This is a law of ecological optics.

The Glass Floor   A floor can be experimentally modified. When the "visual cliff" was being constructed for experiments with young animals by E. J. Gibson and R. D. Walk (1960), observations were made with a large sheet of glass that was horizontal instead of vertical, a glass floor instead of a glass wall. The animal or child can be put down on this surface under two conditions: when it is visible, by virtue of textured paper placed just under the glass, and when it is invisible, with the paper placed far below the glass. The glass affords support under both conditions but provides *optical information* for support only under the first. There is mechanical contact with the feet in both cases but optical information for contact with the feet only in the first.

The animals or babies tested in this experiment would walk or crawl normally when they could both see and feel the surface but would not do so when they could only feel the surface; in the latter case, they froze, crouched, and showed signs of discomfort. Some animals even adopted the posture they would have when falling (E. J. Gibson and Walk, 1960, pp. 65–66). The conclusion seems to be that some animals require optical information for support along with the inertial and tactual information in order to walk normally. For my part, I should feel very uncomfortable if I had to stand on a large observation platform with a transparent floor through which the ground was seen far below.

The optical information in this experiment, I believe, is contradictory to the haptic information. One sees oneself as being up in the air, but one feels oneself in contact with a surface of support and, of course, one feels the normal pull of gravity in the vestibular organ. In such cases of contradictory or conflicting information, the psychologist cannot predict which will be picked up. The perceptual outcome is uncertain.

Note that the perception of the ground and the coperception of the self are inseparable in this situation. One's body *in relation to* the ground is what gets attention. Perception and proprioception are complementary. But the commonly accepted theories of space perception do not bring out this fact.

The Visual Cliff The visual cliff experiments of E. J. Gibson, R. D. Walk, and subsequently others are very well known. They represented a new approach to the ancient puzzle of depth perception, and the results obtained with newborn or dark-reared animals were surprising because they suggested that depth perception was innate. But the sight of a cliff is *not* a case of perceiving the third dimension. One perceives the affordance of its edge. A cliff is a feature of the terrain, a highly significant, special kind of dihedral angle in ecological geometry, a falling-off place. The edge at the top of a cliff is dangerous. It is an occluding edge. But is has the special character of being an edge of the surface of support, unlike the edge of a wall. One can safely walk around the edge of a wall but not off the edge of a cliff. To perceive a cliff is to detect a layout but, more than that, it is to detect an *affordance*, a negative affordance for locomotion, a place where the surface of support ends.

An affordance is for a species of animal, a layout *relative to* the animal and commensurate with its body. A cliff is a drop-off that is large relative to the size of the animal, and a step is a drop-off that is small relative to its size. A falling-off edge is dangerous, but a stepping-down edge is not. What animals need to perceive is not layout as such but the affordances of the layout, as emphasized in the last chapter. Consider the difference between the edge of a horizontal surface and the edge of a vertical surface, the edge of a floor and the edge of a wall. You go *over* the former whereas you can go *around* the latter. Both are dihedral angles, and both are occluding edges. But the meanings of the two kinds of "depth" are entirely different.

Gibson and Walk (1960; Walk and Gibson, 1961) constructed a virtual cliff with the glass-floor apparatus. They tested animals and babies to determine whether or not they would go forward over the virtual cliff. Actually, they provided two edges on either side of a narrow platform, one a falling-off edge and the other a stepping-down edge appropriate to the species of animal being tested. The animals' choices were recorded. Nearly all terrestrial animals chose the shallow edge instead of the deep one.

The results have usually been discussed in terms of depth perception and the traditional cues for depth. But they are more intelligible in terms of the perception of layout and affordances. The separation in depth at an edge of the surface of support is not at all the same thing as the depth dimension of abstract space. As for innate versus learned perception, it is much more sensible to assume an innate capacity to notice falling-off places in terrestrial animals than it is to assume that they have innate ideas or mental concepts of geometry.

Figure 9.4
The invisibly supported object.

The real object is held up in the air by a hidden rod attached to a heavy base. The virtual object appears to be resting on the ground where the bottom edge of the real object hides the ground, so long as vision is monocular and frozen. One sees a concave corner, not an occluding edge. Because the virtual object is at twice the distance of the real object, it is seen as twice the size.

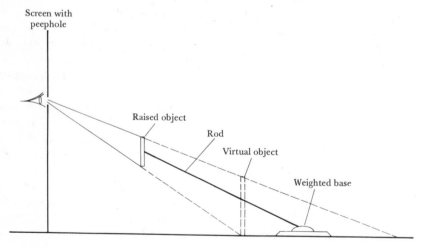

An Object Resting on the Ground   I suggested that one sees the contact of his feet with the ground. This is equally true for other objects than feet. We see whether an object is on the ground or up in the air. How is this contact with or separation from the ground perceived? The answer is suggested by an informal experiment described in my book on the visual world (Gibson, 1950*b*, Fig. 72, pp. 178 ff.), which might be called the *invisibly-supported-object experiment*. I did not clearly understand it at the time, but the optics of occluding edges now makes it more intelligible.

A detached object can be attached to a long rod that is hidden to the observer. The rod can be lowered by the experimenter so that the object rests on the ground or raised so that it stands up in the air. The object can be a cardboard rectangle or trapezoid or a ball, but it must be large enough to hide the rod and its base. An observer who stands at the proper position and looks with two eyes, or with one eye and a normally moving head, perceives a resting object as resting on the surface of support and a raised object as raised above the surface of support. The size and distance of the object are seen correctly. But an observer who looks with one eye and a fixed head, through a peephole or with a biting board, gets an entirely different perception. A resting object is seen correctly, but a raised object is also seen to be resting on the surface. It is seen *at the place where its edge hides the texture of the surface.* It appears farther away and larger than it really is.

This illusion is very interesting. It appears only with monocular arrested vision— a rare and unnatural kind of vision. The increments and decrements of the texture of the ground at the edges of the object have been eliminated, both those of one eye relative to the other and those that are progressive in time at each eye. In traditional theory, the cues of binocular and motion parallax are absent. But it is just these increments and decrements of the ground texture that *specify* the separation of object from ground. The absence of this accretion/deletion specifies contact of the object with the ground. A surface is perceived to "stand up" or "stand out" from the surface that extends behind it only to the extent that the gap is specified. And this depends on seeing from different points of observation, either two points of observation at the same time or different points of observation at different times.

A flat surface that "goes back to" or "lies flat on" the ground will seem to have a different size, shape, and even reflectance than it has when it stands forth in the air. This feature of the illusion is also very interesting, and I have demonstrated it many times. The first published study of it is that of J. E. Hochberg and J. Beck (1954).

EXPERIMENTS WITH THE GROUND AS BACKGROUND

Investigators in the tradition of space perception and the cues for depth have usually done experiments with a background in the frontal plane, that is, a surface facing the observer, a wall, a screen, or a sheet of paper. A form in this plane is most similar to a form on the retina, and extension in this plane might be seen as a simple sensation. This follows from retinal image optics. But investigators of environment perception do experiments with the *ground* as background, studying surfaces instead of forms, and using ecological optics. Instead of studying distance in the air, they study recession along the ground. Distance as such cannot be seen directly but can only be inferred or computed. Recession along the ground can be seen directly.

Distance and Size Perception on the Ground   Although the linear perspective of a street in a painting had been known since the Renaissance, and the converging appearance of a parallel alley of trees in a landscape had been discussed since the eighteenth century, no one had ever studied the perception of a naturally textured ground. Linear perspective was an obvious cue for distance, but the gradient of density or proximity of the texture of the ground was not so obvious. E. G. Boring has described the old experiments with artificial alleys (1942, pp. 290–296), but the first experiment with an ordinary textured field outdoors, I believe, was published at the end of World War II (Gibson, 1947). A plowed field without furrows receding almost to the horizon was used. No straight edges were visible. This original experiment required the judgment of the height of a stake planted in the field at some distance up to half a mile. At such a distance the optical size of the elements of texture and the optical size of the stake itself were extremely small.

Up until that time the unanimous conclusion of observers had been that parallel lines were seen to converge and that objects were seen to be smaller "in the distance." There was a tendency toward "size constancy" of objects, to be sure, but it was usually incomplete. The assumption had always been that size constancy must "break down." It was supposed that an object will cease to be even *visible* at some eventual distance and that presumably it ceases to be visible by way of becoming smaller. (See Gibson, 1950*b*, p. 183, for a statement of this line of reasoning.) With the naive observers in the open field experiment, however, the judgments of the size of the stake did *not* decrease, even when it was a ten-minute walk away and becoming hard to make out. The judgments became more *variable* with distance but not smaller. Size constancy did not break down. The size of the object only became less *definite* with distance, not smaller.

The implication of this result, I now believe, is that certain invariant ratios were picked up unawares by the observers and that the size of the retinal image went unnoticed. No matter how far away the object was, it intercepted or occluded the same number of texture elements of the ground. This is an invariant ratio. For any distance the proportion of the stake extending above the horizon to that extending below the horizon was invariant. This is another invariant ratio. These invariants are not cues but information for direct size perception. The observers in this experiment were aviation trainees and were not interested in the perspective appearance of the terrain and the objects. They could not care less for the patchwork of colors in the visual field that had long fascinated painters and psychologists. They were set to pick up information that would permit a size-match between the distant stake and one of a set of nearby stakes.

The perception of the size and distance of an object on the ground had proved to be unlike the perception of the size and distance of an object in the sky. The invariants are missing in the latter case. The silhouette of an airplane might be a fifty-foot fighter at a one-mile altitude or a hundred-foot bomber at a two-mile altitude. Airplane spotters could be trained to estimate altitude, but only by the method of recognizing the shape, knowing the size by having memorized the wingspan, and inferring the distance from the angular size. Errors were considerable at best. This kind of inferential knowledge is not characteristic of ordinary perception. Baron von Helmholtz called it "unconscious" inference even in the ordinary case, but I am skeptical.

Comparison of Stretches of Distance Along the Ground   The size of an object on the ground is not entirely separable from the sizes of the objects that compose the ground. The terrain is made of clods and particles of earth, or rocks and pebbles, or grass clumps and grass blades. These nested objects might have size constancy just as much as orthodox objects. In the next set of experiments on ground perception, the very distinction between size and distance breaks down. What had to be compared were not stakes or objects but *stretches* of the ground itself, distances between markers placed by the experimenter. In this case distances between *here* and *there* could be compared with distances between *there* and *there*. These open-field experiments were conducted by Eleanor J. Gibson (Gibson and Bergman, 1954; Gibson, Bergman, and Purdy, 1955; Purdy and Gibson, 1955).

Markers could be set down and moved anywhere in a level field of grass up to 350 yards away. The most interesting experiment of the series required the observer to·*bisect* a stretch of distance, which could extend either from his feet to a marker or from one marker to another (Purdy and Gibson, 1955). A mobile marker on wheels had to be stopped by the observer at the halfway point. The ability to bisect a length had been tested in the laboratory with an adjustable stick called a Galton bar but not with a piece of ground on which the observer stood.

All observers could bisect a stretch of distance without difficulty and with some accuracy. The farther stretch could be matched to the nearer one, although the visual angles did not match. The farther visual angle was compressed relative to the nearer, and its surface was, to use a vague term, foreshortened. But no constant error was evident. A stretch from *here* to *there* could be equated with a stretch from *there* to *there*. The conclusion must be that observers were not paying attention to the visual angles; they must have been noticing information. They might have been detecting, without knowing it, the *amount of texture* in a visual angle. The number of grass clumps projected in the farther half of a stretch of distance is exactly the same as the number projected in the nearer half. It is true that the optical texture of the grass becomes denser and more vertically compressed as the ground recedes from the observer, but the rule of *equal amounts of texture for equal amounts of terrain* remains invariant.

This is a powerful invariant. It holds for either dimension of the terrain, for width as well as for depth. In fact, it holds for any regularly textured surface whatever, that is, any surface of the same substance. And it holds for walls and ceilings as well as for floors. To say that a surface is regularly textured is only to assume that bits of the substance tend to be evenly spaced. They do not have to be perfectly regular like crystals in a lattice but only "stochastically" regular.

The implications of this experiment on fractionating a stretch of the ground are radical and far-reaching. The world consists not only of distances from *here*, my world, but also of distances from *there*, the world of another person. These intervals seem to be strikingly equivalent.

The rule of equal amounts of texture for equal amounts of terrain suggests that both size and distance are perceived directly. The old theory that the perceiver *allows for* the distance in perceiving the size of something is unnecessary. The assumption that the cues for distance *compensate for* the sensed smallness of the retinal image is no longer persuasive. Note that the pickup of the *amount of texture* in a visual solid angle of the optic array is not a matter of counting units, that is, of measuring with an arbitrary unit. The other experiments of this open-field series required the observers to make *absolute* judgments, so-called, of distances in terms of yards. They could *learn* to do so readily enough (E. J. Gibson and Bergman, 1954; E. J. Gibson, Bergman, and Purdy, 1955), but it was clear that one had to *see* the distance before one could apply a number to it.

Observations of the Ground and the Horizon   When the terrain is flat and open, the horizon is in the ambient optic array. It is a great circle between the upper and the lower hemisphere separating the sky and the earth. But this is a limiting case. The

---

EVEN SPACING

The fact that the parts of the terrestrial environment tend to be "evenly spaced" was noted in my early book on the visual world (Gibson, 1950*b*, pp. 77–78). This is equivalent to the rule of equal amounts of texture for equal amounts of terrain. The fact can be stated in various ways. However stated, it seems to be a fact that can be seen, not necessarily an intellectual concept of abstract space including numbers and magnitudes. Ecological geometry does not have to be learned from textbooks.

farther stretches of the ground are usually hidden by frontal surfaces such as hills, trees, and walls. Even in an enclosure, however, there has to be a surface of support, a textured floor. The maximum coarseness of its optical texture is straight down, where the feet are, and the density increases outward from this center. These radial gradients projected from the surface of support increase with increasing size of the floor. The densities of texture do not become infinite except when there is an infinitely distant horizon. Only at this limit is the optical structure of the array wholly compressed. But the gradients of density specify where the outdoors horizon would be, even in an enclosure. That is, there exists an implicit horizon even when the earth-sky horizon is hidden.

The concept of a *vanishing point* comes from artificial perspective, converging parallels, and the theory of the picture plane. The *vanishing limit* of optical structure at the horizon comes from natural perspective, ecological optics, and the theory of the ambient optic array. The two kinds of perspective should not be confused, although they have many principles in common (Chapter 5).

The terrestrial horizon is thus an invariant feature of terrestrial vision, an invariant of any and all ambient arrays, at any and all points of observation. The horizon never moves, even when every other structure in the light is changing. This stationary great

Figure 9.5

The base of each pillar covers the same amount of the texture of the ground.

The width of each pillar is that of one paving stone. The pillars will be seen to have the same width if this information is picked up. The height of each pillar is specified by a similar invariant, the "horizon-ratio" relation, described later.

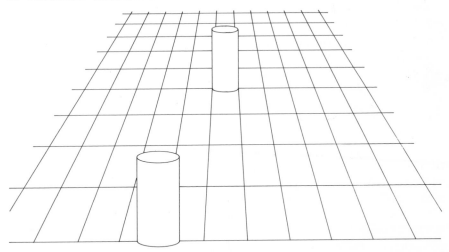

circle is, in fact, that to which all optical motions have reference. It is neither subjective nor objective; it expresses the *reciprocity* of observer and environment; it is an invariant of *ecological* optics.

The horizon is the same as the skyline only in the case of the open ground or the open ocean. The earth-sky contrast may differ from the true horizon because of hills or mountains. The horizon is perpendicular to the pull of gravity and to the two poles of the ambient array at the centers of the two hemispheres; in short, the horizon is horizontal. With reference to this invariant, all other objects, edges, and layouts in the environment are judged to be either *upright* or *tilted*. In fact, the observer perceives *himself* to be in an upright or tilted posture relative to this invariant. (For an early and more complex discussion of visual uprightness and tilt in terms of the retinal image, see Gibson, 1952, on the "phenomenal vertical.")

The facts about the terrestrial horizon are scarcely mentioned in traditional optics. The only empirical study of it is one by H. A. Sedgwick (1973) based on ecological optics. He shows how the horizon is an important source of invariant information for the perception of all kinds of objects. All terrestrial objects, for example, of the same height are cut by the horizon in the same ratio, no matter what the angular size of the object may be. This is the "horizon ratio relation" in its simplest form. Any two trees or poles bisected by the horizon are the same height, and they are also precisely twice my eye-height. More complex ratios specify more complex layouts. Sedgwick showed that judgments of the sizes of objects represented in pictures were actually determined by these ratios.

The perceiving of what might be called *eye level* on the walls, windows, trees, poles, and buildings of the environment in another case of the complementarity between seeing the layout of the environment and seeing oneself in the environment. The horizon is at eye level relative to the furniture of the earth. But this is my eye level, and it goes up and down as I stand and sit. If I want my eye level, the horizon, to rise above all the clutter of the environment, I must climb up to a high place. The perception of *here* and the perception of *infinitely distant from here* are linked.

EXPERIMENTS ON THE PERCEPTION OF SLANT

Experiments on the direct perception of layout began in 1950. From the beginning, the crucial importance of the *density of optical texture* was evident. How could it be varied systematically in an experiment? Along with the outdoor experiments, I wanted to try indoor experiments in the laboratory. I did not then understand ambient light but only the retinal image, and this led me to experiment with texture density in a *window* or *picture*. The density could be increased upward in the display (or downward or rightward or leftward), and the virtual surface would then be expected to *slant* upward (or downward or whatever). The surface should slant *away* in the direction of increasing texture density; it should be inclined from the frontal plane at a certain angle that corresponded to the rate of change of density, the *gradient* of density. Every piece of surface in the world, I thought, had this quality of slant (Gibson, 1950a). The slant of the apparent surface behind the apparent window could be judged by putting the palm of the hand at the same inclination from the frontal plane and recording it with an adjustable "palm board." This appeared to be a neat psychophysical experiment, for it isolated a variable, the gradient of density.

The first experiment (Gibson 1950a) showed that with a uniform density over the display the phenomenal slant is zero and that with increases of density in a given direction one perceives increasing slant in that direction. But the apparent slant was not proportional to the geometrically predicted slant. It was less than it should be theoretically. The experiment has been repeated with modifications by Gibson and J. Cornsweet (1952), J. Beck and J. J. Gibson (1955), R. Bergman and J. J. Gibson (1959), and many other investigators. It is *not* a neat psychophysical experiment.

Figure 9.6
The invariant horizon ratio for terrestrial objects.
The telephone poles in this display are all cut by the horizon in the same ratio. The proportion differs for objects of different heights. The line where the horizon cuts the tree is just as high above the ground as the point of observation, that is, the height of the observer's eye. Hence everyone can see his own *eye-height* on the standing objects of the terrain.

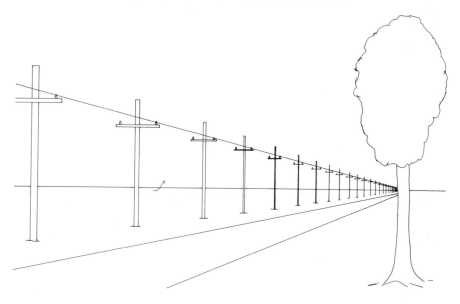

♣

Phenomenal slant does not simply correspond to the gradient. The complexities of the results are described by H. R. Flock (1964, 1965) and by R. B. Freeman (1965).

What was wrong with these experiments? In consideration of the theory of layout, we can now understand it. The kind of slant studied was *optical*, not *geographical*, as noted by Gibson and Cornsweet (1952). It was relative to the frontal plane perpendicular to the line of sight, not relative to the surface of the earth, and was thus merely a new kind of depth, a quality added to each of the flat forms in the patchwork of the visual field. I had made the mistake of thinking that the experience of the layout of the environment could be *compounded* of all the optical slants of each piece of surface. I was thinking of slant as an absolute quality, whereas it is always relative. Convexities and concavities are not made up of elementary impressions of slant but are instead unitary features of the layout.

The impression of slant cannot be isolated by displaying a texture inside a window, for the perception of the occluding edge of the window will affect it; the surface is slanted relative to the surface that has the window in it. The separation of these surfaces is underestimated, as the experimental results showed.

The supposedly absolute judgment of the slant of a surface behind a window becomes more accurate when a graded decrease of *velocity* of the texture across the display is substituted for a graded increase of *density* of the texture, as demonstrated by Flock (1964). The virtual surface "stands back" from the virtual window. It slants away in the direction of decreasing flow of the texture but is perceived to be a rigidly moving surface if the flow gradient is mathematically appropriate. But this experiment belongs not with experiments on surface layout but with those on *changing* surface layout, and these experiments will be described later.

IS THERE EVIDENCE AGAINST THE DIRECT PERCEPTION OF SURFACE LAYOUT?

There are experiments, of course, that seem to go against the theory of a direct perception of layout and to support the opposite theory of a *mediated* perception of layout. The latter theory is more familiar. It asserts that perception is mediated by assumptions, preconceptions, expectations, mental images, or any of a dozen other hypothetical mediators. The demonstrations of Adelbert Ames, once very popular, are well known for being interpreted in this way, especially the Distorted Room and the Rotating Trapezoidal Window.

These demonstrations are inspired by the *argument from equivalent configurations*. A diagram illustrating equivalent configurations is given in Figure 9.7. The argument is that many possible objects can give rise to one retinal image and that hence a retinal image cannot specify the object that gave rise to it. But the image, according to the argument, is all one has for information. The perception of an object, therefore, requires an *assumption* about which of the many possible objects that could exist gave rise to the present image (or to the visual solid angle corresponding to it). The argument is supposed to apply to each of a collection of objects in space.

A distorted room with trapezoidal surfaces can be built so as to give rise to a visual solid angle at the point of observation identical with the solid angle from a normal rectangular room. Or a trapezoidal window with trapezoids for windowpanes can be built and made to rotate so that its changing visual solid angle is identical with the changing solid angle from a rectangular window slanted 45° away from the real distorted window. The window is always one-eighth of a rotation behind itself, as it were. A single and stationary point of observation is taken for granted. An observer who looks with one eye and a stationary head misperceives the trapezoidal surfaces and has the experience of a set of rectangular surfaces, a "virtual" form or window, instead of the actual plywood construction invented by the experimenter. Anomalies of perception result that are striking and curious. The eye has been fooled.

The explanation is that, in the absence of information, the observer has presupposed (assumed, expected, or whatever) the existence of rectangular surfaces causing the solid angles at the eye. That is reasonable, but it is then concluded that presuppositions are necessary for perception in general, since a visual solid angle cannot specify its object. There will always be equivalent configurations for any solid angle or any set of solid angles at a point of observation.

Figure 9.7
Equivalent configurations within the same visual solid angle.

This perspective drawing shows a rectangle and three transparent trapezoids, all of which fit within the envelope of the same visual solid angle. Thus all four quadrangles are theoretically equivalent for a single eye at a fixed point of observation. They are, however, ghosts, not surfaces.

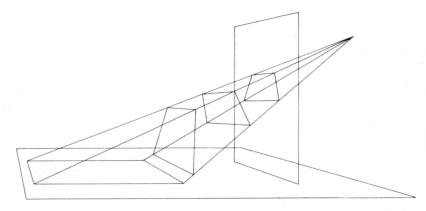

The main fallacy in this conclusion, as the reader will recognize, is the generalization from peephole observation to ordinary observation, the assumption that because the perspective structure of an optic array does not specify the surface layout nothing in the array can specify the layout. The hypothesis of invariant structure that underlies the perspective structure and emerges clearly when there is a shift in the point of observation goes unrecognized. The fact is that when an observer uses two eyes and certainly when one looks from various points of view the abnormal room and the abnormal window are perceived for what they are, and the anomalies cease.

The demonstrations do not prove, therefore, that the perception of layout cannot be direct and must be mediated by preconceptions, as Adelbert Ames and his followers wanted to believe (Ittelson, 1952). Neither do the many other demonstrations that, over the centuries, have purported to prove it.

The diagram of equivalent configurations illustrates one of the perplexities inherent to the retinal image theory of perception: if many different objects can give rise to the same stimulus, how do we ever perceive an object? The other half of the puzzle is this: if the same object can give rise to many different stimuli, how can we perceive the object? (Note that the second question implies a moving object but that neither question admits the fact of a moving observer.) Koffka was perplexed by this dual puzzle (1935, pp. 228 ff.) and many other experimenters have tried to resolve it, but without success (e.g., Beck and Gibson, 1955). The only way out, I now believe, is to abandon the dogma that a retinal stimulus exists in the form of a picture. What specifies an object are invariants that are themselves "formless."

SUMMARY

The experiment of providing either structure or no structure in the light to an eye results in the perception of a surface or no surface. The difference is not between seeing in two dimensions and seeing in three dimensions, as earlier investigators supposed.

The closer together the discontinuities in an experimentally induced optic array, the greater is the "surfaciness" of the perception. This was true, at least, for a 30° array having seven contours at one extreme and thirty-six at the other.

Optical contact of one's body with the surface of support as well as mechanical contact seem to be necessary for some terrestrial animals if they are to stand and walk normally.

Perceiving the meaning of an edge in the surface of support, either a falling-off edge or a stepping-down edge, seems to be a capability that animals develop. This is not abstract depth perception but affordance perception.

Experiments on the perception of distance along the ground instead of distance through the air suggest that such perception is based on invariants in the array instead of cues. The rule of equal amounts of texture for equal amounts of terrain is one such invariant, and the horizon ratio relation is another. On this basis, the dimensions of things on the ground are perceived directly, and the old puzzle of the constancy of perceived size at different distances does not arise.

The fact of the terrestrial horizon in the ambient array should not be confused with the vanishing point of linear perspective in pictorial optics.

A series of experiments on the perception of the slant of a surface relative to the line of sight did not confirm the absolute gradient hypothesis. The implication was that the slants of surfaces relative to one another and to the ground, the depth-shapes of the layout, are what get perceived.

Experiments based on the argument from equivalent configurations do not prove the need to have presuppositions in order to perceive the environment, since they leave out of account the fact that an observer normally moves about.

TEN

EXPERIMENTS ON THE PERCEPTION OF MOTION IN THE WORLD AND MOVEMENT OF THE SELF

Evidence for direct visual perception of the persisting layout of the environment was presented in the last chapter. Persistence, however, is only the complement of change. Is there evidence to suggest that the perception of changing layout is also direct?

THE PERCEPTION OF CHANGING SURFACE LAYOUT

Along with the traditional assumption that form perception in the frontal plane is basic and simpler to understand goes the assumption that *motion* perception in the frontal plane is also basic and simpler to understand. The fallacy of the retinal image and the cues for depth underlies the second assumption as much as the first. But the concept of retinal motion as a "scratching of the retina with pencils of light," as I put it (Gibson, 1968b), is so deep-lying that it is even harder to get rid of than the concept of retinal form. (The retina is a skin for stimuli; a point of light can *prod* the retina and a moving point of light will *scratch* the retina.) Only gradually and reluctantly did I give it up, and only when forced to do so by experiments. My present hypothesis is that the perception of events depends upon nothing less than *disturbances of structure* in the ambient array. I described and listed them in Chapter 6. Disturbances of structure can *specify* events without being *similar* to them.

APPARATUS FOR THE STUDY OF MOTION IN THE FRONTAL PLANE

In order to study a kind of perception, an experimenter must devise an apparatus that will display the information for that kind of perception. Until recently, the principal types of apparatus devised for the perception of motion were as follows.

The Stroboscope and Its Variants   The stroboscope is a device that exposes or flashes different stationary patterns in succession. Cinematography developed from this device (but not television). Since each successive "stimulus" was motionless and the retina was thus never "stimulated" by motion, the motion perceived was said to be only "apparent," not "real." But this assertion is an example of the muddled thinking to which the theory of stimuli can lead. The *stimulus information* for motion is the *change* of pattern, and the information is the same for an intermittent change as for a continuous change. The stroboscope demonstrates only that the motion of an object in the world from one place to another does not have to be copied by a corresponding motion of an image on the retina from one point to another in order for the event to be perceived. But we should never have supposed in the first place that the motion did have to be copied on the retina.

The Moving Endless Belt   A striped or textured surface behind a window in the frontal plane can be made to move continuously in a certain direction and at any chosen speed. Many experiments were carried out with this device before I realized what was wrong. The results for speed and velocity, far from being simple, were complex and puzzling. The just-noticeable speed, for example, could not be determined, although if motion on the retina were a stimulus this variable should have an absolute threshold. Eventually I came to suspect that what the eye was picking up was not the "motion" of the surface relative to the window but the progressive revealing and concealing of the elements of the surface at the occluding edges of the window (Gibson, 1968*b*).

The Rotating Disk Apparatus   If a color wheel is made to rotate slowly instead of rapidly, the motion of the surface of the disk can be seen. The disk can be displayed either behind a circular window or in front of a background. If the observer fixates the center of the disk, no eye movements occur to complicate the retinal image, which is a circle and its surroundings. But does this retinal change constitute a *motion,* as the term is understood in physics, a rotary spin measured in terms of degrees of arc per second of time? No, it does not. I finally came to understand that the wheeling of the circle in its surrounding is actually a *shearing* of the texture of the array at the contour of the circle.

A disk of this sort can also be used as a turntable for a blank circular sheet of paper on which forms are drawn. With rotation of the disk the forms undergo *orbital* motions, and sometimes very curious perceptions result.

The Disk-and-Slot Apparatus   If a spiral line is drawn on such a disk instead of a texture, a perception of expansion (or contraction) is induced when the disk is rotated slowly. And if it is screened except for a slot, the perception of a thing moving along the slot will occur. A. Michotte (1963) has used this device to study the perception of one thing *bumping* another, for example. In these cases, the optical motions in the array of light from the display are radically different from the mechanical motions of the apparatus that produced them. This radical difference has seemed very puzzling to believers in retinal image optics; it becomes intelligible only with the acceptance of ecological optics. The perception of what might be called *slot-motion* with Michotte's apparatus is particularly interesting, for it seems to depend on what happens optically at the *edges of an aperture or window*.

The Method of Shadow Projection   Beginning with the Chinese shadow plays of antiquity, moving shadows have been cast on a screen to induce the perception of moving objects or persons. The light source must be either very small or very distant to make the contour of the silhouette sharp. The opaque object, the shadow caster, is properly said to be *projected* on the screen by radiant light, that is, by rectilinear rays. (Note parenthetically that the light from the screen to the point of observation should *not* be said to be projected, strictly speaking, since it is ambient light and its array consists of visual solid angles, not rays. But I have not conformed to this strict usage.) Projection from a very small, near source is *polar* in that the rays diverge from a point. Projection from a very distant source like the sun is *parallel* inasmuch as the rays do not diverge.

With an opaque screen, the radiant light and the ambient array are on the same side of the screen and the observer can see the shadow caster. With a translucent screen, however, the light to the screen and the array from the screen can be on opposite sides, and the observer cannot see the shadow caster. The visual solid angle of the shadow surrounded by light constitutes information for perceiving an object on an empty background, that is, a virtual object seen as if against the sky.

The shadow caster, an opaque surface or object, can be mounted on a transparent sheet and caused to move by the experimenter. Or the mount can be treated so as to be opaque in some parts and transparent in others, or to vary from opaque to transparent. The latter case is essentially that of the photographic lantern slide. The projection of photographic pictures, either singly or in sequence, is in principle no more than the casting of shadows on a screen corresponding to the varying opacity of the film.

The motion of the virtual object that an observer sees behind the screen corresponds to the motion of the shadow caster, but with certain inverse relationships. Motion away from the observer corresponds to motion away from the point source of light. But the "motion" of the shadow itself on the screen (if it can be called that) is a size change, a minification.

Shadow projection is vastly more flexible and powerful than the other methods for studying the perception of motion. But how to use it for studies of event perception is only now beginning to become clear. The art and technology of the "picture show," as the man in the street calls it, have become fully and elaborately developed in modern times, but without any scientific discipline on which to base them. The production of moving displays with "animated" film, and by means of computer-controlled motions of a cathode ray beam on the screen of an oscilloscope, are both complex elaborations of this method of projection (e.g., Green, 1961; Braunstein, 1962a and b). I will return to the problem of the displaying of optical motions in the last chapter of this book.

EXPERIMENTS ON THE KINETIC DEPTH EFFECT, OR STEREOKINESIS

C. L. Musatti (1924) demonstrated many years ago that a drawing composed of circles or ellipses that looked flat when stationary would go into depth when it underwent an orbital motion on a turntable. Everybody knew that a pair of flat forms having binocular disparity would go into depth when they were looked at in a stereoscope, but the idea of flat drawing being given depth by motion was surprising. Musatti called it the stereokinetic phenomenon.

Figure 10.1
The shadow projecting apparatus set up to show minification or magnification.
In this diagram the displacement of the shadow caster produces a contraction of the shadow on the screen and thus a recession of the virtual object seen by the eye. (From J. J. Gibson, "Optical Motions and Transformations as Stimuli for Visual Perception." *Psychological Review*, 1957, 64, 288–295. Copyright 1957 by the American Psychological Association. Reprinted by permission.)

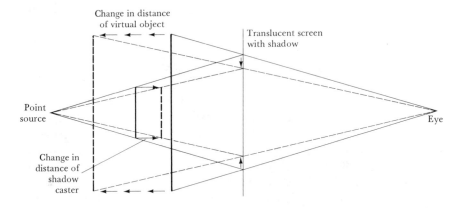

The fact seemed to be that certain motions in the frontal plane could *generate a perception* of motion in depth. The idea was that elementary motions on the retina could combine to give the experience of a real motion in space, the latter being of an entirely different sort from the former. Ten years later, W. Metzger (1934) reported what he called "appearances of depth in moving fields," and much later H. Wallach described what he called the "kinetic depth effect" (Wallach and O'Connell, 1953). No one imagined that a moving volume could be perceived directly, the motion and the volume at the same time, for they assumed that retinal sensations were the necessary basis of perception.

Wallach's kinetic depth effect is obtained when the shadow of a configuartion made of bent wire is projected on a translucent screen and observed from the other side. Without motion the lines appear flat, as if drawn on the screen. But when the wire object is turned the disposition of the wires in space becomes evident. The shift from a flat picture to a moving bent wire is very striking. Why should this occur? Wallach's formula was that the flat pattern went into depth when the lines on the screen changed in both direction and length concurrently (Wallach and O'Connell, 1953).

This formula is not very illuminating. A better one was being worked out at about that time by G. Johansson (1950), to the effect that if a set of several separate motions in the frontal plane can be *resolved* into some single motion of a rigid volume, then this rigid motion will be perceived in depth. This formula is reminiscent of one of Wertheimer's laws of the supposed organization of sensory elements in the brain, the law of "common fate," which says that a collection of spots will be grouped to form a gestalt if they *move in the same way*. But Wertheimer never said exactly what he meant by "the same way."

Johansson's experiments were carried out at first with moving spots or lines projected on a translucent screen. But he later used a set of luminous elements on the screen of a cathode ray tube, which could be programmed to move in any direction, up, down, right, and left. He used vector analysis to determine the "common motion" in the cluster of elements. If the motions were "coherent," or if the cluster were coherent under motion, the elements would be perceived as an object in depth instead of a mere frontal pattern. They would appear to be a *rigidly connected* set of elements, like a three-dimensional lattice in space or a polyhedron of solid geometry.

The hypothesis that individual sensory elements are *grouped* or made to *cohere* in the process of perception is an axiom of Gestalt theory, which assumes that sensations are the necessary basis of perception. If it were not for the process of organization, the individual sensations of motion would yield individual perceptions of object motion in the frontal plane. The theory of organization with reference to motion is adopted by Metzger (1953) as well as by Johansson (1950). But there is another theoretical possibility, namely, that an optical transformation that is *already* coherent does not have to be *made* coherent in the process of perception; it is simply picked up.

EXPERIMENTS WITH PROGRESSIVE MAGNIFICATION
OR MINIFICATION

The first results that began to suggest a direct perception of motion in depth were those of W. Schiff, J. A. Caviness, and J. J. Gibson in 1962. A point-source shadow projector is used with a large translucent screen six feet square and with the point of observation close to the screen. A small, dark silhouette at the center of the screen can be magnified over an interval of several seconds until it fills the screen. The observer sees an indefinite object coming at him and coming up to his face. He gets an experience that might justly be called *visual collision*. Without any mechanical contact, the information for *optical* contact has been provided. The observer has no sensation of touch, but he blinks his eyes and may duck or dodge involuntarily. It seemed to me that this optical change, whatever it was, should be considered a "stimulus" for the blink reflex as much as a puff of air to the cornea of the eye should be (Gibson, 1957). But it was surely not a stimulus in the ordinary meaning of the term. It was an optical expansion or magnification of an intercept angle toward its theoretical limit of 180°. This is the visual solid angle of natural perspective.

Experiments showed that the size and the distance of the virtual object were indefinite but that its approach was perfectly definite. After the shadow filled the screen, the virtual object seemed to be "here," at zero distance. It did not look like a shadow on the screen but looked like an object. The object in fact came out of the screen. This was only to be expected, for, by the laws of natural perspective, the closer an object comes to the point of observation, the closer its solid angle will come to a hemisphere of the ambient array.

There seemed to be a direct perception of an event that could be described as *approach-of-something*. This perception was not based on a sensation of expansion or enlargement. Observers reported that the object did *not* seem to get larger, as a rubber balloon does, and that they did not notice the increasing size of the shadow as such unless the magnification was quite slow. The object appeared to be rigid, not elastic.

The magnification of the visual solid angle of an object normally accelerates as it approaches the limit of a hemispheric angle, as the object comes up to the eye. The accelerated portion of this sequence was called "looming" by Schiff, Caviness, and Gibson (1962). It specifies impending collision, and the *rate* of magnification is proportional to the *imminence* of the collision. Schiff (1965) adapted the looming apparatus to test the behavior of animals. He used monkeys, kittens, chicks, frogs, and fiddler crabs. All of them showed avoidance behavior or withdrawal analogous to the ducking or dodging of the human observer. As a control, the animals were presented with minification of the shadow, the temporal reverse of magnification. The animals showed either no response or one that could be interpreted as curiosity. Presumably, what they saw was something going away in the distance but nothing that threatened collision.

When the screen was simply darkened (or lightened), the animals did not respond. And, of course, the unchanging silhouette on the screen caused no response.

The flinching of the human observer in this experiment usually extinguished after a few repetitions, but that of the animals mostly did not. However, although the human behavior changed, the human perception did not, that is, the awareness of *something approaching* did not extinguish with repetition. The perception evidently did not depend on the learning of a conditioned withdrawal response reinforced by mechanical collision.

In other experiments it was established that when the magnification of the shadow was not symmetrical but skewed, the animal (a crab) dodged appropriately to the left or right, as the path of the virtual object moved to the right or left of the animal's position (Schiff, 1965, pp. 16–18). Human observers see something approaching but approaching a position off to one side instead of the point of observation being occupied, and they can judge how far the ghostly object would pass by on the right or left. Presumably it is this sort of optical information that one uses in dodging a thrown rock, or catching a thrown ball, for that matter. There will be more about magnification in Chapter 13 on locomotion.

The fact that a fiddler crab behaved as if it perceived the same event as the vertebrate animals and the human observers was very suggestive. The crab does not have a camera eye or a retinal image, and retinal image optics cannot be applied to it. But ecological optics works very well for the compound eye, for it is constructed of tubes pointing in different directions (Gibson, 1966*b*, p. 164).

EXPERIMENTS WITH PROGRESSIVE TRANSFORMATIONS

In geometry the magnification or minification of a form is sometimes called a size transformation (or a similarity transformation). But the ordinary meaning of the term is *change* of form, and the most familiar transformation is a perspective transformation. In the theory of perspective drawing, artificial perspective, it is called *foreshortening*. It is the parameter of transformation that converts a rectangle into a trapezoid when the rectangular surface is slanted away from the frontal plane. If a progressive trans- formation was a "stimulus" for space perception, as I thought (Gibson, 1957), then it was more fundamental than the kinetic depth effect and I should carry out a proper psychophysical experiment with this slant transformation. I was still thinking of slant as a basic variable in the perception of layout, and I still had in mind all the experiments that had been done on the perceiving of a constant form with varying slant, the puzzle of form constancy. I was still assuming vaguely that the perceiving of "forms," whatever they were, was basic to other kinds of perceiving.

So my wife and I collaborated in an investigation of what people see with a systematic variation of the amount of foreshortening, using the shadow projection apparatus (Gibson and Gibson, 1957). The shadow projected on the screen was either a regular form (a square), a regular texture (a square of squares), an irregular form (ameboid shape), or an irregular texture (a potato-shaped group of small ameboid shapes). Each of these silhouettes underwent cycles of transformation, the shadow caster being turned back and forth through an angle that varied from 15° to 70°. The observer had to indicate the amount of *change of slant* he perceived, using an adjustable protractor.

All subjects without exception perceived the changing slant of an unchanging rigid surface. It was not an object, to be sure, only the face of an object, a sheet, but its shape was definite and it was not in the least elastic. It simply turned back and forth. If one paid attention to it, one could say that the shadow on the screen was squeezed or compressed, but not the sheet. There was no difference between the regular and the irregular silhouettes in this respect. The angle of the change of slant could be judged with considerable accuracy. The regular patterns, however, did not show more

Figure 10.2
The shadow projecting apparatus set up to show a slant transformation.
In this diagram the rotation of the shadow caster produces a perspective foreshortening of the shadow on the screen and thus an opposite rotation of the virtual object seen by the eye. (From J. J. Gibson and E. J. Gibson, "Continuous Perspective Transformations and the Perception of Rigid Motion," *Journal of Experimental Psychology*, 1957, 54, 129–138. Copyright 1957 by the American Psychological Association. Reprinted by permission.)

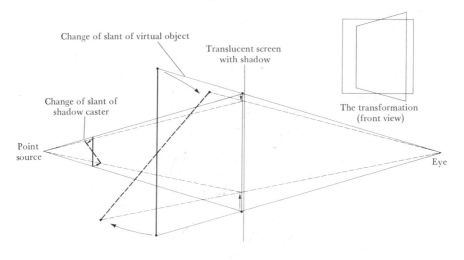

PERCEPTION OF MOTION AND MOVEMENT

accuracy than the irregular, and there was no difference between what I called the forms and the textures.

These results did not fit with the traditional concepts of form and depth perception. They were upsetting. They seemed to imply that a certain *change* of form could yield a *constant* form with a change of *slant*, but this surely involves a muddle of thought. Evidently, the meaning of the term *form* is slippery and, if so, it is nonsense to talk about form perception (Gibson, 1951). What emerged over time during the cycles of change was a distinctive object. The hypothesis that began to suggest itself was that an object is specified by *invariants under transformation*. Far from being forms, these invariants are quite "formless"; they are invariants of structure. Presumably, the four different surfaces in this experiment were specified by different invariants under foreshortening, and the different changes of slant were specified at the same time by different amounts of foreshortening.

An optical transformation, then, was not a set of discrete optical motions, nor was it a cause of depth perception. It was a single, global, lawful change in the array that specified both an unchanging object and its changing position, both at the same time.

THE PUZZLE OF PHENOMENAL RIGIDITY

It began to be clear that the heart of the problem lay in the perception of rigidity and the information to specify rigidity, not in the perception of form and depth. Could it be that certain definable transformations in the optic array were specific to rigid motions and that others specified nonrigid motions? More precisely, the hypothesis would be that certain invariants specified rigidity and that other invariants specified elasticity. This line of thinking had great promise. The elastic *bending* of a sheet or stick preserves connectivity but not proportionality. So does the *stretching* of a sheet or stick. But the *breaking* of it does not even preserve connectivity, except in the broken parts. And the *crumbling* of a surface does not even preserve the surface, which, by disintegrating, ceases to exist. The invariants in this hierarchy are linked both to the meaningful substances of the environment and to abstract mathematics.

What experiments were possible? It was not easy to think of a way to isolate and control an invariant. K. von Fieandt and J. J. Gibson (1959) did a more modest experiment. They presented observers with the transformation of compressing followed by its inverse, and then the transformation of foreshortening followed by its inverse, to see if observers would spontaneously notice the difference and perceive an elastic event in the first case and a rigid event in the second case. They defined *stretching* as change in one dimension only, width or height but not both, as exemplified by square-into-rectangle. *Foreshortening* was exemplified by square-into-trapezoid, as in the Gibson and Gibson experiment described above (1957).

The experimenters projected on the translucent screen the shadow of an irregular elastic fishnet, which was stretched on a frame mounted between the point source and the screen. One end of the frame could be made to slide inward and outward, or the whole frame could be turned back and forth. The frame was invisible, and the texture filled the screen. The motions of the elements on the screen were very similar in the two cases. But observers had no difficulty in distinguishing between the virtual surface in the two cases, elastic in the first and rigid in the second.

Johansson (1964) studied the effects of changing the height and width of a rectangle in a highly ingenious way. He generated a luminous figure on an oscilloscope screen with independent control of its height and width. He could stretch and then compress either dimension in repeated cycles. When both dimensions were increased or decreased at the same time, he got magnification and minification, which yielded clear perception of a rigid object approaching and then receding. But he was interested in elastic motion. So he made the cycles of changing height and width out of phase. But he did not then obtain perceptions of the elastic motions of a variable rectangle as one might expect. Instead, there was a strong tendency to see a virtual rectangular object with *three* parameters of rigid motion, not two, an object turning on a vertical axis, turning on a horizontal axis, and moving forward and backward, *all at the same time in different cycles.*

We do not yet know the exact basis for the perception of rigidity-elasticity, although research is progressing at both Uppsala in Sweden and at Cornell in the U.S.A. These experiments are curious and interesting and have already produced some surprising discoveries.

AN EXPERIMENT ON THE PERCEPTION OF SEPARATION IN DEPTH

What information specifies the connectedness of an object, its unbroken character? The gestalt theorists had emphasized the unity or coherence of the parts of a *form,* but it began to be evident that the unity or coherence of a *substance* was a more basic fact. How do we see the *singleness* of a detached object? A single object has a topologically closed surface; it is a substance completely surrounded by the medium or, in mathematical terms, a surface that returns upon itself. The detached object can be moved without breaking its surface. Its substance is separated from adjacent substances by air. One object becomes two only when its substance has been ruptured. How do we see this unbroken connectedness?

The first experiment to suggest that this basic fact might be specified optically was supposed to be an experiment on motion parallax and depth perception but turned out to be an experiment on the perception of separation in depth (E. J. Gibson, Gibson,

Smith, and Flock, 1959). The point-source shadow projector was set up to throw on the screen two random textures intermixed and filling the screen Actually, there were two transparent sheets of glass, each sprinkled with talcum powder. This kind of texture yields the perception of a surface but not one whose elements are geometrical forms. The phenomenal surface is coherent and continuous but without lines, contours, or definite spots. It looks like the surface of a plaster wall or a cloud.

The two shadow casters could be either motionless or moving. When they were both motionless or moving across the window at the same speed, only one virtual surface was perceived. But when there was a *difference* in speed between the two optical textures, a splitting of the surface in two, a separation in depth, resulted. The perception was of *twoness* instead of *oneness* but not of two *forms*. It was as if the formerly coherent surface had become layered. The striking fact was that although this separation was "in depth" the difference in depth was equivocal. The faster motion was

Figure 10.3
The shadow projecting apparatus set up to show intermixed shadows
that do not cohere.

This is a view from above. The two textured sheets of glass are indicated by the parallel dashed lines. They move together on the same carriage, but their separation can be increased from zero. In a unit of time, the shadow at the center of one sheet sweeps through a certain angle, and the corresponding shadow on the other sheet sweeps through a different angle, as shown. The ratio of the lesser to the greater visual angle is the inverse of the ratio of the distances of their respective sheets from the point source.

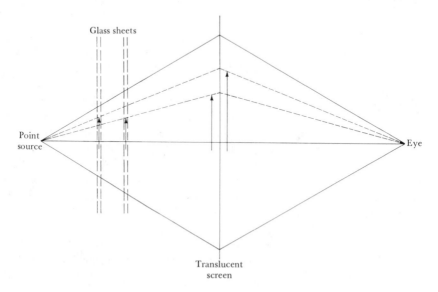

not necessarily seen in front of the other, as the law of motion parallax would predict. The surface in front had to appear semitransparent, of course, but every now and then the front-back relation between the two surfaces would spontaneously be reversed.

Wherein lay the information for this splitting? One half of the interspersed elements of texture all moved with one velocity, and the other half all moved with another velocity. Hence, there was a *permutation of the adjacent order* of the texture elements. When some caught up with and passed others, the adjacent order was destroyed. The permutation was not complete, to be sure, for each set of elements preserved adjacent order, but the original connectivity had been destroyed. Hence, the phenomenal continuity of the original surface gave way to the perception of two continuous surfaces, the nearest being transparent (E. J. Gibson, Gibson, Smith, and Flock, 1959, pp. 45 ff.). Thus, the available information in an optic array for continuity could be described as the *preservation of adjacent order*, which is to say, the absence of its permutation.

A permutation of adjacent order is a more radical change than a transformation that leaves adjacent order invariant. A size transformation and the rigid transformation of foreshortening, as well as the nonrigid transformation of stretching, leave order invariant. A still more radical change than permutation is possible, however, and this was suggested by another experiment. It is a change that *subtracts* elements of the array on one side of a contour or *adds them on*. I have called this change *progressive deletion or accretion of structure*. But this belongs in the next chapter.

EXPERIMENTS ON THE PERCEPTION OF COLLISION

In Chapter 6 the kind of mechanical event called a *collision* was described. In the simplest case, a collision may be one elastic object such as a billiard ball bumping another and causing it to move. Michotte (1963) used the disk-and-slot apparatus to study the optical and temporal conditions for this perception. He found, contrary to the assertion of David Hume, that the actual "launching" of one object by another can be seen, not just the succession of two discrete motions. In other words, one gets a direct causal perception over and above the kinetic sensations when the time intervals fall within certain limits.

Michotte was concerned with the phenomenology of the causal impression. He did not consider the hypothesis that there could be a display of optical *information* for the perception of one object launching another. His results are consistent with that hypothesis, however. S. Runeson (1977) has based a series of experiments on it. He has studied the perception of two-body linear collisions that vary from elastic to damped. In a real collision, the relative velocity difference between the motions before and after contact is invariant and specifies the nature of the substances. This is what he varied.

In his experiments, not only was the collision perceived as such, but the hardness or softness of the objects themselves were also. Yet, all the observer could ever "see" was a pair of moving patches on the screen of an oscilloscope.

Runeson had studied ecological dynamics. He had discovered an informative invariant and had controlled it in his display. We shall begin to understand event perception if we follow this lead.

THE COPERCEPTION OF ONE'S OWN MOVEMENT

So far we have been considering the perception of motion in the world. We now come to the problem of the perceiver's awareness of *his own* motion in the world, that is, the awareness of *locomotion*.

THE DISCOVERY OF VISUAL KINESTHESIS

In the 1940s, great numbers of students were being trained to fly military airplanes, and considerable numbers were failing. It seemed sensible to try and find out whether a student could see what was necessary in order to land a plane before taking him up and trying to teach him to land it without crashing. One thing he had to see was the aiming point of a landing glide, the direction in which he was going. A test was devised consisting of a series of motion picture shots with a camera dollying down toward a model runway (Gibson, 1947, Ch. 9). The testee had to say whether he was aiming at spot *A*, *B*, *C*, or *D*, all marked on the runway. This was a test of "landing judgment," and it was the beginning of an inquiry that went on for years.

It turns out that the aiming point of any locomotion is the center of the centrifugal flow of the ambient optic array. Whatever object or spot on the ground is specified at that null point is the object or spot you are approaching. This is an exact statement. But since I could not conceive of the ambient optic array in 1947, only the retinal image, I first tried to state the flow in terms of retinal motion and gradients of retinal velocity. Such a statement cannot be made exact and leads to contradictions. Not until later were the principles of the two foci of radial outflow and inflow in the whole array at a moving point of observation described precisely (Gibson, Olum, and Rosenblatt, 1955).

In the 1955 paper, the authors gave a mathematical description of "motion perspective" in the optic array, for any direction of locomotion relative to a flat earth. All optical flow vanishes at the horizon and also at the two centers that specify *going toward* and *coming from*. Motion perspective was much more than the "cue" of motion parallax. As this had been formulated by Helmholtz, it was no more than a rule for "drawing conclusions" about the distance of an object, and in any case the rule did not hold for an object on the line of locomotion. Motion perspective did not refer to "apparent" motions of objects but referred to the layout of the earth. And it "told" the observer not only about the earth but also about himself, the fact of his locomotion and the direction of it. The focus of outflow (or the center of optical expansion) is not a sensory cue but an optical invariant, a nonchange in the midst of change. The focus is formless and is the same for any kind of structure, for grass, trees, a brick wall, or the surface of a cloud.

Student pilots see where they are going on the basis of this invariant and get better with practice. Drivers of cars see where they are going, if they pay attention. Viewers of a Cinerama screen see where they are going in the represented environment. A bee that lands on a flower must see where it is going. And all of them at the same time *see the layout of the environment through which they are going.* This is a fact with extremely radical implications for psychology, for it is difficult to understand how a train of signals coming in over the optic nerve could explain it. How could signals have two meanings at once, a subjective meaning and an objective one? How could signals yield an experience of self-movement and an experience of the external world at the same time? How could visual motion sensations get converted into a stationary environment and a moving self? The doctrine of the special senses and the theory of sensory channels come into question. A perceptual system must be at work that extracts invariants. Exteroception and proprioception must be complementary.

There are various ways of putting this discovery, although old words must be used in new ways since age-old doctrines are being contradicted. I suggested that vision is *kinesthetic* in that it registers movements of the body just as much as does the muscle-joint-skin system and the inner ear system. Vision picks up both movements of the whole body relative to the ground and movement of a member of the body relative to the whole. Visual kinesthesis goes along with muscular kinesthesis. The doctrine that vision is exteroceptive, that it obtains "external" information only, is simply false. Vision obtains information about *both* the environment *and* the self. In fact, all the senses do so when they are considered as perceptual systems (Gibson, 1966b).

Vision, of course, is also *statesthetic*, if one wants to be precise about words, in that it picks up *nonmovement* of the body and its members. But since nonmovement is actually only a limiting case of movement, the term *kinesthesis* will do for both. The point is that a flowing and an arrested optic array specify respectively an observer in locomotion and an observer at rest, relative to a fixed environment. Motion and rest are in fact what an observer experiences with flow and nonflow of the array.

Optical motion perspective is not the same as visual kinesthesis. *Motion perspective* is an abstract way of describing the information in an ambient array at a moving point of observation. If the information is picked up, both visual layout perception and visual kinesthesis will occur⌈But motion perspective is analyzed for an ambient array at an unoccupied point of observation. In visual kinesthesis, on the other hand, the nose and the body are visible. There is information for coperceiving the self as well as for perceiving the layout.⌋

Another preliminary point should be made. It is most important not to confuse visual kinesthesis with visual *feedback,* a term that has currency in psychology and physiology today but is not very clear. The term is used with reference to voluntary movement in connection with the control of purposive action. If a movement is caused by a *command* in the brain, the efferent impulses in motor nerves are followed by afferent impulses in sensory nerves that are actually reafferent, that is, impulses that are *fed back* into the brain. Feedback, therefore, comes with an active movement. But not all movements are active; some are passive, as when a bird is moved in the wind or a person is moved in a vehicle. Visual kinesthesis is the same for a passive as for an active movement, but visual feedback is absent with a passive movement. The problem of the *information* for a given movement should not be confounded with the additional problem of the *control* of movement. Visual kinesthesis is important in the control of locomotion but is not the same thing. It is true that we often need to see how we have just moved in order to decide how to move next. But the first question is, how do we see how we have just moved?

The current confusion between kinesthesis and feedback helps to explain why visual kinesthesis is not recognized as a fact of psychology. But it *is* a fact, shown by the following experiments on the inducing of the experience of passive movement.

EXPERIMENTS WITH VISUAL KINESTHESIS

Until recently, most of the evidence about induced ego movement had to come from motion pictures, or simulators for training, or amusement park devices. The flow of the optic array in a glide path can be represented, more or less, in a motion picture (Gibson, 1947, pp. 230 ff.); the observer will see himself moving down toward a pseudoairfield, however much he is still aware of being seated in a room and looking at a screen. With a Cinerama screen, the virtual window may sample as much as 160° of the ambient array, instead of the mere 20° or 30° of the usual movie theater, and the illusion of locomotion may then be compelling, uncomfortably so. Training devices with a panoramic curved screen of 200° from side to side have been used; for example, one such device simulates flight in a helicopter, and the experience of rising, flying, banking, and landing is so vivid that the illusion of reality is almost complete, although the observer's body is always anchored to the floor. Attempts have also been made to simulate automobile driving.

In the best of these displays, the laws of both natural angular perspective and motion perspective have been observed. The virtual world, the layout of earth and objects, appears to be stationary and rigid. Only the observer moves. But if the projection system or the lens system that creates the display is imperfect, stretching or rubbery motions of the layout will be seen. Then the nonrigid appearance of the environment is not only disconcerting but also often leads to nausea.

The laws of motion perspective for flight over the earth with its horizon can even be set into a computer, which then generates a display on a television screen that simulates any desired maneuver. But all these experiments, if they can be called that, have been done in the interests of the aviation industry rather than those of understanding perception, and the reports are found only in the technical engineering literature.

The reader may have observed that what is called a *dolly shot* in cinematography will give the viewer the experience of being a spectator following behind or moving ahead of a character who is walking along. The arrangement of the surfaces and other persons in the scene is more vividly given than it is in a stationary shot. The dolly shot is to be distinguished from the *panning shot,* where the viewer gets the experience not of locomotion but of *turning the head* while keeping the same point of observation.

The Gliding Room Experiment   Recently, a laboratory apparatus has been constructed for the stated purpose of investigating visual kinesthesis during locomotion and separating it from the kinesthesis of the muscle-joint-skin system and the vestibular system (Lishman and Lee, 1973). The flow of the ambient array is produced by a moving enclosure, a room of sorts with walls and ceilings that can be made to glide over the real floor since it is hung by its corners from a great height barely above the floor. I am tempted to call it an *invisibly* moving room because, except for the floor, there is no information for the room's motion relative to the earth. It is a pseudoenvironment. If contact of the feet with the surface of support is obscured and if the floor is hidden, the illusion of being moved forward and backward in the room is compelling. This is accomplished by what Lishman and Lee call a trolley, in which the observer stands (cf. also Lee, 1974).

Rotations of the Body: Swinging, Tilting, Turning   Besides the linear locomotions of the body, there are the movements of rotation, which can occur on a lateral axis, a front-back axis, or a head-foot axis. The movement of a child in a swing has a component of rotation on a lateral axis, like a somersault. The movement of tilting sideways is a rotation on a front-back axis. The movement of being turned in a swivel chair or of turning the head is rotation on a head-foot axis. Pure visual kinesthesis of all these rotations can be induced with an invisibly moving room, that is, by putting the observer in an enclosure, supporting him on an inconspicuous surface attached to the earth, and then rotating the enclosure.

An amusement park device called the Haunted Swing used to be popular. A couple entered what appeared to be an ordinary room and were seated in a swing hanging from a bar running horizontally across the room. The room, not the seat, then began to swing on the shaft from which the seat was suspended. When the room eventually made a complete revolution, the occupants felt themselves go head over heels. What a sensation! It should be noted that the illusion vanished if the eyes were shut, as would be expected with visual kinesthesis. An account of the experience and the original reference are given by Gibson and Mowrer (1938).

An experimental room can be made to tilt on a front-back axis, with an observer in an upright seat. Tilting rooms of this sort have been built in laboratories, and they produced a large literature some twenty years ago (for example, Witkin, 1949). As the room invisibly rotates, both one's body and the chair seem to rotate in the room. Some part of the experienced body tilt usually remains even after the room has become stationary. This latter fact, the feeling of one's *posture* as dependent on both the visual sense and the bodily senses, was what aroused the greatest interest of experimenters. The arguments in terms of sensations were inconclusive, however. For a discussion of the "phenomenal vertical" in terms of stimuli and cues, see Gibson (1952).

Finally, an experimental room can be made to rotate on a vertical axis. This is a common apparatus in many laboratories, going under the name of an *optokinetic drum*. (See, for example, Smith and Bojar, 1938). It has usually been thought of as a device for studying the eye movements of animals instead of visual kinesthesis, but it can be adapted for the human observer. A textured enclosure, usually a vertically striped cylinder, is rotated around the animal, whose head-eye system then shows the same compensatory movements that it would if the animal were really being turned. Optically, although not inertially, it *is* being turned. Human subjects usually say that they *feel* themselves being turned. There must be a real surface of support, however, and, in my experiments, the illusion seemed to depend on not seeing it, or not paying attention to the floor under one's feet. You could anchor yourself to that, if you tried, and then you become aware of the hidden environment *outside* the room.

What is picked up in these three cases of swinging, tilting, and turning must be a relation between the ambient optic array specifying the world and the edges of the field of view specifying the self. As already suggested, the upper and lower edges of the field of view *sweep* over the ambient array in swinging; the field of view *wheels* over the array in tilting; and the lateral edges of the field *sweep across* the array in turning. These three kinds of information were described in Chapter 7.

It should be noted that, insofar as the three rotations of the body occur without locomotion through the environment, motion perspective does not arise and the ambient array does not flow. The information for the perception of layout is thus minimal.

To speak of the environment being rotated relative to the observer in these cases (instead of the body being rotated relative to the environment) would be simply nonsense. The environment, in the sense of the *persisting* environment, is that *with reference to which* objects move, animals move, and surfaces deform. There has to be an underlying nonchange if change is to be specified. The principle of the relativity of motion cannot be applied to rotation of the body.

Visual Kinesthesis of the Limbs and Hands Chapter 7, on the optical information for perceiving one's body and its movements, contained a section on the limbs and hands. Certain shapes protrude into the field of view, or else the field sweeps down to reveal them. If they squirm restlessly and are five-pronged, they specify hands. Every manipulation is specified by a corresponding change in the five-pronged silhouette. Reaching, grasping, letting go, plucking, and twisting are controlled by the ongoing optical motions that specify them, as I shall emphasize in Chapter 13.

There are no experiments, however, on this kind of visual kinesthesis. Only so-called eye-hand coordination has been recognized, as if sensations from the eye and the hand had to be associated and that were the end of it.

SUMMARY

Evidence for the direct perception of changing layout in the environment and evidence for the direct perception of the movement of the self relative to the environment have been summarized. The awareness of the world and the awareness of the self in the world seemed to be concurrent. Both event motion in the world and locomotion of the self can be given by vision, the former by a local change in the perspective structure and the latter by a global change of the perspective structure of the ambient optic array.

The visual perception of motion in general has been taken to depend on a set of discrete motions of stimuli over the retina. If this is so, an explanation is required of how they are made to cohere in the process of perception. Experiments on the "grouping" of spot motions are inspired by this requirement, as are theories of so-called kinetic depth. But if a change in the optic array is already coherent, its elements do not have to be made coherent.

Experiments with progressive magnification and experiments with progressive transformation suggested that a coherent change in the optic array could be picked up by the visual system. The first kind yielded a direct perception of an approaching object and the second kind that of a turning surface. The perception of these two events was vivid and precise. The imminence of collision and the angular degree of turning could be judged correctly.

The virtual object in these experiments did not change size or shape. It was rigid. The changing perspective shadows on the screen were not noticed.

The distinguishing of nonrigid motions such as stretching, bending, and twisting seems to be possible along with the perception of approaching and turning. The Uppsala experiments show this clearly.

The perception of the rupturing of a surface by separation in depth seems to be possible along with the perception of its displacement. This experiment suggests that the optical information for "surfaciness" is not just the proximity of the units in the array, as was implied in the last chapter, but is the nonpermutation of the adjacent order of these persisting units over time.

Experiments on visual kinesthesis are even harder to set up in the laboratory than experiments on visual event perception. One needs a panoramic motion picture screen, or a pseudoenvironment like the invisibly moving room, to produce the full illusion of passive locomotion. And there is danger of falling into epistemological confusion about the real environment. But the evidence is enough to show that the theory of motion perspective in the ambient array applies to the awareness of locomotion.

Moreover, the awareness of swinging, tilting, and turning of the observer's body can be induced if an enclosure, a pseudoenvironment, is rotated around the observer on the appropriate axis.

ELEVEN

THE DISCOVERY OF THE OCCLUDING EDGE AND ITS IMPLICATIONS FOR PERCEPTION

The facts of occlusion have been described in Chapter 5. They are part of ecological optics. But they were not recognized as facts until observations and experiments made them compelling. The experiments described in the last two chapters about surfaces, layout, change, and kinesthesis were radical enough, but they culminated in the most radical of all, in what I can only call the *discovery of the occluding edge*. This discovery is radical for the following reason. If it is true that there are places where opaque surfaces are seen one behind another, if it is true that one can perceive a *hidden* surface, a paradox arises. For we are not now allowed to say that a hidden surface is *perceived*; we can only say that it is *remembered*. To be perceived, a thing must be "present to the senses"; it must be stimulating receptors. If it is not, it can only be experienced by means of an *image*; it can be recalled, imagined, conceived, or perhaps known, but not perceived. Such is the accepted doctrine, the theory of sensation-based perception. If an occluded surface is perceived, the doctrine is upset.

KAPLAN'S EXPERIMENT

The crucial experiment, which was performed by G. A. Kaplan (1969), involved kinetic, not static, displays of information. Each display was a motion picture shot of a random texture filling the screen, with a progressive deletion (or accretion) of the optical structure on one side of a contour and preservation of the structure on the other side. Photographs of a randomly textured paper were taken frame by frame, and successive frames were modified by careful paper-cutting. No contour was ever visible on any single frame, but progressive decrements of the texture were produced on one side of the invisible line by cutting off thin slices of paper in succession. Progressive increments of the texture could be obtained by reversing the film. This particular kind of decrementing or incrementing of structure had not previously been achieved in a visual display.

In effect, a reversible disturbance of structure in a sample of the optic array had been isolated and controlled, a reversible transition. It is called a *transition, not a transformation*, since elements of structure were lost or gained and one-to-one correspondence was not preserved. What was perceived?

All observers, without exception, saw one surface *going behind* another (or *coming from* behind another) that was always concealing (or revealing) the first. Deletion always caused the perception of covering, and accretion always caused the perception of uncovering. The surface going out of sight was never seen to go out of existence, and the surface coming into sight was never seen to come into existence. In short, one surface was seen in a legitimate sense *behind* another *at an occluding edge*.

When the array was arrested by stopping the film, the edge perception ceased and a wholly continuous surface replaced it; when the optical transition was resumed, the edge perception began. The "motion" of the display as such, however, had nothing to do with the occluding edge; what counted was accretion or deletion and whether it was on one side or the other.

These results were striking. There were no uncertainties of judgment, no guessing as in the usual psychophysical experiment. What the observers saw was an edge, a *cut* edge, the edge of a *sheet,* and another surface behind it. But this depended on an array changing in time.

The surface that was being covered was seen to persist after being concealed, and the surface that was being uncovered was seen to pre-exist before being revealed. The hidden surface could not be described as remembered in one case or expected in the other. A better description would be that it was perceived retrospectively and prospectively. It is certainly reasonable to describe perception as extending into the past and the future, but note that to do so violates the accepted doctrine that perception is *confined* to the present.

The crucial paper by Kaplan (1969) was published along with a motion picture film called *The Change from Visible to Invisible: A Study of Optical Transitions* (Gibson, 1968) and an article having the same title by Gibson, Kaplan, Reynolds, and Wheeler (1969). A sharp distinction was made between *going out of sight* and *going out of existence,* and it was proposed that there is information to specify the two cases. I have described the information in Chapters 5 and 6. The former is a *reversing* transition, but the latter is not.

ANTICIPATIONS OF THE OCCLUDING EDGE

The important result of Kaplan's experiment was not the perceiving of depth at the occluding edge but the perceiving of the persistence of the occluded surface. Depth perception requires no departure from traditional theories, but persistence perception is radically inconsistent with them. Only in the experimental work of Michotte had anything like persistence perception ever been hinted at (Michotte, Thinès, and Crabbé, 1964). He discovered what he called the "tunnel phenomenon" or the "tunnel effect," the perception of a moving object during the interval between going into a tunnel and coming out of it. He ascribed it, however, not to progressive deletion and accretion of structure for going in and coming out but to a tendency for perception to be completed across a gap, in the style of gestalt theorizing. He did not realize how universal occlusion is during locomotion of the observer. But he was very much aware of the paradox of asserting that an object could be seen during an interval when there was no sensory basis for seeing it. The "screening" or "covering" of an object, he realized, was a fact of visual perception. But he could only suppose that the perception of an object must somehow persist after the sensory input ends; he did not entertain the more radical hypothesis that the persistence of the object is perceived as a fact in its own right. There is a vast difference between the persistence of a percept and the perception of persistence.

It had long been recognized that in pictures, or other displays with a frozen array, the appearance of *superposition* could be obtained. Likewise, Rubin's discovery that a closed contour or *figure* in a display involved the appearance of a *ground* that seemed to extend without interruption behind the figure was well known. But these demonstrations were concerned with the seeing of contours and lines and the perceiving of forms, not with the perceiving of the occluding edges of surfaces in a cluttered terrestrial environment. They showed that what might be called depth-by-superposition could be induced by a picture but not that an occluded surface is seen to persist.

The occluding edge seems to have escaped notice in both physics and psychology. In truth, it is not a fact of physics or a fact of psychology as these disciplines have been taught. It depends on the combined facts of a surface layout and a point of observation.

THE THEORY OF REVERSIBLE OCCLUSION

The theory of reversible occlusion was formulated in Chapter 5 in terms of what I called projected and unprojected surfaces for an ambient optic array at a given time. Reversible occlusion was said to be a consequence of the reversibility of locomotions and motions in the medium, and this was contrasted in Chapter 6 with the unreversibility of changes such as disintegration, dissolution, and the change from a solid to a liquid or a gas. These changes, I said, were not such that the waning of a surface was the temporal inverse of waxing, not such that if a film of one event were *run backward* it would represent the opposite event (Gibson and Kaushall, 1973).

Then, in Chapter 7 on the self, the principle of reversible occlusion was extended to the head turning of the observer, and the margins of the field of view were compared to the occluding edges of a window. The principle is widely applicable. It would be useful to bring together all this theorizing and to summarize it in a list of propositions.

TERMINOLOGY

The reader should be reminded again that many pairs of terms can be used to denote what I have called *occlusion*. In what follows, the words *hidden* and *unhidden* are chosen to have a general meaning (although they have the unwanted flavor of buried treasure!). *Unprojected* and *projected*, the terms used in Chapter 5, are all right except for the implication of throwing an image on a screen, which gives precisely the wrong emphasis. *Covered* and *uncovered* are possible terms, or *screened* and *unscreened*, and these were employed by Michotte. Other possibilities are *concealed* and *revealed*, or *undisclosed* and *disclosed*. All these terms refer to various kinds of occlusion. The most general terms are *out of sight* and *in sight*, which contrast with *out of existence* and *in existence*. It should be kept in mind that all these terms refer to reversible transitions, that is, to *becoming* hidden or unhidden, to *going* out of sight or *coming* into sight. Terms that should *not* be employed are *disappear* and *appear*. Although in common use, these words are ambiguous and promote sloppy thinking about the psychology of perception. The same is true of the words *visible* and *invisible*.

There seem to be a number of different ways of going out of sight, some not by occlusion and some by occlusion. The latter always involves an occluding edge with progressive deletion on one side of a contour, but the former does not. I can think of three kinds of going out of sight *not* by occlusion: first, going into the distance by minification of the solid angle to a so-called vanishing point in the sky or on the horizon; second, going out of sight in "the dark" by reduction of illumination; and third, going out of sight by closure or covering of the eyes. Perhaps going out of sight in fog or mist is another kind, but it is similar to loss of structure by darkness (Chapter 4). I can also think of three kinds of occlusion other than self-occlusion (Chapter 5): first, at the edge of an opaque covering surface; second, at the edge of the field of view of an observer; and third, for celestial bodies, at the horizon of the earth. As for the going out of *existence* of a surface, there seem to be many kinds of destruction, so many that only a list of examples could be given in Chapter 6 on ecological events.

LOCOMOTION IN A CLUTTERED ENVIRONMENT

The following seven statements about reversible occlusion are taken from Chapters 1 to 5.

1. The substances of the environment differ in the degree to which they persist, some resisting dissolution, disintegration, or vaporization more than others.

2. The surfaces of the environment, similarly, differ in the degree to which they persist, some being transitory and others being relatively permanent. A surface goes out of existence when its substance dissolves, disintegrates, or evaporates.

3. Given an illuminated medium, a surface is unhidden at a fixed point of observation if it has a visual solid angle in the ambient optic array at that point. If it does not (but has at another point of observation), it is hidden.

4. For any fixed point of observation, the persisting layout of the environment is divided into hidden and unhidden surfaces. Conversely, for every persisting surface, the possible points of observation are divided into those at which it is hidden and those at which it is not.

5. A surface that has no visual solid angle at any point of observation is neither hidden nor unhidden. It is out of existence, not out of sight.

6. Any movement of a point of observation that hides previously unhidden surfaces has an opposite movement that reveals them. Thus, the hidden and the unhidden interchange. This is the _law of reversible occlusion_ for locomotion in a cluttered habitat. It implies that after a sufficient sequence of reversible locomotions *all* surfaces will have been both hidden and unhidden.

7. The loci of occlusion are those places at which the hidden and unhidden surfaces into which a layout is temporarily divided are separated at occluding edges, there being two sorts, apical and curved. They are also the places where the hidden and unhidden surfaces are *joined* at occluding edges. Thus, to perceive an occluding edge of an object, even a fixed occluding edge at a fixed point of observation, is to perceive both the separation and the junction of its far and near surfaces.

THE MOTIONS OF DETACHED OBJECTS

Three more statements about reversible occlusion follow; they are taken from Chapter 5.

8. For any opaque object, the near surface, the temporary "front," hides the far surface, the temporary "back," at a fixed point of observation. The two interchange, however, when the object is rotated. The near surface also hides the *background* of the object, if present, but when the object is displaced the parts that go behind at one edge come from behind at the other. These facts can be observed in the film entitled *The Change from Visible to Invisible: A Study of Optical Transitions* (Gibson, 1968).

9. For both solidity and superposition, any motion of an object that conceals a surface has a reverse motion that reveals it.

THE OCCLUDING EDGE AND ITS IMPLICATIONS

10. To the extent that the objects of the environment have moved or been moved, the near and far sides of every object will have interchanged many times. This holds true over and above the extent to which the observer has moved around.

HEAD TURNING

Following is the theorem about reversible occlusion when the observer looks around by turning her head. It is now assumed that the point of observation is occupied (Chapter 7).

11. For any fixed posture of the head, surfaces of the surrounding layout are divided into those inside the boundaries of the field of view and those outside the boundaries of the field. But with every turn of the head surfaces come into sight at the leading edge of the field of view and go out of sight at the trailing edge. The observer who looks around can thus see undivided surroundings and see herself in the middle of them.

NONPERSISTING SURFACES

The next theorem is about the unreversing destruction and creation of surfaces and the unreversing optical transitions that accompany them (Chapter 6).

12. The going out of existence of a surface is not the reverse of its coming into existence, nor is the disturbance of optical structure that specifies one the reverse of the disturbance of structure that specifies the other. Hence, the disappearance of a surface by, say, dissolution can be distinguished from its disappearance by occlusion if the observer has learned to see the difference between the optical transitions. Such evidence as there is suggests that the two kinds of disappearance are usually distinguished (Gibson, Kaplan, Reynolds, and Wheeler, 1969). This is not to say that infants notice the difference, or even that adults always notice the difference. The difference may sometimes be hard to notice, as when a conjurer is playing tricks with one's perception. It is only to say that anyone can learn to see the difference.

The occlusion of a surface can be nullified, whereas the destruction of a surface cannot. Occlusion can be canceled by a movement of the body, head, or limbs in the opposite direction. Destruction, although it can sometimes be remedied, cannot simply be canceled by an opposite movement. It seems to me that young children must notice the optical transitions that can be thus nullified and those that cannot. How could they fail to pay attention to them? They play peek-a-boo, turn their heads, and watch their hands, all cases of reversible occlusion, and they also spill the milk, break the glass, and knock down the tower of blocks, things that cannot be reversed. But this hypothesis has not been tested with babies, because the only experiments carried out are in the spirit of rationalism promoted by J. Piaget, which asserts that children must form a concept of persistence or permanence and emphasizes what the children believe instead of what they see (for example, Bower, 1974, Ch. 7).

WHAT IS SEEN AT THIS MOMENT FROM THIS POSITION DOES NOT COMPRISE WHAT IS SEEN

The old approach to perception took the central problem to be how one could see into the distance and never asked how one could see into the past and the future. These were not problems for perception. The past was remembered, and the future was imagined. Perception was of the present. But this theory has never worked. No one could decide how long the present lasted, or what distinguished memory from imagination, or when percepts began to be stored, or which got stored, or any other question to which this doctrine led. The new approach to perception, admitting the coperception of the self to equal status with the perception of the environment, suggests that the latter is timeless and that present-past-future distinctions are relevant only to the awareness of the self.

The environment seen-at-this-moment does not constitute the environment that is seen. Neither does the environment seen-from-this-point constitute the environment that is seen. The seen-now and the seen-from-here specify the self, not the environment. Consider them separately.

What is seen now is a very restricted sample of the surfaces of the world, limited to those that are inside the boundaries of the field of view at this head-posture. It is even limited to that surface being fixated at this eye-posture, if by *seen* one means *clearly seen*. This is at most less than half of the world and perhaps only a detail of that.

What is seen from here is at most the optically uncovered surfaces of the world at this point of observation, that is, the near sides of objects, the unhidden portions of the ground, the walls, and the bits that project through windows and doors.

The fact is that, although one can become aware of the seen-now and the seen-from-here if one takes the attitude of introspection, what one perceives is an environment that surrounds one, that is everywhere equally clear, that is in-the-round or solid, and that is all-of-a-piece. This is the experience of what I once called the visual world (Gibson, 1950*b*, Ch. 3). It has vistas that are connected and places that adjoin, with a continuous ground beneath everything, below the clutter, receding into the distance, out to the horizon.

The surface being fixated now at this momentary eye-posture is not a depthless patch of color, and the surfaces inside the field of view seen now at this head-posture are not a depthless patchwork of colors, for they have the quality that I called *slant* in the last chapter. The seen-at-this-moment is not the same, therefore, as the supposedly flat visual *field* analogous to the colors laid on a canvas by a painter that the old theory of color sensations asserted. I once believed that you could with training come to see the world as a picture, or almost do so, but I now have doubts about it. That comes close to saying that you can almost see your retinal image, which is a ridiculous assertion.

The seen-from-here, from this stationary point of observation, is also not the supposedly flat visual field of tradition, for it is ambient. But it might justly be called *viewing the world in perspective*, or *noticing the perspectives of things*. This means the

Figure 11.1
The surfaces viewed now from here by an observer seated in a room.
At this temporary eye posture and this temporary head posture, the surfaces projected into the retinal image are indicated by solid lines and the remaining surfaces by dashed lines. The awareness of the here-and-now surfaces might be called *viewing* the room as distinguished from *seeing* the room. This is a vertical section of the observer and his monocular field of view.

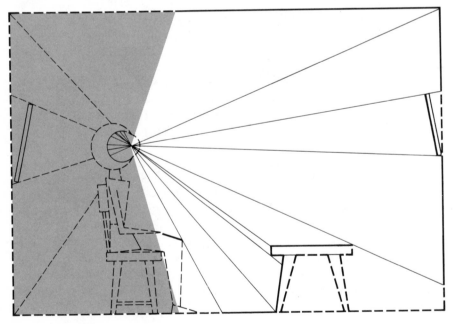

natural perspective of ancient optics, not the artificial perspective of the Renaissance; it refers to the set of surfaces that create visual solid angles in a frozen ambient optic array. This is a very small sample of the whole world, however, and what we perceive is the world.

PERCEPTION OVER TIME FROM PATHS
OF OBSERVATION

It is obvious that a motionless observer can see the world from a single fixed point of observation and can thus notice the perspectives of things. It is not so obvious but it is true that an observer who is moving about sees the world at *no* point of observation and thus, strictly speaking, *cannot* notice the perspectives of things. The implications are radical. Seeing the world at a traveling point of observation, over a long enough time for a sufficiently extended set of paths, begins to be perceiving the world at *all* points of observation, as if one could be everywhere at once. To be everywhere at once with nothing hidden is to be all-seeing, like God. Each object is seen from all sides, and each place is seen as connected to its neighbor. The world is *not* viewed in perspective. The underlying invariant structure has emerged from the changing perspective structure, as I put it in Chapter 5.

Animals and people do in fact see the environment during locomotion, not just in the pauses between movements. They probably see better when moving than when stationary. The arrested image is only necessary for a photographic camera. An observer who is getting around in the course of daily life sees from what I will call a *path* of observation. A path does not have to be treated as an infinite set of adjacent points at an infinite set of successive instants; it can be thought of as a unitary movement, an excursion, a trip, or a voyage. A path of observation is the normal case, short paths for short periods of observation and long paths for hours, days, and years of observation. The medium can be thought of as composed not so much of points as of paths.

It sounds very strange to say that one can perceive an object or a whole habitat at no fixed point of observation, for it contradicts the picture theory of perception and the retinal image doctrine on which it is based. But it has to be true *if it is acknowledged that one can perceive the environment during locomotion.* The perception of the environment is understood to accompany the visual proprioception of the locomotion, of course, and the hypothesis of invariant structure underlying the changing perspective structure is required for this to be intelligible. These are unfamiliar notions. But the notion of ambulatory vision is not more difficult, surely, than the notion of successive snapshots of the flowing optic array taken by the eye and shown in the dark projection room of the skull.

THE PROBLEM OF ORIENTATION

Animals and humans are capable of being oriented to the habitat. This state is the opposite of being *disoriented* or "lost." The rat who can find its way directly to the goal box of a maze is said to be oriented to the goal. If there are many paths to the goal, the animal is capable of taking the shortest path. A person, similarly, can learn the way to work, to the post office, to the grocery store, and back home again through the passageways of his town. When he can do so in an unfamiliar town, he has become oriented in the new habitat. Both animals and humans are capable of homing. More generally, they are capable of way-finding. Or, in still other terms, they can do place-learning. Observers can go to the places in their environment that have affordances for them. If they are human observers, moreover, they may be able to *point* to these places, that is, to indicate their direction from here through the walls or other surfaces that hide them.

Two current explanations of how animals learn to find their way to hidden places are the theory of response chains and the theory of cognitive maps. Neither is adequate. Way-finding is surely not a sequence of turning responses conditioned to stimuli. But neither is it the consulting of an internal map of the maze, for who is the internal perceiver to look at the map? The theory of reversible occlusion can provide a better explanation.

An alley in a maze, a room in a house, a street in a town, and a valley in a countryside each constitutes a place, and a place often constitutes a *vista* (Gibson, 1966*b*, p. 206), a semienclosure, a set of unhidden surfaces. A vista is what is seen from here, with the proviso that "here" is not a point but an extended region. Vistas are serially connected since at the end of an alley the next alley opens up; at the edge of the doorway the next room opens up; at the corner of the street the next street opens up; at the brow of the hill the next valley opens up. To go from one place to another involves the opening up of the vista ahead and closing in of the vista behind. A maze or a cluttered environment provides a choice of vistas. And thus, to find the way to a hidden place, one needs to see which vista has to be opened up next, or which occluding edge hides the goal. One vista leads to another in a continuous set of reversible transitions. Note that in a terrestrial environment of semienclosed places each vista is unique, unlike the featureless passageways of a maze. Each vista is thus its own "landmark" inasmuch as the habitat never duplicates itself.

When the vistas have been put in order by exploratory locomotion, the invariant structure of the house, the town, or the whole habitat will be apprehended. The hidden and the unhidden become one environment. One can then perceive the ground below the clutter out to the horizon, and at the same time perceive the clutter. One is oriented to the environment. It is not so much having a bird's-eye view of the terrain as it is being everywhere at once. The getting of a bird's-eye view is helpful in becoming oriented, and the explorer will look down from a high place if possible. Homing pigeons are better at orientation than we are. But orientation to goals behind the walls, beyond the trees, and over the hill is not just a looking-down-on, and it is certainly not the having of a map, not even a "cognitive" map supposed to exist in the mind instead of on paper. A map is a useful artifact when the hiker is lost, but it is a mistake to confuse the artifact with the psychological state the artifact promotes.

Note that the perception of places and the perception of detached objects are quite different. Places cannot be displaced, whereas objects can be, and animate objects displace themselves. Places merge into adjacent places, whereas objects have boundaries. Orientation to hidden places with their attached objects can be learned once and for all, whereas orientation to movable objects has to be relearned continually. I know

Figure 11.2
The opening up of a vista at an occluding edge, as seen from above.

This is a plan view of a passageway that opens on a courtyard from which another passageway leads. As an observer moves along the corridor, the surfaces behind his head progressively go out of sight, and surfaces in front progessively come into sight at one occluding edge and then the other. The hidden portions of the ground are indicated by hatching. The hidden portions of the walls are indicated by dashed lines. The position of the observer is indicated by a black dot.

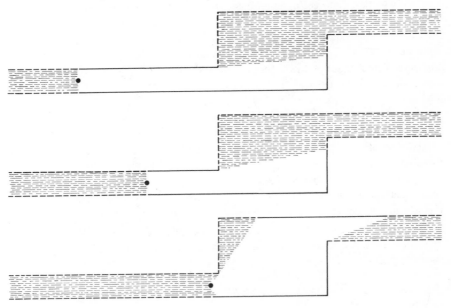

where the kitchen sink is, I think I know where the ski boots are stored, but I don't always know where my child is. One can only go to the last known locus of a detached object. Hidden objects can be moved without that event being perceived, and the unhappy state of the man whose car keys are seldom where he left them is notorious.

In the pages above I have formulated a theory of orientation to the places of the habitat. The perceiving of the world entails the coperceiving of where one is in the world and of being in the world at that place. This is a neglected fact that is neither subjective nor objective. To the extent that one has moved from place to place, from vista to vista, one can stand still in one place and see where one is, which means where one is relative to where one might be. One does not need a map with a circle on it labeled, "You are here." I suggest that this constitutes the state of being oriented.

THE PROBLEM OF PUBLIC KNOWLEDGE

The hypothesis of reversible optical transformations and occlusions resolves the puzzle of how, although the perspective appearances of the world are different for different observers, they nevertheless perceive the same world. Perspective appearances are not the necessary basis of perception.

It is true that there is a different optic array for each point of observation and that different observers must occupy different points at any one time. But observers move, and the same path may be traveled by any observer. If a set of observers move around, the same invariants under optical transformations and occlusions will be available to all. To the extent that the invariants are detected, all observers will perceive the same world. Each will also be aware that his or her place in the world is different here and now from that of any other.

Points, of course, are geometrical concepts, whereas places are ecological layouts, but the above theory can also be put geometrically: although at a given instant some points of observation are occupied and the remainder unoccupied, the one set can go into the other.

The theory asserts that an observer can perceive the persisting layout from other places than the one occupied at rest. This means that the layout can be perceived from the position of another observer. The common assertion, then, that "I can put myself in your position" has meaning in ecological optics and is not a mere figure of speech. To adopt the point of view of another person is not an advanced achievement of conceptual thought. It means, *I can perceive surfaces hidden at my point of view but unhidden at yours.* This means, *I can perceive a surface that is behind another.* And if so, *we can both perceive the same world.*

THE PUZZLE OF EGOCENTRIC AWARENESS

Psychologists often talk about egocentric perception. An egocentric perceiver is supposed to be one who can see the world only from his own point of view, and this habit is sometimes thought to characterize an egocentric *person*. Egoism is thought to come naturally to humans because they are innately aware of their private experiences and do not easily learn to adopt the point of view of others. This line of thinking now seems mistaken. Perception and proprioception are not alternatives or opposing tendencies of experience but complementary experiences.

The sensation-based theories of perception assume that the perspective appearances of the world are all that a newborn infant is given. They are the data for perception. Hence, the young child is necessarily egocentric, and cognitive development is a matter of progressing from subjective sensations to objective perceptions. The child's ego encompasses the world, and at the same time she is supposed to be confined to the awareness of her fleeting sensations. But there is a reason to be suspicious of all these speculations. The evidence about the earliest visual experiences of infants does not suggest that they are confined to surfaces seen-now-from-here, and the evidence definitely contradicts the doctrine that what they see is a flat patchwork of color sensations. I therefore suspect that the supposed egocentricity of the young child is a myth.

HIDING, PEEKING, AND PRIVACY

In Chapter 8 on affordances, I described how some of the places of an environment are *hiding* places. That is, they afford the hiding of oneself or of one's property from the sight of other observers. The phenomenon of seeing without being seen illustrates the application of optical occlusion to social psychology. The passage on hiding places in Chapter 8 should be reread.

The perceiving of occluded places and objects does occur and can be shared with other perceivers. To this extent, we all perceive the same world. But there is also ignorance of occluded things, and if you hide from me your private property, your hideaway in the hills, your secret lover, or the birthmark on your buttocks, then you and I do not perceive quite the same world. Public knowledge is possible, but so is its reciprocal, private knowledge.

Not only do babies like to play peek-a-boo and children to play hide-and-seek, but animals who are preyed upon hide from the predator, and the predator may hide from the prey in ambush. One observer often wants to spy upon others, to see without being seen. He peers through a peephole or peeks around the occluding edge of a corner. In opposition to this is the striving *not* to be seen by others, the need for privacy. Burrows, caves, huts, and houses afford not only shelter from wind, cold, and rain but also the state of being out of sight, or out of the "public eye."

The human habit of covering the body with clothing whenever one is in sight of others is a matter of hiding some skin surfaces but not others, depending on the conventions of the culture. To display the usually covered surfaces is improper or immodest. The providing of some information for the layout of these hidden surfaces, however, is the aim of skillful clothing designers. And the careful manipulation of the occluding edges of clothing with progressive revealing of skin is a form of the theatrical art called stripping.

SUMMARY

The demonstration that reversible occlusion is a fact of visual perception has far-reaching implications. It implies that an occluding edge is seen as such, that the persistence of a hidden surface is seen, and that the connection of the hidden with the unhidden is perceived. This awareness of what-is-behind, and of the togetherness of the far side and the near side of any object, puts many of the problems of psychology in a new light.

The doctrine that all awareness is memory except that of the present moment of time must be abandoned. So must the theory of depth perception. The importance of the fixed point of view in vision is reduced. But a new theory of orientation, of way-finding, and of place-learning in the environment becomes possible. And the puzzles of public knowledge, of egocentricity, and of privacy begin to be intelligible.

TWELVE

LOOKING WITH THE HEAD AND EYES

We modern, civilized, indoors adults are so accustomed to looking at a page or a picture, or through a window, that we often lose the feeling of being *surrounded* by the environment, our sense of the *ambient* array of light. Even when outdoors under the sky, one is apt to be driving an automobile and looking only through the windshield, or traveling in a vehicle where the window to the outside world is constricted to a small angle. We do not look *around*.

We live boxed-up lives. Our ancestors were always looking around. They surveyed the environment, for they needed to know where they were and what there was in all directions. Children pay attention to their surroundings when allowed to do so. Animals must do so. But we adults spend most of our time *looking at* instead of *looking around*. In order to look around, of course, one must turn one's head.

LOOKING AROUND AND LOOKING AT

The reason why humans must turn their heads in order to look around is that their eyes are set in the front of their heads instead of on either side, as they are in horses or rabbits. The orbits in the human skull are frontal, not lateral. The horse can see most of its surroundings (but not all) without having to turn its head; it can *see* around fairly well without having to *look* around. Thus, an enemy can sneak up on a person from behind, sometimes, but the hunter cannot sneak up on a rabbit. It has been suggested that animals who are preyed upon need a more panoramic field of view, whereas predatory animals such as cats can afford to have eyes in the front of the head (Walls, 1942). It has also been argued that the frontal eyes of primates living in the trees afford better "depth perception," but this argument presupposes the entrenched fallacy of depth perception that this book has been at such pains to destroy. Even if depth were perceived, it would be another error to assume that the only kind of depth perception is "binocular," that is, the kind that rests on binocular disparity.

With lateral eyes, the blind region behind the animal is minimal, but the overlap of the fields of view ahead of the animal is sacrificed. With frontal eyes, the overlap of the fields of view ahead is maximal, but the scope of the field of view is sacrificed and the blind region is large. Complete simultaneous ambience of perception is impossible. There has to be some gap in the combined field of view simply because the body of the animal itself is there, that is, its body is bound to hide some of the surfaces of the surrounding environment. Simultaneous ambience of perception is unnecessary in any case if the animal can always turn its head. There is no need to perceive everything at once if everything can be perceived in succession.

The gap in the combined field of view of the eyes is that portion of the ambient optic array filled by the head and body of the observer himself. It is a visual solid angle with a closed envelope, *a closed boundary in the array that specifies the body*. It has a meaning, and it carries information. I have already made this point at some length in Chapter 7 on the self. The portion of the environmental layout that is hidden by the body is continually interchanging with the unhidden remainder as the head turns and the body moves.

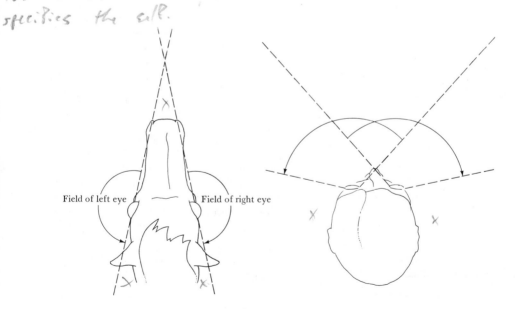

Figure 12.1

The lateral eyes of a horse and the frontal eyes of a man and the respective fields of view approximately.

Field of left eye   Field of right eye

The difference between the way a horse perceives its environment and the way a human does is therefore not so profound as you might assume. The blind region caused by the head and body of the horse is a small part of the ambient array, whereas the blind region caused by the head of a human is a large part, in fact, a visual solid angle of about 180°, approximating a hemisphere of the array. But it is not actually a blind region, of course; it is the head. A small turn of the head enables the horse to see what is behind, and a large turn of the head enables a person to see what is behind, but in both cases the observer sees himself in the middle of an environment. Are you doubtful that a horse can see itself? Why shouldn't the horse see itself just as much as the human does, if vision yields proprioception as well as exteroception? The horse's blind area is differently shaped than the human's—the boundaries of its field of view are different—but the blind area means the same thing to the horse as it does to the human. Egoreception and exteroception are inseparable kinds of experience. The seeing of oneself is not a complex intellectual experience but a simple primitive one. The orthodox dogma that no animal but the human animal has *self-consciousness* is surely false.

WITH WHAT DOES ONE SEE THE WORLD?

We human observers take it for granted that one sees the environment with one's eyes. The eyes are the organs of vision just as the ears are the organs of hearing, the nose is the organ of smelling, the mouth is the organ of tasting, and the skin is the organ of touching. The eye is considered to be an instrument of the mind, or an organ of the brain. But the truth is that each eye is positioned in a head that is in turn positioned on a trunk that is positioned on legs that maintain the posture of the trunk, head, and eyes relative to the surface of support. Vision is a whole perceptual system, not a channel of sense (Gibson, 1966*b*). One sees the environment not with the eyes but with the eyes-in-the-head-on-the-body-resting-on-the-ground. Vision does not have a *seat* in the body in the way that the mind has been thought to be seated in the brain. The perceptual capacities of the organism do not lie in discrete anatomical parts of the body but lie in systems with nested functions.

Even so, it might be argued, one surely *looks* with the eyes even if one does not *see* with the eyes. But looking with the eyes alone is mere looking *at*, not looking *around*. It is the scanning of an object, a page of print, or a picture. One also looks with the head, not just with the eyes, more exactly with the head-eye system, as I said at the outset.

The exclusive concern with eye turning to the neglect of head turning is one of the deep errors of the snapshot theory of vision and goes back at least a century.

Helmholtz asserted in *Physiological Optics* that "the intent of vision is to see as distinctly as possible various objects or parts of an object in succession. This is accomplished by so pointing the eyes that an image of the given object is projected on the fovea of each retina. The governing of the ocular movements is wholly subordinated to this end; both eyes are adjusted and accommodated together so as to permit this light absorptive pointing. Any . . . eye movement not having for its end the attaining of distinct imaging of an object cannot be performed" (Helmholtz, trans. 1925, p. 56). He assumed that objects and parts of objects are what we perceive and that these are limited to objects in the fixed field of view. He would be astonished at the assertion that a man perceives his surroundings, including the environment behind his head, for that is not "the intent of vision."

THE AWARENESS OF THE ENVIRONMENT
AND THE EGO

Despite what Helmholtz said, some psychologists have insisted that a man *is* aware of the environment behind his head. Koffka was one who did so. Phenomenal space, he said, extends to the sides; yonder is the wall of the room and there are walls to the right and left, but phenomenal space also extends *behind*. You would be vividly aware of the space behind if the edge of a cliff were there. "Behavioral space does not confront me but encloses me." What is it that lies between the "in front" and the "behind"? It is, he says, "just that phenomenal object we call the Ego." It is a segregated object, like others in phenomenal space (Koffka, 1935, p. 322). It is only a step from this description to the theory that the head and body of the observer *hide* the surfaces of the world that are outside the occluding edges of the field of view. Koffka made no reference to head turning and failed to recognize the interchange of the hidden and the unhidden, and that is an important step, but he did recognize a fact of perception.

When I distinguished, years ago, between the visual field as one kind of experience and the visual world as a radically different kind (Gibson, 1950*b*, Ch. 3), I was elaborating on Koffka. The visual field, I suggested, consists of a patchwork of colors something like a picture, whereas the visual world consists of familiar surfaces and objects one behind another. The *visual field* has boundaries, roughly oval in shape, and it extends about 180° from side to side and about 140° up and down. The boundaries are not sharp, but they are easily observed when attended to. The *visual world*, however, has no such boundaries; it is unbounded, like the surface of a sphere extending all the way around me. The visual field is clear in the center and vague in the periphery—that is, less definite toward the boundaries—but the visual world has no such center of definition and is everywhere clear. The oval boundaries of the visual field sweep across the array whenever I turn my head and wheel over the array whenever I tilt my head, but the visual world is perfectly stationary and always upright. The patchwork of the visual field deforms as I move and, in particular, flows outward from a center when I move in the direction of that center, but the phenomenal surfaces of the world are always perfectly rigid.

The visual field is a special kind of experience that can arise from a sample of the ambient array taken with the head and eyes fixed. In its purest form, the visual field arises with a single fixed eye. The visual world is the kind of experience that arises naturally from the whole ambient array when one is looking around and looking with two eyes at two slightly different points of observation. The field of view of the two eyes is a sort of mixed cross-section of the overlapping solid angles registered by the eyes. The field of one eye would correspond to a plane picture cutting the solid angle for that eye. It would correspond in the sense that a faithful picture could be substituted for the angular sample so as to yield almost the same phenomenal experience. But the visual world is a kind of experience that *does not correspond to anything*, not any possible picture, not any motion picture, and not even any "panoramic" motion picture. The visual world is not a *projection* of the ecological world. How could it be? The visual world is the outcome of the picking up of invariant information in an ambient optic array by an exploring visual system, and the awareness of the observer's own body in the world is a part of the experience.

The awareness of "out there" and of "here" are complementary. The occluding boundary of the field of view constitutes "here." The content and details of the field of view are "out there," and the smaller the detail the farther away it is.

THE VISUAL EGO

Ecological optics distinguishes between an unoccupied point of observation in the medium and an occupied point (Chapter 7). The former is a position where an observer *might* be situated and the latter is a position where an observer *is* situated. The ambient optic array is then altered, for it includes a solid angle filled by the observer, having a boundary that is unique to the observer's particular anatomy. It is called the *blind*

TERMINOLOGICAL NOTE

I should never have entitled my 1950 book *The Perception of the Visual World*, for it has promoted confusion. A better title would have been *The Visual Perception of the World*. The term *visual world* should be reserved for the awareness of the environment obtained by vision.

region in physiological optics. But it is blind only for exteroception, not for proprioception. It *looks like oneself.* Its shape depends on the shape of one's nose, the shape of one's head, and the shape of one's limbs. It is altered when a person puts on eyeglasses or when a horse is made to wear blinders. Thus, whenever a point of observation is occupied, the occupier is uniquely specified, whether adult or child, monkey or dog.

An observer perceives the position of *here* relative to the environment and also his body as *being* here. His limbs protrude into the field of view, and even his nose is a sort of protuberance into the field. Undoubtedly, the length of a man's nose determines how he sees himself. (Consider the ego of a baboon in this respect, and think what the ego of an elephant would be!) For us, the nose is the leftward edge of the right eye's field of view and the rightward edge of the left eye's field of view. Hence, it yields a kind of subjective sensation called a *double image* in the theory of binocular vision, in fact, the maximum limit of *crossed diplopia.* It would therefore be a theoretical zero for the dimension of distance from here.

Since the occupied point of observation is normally a moving position, not a stationary one, the animal sees its body moving relative to the ground. It sees that part of the enviironment toward which it is moving; it sees the movements of its feet, relative to its body and also over the ground. When it looks around during locomotion, it sees the turning of its head. These are all cases of visual kinesthesis.

THE PERSISTING ENVIRONMENT: PERSISTENCE, COEXISTENCE, AND CONCURRENCE

To say that one is aware of the environment behind one's head is to say that one is aware of the *persistence* of the environment. Things go out of sight and come into sight as the head turns in looking around, but they persist while out of sight. Whatever

---

THE INFORMATION FOR PERSISTENCE

The perceiving of the persistence of the environment is not, of course, an achievement of the visual system alone. It is a nonmodal form of perception, cutting across the perceptual systems and transcending the "senses." Touching and listening accompany looking. The young child who goes for a walk and looks around at the strange wide world can cling to the mother's hand, confirming her persistence while she is temporarily out of sight. Similarly, the persistence of the mother when she goes around the corner, or goes out of sight in the dark, is confirmed by hearing her voice. The information to specify the continued existence of something may be carried by touch or sound as well as by light. Incessant stimulation is not necessary for the perceiving of persistence.

leaves the field as one turns to the right re-enters the field as one turns to the left. The structure that is deleted is later accreted; this is a reversible transition, and therefore the structure can be said to be *invariant* under the transition. To pick up the invariant is to perceive the persistence of a surface, so my argument runs. If this is true, there is no need to appeal to a concept of "object permanence" or to any theory of how the concept might develop.

To perceive the persistence of surfaces that are out of sight is also to perceive their coexistence with those that are in sight. In short, the hidden is continuous with the unhidden; they are *connected.*

Separated places and objects are perceived to coexist. This means that separated *events* at these places are perceived to be concurrent. What happens at one end of a corridor is seen to co-occur with what happens at the other end, even though one must look back and forth between the two. Different concurrent events, thus, can be sampled in succession without destroying their concurrence, just as different coexisting places can be sampled in succession without destroying their coexistence.

implications for memory?

HOW DOES THE EYE-HEAD SYSTEM WORK?
OUTLINE OF A NEW THEORY

Looking-around and looking-at are acts that naturally go together, but they can be studied separately. In fact, looking-at has been studied almost exclusively by visual physiologists. What they have recorded and measured are so-called eye movements, that is, movements of the eyes *relative to the head.* The head is usually fixed in an apparatus. The eyes are then allowed to scan a display of some sort within the field of view of the stationary head, a pattern of luminous points in the dark, or a line of print on a page, or a picture. The eyes rotate in rapid jumps from one fixation to another, and these are called *saccadic movements.* In terms of the retinal image theory, the fovea of each retina is moved so that an image of the particular "object of interest" falls on the retinal point of highest acuity where the photoreceptors, the cones, are most densely packed together. The anatomical fovea corresponds to the psychological "center of clearest vision." The fine details of the optical image are said to be best "resolved" at the fovea. All this is implied in the quotation from Helmholtz, above.

THE RECOGNIZED TYPES OF EYE MOVEMENT

There are other kinds of ocular movements besides scanning, however, and the accepted classification goes back to R. Dodge (1903), who was the first investigator to record and measure them by photography. They have since been studied with ever-increasing ingenuity and precision, but Dodge's list has never been challenged by physiologists. He never doubted the eye-camera analogy; he only forced us to consider that the eyes were *movable* cameras at the ends of flexible cables leading to the brain. The list is approximately as given below.

1.   *Fixation*: Not strictly a "movement," fixation is nevertheless an important kind of ocular behavior. It should be called a *posture* of the eye, a *pointing at*.

2.   *Saccadic movement*: A saccadic movement is a rapid rotation of the eyeball from one fixation to another. It has long been taken for granted that the movement is a response of the eye muscles to a stimulus at the periphery of the retina such as to bring that stimulus to the center of the retina, the fovea. But I shall challenge this assumption.

3.   *Pursuit movement*: This kind of movement is said to be fixation of the eye on a moving object in the world, often nowadays called *tracking*. It is much slower than a saccadic movement.

4.   *Convergence and divergence*: Convergence is the inward rotation of each eye so as to permit both eyes to fixate on the same near object. Divergence is the opposite, a return of the ocular axes to parallel so as to permit both eyes to fixate on the same distant object. In retinal image optics, it is assumed that these movements occur so that the two similar but more or less disparate images of the object can be "fused" in the brain to yield a single phenomenal object with depth. They are said to be governed by what is called a *fusion reflex*, but this is not consistent with the notion of a reflex as a response to a stimulus. Note that in both saccadic and pursuit movements the two eyes fixate together and rotate together as if they were linked. They are said to be *conjugated*. But they rotate in opposite directions during the vergence movements. All three types of movement, however, can be said to work in the interest of fixation.

5.   *Compensatory movement*: This movement is quite different from the others. Like them, it is a rotation of each eye in the head but in precisely the opposite direction from that of the head, and to exactly the same degree. It *compensates* for the turning of the head. Thus, it is a *nonmotion* of the eyes relative to the *environment*, a posture, like fixation. Anyone can note how exact this compensation normally is by looking at one eye in his mirror image and then moving his head around, left and right, up and down; the eye never swerves from its fixed orientation in space. It is as if anchored to the environment. When the head starts, the eye starts; when the head stops, the eye stops.

If the head turns through an angle too great for compensation, the eye jumps rapidly to a new orientation and holds it. Thus, a man on a mountaintop who turns around completely, taking several seconds for the act, keeps his eyes anchored to the dual ambient array for the whole period except for a small part of the time, totaling only a fraction of a second, during which the jumps have occurred. This is what happens in "looking around," and the result is a vivid perception of the whole environment. This is the natural exploratory activity of the visual system.

What experimenters do, however, is to put the subject in a rotating chair and turn him passively. In this unnatural situation a reflex response of the eyes is aroused to the stimulus of acceleration in the semicircular canals of the inner ear. It is called *nystagmus*. The compensatory turning of the eyes then has a certain latency; it does not begin with the turning of the head as does the compensatory turning of the eyes with an *active* head movement. The latter is not a reflex to a stimulus but a coordination. The head turning and the eye turning are concurrent movements of a single act. The active turning of the head *involves* the opposite turning of the eyes in much the same way that the contracting of the extensor muscles of a limb involves the relaxing of the flexor muscles. The neck muscles and the eye muscles are innervated at the same time, reciprocally. But the passive movement of the eyes in response to a passive movement of the head has received by far the most attention from experimenters. Physiologists are preoccupied with reflexes to stimuli, probably because they assume that reflexes are basic for behavior.

Experiments on ocular nystagmus with passive rotation often bring about a kind of disorientation of the eyes to the environment called *vertigo*. After stopping such rotation, the eyes will compensate for a nonexistent turning of the head. The experimenter has overstrained the capacity of the system. The observer reports that the world seems to be going around and usually that he feels as if his body were also being rotated. These two experiences are inconsistent. He usually just says that he is dizzy. He is at any rate disoriented to the environment: he cannot point to things, he will stagger, and somtimes fall down. I have described the limitations of the vestibular apparatus in my chapter on the basic orienting system (Gibson, 1966*b*, Ch. 4.). The study of dizziness, however interesting and important for neurology, tells us nothing about the normal working of the eye-head system. I would explain it by saying that the normal complementarity of exteroception and proprioception has broken down.

A RECONSIDERATION OF EYE MOVEMENTS

Ecological optics as distinguished from eyeball optics calls for a re-examination of the traditional eye movements. We must consider how the visual system works, not just how the eyes move. Eyeball optics is appropriate for visual physiology and the prescribing of eyeglasses but not for the psychology of visual perception.

Fixation The prolonged fixing of the eyes on an "object or part of an object," the bringing of its image to the fovea and keeping it there, does not occur in life. It is a laboratory artifice, brought about when an experimenter tells an observer to stare at a "fixation point" that is usually of no interest to her. No one stares at a fixed point in the world for long unless she is so preoccupied that she is actually not seeing what she looks at. Seeming exceptions arise in the aiming of a rifle or the threading of a needle, but these are actually cases where different objects are *aligned*, not where a single object is fixated. The eyes normally search, explore, or scan, and there are seldom fewer than several saccadic jumps per second. They *look at* but do not *fixate*.

Even when fixation is artificially prolonged in the laboratory, it turns out not to be pure fixation, a steady posture. The eye is never literally fixed. It undergoes a series of miniature movements or microsaccades. The recording of such eye movements has become very precise in recent years, and the evidence now suggests that looking at a tiny thing consists of making tiny movements. If so, looking is always exploring, even so-called fixating. On the smallest scale, the eyes could never be perfectly steady, for the eye muscles that control their posture undergo tremor and the eyes tremble in the same way that the hand does when you hold it out. There does not seem to be any clear separation between large saccades, small saccades, microsaccades, and tremor. Perhaps the general conclusion should be that *an eye-posture is nothing but movements that are very small.*

This conclusion is consistent with my conception of the ambient optic array. It consists of adjacent visual solid angles that are *nested*, each solid angle having its base in a feature or face or facet of the environmental layout, the features being *themselves* nested in superordinate and subordinate units. The eyes can explore the large details of large solid angles. And the eye-head system can explore the hemispheric solid angles of the sky and the earth or of the mountains to the east and the valley to the west. We perceive a large mural painting with sweeps of the eyes. We perceive a page of print with small saccades. And one puts a thread into the eye of a needle with the tiniest saccades of all.

Saccadic Movement   The jump of the eyeball from one fixation to another, it seems, can vary from an angle of many degrees to one of a few minutes of arc or less. So, just as there is no pure fixation, there is also no pure movement. There are postures of the eyes that are relatively stable and movements of the eyes from one such posture to another, but they grade into each other. Moving and fixating are complementary. They combine in the act of scanning.

It is certainly a fallacy to assume that a saccadic movement is a response to a "stimulus" on the periphery of the retina that brings it to the fovea. There are no stimuli in an optic array. That assumption comes from experiments in which a point of light is flashed on in utter darkness; the eyes then turn so as to foveate it, but this experimental situation does not apply to everyday vision. Visual physiologists, however, presuppose an array of stimuli and assume that a localizing movement, a "fixation reflex," tends to occur for each retinal point when it is stimulated.

It is also a fallacy, if a little more plausible, to assume that a series of fixations is a series of acts of selective attention to the different *objects* in the world. Each fixation would then be a centering of foveal attention on one object to the exclusion of other objects. Each saccade must then be a *movement* of attention from one object to another. But the truth is that attention is not only selective, it is also integrative. Attention can be distributed as well as being concentrated. The awareness of details is not inconsistent with the awareness of wholes. Each in fact implies the other. One can perfectly well pay attention to some aspect of the environment that extends over a large angle of the ambient array, such as the gradient of the ground that goes all the way from one's feet out to the horizon. Hence, a whole series of fixations can be a single act of attention.

Pursuit Movement   Not just a fixation of the eyes on a moving object in the world, pursuit movement is also, and usually, an adjustment of the ocular system to the flowing ambient array during locomotion of the observer. The centrifugal outflow of the optic array from the direction in which one is traveling must be attended to in order to see where one is going, and in order to control one's locomotion. The eyes are pointed at one element of the flowing array so that all the other elements of the flow pattern that fall into lawful relationships to it can be picked up. This is what happens when you drive your car down the road: your eyes fix on a piece of the layout and track it downward, then jump ahead to a new piece. These drifts and jumps are somewhat similar to the compensatory nystagmus with head turning, but the drifts during locomotion are not the same as the drifts during compensation.

Convergence and Divergence   Retinal image optics assumes that if one object in space has an image in each of the two eyes the two images have to be fused into one picture in the brain. It further assumes that convergence or divergence of the eyes somehow works in the interests of this fusion process. If the physiological images were not combined or unified, we should see two objects instead of one. Ecological optics makes no such assumptions, rejecting the very idea of a physiological image transmitted to the brain. It supposes that two eyes have no more difficulty in perceiving one object than two hands do in feeling one object, or than two ears do in perceiving one event. The dual ocular system registers both the *matching* of structure between the optic arrays at the different points of observation of the two eyes and the perspective *mismatch* of their structure, both the congruence and the disparity, at the same time. The two eyes are not two channels of sensation but a single system. The converging and diverging of the eyes presumably work in the interests of picking up the congruity/disparity information.

Note that two arrays could not possibly be fused in the sense of being united in one location. Neither could two optical images be mixed or combined. They do not need to be. The fallacy of the traditional theory comes from supposing that two *physiological* images have to be fused in the brain, as if one picture were picked up and superposed on the other and then compared, in the manner of a photographer who puts one transparent film on top of another and looks to see if they match. The error is to assume that a unitary mental image can only arise from a unitary brain image, a process in the brain that occurs in one locus.

The human binocular system extracts the similarities of structure between two arrays, I suggest, just as each eye extracts the invariants of structure in its own array. Varying convergence of the binocular system is a kind of exploration, like the varying fixation of each monocular system. The dual array is available for exploration just as much as the single array is. The difference in perspective structure between two arrays is the same as the *change* in perspective structure of one array when one eye moves sideways through the interocular distance. This disparity is neither identity at one extreme nor discrepancy at the other. If the structures were completely identical, nothing would be specified but a hypothetical and ecologically impossible surface called a *horopter*. If the structures were completely discrepant, another kind of impossibility would be specified, and this discrepancy can actually be imposed on the binocular system with a device called a *haploscope*. For example, the array to one eye may consist of vertical stripes and the array to the other of horizontal stripes. In this case the binocular system fails, and the use of one eye is suppressed. The system becomes monocular. Typically, the suppression shifts from one eye to the other, and the result is called *binocular rivalry*. You see horizontal stripes or vertical stripes, or horizontal in one part of the field and vertical in the other, but never horizontal stripes and vertical stripes in the same place at the same time.

This kind of contradiction is very interesting. It is not logical contradiction of the

---

On Binocular Disparity

The idea of disparity between two arrays is quite new. It is not the same as the old idea of disparity between two retinal images defined by noncorresponding points on two retinas considered as receptive mosaics. Array disparity rests on ecological optics instead of on physiological optics.

The application of the new optics to binocular disparity has been worked out by Barrand (1978). Although anticipated by the gestalt theorists in the assumption that binocular disparity was "relational," it is a departure from the classical theory of stereopsis. It can handle the neglected fact of occluding edges in stereopsis, for example, which the classical theory cannot.

sort that philosophers have studied since Aristotle. It might be called *ecological con-tradiction*. It is a discrepancy of information. There will be more about this in Chapter 14 on depiction.

Compensatory Movement   When we consider the ambient optic array at the point of observation occupied by an eye instead of the retinal image of an object formed in the eye by light rays, we begin to understand the purpose of the compensatory eye-head coordination. Its purpose is to keep the eye oriented to the unchanging features of the environment for as much of the time as possible while the observer looks around and gets about. It prevents both eyes from wandering or drifting aimlessly. They are linked to the layout of the surfaces. Only if they are stable relative to the world can they look at the world. The eyes do tend to drift or wander when the ambient light is homogeneous, as it is in the presence of an unstructured total field like the blue sky or a dense fog or in ambient darkness. The compensation is automatic, but it is not a reflex response to a stimulus. If the eyes were not anchored, the phenomenal world would "swing" instead of being the fixed frame of reference it is. Indeed, the experience of

Figure 12.2
The turning of the eyes in the head to compensate for the turning of
the head in the world.

As the head turns to the right, the eyes turn to the left through the same angle. In this diagram the eyes are converged. (From *The Perception of the Visual World* by James Jerome Gibson and used with the agreement of the reprint publisher, Greenwood Press, Inc.)

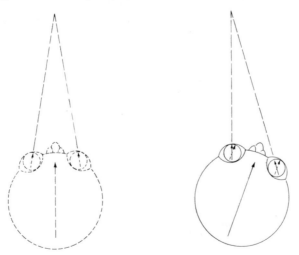

vertigo does arise whenever the coordinate compensation breaks down after the stopping of prolonged passive rotation in a swivel chair.

The so-called *swinging of the scene* can be artificially induced in another way when the structure of the field of view of the eye is distorted or reversed by a prism or lens attached to the head by a spectacle frame. The field of view no longer sweeps over the ambient array in the normal manner when the head turns. Thus, the compensatory eye movements no longer serve their purpose, for the sampling of the array by head turning has been disturbed. The eyes are no longer anchored to the environment. The results of experiments on perception when distorting spectacles are worn can only be understood in the light of this fact (Kohler, 1964).

OTHER ADJUSTMENTS OF THE VISUAL SYSTEM

The movements and postures of the eye-head system have now been described. But vision is a highly tuned and elaborate mode of perception, and several other kinds of adjustment occur in the activity of looking. The eyes blink, the tear glands secrete, the pupils enlarge or contract, the lens accommodates, and the retina adjusts for either daytime or nighttime illumination. All these adjustments subserve the pickup of information.

Eye-blinking   The eyelids close and reopen at intervals during waking hours to keep the transparent surface of the cornea washed clean and prevent it from drying out. The retina is of course deprived of stimulation during these brief moments of eye-closing, but the interesting fact is that no sensation of darkening is noticed, although even the briefest dimming of the illumination when the electric light falters is noticed. The explanation, perhaps, is simply that this particular kind of flicker is propriospecific. A dimming obtained with an eye-blink is experienced as an eye-blink; a dimming imposed by the illumination is experienced as coming from the world.

The ordinary eye-blink is not a triggered reflex. It may sometimes be stimulated by a puff of air or a cinder on the cornea, but it usually operates to prevent stimulation, not to respond to it. Like the closing of the eyes during sleep, it is an adjustment.

The eyelids work in cooperation with the tear glands. The reason for keeping the surface of the cornea clear is (by analogy with a windshield wiper) that dirt or foreign particles reduce its transparency. The structure of the optic array when the air is clear can be extremely fine, and these very small solid angles specify both the small-scale structure of the near environment and the large-scale structure of the far environment. A dirty cornea still admits light to the eye but degrades the information in the array of light.

The Accommodation of the Lens   The combined cornea and lens of the eye constitute a lens system that is said to focus an image of an object on the retina, in accordance with the classical theory formulated by Johannes Kepler. To each radiating point on the near surface of the object there corresponds, ideally, one focus point in the retinal image. The function of the lens is to make it a true point instead of a "blur circle," whatever the distance of the object. The lens accommodates for distance and minimizes the blur (Chapter 4).

The theory of ambient light and its structure is not consistent with this, or at least I do not now understand how it could be made consistent. The notion of nested solid angles based on a nested layout of surfaces, the solid angles being ever changing and never frozen, is of a different order from the notion of radiation from the atoms of a surface and the bringing to a focus of a pencil of these rays from each point of the surface. I do not understand how the former notion could be reduced to the latter, for they are in different realms of discourse.

The focusing of the lens of a photographic camera for a given distance or range of distances is not as similar to the accommodating of the lens of an eye as we have been taught. There is just enough similarity to make optometry and the prescribing of eyeglasses a useful technology. But the eye's lens works as part of the exploratory mechanism of the visual system, along with fixation and convergence, and nothing in the photographic camera is comparable to this. Photographic film does not scan, or look at, or pick up disparity. We are so accustomed to think of deficiencies in accommodation in terms of an acuity chart that we tend to forget this fact. Distinct vision with a fixated eye is not the only test for good visual perception, but that is all the optometrist tries to measure.

The function of the retina is to register *invariants of structure*, not the *points of an image*. The point-to-point correspondence of the theory of image formation does not apply. Ecological optics will have to explain the action of the ocular lens in a different way than does classical geometrical optics. The explanation is not simple.

The Adjustment of the Pupil   In Chapter 4, I distinguished carefully between stimulus energy and stimulus information, between ambient light and the ambient array. Light as energy is necessary if the photochemicals in the photoreceptors of the retina are to react, but light as a structural array is necessary if the visual system is to pick up information about the world. Although a clear distinction should be made, it must not be forgotten that stimulus information is *carried* by stimulus energy. There is no information in utter darkness. And, at the other extreme, perception fails in blazing illumination. The photoreceptors are then swamped by the intense light, and the information cannot be extracted by the perceptual system. We describe the accompanying sensation as *dazzle*, and it is propriospecific. The contracting of the pupil of the eye is an adjustment that reduces the tendency of the photoreceptors to be over-whelmed by excessive stimulation.

Physiological optics, concerned with receptors and stimulus energy, is adequate to explain the pupillary adjustment. Ecological optics, concerned with perceptual organs and the information in light, is not required. The different levels of optics correspond to different levels of activity in the visual system. It should nevertheless be noted that the contraction of the pupil in strong illumination and its enlargement in weak illumination work in the interests of information pickup. And the continuous adjustment of pupil size to light intensity is not a series of responses to stimuli but an optimizing process.

The Dark Adaptation of the Retina One kind of adjustment of the retina to the level of illumination involves no movement at all. This is a shift between the functioning of one set of photoreceptors and another set containining different photochemicals and with a different level of sensitivity. We have what is called a *duplex retina*, and the duplicity theory of the retina is one of the triumphs of the study of vision at the cellular level. The cones provide for daylight vision and the rods for night vision. The shift of function from cones to rods and the reverse is supplementary to the adjustment of the pupil, which by itself is insufficient for the million-to-one intensity difference between daylight and nightlight.

I have described the advantages of a night retina, a day retina, and a duplex retina in the chapter on the evolution of the visual system in *The Senses Considered as Perceptual Systems* (Gibson, 1966b, Ch. 9). Animals of our sort are able to perceive well enough in either a brightly or a dimly lighted environment and thus do not have to make a choice between a diurnal and a nocturnal way of life.

CONCLUSION: THE FUNCTIONS OF
THE VISUAL SYSTEM

The anatomical parts of the visual system are, approximately, the body, the head, the eyes, the appurtenances of an eye (eyelid, pupil, and lens), and finally the retina of an eye, which is composed of photocells and nerve cells. The body includes all the other parts, and the cell includes none of the others. All these components are connected with the nervous system, and all are active. All are necessary for visual perception. Both the parts and their activities form a hierarchy of organs. At the top is the body, then the head, and then the eyes. Being equipped with muscles, the parts can move, each in its own way—the eyes relative to the head, the head relative to the body, and the body relative to the environment. Hence, all move relative to the environment, and I suggested that their purpose is perceptual exploration. At the level of the single eye, the eylid wipes, the lens accommodates, and the pupil adjusts. Muscles are also required for these activities, but they are not bodily movements in the sense used above. At the bottom level, the retina and its cells adapt to external conditions but the activity of the retina does not depend on muscles. At all levels the activities are *adjustments* of the system instead of reflex reactions to stimuli, or "motor" responses, or responses of any kind, for that matter.

The body explores the surrounding environment by locomotion; the head explores the ambient array by turning; and the eyes explore the two samples of the array, the fields of view, by eye movements. These might be called *exploratory adjustments*. At the lower levels, eyelid, lens, pupil, and retinal cells make what might be called *optimizing adjustments*. Both the global structure and the fine structure of an array constitute information. The observer needs to look around, to look at, to focus sharply, and to neglect the amount of light. Perception needs to be both comprehensive and clear. The visual system *hunts* for comprehension and clarity. It does not rest until the invariants are extracted. Exploring and optimizing seem to be the functions of the system.

THE FALLACY OF THE STIMULUS SEQUENCE THEORY

The traditional assumption has been that we perceive the world by means of a sequence of stimuli. When we look at the scene in front of us, we see it in a succession of *glimpses* analogous to snapshots, each glimpse corresponding to a pure fixation. Similarly, when we look around at the whole environment, we perceive it as a sequence of *visual fields* analogous to pictures, each field corresponding to a posture of the head.

The Lorgnette Tachistoscope

I once devised a sort of test of what perception would be like if it really consisted of a sequence of snapshots. I mounted the shutter of a camera on a handle so that it could be held close to one eye and triggered with a finger, giving a wide-angle glimpse of the environment for a fifth of a second or less. The other eye was covered. The subject was led up to a table on which was a collection of familiar objects and told to keep looking until he knew what was there. Because he couldn't scan the table with his eye, he had to scan with his head and trigger the shutter for each new fixation.

Perception was seriously disturbed, and the task was extremely difficult. What took only a few seconds with normal looking required many fixations with the lorgnette tachistoscope, and there were many errors. I now begin to understand why.

Both the glimpses and the pictures of the world have been vaguely identified with retinal images. But this assumption that we perceive in a sequence of pictures, either glimpses or fields, is quite false.

A visual fixation is not at all comparable to a snapshot, that is, a momentary exposure. The eye has no shutter. The eye scans over the field. The fovea is transposed over the sample of the array, and the structure of the array remains invariant. Not even a visual field at a head-posture is comparable to a picture in a sequence of pictures (although I used to think it was). The field sweeps over the ambient array with progressive gain and loss at its leading and trailing edges, and the ambient structure remains invariant. No succession of discrete images occurs, either in scanning or in looking around.

The transposition of the fovea over the sample of the array and the sweeping of the edges of the field of view over the ambient array are propriospecific; they specify eye turning and head turning respectively, which is precisely what they should do. The former is visual kinesthesis for an eye movement, and the latter is visual kinesthesis for a head movement.

The formula of visual kinesthesis for the exploratory movements of the eyes, and of the head and eyes together, resolves a number of long-standing puzzles concerning visual sensations. It cuts a Gordian knot. The century-old problem of why the world does not seem to move when the eyes move and the analogous problem of why the room does not appear to go around when one looks around are unnecessary. They only arise from the assumption that visual stimuli and visual sensations are the elements of visual perception. If the visual system is assumed instead to detect its own movements along with extracting the information about the world from the ambient light, the puzzles disappear. I shall have more to say about this later.

The false problems stem from the false analogy between photography and visual perception that everyone has taken for granted. A photograph is an arrested moment of a changing array. The film has to be exposed, and the so-called latent image must be developed, fixed, and printed before it becomes a picture. But there is nothing even faintly comparable to a latent image in the retina. It is misleading enough to compare the eye with a camera, but it is even worse to compare the retina with a photographic film.

The stimulus-sequence theory of perception underlies much of modern thought, not only the thinking of philosophers, psychologists, and physiologists but that of the man in the street. It is reinforced by comic strips and cartoons and news photographs, and the movies above all. As children we do learn much about the world at second hand from picture sequences, so much that we are strongly tempted to interpret firsthand experience in the same way. Everybody knows what pictures are, and textbooks tell us that retinal images are pictures. I said so myself in my book on the visual world, and the only problem that bothered me was how a *sequence* of images could be converted into a *scene* (Gibson, 1950*b*, Ch. 8, pp. 158 ff.). I did realize that something was wrong with this assertion, but it took me years to detect the fallacy.

THE THEORY OF THE CONVERSION OF
A SEQUENCE INTO A SCENE

It sounds plausible to assert that a sequence of images is converted into a scene. "At the circus, for example, you may watch the tightrope walker, then look at the performing seals, pause to observe a clown, and return to the tightrope walker. Although you have had a succession of impressions the events are perceived as coexisting" (Gibson, 1950*b*, p. 158). You are aware of three concurrent events in three different places, all going on at the same time, but you are not aware of the successive order in which they have been fixated. An adjacent order of places, a whole scene, must have been obtained from a successive order of sensory inputs, a sequence, by some sort of *conversion*. The sequence of smaller fixations with which you observe the tightrope walker in his smaller situation is noticed even less. You look back and forth between his feet and his hands, say, but what you see is the whole act.

The hypothesis of *conversion* is consistent with the traditional theory that successive inputs of a sensory nerve are *processed*, that a series of signals is *interpreted*, or that the incoming data of sense are *operated on* by the mind. Sensations are converted into perceptions, and the question is, how does this come about? In the case of successive retinal images, the process is supposed to be that of memory. It may be called short-term or primary memory, or immediate memory as distinguished from long-term memory, but the basic assumption is that each image has to be held over, or stored in some sense, in order for the sequence to be integrated, that is, combined into a unit. The present percept is nothing without past percepts, but past percepts cannot combine with the present except as memories. Every item of experience has to be carried forward into the present in order to make possible perception in the present. Memories have to *accumulate*. This is the traditional theory of memory made explicit. It is full of difficulties, but it has seemed to provide the only explanation of how images could be integrated.

The error was to suppose in the first place that perception of the environment is based on a sequence of discrete images. If it is based instead on invariance in a flow of stimulation, the problem of integration does not arise. There is no need to unify or combine different pictures if the scene is *in* the sequence, is specified by the invariant structure that underlies the samples of the ambient array.

The problem of explaining the experience of what I once called the unbounded visual world (Gibson, 1950*b*, Ch. 8) or what I would now call the surrounding environment is a false problem. The retinal image is bounded, to be sure, and the foveal image has even smaller bounds, but the ambient array is unbounded. If the stimulation of the retina, or that of the fovea, is accepted as basic, another problem arises as well, how to explain the experience of a *stable* visual world. The stimulation of the retina is continually shifting, but this is also a false problem, for the structure of the ambient array is quite stable.

SUMMARY

One sees the environment not just with the eyes but with the eyes in the head on the shoulders of a body that gets about. We look at details with the eyes, but we also look around with the mobile head, and we go-and-look with the mobile body.

A theory of how the eye-head system works has been formulated in this chapter. A theory of how the system works during locomotion was formulated in the last chapter. The exploratory adjustments of the eye-head system (fixation, saccadic movements, pursuit movements, convergence-divergence, and compensatory movements) are easier to understand. Even the optimizing adjustments of the lens, the pupil, and the photoreceptors are more intelligible when we consider optical information instead of stimuli.

The flow of optical stimulation is not a sequence of stimuli or a series of discrete snapshots. If it were, the sequence would have to be converted into a scene. The flow is sampled by the visual system. And the persistence of the environment together with the coexistence of its parts and the concurrence of its events are all perceived together.

THIRTEEN

LOCOMOTION AND MANIPULATION

The theory of affordances implies that to see things is to see how to get about among them and what to do or not do with them. If this is true, visual perception serves behavior, and behavior is controlled by perception. The observer who does not move but only stands and looks is not behaving at the moment, it is true, but he cannot help seeing the affordances for behavior in whatever he looks at.

Moving from place to place is supposed to be "physical" whereas perceiving is supposed to be "mental," but this dichotomy is misleading. Locomotion is guided by visual perception. Not only does it depend on perception but perception depends on locomotion inasmuch as a moving point of observation is necessary for any adequate acquaintance with the environment. So we must perceive in order to move, but we must also move in order to perceive.

Manipulation is another kind of behavior that depends on perception and also facilitates perception. Let us consider in this chapter how vision enters into these two kinds of behavior.

THE EVOLUTION OF LOCOMOTION AND MANIPULATION

SUPPORT

Animals, no less than other bodies, are pulled downward by the force of gravity. They fall unless supported. In water the animal is supported by the medium, which has about the same density as its body. But in air the animal must have a substantial surface below if it is not to become a Newtonian falling body.

Locomotion has evolved from swimming in the sea to crawling and walking on land to clinging and climbing on the protuberances that clutter up the land and, finally, to flying through the air, the most rapid kind of locomotion but the most risky. Fish are supported by the medium, terrestrial animals by a substantial surface on the underside, and birds (when they are not at rest) by airflow, the aerodynamic force called *lift*. Zoologists sometimes classify animals as aquatic, terrestrial, or aerial, having in mind the different ways of getting about in water, on land, or in the air.

VISUAL PERCEPTION OF SUPPORT

A terrestrial animal must have a surface that pushes up on its feet, or its underside. The experiments reported in Chapter 4 with the glass floor apparatus suggest that many terrestrial animals cannot maintain normal posture unless they can see their feet on the ground. With optical information to specify their feet *off* the ground, they act as if they were falling freely, crouching and showing signs of fear. But when a textured surface is brought up under the glass floor, the animals stand and walk normally (E. J. Gibson, 1969, pp. 267–270).

This result implies that contact of the feet with the surface of support as against separation of the feet from the surface is specified optically, at the occluding edges of the feet. The animal who moves its head or uses two eyes can perceive either *no* separation in depth between its feet and the floor or the kind of separation it would see if it were suspended in air. Contact is specified both optically and mechanically.

Note that a rigid surface of earth can be distinguished from a nonrigid surface of water by its color, texture, and the absence or presence of ripples. A surface of water does not afford support for chicks, but it does for ducklings. The latter take to the water immediately after hatching; the former do not.

MANIPULATION

Manipulation presumably evolved in primates, along with bipedal locomotion and the upright posture, by the conversion of the forelimbs from legs into arms and of the forepaws into what we call hands. Walking on two legs, it is sometimes said, leaves the hands free for other acts. The hands are specified by "five-pronged squirming protrusions" into the field of view from below (Chapter 7). They belong to the self, but they are constantly touching the objects of the outer world by reaching and grasping. The shapes and sizes of objects, in fact, are perceived in *relation* to the hands, as graspable or not graspable, in terms of their affordances for manipulation. Infant primates learn to see objects and their hands in conjunction. The perception is constrained by manipulation, and the manipulation is constrained by perception.

THE CONTROL OF LOCOMOTION
AND MANIPULATION

Locomotion and manipulation, like the movements of the eyes described in the last chapter, are kinds of behavior that cannot be reduced to responses. The persistent effort to do so by physiologists and psychologists has come to a dead end. But the ancient Cartesian doctrine still hangs on, that animals are reflex mahines and that humans are the same except for a soul that rules the body by switching impulses at the center of the brain. The doctrine will not do. Locomotion and manipulation are not triggered by stimuli from outside the body, nor are they initiated by commands from inside the brain. Even the classification of incoming impulses in nerves as *sensory* and outgoing impulses as *motor* is based on the old doctrine of mental sensations and physical movements. Neurophysiologists, most of them, are still under the influence of dualism, however much they deny philosophizing. They still assume that the brain is the seat of the mind. To say, in modern parlance, that it is a computer with a program, either inherited or acquired, that plans a voluntary action and then commands the muscles to move is only a little better than Descartes's theory, for to say this is still to remain confined within the doctrine of responses.

Locomotion and manipulation are neither triggered nor commanded but *controlled*. They are constrained, guided, or steered, and only in this sense are they ruled or governed. And they are controlled not by the brain but by information, that is, by seeing oneself in the world. Control lies in the animal-environment system. Control is by the animal *in* its world, the animal itself having subsystems for perceiving the environment and concurrently for getting about in it and manipulating it. The rules that govern behavior are not like laws enforced by an authority or decisions made by a commander; behavior is regular without being regulated. The question is how this can be.

What Happens to Infant Primates Deprived of
the Sight of Their Hands?

Monkeys reared from birth in a device that kept them from seeing the hands and body but not from feeling them move and touching things were very abnormal monkeys. When freed from the device, they acted at first as if they could not reach for and grasp an object but must grope for it. An opaque shield with a cloth bib fitted tightly around the monkey's neck had eliminated visual kinesthesis and had thus prevented the development of visual control of reaching and grasping. So I interpret the results of an experiment by R. Held and J. A. Bauer (1974). See my discussion of the optical information for hand movement in Chapter 7.

THE MEDIUM CONTAINS THE INFORMATION
FOR CONTROL

It should be kept in mind that animals live in a medium that, being insubstantial, permits them to move about, if supported. We are tempted to call the medium "space," but the temptation should be resisted. For the medium, unlike space, permits a steady state of reverberating illumination to become established such that it contains information about surfaces and their substances. That is, there is an array at every point of observation and a changing array at every moving point of observation. The medium, as distinguished from space, allows compression waves from a mechanical event, sound, to reach all points of observation and also allows the diffusion field from a volatile substance, odor, to reach them (Gibson, 1966*b*, Ch. 1). The odor is specific to the volatile substance, the sound is specific to the event, and the visual solid angle is the most specific of all, containing all sorts of structured invariants for perceiving the affordance of the object. This is why to perceive something is also to perceive how to approach it and what to do about it.

Information in a medium is not propagated as signals are propagated but is *contained*. Wherever one goes, one can see, hear, and smell. Hence, perception in the medium accompanies locomotion in the medium.

VISUAL KINESTHESIS AND CONTROL

Before getting into the problem of control, we should be clear about the difference between active and passive movement, a difference that is especially important in the case of locomotion. For animal locomotion may be uncontrolled; the animal may be simply transported. This can happen in various ways. A flow of the medium can transport the animal, as happens to the bird in a wind and the fish in a stream. Or an individual may be transported by another animal, as happens to a monkey clinging to its mother or a baby carried in a cradleboard. Or the observer may be a passenger in a vehicle. In all these cases, the animal can *see* its locomotion without initiating, governing, or steering it. The animal has the information for transportation but cannot regulate it. In my terminology, the observer has visual kinesthesis but no visual control of the movement. This distinction is essential to an understanding of the problem of control. The traditional theory of the senses is incapable of making it, however, and followers of the traditional theory become mired in the conceptual confusion arising from the slippery notion of feedback.

Visual kinesthesis specifies locomotion relative to the environment, whereas the other kinds of kinesthesis may or may not do so. The control of locomotion in the environment must therefore be visual. Walking, bicycling, and driving involve very different kinds of classical kinesthesis but the same visual kinesthesis. The muscle movements must be governed by vision. If you want to go somewhere, or to know where you are going, you can only trust your eyes. The bird in a wind even has to fly in order to stay in the same place. To prevent being carried away, it must arrest the flow of the ambient array.

Before we can hope to understand controlled locomotion, therefore, we must answer several preliminary questions about the information in ambient light. I can think of four. What specifies locomotion or stasis? What specifies an obstacle or an opening? What specifies imminent contact with a surface? What specifies the benefit or the injury that lies ahead? These questions must be answered before we can begin to ask what the *rules* are for starting and stopping, for approaching and retreating, for going this way or that way, and so on.

THE OPTICAL INFORMATION NECESSARY
FOR CONTROL OF LOCOMOTION

For each of the four questions above, I shall list a number of assertions about optical information. I will try to put together what the previous chapters have established.

WHAT SPECIFIES LOCOMOTION OR STASIS?

1. *Flow of the ambient array specifies locomotion, and nonflow specifies stasis.* By *flow* is meant the change analyzed as *motion perspective* (Gibson, Olum, and Rosenblatt, 1955) for the abstract case of an uncluttered environment and a moving point of observation. A better term would be *flow perspective*, or *streaming perspective*. It yields the "melon-shaped family of curves" illustrated in Figure 13.1 and is based on rays of light from particles of the terrain, not on solid angles from features of the terrain. Thus, it has the great advantages of geometrical analysis but also has its disadvantages. Nevertheless, the flow as such specifies locomotion and the invariants specify the layout of surfaces in which locomotion occurs.

2. *Outflow specifies approach to and inflow specifies retreat from.* An invariant feature of the ambient flow is that one hemisphere is centrifugal and the other centripetal. Outflow entails magnification, and inflow entails minification. There is always both a going-to and a coming-from during locomotion. A creature with semipanoramic vision can register both the outflow and the inflow at the same time, but human creatures can sample only one or the other, by looking "ahead" or by looking "behind." Note that a reversal of the flow pattern specifies a reversal of locomotion.

3. *The focus or center of outflow specifies the direction of locomotion in the environment.* More exactly, that visual solid angle at the center of outflow specifies the surface in the environment, or the object, or the opening, toward which the animal is moving. This statement is not analytical. Because the overall flow is radial in both hemispheres, the two foci are implicit in any sufficiently large sample of the ambient

Figure 13.1
The flow velocities in the lower hemisphere of the ambient optic array with locomotion parallel to the earth.
The vectors are plotted in angular coordinates, and all vectors vanish at the horizon. This drawing should be compared with Figure 7.3 showing the motion perspective to a flying bird. (From Gibson, Olum, and Rosenblatt, 1955. © 1955 by the Board of Trustees of the University of Illinois. Reprinted by permission of the University of Illinois Press.)

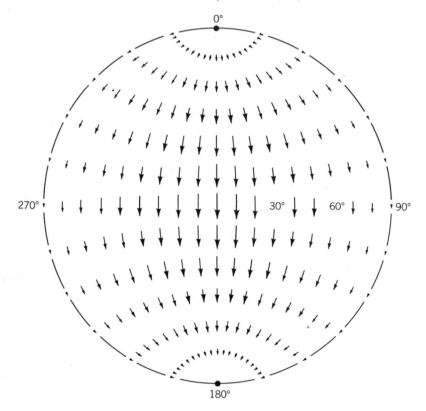

array, and even humans can thus *see* where they are going without having to *look* where they are going. The "melon-shaped family of curves" continues outside the edges of the temporary field of view.

4. *A shift of the center of outflow from one visual solid angle to another specifies a change in the direction of locomotion, a turn, and a remaining of the center within the same solid angle specifies no change in direction.* The ambient optic array is here supposed to consist of nested solid angles, not of a bundle of lines. The direction of locomotion is thus anchored to the layout, not to a coordinate system. The flow of the ambient array can be *transposed over the invariant structure of the array, so that where one is going is seen relative to the surrounding layout*. This unfamiliar notion of invariant structure underlying the changing perspective structure is one that I tried to make explicit in Chapter 5; here is a good example of it. The illustrations in Chapter 7 showing arrows superposed on a picture of the terrain were supposed to suggest this invariance under change but, of course, it cannot be pictured.

5. *Flow of the textured ambient array just behind certain occluding protrusions into the field of view specifies locomotion by an animal with feet.* If you lower your head while walking, a pair of moving protrusions enters the field of view from its lower edge (Chapter 7), and these protrusions move up and down alternately. A cat sees the same thing except that what it sees are *front* feet. The extremities are in optical contact with the flowing array at the locus of maximal flow and maximally coarse texture. They occlude parts of the surface, but it is seen to extend behind them. Convexities and concavities in the surface will affect the timing of contact, and therefore you and the cat must place your feet with regard to the *footing*.

WHAT SPECIFIES AN OBSTACLE OR AN OPENING?

I distinguish two general cases for the affording of locomotion, which I will call *obstacle* and *opening*. An *obstacle* is a rigid object, detached or attached, a surface with occluding edges. An *opening* is an aperture, hole, or gap in a surface, also with occluding edges. An obstacle affords collision. An opening affords passage. Both have a closed or nearly closed contour in the optic array, but the edge of the obstacle is inside the contour,

---

ON LOOKING AT THE ROAD WHILE DRIVING

It must be admitted that when I turn around while driving our car and reply to my wife's protests that I can perfectly well see where I am going without having to look where I am going because the focus of outflow is implicit, she is not reassured.

whereas the edge of the opening is outside the contour. A round object hides in one direction, and a round opening hides in the opposite direction. The way to tell the difference between an obstacle and an opening, therefore, is as follows.

6. *Loss (or gain) of structure outside a closed contour during approach (or retreat) specifies an obstacle. Gain (or loss) of structure inside a closed contour during approach (or retreat) specifies an opening.* This is the only absolutely trustworthy way to tell the difference between an obstacle and an opening. In both cases the visual solid angle goes to a hemisphere as you approach it, but you collide with the obstacle and enter the opening. Magnification of the form as such, the outline, does not distinguish them. But as you come up to the obstacle it hides more and more of the vista, and as you come up to the opening it reveals more and more of the vista. Deletion outside the occluding edge and accretion inside the occluding edge will distinguish the two. Psychologists and artists alike have been confused about the difference between things and holes, surfaces and apertures. The figure-ground phenomenon that so impressed the gestalt psychologists and that is still taken to be a prototype of perception is misleading. A closed contour as such in the optic array does *not* specify an object in the environment.

What specifies the near edge of an opening in the ground, a hole or gap in the surface of support? This is very important information for a terrestrial animal.

7. *Gain of structure above a horizontal contour in the ambient array during approach specifies a brink in the surface of support.* A *brink* is a drop-off in the ground, a step, or the edge of a perch. It is the essential feature of the experiments on the visual cliff that were described in Chapter 9 (for example, E. J. Gibson and Walk, 1960). It is depth downward at an occluding edge, and depending on the amount of depth relative to the size of the animal, it affords stepping-down or falling-off. The rat, chick, or human infant who sees its feet close to such an occluding edge needs to take care. The experimental evidence suggests that the changing occlusion at the edge, not the abrupt increase in the density of optical texture, is the effective information for the animal.

This formula applies to a *horizontal* contour in the array coming from the ground. What about a *vertical* contour in the array coming from a wall?

8. *Gain of structure on one side of a vertical contour in the ambient array during approach specifies the occluding edge of a barrier, and the side on which gain occurs is the side of the edge that affords passage.* This is the edge of a house, the end of a wall, or the vertical edge of a doorway, often loosely called a corner. On one side of the edge the vista beyond is hidden, and on the other side it is revealed; on one side there is potential collision, and on the other potential passage. The trunk of a tree has two such curved edges not far apart. To "go around the corner" is to reveal the surfaces of the new vista. Rats do it in mazes, and people do it in cities. To find one's way in

a cluttered environment is to go around a series of occluding edges, and the problem is to choose the correct edges to go around (see Figure 11.2).

WHAT SPECIFIES IMMINENT CONTACT
WITH A SURFACE?

In an early essay on the visual control of locomotion (Gibson, 1958), I wrote:

Approach to a solid surface is specified by a centrifugal flow of the texture of the optic array. Approach to an object is specified by a magnification of the closed contour in the array corresponding to the edges of the object. A uniform *rate of approach is accompanied by an* accelerated *rate of magnification. At the theoretical point where the eye touches the object, the latter will intercept a visual angle of 180°. The magnification reaches an explosive rate in the last moments before contact. This accelerated expansion . . . specifies imminent collision.*

This was true enough as far as it went. I was thinking of the problem of how a pilot lands on a field or how a bee lands on a flower. The explosive magnification, the "looming" as I called it, has to be canceled if a "soft" landing is to be achieved. I never thought of the entirely different problem of steering through an opening. The optical information provided by various kinds of magnification is evidently not as simple as I thought in 1958.

The complexities were not clarified by the empirical studies of Schiff, Caviness, and Gibson (1962) and Schiff (1965), who provided the optical information for the approach *of* an object in space instead of the information for approach *to* a surface in the environment. They displayed an expanding dark silhouette in the center of a luminous translucent screen, as described in Chapter 10. No one saw himself being transposed; everyone saw something indefinite coming toward them, as if it were in the sky. The display consisted of an expanding single form, a shadow or silhouette, not the magnifying of a nested structure of subordinate forms that characterizes approach to a real surface. The magnifying of detail *without limit* was missing from the display.

9. *The magnification of a nested structure in which progressively finer details keep emerging at the center specifies approach of an observer to a surface in the environment.* This formula emphasizes the facets within the faces of a substantial surface, such as that of an obstacle, an object, an animate object, or a surface of rest that the observer might encounter. In order to achieve contact without collision, the nested magnification must be made to cease at the appropriate level instead of continuing to its limit. There seems to be an optimal degree of magnification for contact with a surface, depending on what it affords. For food one moves up to *eating* distance; for

manipulating one moves up to *reaching* distance; for print one moves up to *reading* distance.

WHAT SPECIFIES THE BENEFIT OR INJURY
THAT LIES AHEAD?

Bishop Berkeley suggested in 1709 that the chief end of vision was for animals "to foresee the benefit or injury which is like to ensue upon the application of their own bodies to this or that body which is at a distance." What the philosopher called foresight is what I call the *perception of the affordance*. To see at a distance what the object affords on contact is "necessary for the preservation of an animal."

I differ from Bishop Berkeley in assuming that information is available in the light to the animal for what an encounter with the object affords. But I agree with him about the utility of vision.

10. *Affordances for the individual upon encountering an object are specified in the optic array from the object by invariants and invariant combinations. Tools, food, shelter, mates, and amiable animals are distinguished from poisons, fires, weapons, and hostile animals by their shapes, colors, textures, and deformations.* The positive and negative affordances of things in the environment are what makes locomotion through the medium such a fundamental kind of behavior for animals. Unlike a plant, the animal can go to the beneficial and stay away from the injurious. But it must be able to perceive the affordances from afar. A rule for the visual control of locomotion might be this: so move as to obtain beneficial encounters with objects and places and to prevent injurious encounters.

RULES FOR THE VISUAL CONTROL
OF LOCOMOTION

I suggested at the beginning that behavior was controlled by information about the world and the self conjointly. The information has now been described. What about the control?

I asserted that behavior was controlled by *rules*. Surely, however, they are not rules enforced by an authority. The rules are not commands from a brain; they emerge from the animal-environment system. But the only way to describe rules is in words, and a rule expressed in words is a command. I am faced with a paradox. The rules for the control of locomotion will sound like commands, although they are not intended to. I can only suggest that the reader should interpret them as rules *not formulated in words*.

The rules that follow are for *visual control*, not muscular, articular, vestibular, or cutaneous control. The visual system normally supersedes the haptic system for locomotion and manipulation, as I tried to explain in *The Senses Considered as Perceptual Systems* (Gibson, 1966*b*). This means that the rules for locomotion will be the same for crawling on all fours, walking, running, or driving an automobile. The particular muscles involved do not matter. Any group of muscles will suffice if it brings about the relation of the animal to its environment stated in the rule.

Standing. The basic rule for a pedestrian animal is *stand up*; that is, keep the feet in contact with a surface of support. It is also well to keep the oval boundaries of the field of view normal with the implicit horizon of the ambient array; if the head is upright the rest of the body follows.

Starting, stopping, going back. To start, make the array flow. To stop, cancel the flow. To go back, make the flow reverse. According to the first two formulas listed in the previous pages, to cause outflow is to get closer and to cause inflow is to get farther away.

Steering. To turn, shift the center of outflow from one patch in the optic array to another, according to the the third and fourth formulas. Steering requires that openings be distinguished from barriers, obstacles, and brinks. The rule is: *To steer, keep the center of outflow outside the patches of the array that specify barriers, obstacles, and brinks and within a patch that specifies an opening* (sixth, seventh, and eighth formulas). Following this rule will avert collisions and prevent falling off.

Approaching. To approach is to magnify a patch in the array, but magnification is complicated (formulas two and six). There are many rules involving magnification. Here are a few. *To permit scrutiny, magnify the patch in the array to such a degree that the details can be looked at. To manipulate something graspable, magnify the patch to such a degree that the object is within reach. To bite something, magnify the patch to such an angle that the mouth can grasp it. To kiss someone, magnify the face-form, if the facial expression is amiable, so as almost to fill the field of view.* (It is absolutely essential for one to keep one's eyes open so as to avoid collision. It is also wise to learn to discriminate those subtle invariants that specify amiability.) *To read something, magnify the patch to such a degree that the letters become distinguishable.* The most general rule for approach is this: *To realize the positive affordances of something, magnify its optical structure to that degree necessary for the behavioral encounter.*

Entering enclosures. An enclosure such as a burrow, cave, nest, or hut affords various benefits upon entry. It is a place of warmth, a shelter from rain and wind, and a place for sleep. It is often a home, the place where mate and offspring are. It is also a place of safety, a hiding place affording both concealment from enemies and a barrier to their locomotion. An enclosure must have an opening to permit entry, and the opening must be identified. The rule seems to be as follows: *to enter an enclosure, magnify the angle of its opening to 180° and open up the vista. Make sure that there is gain of structure inside the contour and not loss outside, or else you will collide with an obstacle* (formulas six and nine).

Keeping a safe distance. The opposite of approach is retreat. Psychologists have sometimes assumed that the *alternative* to approach is retreat. Kurt Lewin's theory of behavior, for example, was based on approach to an object with a positive "valence" and retreat from an object with a negative "valence." This fits with a theory of conflict between approach and retreat, and a compromise between opposite tendencies. But it is wrong to assume that approach and retreat are alternatives. There is no need to flee from an obstacle, a barbed-wire fence, the edge of a river, the edge of a cliff, or a fire. The only need is to maintain a safe distance, a "margin of safety," since these things do not pursue the observer. A ferocious tiger has a negative valence, but a cliff does not. The rule is this, I think: *To prevent an injurious encounter, keep the optical structure of the surface from magnifying to the degree that specifies an encounter* (formulas two and ten).

For moving predators and enemies, *flight* is an appropriate form of action since they can approach. The rule for flight is, *so move as to minify the dangerous form and to make the surrounding optic array flow inward.* If, despite flight, the form magnifies, the enemy is catching up; if it minifies, one is getting away. At the predator's point of observation, of course, the rule is opposite to that for the prey: *so move as to magnify the succulent form by making the surrounding array flow outward until it reaches the proper angular size for capturing.*

RULES FOR THE VISUAL CONTROL
OF MANIPULATION

The rules for the visual control of the movements of the hands are more complex than those for the control of locomotion. But the human infant who watches these squirming protuberances into his field of view is not formulating rules and, in any case, complexity does not seem to cause trouble for the nervous system. I am unable to formulate the rules in words except for a few easy cases.

Locomotor approach often terminates in reaching and grasping. *Reaching* is an elongation of the arm-shape and a minification of the five-pronged hand-shape until contact occurs. If the object is hand-size, it is graspable; if too large or too small, it is not. Children learn to see sizes in terms of prehension: they see the span of their grasp and the diameter of a ball at the same time (Gibson, 1966*b*, fig. 7.1, p. 119). Long before the child can discriminate one inch, or two, or three, he can see the fit of the object to the pincerlike action of the opposable thumb. The child learns his scale of sizes as commensurate with his body, not with a measuring stick.

The affordance of an elongated object for pounding and striking is easily learned. The skill of hammering or striking a target requires visual control, however. It involves what we vaguely call *aiming*. I will not try to state the rules for aiming except to suggest that it entails a kind of centering or symmetricalizing of a diminishing form on a fixed form.

Throwing as such is easy. Simply cause the visual angle of the object you have in your hand to shrink, and it will "zoom" in a highly interesting manner. You have to let go, of course, and this is a matter of haptic control, not visual control. Aimed throwing is much harder, as ballplayers know. It is a sort of reciprocal of steered locomotion.

Tool-using in general is rule governed. The rule for pliers is analogous to that for prehending, the tool being metaphorically an extension of the hand. The use of a stick as a rake for getting a banana outside the cage was one of the achievements of a famous chimpanzee (Köhler, 1925).

Knives, axes, and pointed objects afford the cutting and piercing of other objects and surfaces, including other animals. But the manipulation must be carefully controlled, for the observer's own skin can be cut or pierced as well as the other surface. The tool must be grasped by the handle, not the point; that is, the rule for reaching and the rules for maintaining the margin of safety must both be followed. Visual contact with one part of the surface is beneficial but with another part is injurious, and the "sharp" part is not always easy to discriminate. The case is similar to that of walking along a cliff edge in this respect: one must steer the movement so as to skirt the danger.

The uses of the hands are almost unlimited. And manipulation subserves many other forms of behavior of which it is only a part, eating, drinking, transporting, nursing, caressing, gesturing, and the acts of trace-making, depicting, and writing, which will concern us in Part IV.

The point to remember is that the visual control of the hands is inseparably connected with the visual perception of objects. The act of throwing complements the perception of a throwable object. The transporting of things is part and parcel of seeing them as portable or not.

Conclusion about manipulation. One thing should be evident. The movements of the hands do not consist of responses to stimuli. Manipulation cannot be understood in those terms. Is the only alternative to think of the hands as instruments of the mind? Piaget, for example, sometimes seems to imply that the hands are tools of a child's intelligence. But this is like saying that the hand is a tool of an inner child in more or less the same way that an object is a tool for a child with hands. This is surely an error. The alternative is not a return to mentalism. We should think of the hands as neither triggered nor commanded but *controlled.*

MANIPULATION AND THE PERCEIVING
OF INTERIOR SURFACES

Finally, it should be noted that a great deal of manipulation occurs for the sake of perceiving hidden surfaces. I can think of three kinds of such manipulation: *opening up, uncovering,* and *taking apart.* Each of these has an opposite, as one would expect from the law of reversible occlusion: *closing, covering,* and *putting together.*

Opening and *closing* apply to the lids and covers of hollow objects and also to drawers, compartments, cabinets, and other enclosures. Children are fascinated by the act of opening so as to reveal the interior and closing so as to conceal it. They then come to perceive the continuity between the inner and the outer surfaces. The closed box and the covered pot are then seen to have an inside as well as an outside.

Covering and *uncovering* apply to a cloth, or a child's blanket, or to revealing and concealing by an opaque substance, as in a sandbox. The movement of the hand that conceals the object is not always so clearly the reverse of the movement that reveals it as it is in the case of closing-opening, however. The perceiving of hidden surfaces may well be more difficult in this case.

Taking apart and *putting together* apply to an object composed of smaller objects, that is, a composite that can be disassembled and assembled. There are toys of this sort. Blocks that can be fitted together make such a composite object. Taking apart is usually a simpler act of manipulation than putting together. Children need to see what is inside these compound objects, and it is only to be expected that they should take them apart, or break them apart if need be. After such visual-manual cooperation, they can perceive the interior surfaces of the object together with the cracks, joins, and apertures that separate them. This is the way children come to apprehend a mechanism such as a clock or an internal combustion engine.

SUMMARY

Active locomotor behavior, as contrasted with passive transportation, is under the continuous control of the observer. The dominant level of such control is visual. But this could not occur without what I have called *visual kinesthesis,* the awareness of movement or stasis, of starting or stopping, of approaching or retreating, of going in one direction or another, and of the imminence of an encounter. Such awarenesses are necessary for control.

Also necessary is an awareness of the affordance of the encounter that will terminate the locomotor act and of the affordances of the openings and obstacles, the brinks and barriers, and the corners on the way (actually the occluding edges).

＃

When locomotion is thus visually controlled, it is regular without being a chain of responses and is purposive without being commanded from within.

Manipulation, like active locomotion, is visually controlled. It is thus dependent on an awareness of both the hands as such and the affordances for handling. But its regularities are not so easy to formulate.

FOURTEEN

THE THEORY OF INFORMATION PICKUP AND ITS CONSEQUENCES

In this book the traditional theories of perception have been abandoned. The perennial doctrine that two-dimensional images are restored to three-dimensional reality by a process called depth perception will not do. Neither will the doctrine that the images are transformed by the cues for distance and slant so as to yield constancy of size and shape in the perception of objects. The deep-seated notion of the retinal image as a still picture has been abandoned.

The simple assumption that perceptions of the world are caused by stimuli from the world will not do. The more sophisticated assumption that perceptions of the world are caused when sensations triggered by stimuli are supplemented by memories will not do either. Not even the assumption that a sequence of stimuli is converted into a phenomenal scene by memory will do. The very notion of stimulation as typically composed of discrete stimuli has been abandoned.

The established theory that exteroception and proprioception arise when exteroceptors and proprioceptors are stimulated will not do. The doctrine of special channels of sensation corresponding to specific nerve bundles has been abandoned.

The belief of empiricists that the perceived meanings and values of things are supplied from the past experience of the observer will not do. But even worse is the belief of nativists that meanings and values are supplied from the past experience of the race by way of innate ideas. The theory that meaning is attached to experience or imposed on it has been abandoned.

Not even the current theory that the inputs of the sensory channels are subject to "cognitive processing" will do. The inputs are described in terms of information theory, but the processes are described in terms of old-fashioned mental acts: recognition, interpretation, inference, concepts, ideas, and storage and retrieval of ideas. These are still the operations of the mind upon the deliverances of the senses, and there are too many perplexities entailed in this theory. It will not do, and the approach should be abandoned.

What sort of theory, then, will explain perception? Nothing less than one based on the pickup of information. To this theory, even in its undeveloped state, we should now turn.

Let us remember once again that it is the perception of the environment that we wish to explain. If we were content to explain only the perception of forms or pictures on a surface, of nonsense figures to which meanings must be attached, of discrete stimuli imposed on an observer willy-nilly, in short, the items most often presented to an observer in the laboratory, the traditional theories might prove to be adequate and would not have to be abandoned. But we should not be content with that limited aim. It leaves out of account the eventful world and the perceiver's awareness of being in the world. The laboratory does not have to be limited to simple stimuli, so-called. The experiments reported in Chapters 9 and 10 showed that information can be displayed.

WHAT IS NEW ABOUT THE PICKUP
OF INFORMATION?

The theory of information pickup differs radically from the traditional theories of perception. First, it involves a new notion of perception, not just a new theory of the process. Second, it involves a new assumption about what there is to be perceived. Third, it involves a new conception of the information for perception, with two kinds always available, one about the environment and another about the self. Fourth, it requires the new assumption of perceptual systems with overlapping functions, each having outputs to adjustable organs as well as inputs from organs. We are especially concerned with vision, but none of the systems, listening, touching, smelling, or tasting, is a channel of sense. Finally, fifth, optical information pickup entails an activity of the system not heretofore imagined by any visual scientist, the concurrent registering of both persistence and change in the flow of structured stimulation. This is the crux of the theory but the hardest part to explicate, because it can be phrased in different ways and a terminology has to be invented.

Consider these five novelties in order, ending with the problem of detecting variants and invariants or change and nonchange.

A REDEFINITION OF PERCEPTION

Perceiving is an achievement of the individual, not an appearance in the theater of his consciousness. It is a keeping-in-touch with the world, an experiencing of things rather than a having of experiences. It involves awareness-of instead of just awareness. It may be awareness of something in the environment or something in the observer or both at once, but there is no content of awareness independent of that of which one is aware. This is close to the act psychology of the nineteenth century except that perception is not a mental act. Neither is it a bodily act. Perceiving is a psychosomatic act, not of the mind or of the body but of a living observer.

The act of picking up information, moreover, is a continuous act, an activity that is ceaseless and unbroken. The sea of energy in which we live flows and changes without sharp breaks. Even the tiny fraction of this energy that affects the receptors in the eyes, ears, nose, mouth, and skin is a flux, not a sequence. The exploring, orienting, and adjusting of these organs sink to a minimum during sleep but do not stop dead. Hence, perceiving is a stream, and William James's description of the stream of consciousness (1890, Ch. 9) applies to it. Discrete percepts, like discrete ideas, are "as mythical as the Jack of Spades."

The continuous act of perceiving involves the coperceiving of the self. At least, that is one way to put it. The very term *perception* must be redefined to allow for this fact, and the word *proprioception* must be given a different meaning than it was given by Sherrington.

A NEW ASSERTION ABOUT WHAT IS PERCEIVED

My description of the environment (Chapters 1–3) and of the changes that can occur in it (Chapter 6) implies that places, attached objects, objects, and substances are what are mainly perceived, together with events, which are changes of these things. To see these things is to perceive what they afford. This is very different from the accepted categories of what there is to perceive as described in the textbooks. Color, form, location, space, time, and motion—these are the chapter headings that have been handed down through the centuries, but they are not what is perceived.

Places   A *place* is one of many adjacent places that make up the habitat and, beyond that, the whole environment. But smaller places are nested within larger places. They do not have boundaries, unless artificial boundaries are imposed by surveyors (my piece of land, my town, my country, my state). A place at one level is what you can see from here or hereabouts, and locomotion consists of going from place to place in this sense (Chapter 11). A very important kind of learning for animals and children is place-learning—learning the affordances of places and learning to distinguish among them—and way-finding, which culminate in the state of being oriented to the whole habitat and knowing where one is in the environment.

A place persists in some respects and changes in others. In one respect, it cannot be changed at all—in its location relative to other places. A place cannot be *displaced* like an object. That is, the adjacent order of places cannot be permuted; they cannot be shuffled. The sleeping places, eating places, meeting places, hiding places, and falling-off places of the habitat are immobile. Place-learning is therefore different from other kinds.

Attached Objects   I defined an *object* in Chapter 3 as a substance partially or wholly surrounded by the medium. An object attached to a place is only partly surrounded. It is a protuberance. It cannot be displaced without becoming detached. Nevertheless, it has a surface and enough of a natural boundary to constitute a unit. Attached objects can thus be counted. Animals and children learn what such objects are good for and how to distinguish them. But they cannot be separated from the places where they are found.

Detached Objects   A fully detached object can be displaced or, in some cases, can displace itself. Learning to perceive it thus has a different character from learning to perceive places and attached objects. Its affordances are different. It can be put side by side with another object and compared. It can therefore be grouped or classed by the manipulation of sorting. Such objects when grouped can be rearranged, that is, permuted. And this means not only that they can be counted but that an abstract number can be assigned to the group.

It is probably harder for a child to perceive "same object in a different place" than it is to perceive "same object in the same place." The former requires that the information for persistence-despite-displacement should have been noticed, whereas the latter does not.

Inanimate detached objects, rigid or nonrigid, natural or manufactured, can be said to have features that distinguish them. The features are probably not denumerable, unlike the objects themselves. But if they are compounded to specify affordances, as I argued they must be, only the relevant compounds need to be distinguished. So when it comes to the natural, nonrigid, animate objects of the world whose dimensions of difference are overwhelmingly rich and complex, we pay attention only to what the animal or person affords (Chapter 8).

Persisting Substances   A *substance* is that of which places and objects are composed. It can be vaporous, liquid, plastic, viscous, or rigid, that is, increasingly "substantial." A substance, together with what it affords, is fairly well specified by the color and texture of its surface. Smoke, milk, clay, bread, and wood are polymorphic in layout but invariant in color-texture. Substances, of course, can be smelled and tasted and palpated as well as seen.

The animal or child who begins to perceive substances, therefore, does so in a different way than one who begins to perceive places, attached objects, and detached objects. Substances are formless and cannot be counted. The number of substances, natural compositions, or mixtures is not fixed. (The number of chemical elements is fixed, but that is a different matter.) We discriminate among surface colors and textures, but we cannot group them as we do detached objects and we cannot order them as we do places.

We also, of course, perceive changes in otherwise persisting substances, the ripening of fruit, and the results of boiling and baking, or of mixing and hardening. But these are a kind of event.

Events   As I used the term, an *event* is any change of a substance, place, or object, chemical, mechanical, or biophysical. The change may be slow or fast, reversible or nonreversible, repeating or nonrepeating. Events include what happens to objects in general, plus what the animate objects *make* happen. Events are nested within superordinate events. The motion of a detached object is not the prototype of an event that we have been led to think it was. Events of different sorts are perceived as such and are not, surely, reducible to elementary motions.

Motion is not an event but the effect of motion is change in layout which would be an event.

THE INFORMATION FOR PERCEPTION

Information, as the term is used in this book (but not in other books), refers to specification of the observer's environment, not to specification of the observer's receptors or sense organs. The qualities of objects are specified by information; the qualities of the receptors and nerves are specified by sensations. Information about the world cuts right across the qualities of sense.

The term *information* cannot have its familiar dictionary meaning of *knowledge communicated to a receiver.* This is unfortunate, and I would use another term if I could. The only recourse is to ask the reader to remember that picking up information is not to be thought of as a case of communicating. The world does not speak to the observer. Animals and humans communicate with cries, gestures, speech, pictures, writing, and television, but we cannot hope to understand perception in terms of these channels; it is quite the other way around. Words and pictures convey information, carry it, or transmit it, but the information in the sea of energy around each of us, luminous or mechanical or chemical energy, is not conveyed. It is simply there. The assumption that information can be transmitted and the assumption that it can be stored are appropriate for the theory of communication, not for the theory of perception.

The vast area of speculation about the so-called media of communication had a certain discipline imposed on it some years ago by a mathematical theory of communication (Shannon and Weaver, 1949). A useful measure of information transmitted was formulated, in terms of "bits." A sender and receiver, a channel, and a finite number of possible signals were assumed. The result was a genuine discipline of communications engineering. But, although psychologists promptly tried to apply it to the senses and neuropsychologists began thinking of nerve impulses in terms of bits and the brain in terms of a computer, the applications did not work. Shannon's concept of information applies to telephone hookups and radio broadcasting in elegant ways but not, I think, to the firsthand perception of being in-the-world, to what the baby gets when first it opens its eyes. The information for perception, unhappily, cannot be defined and measured as Claude Shannon's information can be.

The information in ambient light, along with sound, odor, touches, and natural chemicals, is inexhaustible. A perceiver can keep on noticing facts about the world she lives in to the end of her life without ever reaching a limit. There is no threshold for information comparable to a stimulus threshold. Information is not lost to the environment when gained by the individual; it is not conserved like energy.

Information is not specific to the banks of photoreceptors, mechanoreceptors, and chemoreceptors that lie within the sense organs. Sensations are specific to receptors and thus, normally, to the kinds of stimulus energy that touch them off. But information is not energy-specific. Stimuli are not always imposed on a passive subject. In life one *obtains* stimulation in order to extract the information (Gibson, 1966*b*, Ch. 2). The information can be the same, despite a radical change in the stimulation obtained.

Finally, a concept of information is required that admits of the possibility of illusion. Illusions are a theoretical perplexity in any approach to the study of perception. Is information always valid and illusion simply a failure to pick it up? Or is the information picked up sometimes impoverished, masked, ambiguous, equivocal, contradictory, even false? The puzzle is especially critical in vision.

In Chapter 14 of *The Senses Considered as Perceptual Systems* (Gibson, 1966*b*) and again in this book I have tried to come to terms with the problem of misperception. I am only sure of this: it is not one problem but a complex of different problems. Consider, first, the mirage of palm trees in the desert sky, or the straight stick that looks bent because it is partly immersed in water. These illusions, together with the illusion of Narcissus, arise from the regular reflection or refraction of light, that is, from exceptions to the ecological optics of the scatter-reflecting surface and the perfectly homogeneous medium. Then consider, second, the misperception in the case of the shark under the calm water or the electric shock hidden in the radio cabinet. Failure to perceive the danger is not then blamed on the perceiver. Consider, third, the sheet of glass mistaken for an open doorway or the horizontal sheet of glass (the optical cliff) mistaken for a void. A fourth case is the room composed of trapezoidal surfaces or the trapezoidal window, which look normally rectangular so long as the observer does not open both eyes and walk around. Optical misinformation enters into each of these cases in a different way. But in the last analysis, *are* they explained by misinformation? Or is it a matter of failure to pick up *all* the available information, the inexhaustible reservoir that lies open to further scrutiny?

The misperceiving of affordances is a serious matter. As I noted in Chapter 8, a wildcat may look like a cat. (But *does* he look just like a cat?) A malevolent man may act like a benevolent one. (But *does* he exactly?) The line between the pickup of misinformation and the failure to pick up information is hard to draw.

Consider the human habit of picture-making, which I take to be the devising and displaying of optical information for perception by others. It is thus a means of communication, giving rise to mediated apprehension, but it is more like direct pickup than word-making is. Depiction and its consequences are deferred until later, but it can be pointed out here that picture-makers have been experimenting on us for centuries with artificial displays of information in a special form. They enrich or impoverish it, mask or clarify it, ambiguate or disambiguate it. They often try to produce a discrepancy of information, an equivocation or contradiction, in the same display. Painters invented the cues for depth in the first place, and psychologists looked at their paintings and began to talk about cues. The notions of counterbalanced cues, of figure-ground reversals, of equivocal perspectives, of different perspectives on the same object, of "impossible" objects—all these come from artists who were simply experimenting with frozen optical information.

An important fact to be noted about any pictorial display of optical information is that, in contrast with the inexhaustible reservoir of information in an illuminated medium, it cannot be looked at close up. Information to specify the display as such, the canvas, the surface, the screen, can always be picked up by an observer who walks around and looks closely.

THE CONCEPT OF A PERCEPTUAL SYSTEM

The theory of information pickup requires perceptual systems, not senses. Some years ago I tried to prove that a perceptual system was radically different from a sense (Gibson, 1966*b*), the one being active and the other passive. People said, "Well, what I mean by a sense is an *active* sense." But it turned out that they still meant the passive inputs of a sensory nerve, the activity being what occurs in the brain when the inputs get there. That was not what I meant by a perceptual system. I meant the activities of looking, listening, touching, tasting, or sniffing. People then said, "Well, but those are responses to sights, sounds, touches, tastes, or smells, that is, motor acts resulting from sensory inputs. What you call a perceptual system is nothing but a case of feedback." I was discouraged. People did not understand.

I shall here make another attempt to show that the senses considered as special senses cannot be reconciled with the senses considered as perceptual systems. The five perceptual systems correspond to five modes of overt attention. They have overlapping functions, and they are all more or less subordinated to an overall orienting system. A system has organs, whereas a sense has receptors. A system can orient, explore, investigate, adjust, optimize, resonate, extract, and come to an equilibrium, whereas a sense cannot. The characteristic activities of the visual system have been described in Chapter 12 of this book. The characteristic activities of the auditory system, the haptic system, and the two related parts of what I called the "chemical value system" were described in Chapters 5–8 of my earlier book (Gibson, 1966b). Five fundamental differences between a sense and a perceptual system are given below.

1. A special sense is defined by a bank of receptors or receptive units that are connected with a so-called projection center in the brain. Local stimuli at the sensory surface will cause local firing of neurons in the center. The adjustments of the organ in which the receptors are incorporated are not included within the definition of a sense.

A perceptual system is defined by an organ and its adjustments at a given level of functioning, subordinate or superordinate. At any level, the incoming and outgoing nerve fibers are considered together so as to make a continuous loop.

The organs of the visual system, for example, from lower to higher are roughly as follows. First, the lens, pupil, chamber, and retina comprise an organ. Second, the eye with its muscles in the orbit comprise an organ that is both stabilized and mobile. Third, the two eyes in the head comprise a binocular organ. Fourth, the eyes in a mobile head that can turn comprise an organ for the pickup of ambient information. Fifth, the eyes in a head on a body constitute a superordinate organ for information pickup over paths of locomotion. The adjustments of accommodation, intensity modulation, and dark adaptation go with the first level. The movements of compensation, fixation, and scanning go with the second level. The movements of vergence and the pickup of disparity go with the third level. The movements of the head, and of the body as a whole, go with the fourth and fifth levels. All of them serve the pickup of information.

2. In the case of a special sense, the receptors can only receive stimuli, passively, whereas in the case of a perceptual system the input-output loop can be supposed to obtain information, actively. Even when the theory of the special senses is liberalized by the modern hypothesis of receptive units, the latter are supposed to be triggered by complex stimuli or modulated in some passive fashion.

3. The inputs of a special sense constitute a repertory of innate sensations, whereas the achievements of a perceptual system are susceptible to maturation and learning. Sensations of one modality can be combined with those of another in accordance with the laws of association; they can be organized or fused or supplemented or selected, but *no new sensations can be learned*. The information that is picked up, on the other hand, becomes more and more subtle, elaborate, and precise with practice. One can keep on learning to perceive as long as life goes on.

4. The inputs of the special senses have the qualities of the receptors being stimulated, whereas the achievements of the perceptual systems are specific to the qualities of things in the world, especially their affordances. The recognition of this limitation of the senses was forced upon us by Johannes Müller with his doctrine of specific "nerve energies." He understood clearly, if reluctantly, the implication that, because we can never know the external causes of our sensations, we cannot know the outer world. Strenuous efforts have to be made if one is to avoid this shocking conclusion. Helmholtz argued that we must deduce the causes of our sensations because we cannot detect them. The hypothesis that sensations provide clues or cues for perception of the world is similar. The popular formula that we can interpret sensory signals is a variant of it. But it seems to me that all such arguments come down to this: we can perceive the world only if we already know what there is to be perceived. And that, of course, is circular. I shall come back to this point again.

The alternative is to assume that sensations triggered by light, sound, pressure, and chemicals are merely incidental, that information is available to a perceptual system, and that the qualities of the world in relation to the needs of the observer are experienced directly.

5. In the case of a special sense the process of attention occurs at centers within the nervous system, whereas in the case of a perceptual system attention pervades the whole input-output loop. In the first case attention is a consciousness that can be focused; in the second case it is a skill that can be educated. In the first case physiological metaphors are used, such as the filtering of nervous impulses or the switching of impulses from one path to another. In the second case the metaphors used can be terms such as *resonating, extracting, optimizing,* or *symmetricalizing* and such acts as orienting, exploring, investigating, or adjusting.

I suggested in Chapter 12 that a normal act of visual attention consists of scanning a whole feature of the ambient array, not of fixating a single detail of the array. We are tempted to think of attention as strictly a narrowing-down and holding-still, but actually this is rare. The invariants of structure in an optic array that constitute information are more likely to be gradients than small details, and they are scanned over wide angles.

THE REGISTERING OF BOTH PERSISTENCE
AND CHANGE

The theory of information pickup requires that the visual system be able to detect both persistence and change—the persistence of places, objects, and substances along with whatever changes they undergo. Everything in the world persists in some respects and changes in some respects. So also does the observer himself. And some things persist for long intervals, others for short.

The perceiving of persistence and change (instead of color, form, space, time, and motion) can be stated in various ways. We can say that the perceiver *separates* the change from the nonchange, *notices* what stays the same and what does not, or *sees* the continuing identity of things along with the events in which they participate. The question, of course, is how he does so. What is the information for persistence and change? The answer must be of this sort: The perceiver extracts the invariants of structure from the flux of stimulation while still noticing the flux. For the visual system in particular, he tunes in on the invariant structure of the ambient optic array that underlies the changing perspective structure caused by his movements.

The hypothesis that invariance under optical transformation constitutes information for the perception of a rigid persisting object goes back to the moving-shadow experiment (Gibson and Gibson, 1957). The outcome of that experiment was paradoxical; it seemed at the time that a changing form elicited the perception of a constant form with a changing slant. The solution was to postulate invariants of optical structure for the persisting object, "formless" invariants, and a particular disturbance of optical structure for the motion of the object, a perspective transformation. Separate terms needed to be devised for physical motions and for the optical motions that specified them, for events in the world and for events in the array, for geometry did not provide the terms. Similarly, different terms need to be invented to describe invariants of the changing world and invariants of the changing array; the geometrical word *form* will not do. Perhaps the best policy is to use the terms *persistence* and *change* to refer to the environment but *preservation* and *disturbance* of structure to refer to the optic array.

The stimulus-sequence theory of perception, based on a succession of discrete eye fixations, can assume only that the way to apprehend persistence is by an act of comparison and judgment. The perception of what-it-is-now is compared with the memory of what-it-was-then, and they are judged *same*. The continuous pickup theory of perception can assume that the apprehension of persistence is a simple act of invariance detection. Similarly, the snapshot theory must assume that the way to apprehend change is to compare what-it-is-now with what-it-was-then and judge *different*, whereas the pickup theory can assume an awareness of transformation. The congruence of the array with itself or the disparity of the array with itself, as the case may be, is picked up.

The perception of the persisting identity of things is fundamental to other kinds of perception. Consider an example, the persisting identity of another person. How does a child come to apprehend the identity of the mother? You might say that when the mother-figure, or the face, is continually fixated by the child the persistence of the sensation is supported by the continuing stimulus. So it is when the child clings to the mother. But what if the mother-figure is scanned? What if the figure leaves and returns to the field of view? What if the figure goes away and comes back? What is perceived when it emerges from the distance or from darkness, when its back is turned, when its clothing is changed, when its emotional state is altered, when it comes back into sight after a long interval? In short, how is it that the phenomenal identity of a person agrees so well with the biological identity, despite all the vicissitudes of the figure in the optic array and all the events in which the person participates?

The same questions can be asked about inanimate objects, attached objects, places, and substances. The features of a person are invariant to a considerable degree (the eyes, nose, mouth, style of gesture, and voice). But so are the analogous features of other things, the child's blanket, the kitchen stove, the bedroom, and the bread on the table. All have to be identified as continuing, as persisting, as maintaining existence. And this is not explained by the constructing of a concept for each.

We are accustomed to assuming that successive stimuli from the same entity, sensory encounters with it, are united by an act of recognition. We have assumed that perception ceases and memory takes over when sensation stops. Hence, every fresh glimpse of anything requires the act of linking it up with the memories of that thing instead of some other thing. The judgment, "I have seen this before," is required for the apprehension of "same thing," even when the observer has only turned away, or

---

THE EFFECT OF PERSISTING STIMULATION ON PERCEPTION

We have assumed that perception stops when sensation stops and that sensation stops when stimulation stops, or very soon thereafter. Hence, a persisting stimulus is required for the perception of a persisting object. The fact is, however, that a truly persisting stimulus on the retina or the skin specifies only that the observer does not or cannot move his eye or his limb, and the sense perception soon fades out by sensory adaptation (Chapter 4). The persistence of an object is specified by invariants of structure, not by the persistence of stimulation.

The seeing of persistence considered as the picking up of invariants under change resolves an old puzzle: the phenomenal identity of the spots of a retinal pattern when the image is transposed over the retina stroboscopically. The experiments of Josef Ternus first made this puzzle evident. See Gibson (1950, p. 56 ff.) for a discussion and references.

I used to think that the aftereffects of persisting stimulation of the retina obtained by the prolonged fixation of a display could be very revealing. Besides ordinary afterimages there are all sorts of perceptual aftereffects, some of which I discovered. But I no longer believe that experiments on so-called perceptual adaptation are revealing, and I have given up theorizing about them. The aftereffects of prolonged scrutiny are of many sorts. Until we know more about information pickup, this field of investigation will be incoherent.

has only glanced away for an instant. The classical theory of sense perception is reduced to an absurdity by this requirement. The alternative is to accept the theory of invariance detection.

The quality of familiarity that can go with the perception of a place, object, or person, as distinguished from the quality of unfamiliarity, is a fact of experience. But is familiarity a result of the percept making contact with the traces of past percepts of the same thing? Is unfamiliarity a result of not making such contact? I think not. There is a circularity in the reasoning, and it is a bad theory. The quality of familiarity simply accompanies the perception of persistence.

The perception of the persisting identity of places and objects is more fundamental than the perception of the differences among them. We are told that to perceive something is to categorize it, to distinguish it from the other types of things that it might have been. The essence of perceiving is discriminating. Things differ among themselves, along dimensions of difference. But this leaves out of account the simple fact that the substance, place, object, person, or whatever has to last long enough to be distinguished from other substances, places, objects, or persons. The detecting of the invariant features of a persisting thing should not be confused with the detecting of the invariant features that make different things similar. Invariants over time and invariants over entities are not grasped in the same way.

In the case of the persisting thing, I suggest, the perceptual system simply extracts the invariants from the flowing array; it *resonates* to the invariant structure or is *attuned* to it. In the case of substantially distinct things, I venture, the perceptual system must *abstract* the invariants. The former process seems to be simpler than the latter, more nearly automatic. The latter process has been interpreted to imply an intellectual act of lifting out something that is mental from a collection of objects that are physical, of forming an abstract concept from concrete percepts, but that is very dubious. Abstraction is invariance detection across objects. But the invariant is only a similarity, not a persistence.

SUMMARY OF THE THEORY OF PICKUP

According to the theory being proposed, *perceiving is a registering of certain definite dimensions of invariance in the stimulus flux together with definite parameters of disturbance*. The invariants are invariants of structure, and the disturbances are disturbances of structure. The structure, for vision, is that of the ambient optic array.

The invariants specify the persistence of the environment and of oneself. The disturbances specify the changes in the environment and of oneself. A perceiver is aware of her existence in a persisting environment and is also aware of her movements relative to the environment, along with the motions of objects and nonrigid surfaces relative to the environment. The term *awareness* is used to imply a direct pickup of the information, not necessarily to imply consciousness.

There are many dimensions of invariance in an ambient optic array over time, that is, for paths of observation. One invariant, for example, is caused by the occluding edge of the nose, and it specifies the self. Another is the gradient of optical texture caused by the material texture of the substratum, and it specifies the basic environment. Equally, there are many parameters of disturbance of an ambient optic array. One, for example, is caused by the sweeping of the nose over the ambient optic array, and it specifies head turning. Another is the deletion and accretion of texture at the edges of a form in the array, and it specifies the motion of an object over the ground.

For different kinds of events in the world there are different parameters of optical disturbance, not only accretion-deletion but also polar outflow-inflow, compression, transformation, substitution, and others. Hence, the same object can be seen undergoing different events, and different objects can be seen undergoing the same event. For example, an apple may ripen, fall, collide, roll, or be eaten, and eating may happen to an apple, carrot, egg, biscuit, or lamb chop. If the parameter of optical disturbance is distinguished, the event will be perceived. Note how radically different this is from saying that if stimulus-event A is invariably followed by stimulus-event B we will come to expect B whenever we experience A. The latter is classical association theory (or conditioning theory, or expectancy theory). It rests on the stimulus-sequence doctrine. It implies that falling, colliding, rolling, or eating are not units but sequences. It implies, with David Hume, that even if B has followed A a thousand times there is no certainty that it will follow A in the future. An event is only known by a conjunction of atomic sensations, a contingency. If this recurrent sequence is experienced again and again, the observer will begin to anticipate, or have faith, or learn by induction, but that is the best he can do.

The process of pickup is postulated to depend on the input-output loop of a perceptual system. For this reason, the information that is picked up cannot be the familiar kind that is transmitted from one person to another and that can be stored. According to pickup theory, information does not have to be stored in memory because it is always available.

The process of pickup is postulated to be very susceptible to development and learning. The opportunities for educating attention, for exploring and adjusting, for extracting and abstracting are unlimited. The increasing capacity of a perceptual system to pick up information, however, does not in itself constitute information. The ability to perceive does not imply, necessarily, the having of an idea of what can be perceived. The having of ideas is a fact, but it is not a prerequisite of perceiving. Perhaps it is a kind of extended perceiving.

THE TRADITIONAL THEORIES OF
PERCEPTION: INPUT PROCESSING

The theory of information pickup purports to be an alternative to the traditional theories of perception. It differs from all of them, I venture to suggest, in rejecting the assumption that perception is the processing of inputs. *Inputs* mean sensory or afferent nerve impulses to the brain.

Adherents to the traditional theories of perception have recently been making the claim that what they assume is the processing of information in a modern sense of the term, not sensations, and that therefor they are not bound by the traditional theories of perception. But it seems to me that all they are doing is climbing on the latest bandwagon, the computer bandwagon, without reappraising the traditional assumption that perceiving is the processing of inputs. I refuse to let them pre-empt the term *information*. As I use the term, it is not something that has to be processed. The inputs of the receptors have to be processed, of course, because they in themselves do not specify anything more than the anatomical units that are triggered.

All kinds of metaphors have been suggested to describe the ways in which sensory inputs are processed to yield perceptions. It is supposed that sensation occurs first, perception occurs next, and knowledge occurs last, a progression from the lower to the higher mental processes. One process is the filtering of sensory inputs. Another is the organizing of sensory inputs, the grouping of elements into a spatial pattern. The integrating of elements into a temporal pattern may or may not be included in the organizing process. After that, the processes become highly speculative. Some theorists propose mental operations. Others argue for semilogical processes or problem-solving. Many theorists are in favor of a process analogous to the decoding of signals. All theorists seem to agree that past experience is brought to bear on the sensory inputs, which means that memories are somehow applied to them. Apart from filtering and organizing, the processes suggested are cognitive. Consider some of them.

MENTAL OPERATIONS ON THE SENSORY INPUTS

The a priori categories of understanding possessed by the perceived, according to Kant

The perceiver's presuppositions about what is being perceived

Innate ideas about the world

SEMILOGICAL OPERATIONS ON THE SENSORY INPUTS

Unconscious inferences about the outer causes of the sensory inputs, according to Helmholtz (the outer world is deduced)

Estimates of the probable character of the "distant" objects based on the "proximal" stimuli, according to Egon Brunswik (1956), said to be a quasirational, not a fully rational, process

DECODING OPERATIONS ON THE SENSORY INPUTS

The interpreting of the inputs considered as signals (a very popular analogy with many variants)

The decoding of sensory messages

The utilizing of sensory cues

The understanding of signs, or indicators, or even *clues*, in the manner of a police detective

THE APPLICATION OF MEMORIES TO THE SENSORY INPUTS

The "accrual" of a context of memory images and feelings to the core of sensations, according to E. B. Titchener's theory of perception (1924)

This last hypothetical process is perhaps the most widely accepted of all, and the most elaborated. Perceptual learning is supposed to be a matter of enriching the input, not of differentiating the information (Gibson and Gibson, 1955). But the process of combining memories with inputs turns out to be not at all simple when analyzed. The appropriate memories have to be retrieved from storage, that is, aroused or summoned; an image does not simply accrue. The sensory input must fuse in some fashion with the stored images; or the sensory input is assimilated to a composite memory image, or, if this will not do, it is said to be assimilated to a class, a type, a schema, or a concept. Each new sensory input must be categorized—assigned to its class, matched to its type, fitted to its schema, and so on. Note that categories cannot become established until enough items have been classified but that items cannot be classified until categories have been established. It is this difficulty, for one, that

Figure 14.1

The commonly supposed sequence of stages in the visual perceiving of an object.

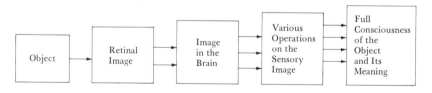

compels some theorists to suppose that classification is a priori and that people and animals have innate or instinctive knowledge of the world.

The error lies, it seems to me, in assuming that either innate ideas or acquired ideas must be applied to bare sensory inputs for perceiving to occur. The fallacy is to assume that because inputs convey no knowledge they can somehow be made to yield knowledge by "processing" them. Knowledge of the world must come from somewhere; the debate is over whether it comes from stored knowledge, from innate knowledge, or from reason. But all three doctrines beg the question. Knowledge of the world cannot be explained by supposing that knowledge of the world already exists. All forms of cognitive processing imply cognition so as to account for cognition.

All this should be treated as ancient history. Knowledge of the environment, surely, develops as perception develops, extends as the observers travel, gets finer as they learn to scrutinize, gets longer as they apprehend more events, gets fuller as they see more objects, and gets richer as they notice more affordances. Knowledge of this sort does not "come from" anywhere; it is got by looking, along with listening, feeling, smelling, and tasting. The child also, of course, begins to acquire knowledge that comes from parents, teachers, pictures, and books. But this is a different kind of knowledge.

(indirect knowledge?)

THE FALSE DICHOTOMY BETWEEN PRESENT AND PAST EXPERIENCE

The division between present experience and past experience may seem to be self-evident. How could anyone deny it? Yet it is denied in supposing that we can experience both change and nonchange. The difference between present and past blurs, and the clarity of the distinction slips away. The stream of experience does not consist of an instantaneous present and a linear past receding into the distance; it is not a "traveling razor's edge" dividing the past from the future. Perhaps the present has a certain duration. If so, it should be possible to find out when perceiving stops and remembering begins. But it has not been possible. There are attempts to talk about a "conscious" present, or a "specious" present, or a "span" of present perception, or a span of "immediate memory," but they all founder on the simple fact that there is no dividing line between the present and the past, between perceiving and remembering. A special sense impression clearly ceases when the sensory excitation ends, but a perception does not. It does not become a memory after a certain length of time. A perception, in fact, does not *have* an end. Perceiving goes on.

Perhaps the force of the dichotomy between present and past experience comes from language, where we are not allowed to say anything intermediate between "I see you" and "I saw you" or "I am seeing you" and "I was seeing you." Verbs can take the present tense or the past tense. We have no words to describe my continuing awareness of you, whether you are in sight or out of sight. Language is categorical. Because we are led to separate the present from the past, we find ourselves involved in what I have called the "muddle of memory" (Gibson, 1966a). We think that the past ceases to exist unless it is "preserved" in memory. We assume that memory is the bridge between the past and the present. We assume that memories accumulate and are stored somewhere; that they are images, or pictures, or representations of the past; or that memory is actually physiological, not mental, consisting of engrams or traces; or that it actually consists of neural connections, not engrams; that memory is the basis of all learning; that memory is the basis of habit; that memories live on in the unconscious; that heredity is a form of memory; that cultural heredity is another form of memory; that any effect of the past on the present is memory, including hysteresis. If we cannot do any better than this, we should stop using the word.

The traditional theories of perception take it for granted that what we see *now*, present experience, is the sensory basis of our perception of the environment and that what we have seen *up to now*, past experience, is added to it. We can only understand the present in terms of the past. But what we see *now* (when it is carefully analyzed) turns out to be at most a peculiar set of surfaces that happen to come within the field of view and face the point of observation (Chapter 11). It does not comprise what we see. It could not possibly be the basis of our perception of the environment. What we see *now* refers to the self, not the environment. The perspective appearance of the world at a given moment of time is simply what specifies to the observer where he is at that moment. The perceptual process does not begin with this peculiar projection, this momentary pattern. The perceiving of the world begins with the pickup of invariants.

Evidently the theory of information pickup does not need memory. It does not have to have as a basic postulate the effect of past experience on present experience by way of memory. It needs to explain learning, that is, the improvement of perceiving with practice and the education of attention, but not by an appeal to the catch-all of past experience or to the muddle of memory.

The state of a perceptual system is altered when it is attuned to information of a certain sort. The system has become sensitized. Differences are noticed that were previously not noticed. Features become distinctive that were formerly vague. But this altered state need not be thought of as depending on a memory, an image, an engram, or a trace. An image of the past, if experienced at all, would be only an incidental symptom of the altered state.

This is not to deny that reminiscence, expectation, imagination, fantasy, and dreaming actually occur. It is only to deny that they have an essential role to play in

perceiving. They are kinds of visual awareness other than perceptual. Let us ___
consider them in their own right.

A NEW APPROACH TO NONPERCEPTUAL
AWARENESS

The redefinition of *perception* implies a redefinition of the so-called higher mental processes. In the old mentalistic psychology, they stood above the lower mental processes, the sensory and reflex processes, which could be understood in terms of the physiology of receptors and nerves. These higher processes were vaguely supposed to be intellectual processes, inasmuch as the intellect was contrasted with the senses. They occurred in the brain. They were operations of the mind. No list of them was ever agreed upon, but *remembering, thinking, conceiving, inferring, judging, expecting,* and, above all, *knowing* were the words used. *Imagining, dreaming, rationalizing,* and *wishful thinking* were also recognized, but it was not clear that they were higher processes in the intellectual sense. I am convinced that none of them can ever be understood as an operation of the mind. They will never be understood as reactions of the body, either. But perhaps if they are reconsidered in relation to ecological perceiving they will begin to sort themselves out in a new and reasonable way that fits with the evidence.

To perceive is to be aware of the surfaces of the environment and of oneself in it. The interchange between hidden and unhidden surfaces is essential to this awareness. These are existing surfaces; they are specified at some points of observation. Perceiving gets wider and finer and longer and richer and fuller as the observer explores the environment. The full awareness of surfaces includes their layout, their substances, their events, and their affordances. Note how this definition includes within perception a part of memory, expectation, knowledge, and meaning—some part but not all of those mental processes in each case.

One kind of remembering, then, would be an awareness of surfaces that have ceased to exist or events that will not recur, such as items in the story of one's own life. There is no point of observation at which such an item will come into sight.

To expect, anticipate, plan, or imagine creatively is to be aware of surfaces that do not exist or events that do not occur but that could arise or be fabricated within what we call the limits of possibility.

To daydream, dream, or imagine wishfully (or fearfully) is to be aware of surfaces or events that do not exist or occur and that are outside the limits of possibility.

These three kinds of nonperceptual awareness are not explained, I think, by the traditional hypothesis of mental imagery. They are better explained by some such hypothesis as this: a perceptual system that has become sensitized to certain invariants and can extract them from the stimulus flux can also operate without the constraints of the stimulus flux. Information becomes further detached from stimulation. The adjustment loops for looking around, looking at, scanning, and focusing are then inoperative. The visual system visualizes. But this is still an activity of the system, not an appearance in the theater of consciousness.

Besides these, other kinds of cognitive awareness occur that are not strictly perceptual. Before considering them, however, I must clarify what I mean by *imaginary* or *unreal*.

THE RELATIONSHIP BETWEEN IMAGINING AND PERCEIVING

I assume that a normal observer is well aware of the difference between surfaces that exist and surfaces that do not. (Those that do not have ceased to exist, or have not begun to, or have not and will not.) How can this be so? What is the information for existence? What are the criteria? It is widely believed that young children are not aware of the differences, and neither are adults suffering from hallucinations. They do not distinguish between what is "real" and what is "imaginary" because perception and mental imagery cannot be separated. This doctrine rests on the assumption that, because a percept and an image both occur in the brain, the one can pass over into the other by gradual steps. The only "tests for reality" are intellectual. A percept cannot validate itself.

We have been told ever since John Locke that an image is a "faint copy" of a percept. We are told by Titchener (1924) that an image is "easily confused with a sensation" (p. 198). His devoted student, C. W. Perky, managed to show that a faint optical picture secretly projected from behind on a translucent screen is sometimes not identified as such when an observer is imagining an object of the same sort on the screen (Perky, 1910). We are told by a famous neurosurgeon that electrical stimulation of the surface of the brain in a conscious patient "has the force" of an actual perception (Penfield, 1958). It is said that when a feeling of reality accompanies a content of consciousness it is marked as a percept and when it does not it is marked as an image. All these assertions are extremely dubious.

I suggest that perfectly reliable and automatic tests for reality are involved in the working of a perceptual system. They do not have to be intellectual. A surface is seen with more or less definition as the accommodation of the lens changes; an image is not. A surface becomes clearer when fixated; an image does not. A surface can be scanned; an image cannot. When the eyes converge on an object in the world, the sensation of crossed diplopia disappears, and when the eyes diverge, the "double image" reappears; this does not happen for an image in the space of the mind. An object can be scrutinized with the whole repertory of optimizing adjustments described in Chapter 11. No image can be scrutinized—not an afterimage, not a so-called eidetic image, not the image in a dream, and not even a hallucination. An imaginary object can undergo an *imaginary* scrutiny, no doubt, but you are not going to discover a new and surprising feature of the object this way. For it is the very features of the object that your perceptual system has already picked up that constitute your ability to visualize it. The most decisive test for reality is whether you can discover new features and details by the act of scrutiny. Can you obtain new stimulation and extract new information from it? Is the information inexhaustible? Is there more to be seen? The imaginary scrutiny of an imaginary entity cannot pass this test.

A related criterion for the existence of a thing is reversible occlusion. Whatever goes out of sight as you move your head and comes into sight as you move back is a *persisting* surface. Whatever comes into sight when you move your head is a *pre-existing* surface. That is to say, it exists. The present, past, or future tense of the verb *see* is irrelevant; the fact is perceived without words. Hence, a criterion for *real* versus *imaginary* is what happens when you turn and move. When the infant turns her head and creeps about and brings her hands in and out of her field of view, she perceives what is real. The assumption that children cannot tell the difference between what is real and what is imaginary until the intellect develops is mentalistic nonsense. As the child grows up, she apprehends more reality as she visits more places of her habitat.

Nevertheless, it is argued that dreams sometimes have the "feeling" of reality, that some drugs can induce hallucinations, and that a true hallucination in psychosis is proof that a mental image can be the same as a percept, for the patient acts as if he were perceiving and thinks he is perceiving. I remain dubious (Gibson, 1970). The dreamer is asleep and cannot make the ordinary tests for reality. The drug-taker is hoping for a vision and does not want to make tests for reality. There are many possible reasons why the hallucinating patient does not scrutinize what he says he sees, does not walk around it or take another look at it or test it.

There is a popular fallacy to the effect that if you can touch what you see it is real. The sense of touch is supposed to be more trustworthy than the sense of sight, and Bishop Berkeley's theory of vision was based on this idea. But it is surely wrong. Tactual hallucinations can occur as well as visual. And if the senses are actually perceptual systems, the haptic system as I described it (Gibson, 1966b) has its own exploratory adjustments and its own automatic tests for reality. One perceptual system does not *validate* another. Seeing and touching are two ways of getting much the same information about the world.

A NEW APPROACH TO KNOWING

The theory of information pickup makes a clear-cut separation between perception and fantasy, but it closes the supposed gap between perception and knowledge. The extracting and abstracting of invariants are what happens in both perceiving and knowing. To perceive the environment and to conceive it are different in degree but not in kind. One is continuous with the other. Our reasons for supposing that seeing something is quite unlike knowing something come from the old doctrine that seeing is having temporary sensations one after another at the passing moment of present time, whereas knowing is having permanent concepts stored in memory. It should now be clear that perceptual seeing is an awareness of persisting structure.

Knowing is an *extension* of perceiving. The child becomes aware of the world by looking around and looking at, by listening, feeling, smelling, and tasting, but then she begins to be *made* aware of the world as well. She is shown things, and told things, and given models and pictures of things, and then instruments and tools and books, and finally rules and short cuts for finding out more things. Toys, pictures, and words are aids to perceiving, provided by parents and teachers. They transmit to the next generation the tricks of the human trade. The labors of the first perceivers are spared their descendants. The extracting and abstracting of the invariants that specify the environment are made vastly easier with these aids to comprehension. But they are not in themselves knowledge, as we are tempted to think. All they can do is facilitate knowing by the young.

These extended or aided modes of apprehension are all cases of information pickup from a stimulus flux. The learner has to hear the speech in order to pick up the message; to see the model, the picture, or the writing; to manipulate the instrument in order to extract the information. But the information itself is largely independent of the stimulus flux.

What are the kinds of culturally transmitted knowledge? I am uncertain, for they have not been considered at this level of description. Present-day discussions of the "media of communication" seem to me glib and superficial. I suspect that there are many kinds merging into one another, of great complexity. But I can think of three obvious ways to facilitate knowing, to aid perceiving, or to extend the limits of comprehension: the use of instruments, the use of verbal descriptions, and the use of pictures. Words and pictures work in a different way than do instruments, for the information is obtained at second hand. Consider them separately.

KNOWING MEDIATED BY INSTRUMENTS

Surfaces and events that are too small or too far away cannot be perceived. You can of course increase the visual solid angle if you approach the item and put your eye close to it, but that procedure has its limits. You cannot approach the moon by walking, and you cannot get your eye close enough to a drop of pond water to see the little animals swimming in it. What can be done is to *enlarge* the visual solid angle from the moon or the water drop. You can convert a tiny sample of the ambient optic array at a point of observation into a magnified sample by means of a telescope or a microscope. The structure of the sample is only a little distorted. The surfaces perceived when the eye is placed at the eyepiece are "virtual" instead of "real," but only in the special sense that they are very much closer to the observer. The invariants of structure are nearly the same when a visual angle with its nested components is magnified. This description of magnification comes from ecological optics. For designing the lens system of the instrument, a different optics is needed.

The discovery of these instruments in the seventeenth century enabled men to know much more about very large bodies and very small bodies than they had before. But this new knowledge was almost like seeing. The mountains of the moon and the motions of a living cell could be observed with adjustments of the instrument not unlike those of the head and eyes. The guarantees of reality were similar. You did not have to take another person's word for what he had seen. You might have to learn to use the instrument, but you did not have to learn to interpret the information. Nor did you have to judge whether or not the other person was telling the truth. With a telescope or a microscope you could look for yourself.

THE UNAIDED PERCEIVING OF OBJECTS IN THE SKY

Objects in the sky are very different from objects on the ground. The heavenly bodies do not come to rest on the ground as ordinary objects do. The rainbow and the clouds are transient, forming and dissipating like mists on earth. But the sun, the moon, the planets, and the stars seem permanent, appearing to revolve around the stationary earth in perfect cycles and continuing to exist while out of sight. They are immortal and mysterious. They cannot be scrutinized.

Optical information for direct perception of these bodies with the unaided eye is lacking. Their size and distance are indeterminate except that they rise and set from behind the distant horizon and are thus very far away. Their motions are very different from those of ordinary objects. The character of their surfaces is indefinite, and of what substances they are composed is not clear. The sun is fiery by day, and the others are fiery at night, unlike the textured reflecting surfaces of most terrestrial objects. What they afford is not visible to the eye. Lights in the sky used to look like gods. Nowadays they look like flying saucers.

All sorts of instruments have been devised for mediating apprehension. Some optical instruments merely enhance the information that vision is ready to pick up; others—a spectroscope, for example—require some inference; still others, like the Wilson cloud chamber, demand a complex chain of inferences.

Some measuring instruments are closer to perception than others. The measuring stick for counting units of distance, the gravity balance for counting units of mass, and the hourglass for time are easy to understand. But the complex magnitudes of physical science are another matter. The voltmeters, accelerometers, and photometers are hard to understand. The child can see the pointer and the scale well enough but has to learn to "read" the instrument, as we say. The direct perception of a distance is in terms of whether one can jump it. The direct perception of a mass is in terms of whether one can lift it. Indirect knowledge of the metric dimensions of the world is a far extreme from direct perception of the affordance dimensions of the environment. Nevertheless, they are both cut from the same cloth.

KNOWING MEDIATED BY DESCRIPTIONS: EXPLICIT KNOWLEDGE

The principal way in which we save our children the trouble of finding out everything for themselves is by describing things for them. We transmit information and convey knowledge. Wisdom is handed down. Parents and teachers and books give the children knowledge of the world at second hand. Instead of having to be extracted by the child from the stimulus flux, this knowledge is communicated to the child.

It is surely true that speech and language convey information of a certain sort from person to person and from parent to child. Written language can even be stored so that it accumulates in libraries. But we should never forget that this is information that has been put into words. It is not the limitless information available in a flowing stimulus array.

Knowledge that has been put into words can be said to be *explicit* instead of *tacit*. The human observer can verbalize his awareness, and the result is to make it communicable. But my hypothesis is that there has to be an awareness of the world before it can be put into words. You have to see it before you can say it. Perceiving precedes predicating.

In the course of development the young child first hears talk about what she is perceiving. Then she begins herself to talk about what she perceives. Then she begins to talk to herself about what she knows—when she is alone in her crib, for example. And, finally, her verbal system probably begins to verbalize silently, in much the same way that the visual system begins to visualize, without the constraints of stimulation or muscular action but within the limits of the invariants to which the system is attuned. But no matter how much the child puts knowledge into words all of it cannot be put into words. However skilled an explicator one may become one will always, I believe, see more than one can say.

Consider an adult, a philosopher, for example, who sees the cat on the mat. He knows *that* the cat is on the mat and believes the proposition and can say it, but all the time he plainly sees all sorts of wordless facts—the mat extending without interruption behind the cat, the far side of the cat, the cat hiding part of the mat, the edges of the cat, the cat being supported by the mat, or resting on it, the horizontal rigidity of the floor under the mat, and so on. The so-called concepts of extension, of far and near, gravity, rigidity, horizontal, and so on, are nothing but partial abstractions from a rich but unitary perception of *cat-on-mat*. The parts of it he can name are called concepts, but they are not all of what he can see.

FACT AND FICTION IN WORDS AND PICTURES

Information about the environment that has been put into words has this disadvantage: The reality testing that accompanies the pickup of natural information is missing. Descriptions, spoken or written, do not permit the flowing stimulus array to be scrutinized. The invariants have already been extracted. You have to trust the original perceiver; you must "take his word for it," as we say. What he presents may be fact, or it may be fiction. The same is true of a depiction as of a description.

The child, as I argued above, has no difficulty in contrasting real and imaginary, and the two do not merge. But the factual and the fictional may do so. In storytelling, adults do not always distinguish between true stories and fairy stories. The child herself does not always separate the giving of an account from the telling of a story. Tigers and dragons are both fascinating beasts, and the child will not learn the difference until she perceives that the zoo contains the former but not the latter.

Fictions are not necessarily fantasies. They do not automatically lead one astray, as hallucinations do. They can promote creative plans. They can permit vicarious learning when the child identifies with a fictional character who solves problems and makes errors. The "comic" characters of childhood, the funny and the foolish, the strong and the weak, the clever and the stupid, occupy a great part of children's cognitive awareness, but this does not interfere in the least with their realism when it comes to perceiving.

The difference between the real and the imaginary is specified by two different modes of operation of a perceptual system. But the difference between the factual and the fictional depends on the social system of communication and brings in complicated questions. Verbal descriptions can be true or false as predications. Visual depictions can be correct or incorrect in a wholly different way. A picture cannot be true in the sense that a proposition is true, but it may or may not be true to life.

KNOWING AND IMAGINING MEDIATED
BY PICTURES

Perceiving, knowing, recalling, expecting, and imagining can all be induced by pictures, perhaps even more readily than by words. Picture-making and picture-perceiving have been going on for twenty or thirty thousand years of human life, and this achievement, like language, is ours alone. The image makers can arouse in us an awareness of what they have seen, of what they have noticed, of what they recall, expect, or imagine, and they do so *without converting the information into a different mode.* The description puts the optical invariants into words. The depiction, however, captures and displays them in an optic array, where they are more or less the same as they would be in the case of direct perception. So I will argue, at least. The justification of this theory is obviously not a simple matter, and it is deferred to the last chapters of this book, Part IV.

The reality-testing that accompanies unmediated perceiving and that is partly retained in perceiving with instruments is obviously lost in the kind of perceiving that is mediated by pictures. Nevertheless, pictures give us a kind of grasp on the rich complexities of the natural environment that words could never do. Pictures do not stereotype our experience in the same way and to the same degree. We can learn from pictures with less effort than it takes to learn from words. It is not like perceiving at first hand, but it is *more* like perceiving than any verbal description can be.

The child who has learned to talk about things and events can, metaphorically, talk to himself silently about things and events, so it is supposed. He is said to have "internalized" his speech, whatever that might mean. By analogy with this theory, a child who has learned to draw might be supposed to picture to himself things and events without movement of his hands, to have "internalized" his picturemaking. A theory of internal language and internal images might be based on this theory. But it seems to me very dubious. Whether or not it is plausible is best decided after we have considered picturemaking in its own right.

SUMMARY

When vision is thought of as a perceptual system instead of as a channel for inputs to the brain, a new theory of perception considered as information pickup becomes possible. Information is conceived as available in the ambient energy flux, not as signals in a bundle of nerve fibers. It is information about both the persisting and the changing features of the environment together. Moreover, information about the observer and his movements is available, so that self-awareness accompanies perceptual awareness.

The qualities of visual experience that are specific to the receptors stimulated are not relevant to information pickup but incidental to it. Excitation and transmission are facts of physiology at the cellular level.

The process of pickup involves not only overt movements that can be measured, such as orienting, exploring, and adjusting, but also more general activities, such as optimizing, resonating, and extracting invariants, that cannot so easily be measured.

The ecological theory of direct perception cannot stand by itself. It implies a new theory of cognition in general. In turn, that implies a new theory of noncognitive kinds of awareness—fictions, fantasies, dreams, and hallucinations.

Perceiving is the simplest and best kind of knowing. But there are other kinds, of which three were suggested. Knowing by means of instruments extends perceiving into the realm of the very distant and the very small; it also allows of metric knowledge. Knowing by means of language makes knowing explicit instead of tacit. Language permits descriptions and pools the accumulated observations of our ancestors. Knowing by means of pictures also extends perceiving and consolidates the gains of perceiving.

The awareness of imaginary entities and events might be ascribed to the operation of the perceptual system with a suspension of reality-testing. Imagination, as well as knowledge and perception, can be aroused by another person who uses language or makes pictures.

These tentative proposals are offered as a substitute for the outworn theory of past experience, memory, and mental images.

FOUR

DEPICTION

FIFTEEN

PICTURES
AND
VISUAL AWARENESS

Having rejected the picture theory of natural perception, we can make a start on picture perception. To see the environment is to extract information from the ambient array of light. What is it, then, to see a picture of something? The information in ambient light consists not of forms and colors but of invariants. Is it implied that the information in a picture does not consist of forms and colors but consists of invariants likewise? That sounds very odd, for we suppose that a picture is entirely composed of forms and colors.

The kind of vision we get from pictures is harder to understand than the kind we get from ambient light, not easier. It should be considered at the end of a treatise on perception, not at the beginning. It cannot be omitted, for pictures are as essential a part of human life as words. They are deeply puzzling and endlessly interesting. What are pictures, and what do they do for us? There are obviously two kinds: still pictures and motion pictures. This chapter is concerned with the first and the following chapter with the second. The motion picture is more like natural vision than the still picture, for the latter is an arrested image. The pictorial array is frozen in time and fixed at a single, unmoving point of observation. The cinematic array can display not only the information for seeing events but also that for a moving observer. It is technologically complex, however, and we had better treat it later.

THE SHOWING OF DRAWINGS AND THE
STUDY OF PERCEPTION

For countless centuries, certainly since the cavemen, artists have been making drawings, showing them to their neighbors, and asking what they saw. Sometime around a century ago, psychologists thought of presenting drawings to observers under controlled conditions and finding out what was perceived with systematic variation of the drawings. This made the procedure an experiment with an independent variable and a dependent variable consisting of the verbal (or other) response. But actually the artist as much as the psychologist, was experimenting with perception all along, even if not formally.

This ancient procedure is easy to carry out, but it is not a good way to begin the study of perception, for the observer is never quite sure how to answer the question, "What do you see?" A drawing does not have ecological validity. I use *drawing* in a general sense that includes a scribble, a form, or a pattern as well as a picture. It is the procedure that perceptionists use, however, on the assumption that a form on the retina is the basic stimulus and that form perception is the primary kind. A drawn form on paper is also said to be a stimulus, loosely speaking, and thus an experimenter can "apply" it to an animal or a baby as well as an adult. But is this a good way to begin the study of perception?

My own first effort in psychology was an experiment on the perception of drawings (Gibson, 1929), and I have been puzzling about such experiments ever since. My subjects had to reproduce the figures shown, but one could have them recognized, or matched, or described in words, or completed from a part. One could present line drawings or silhouettes, closed outlines or open, nonsense figures or meaningful ones, regular or irregular forms, simple or complex forms, scribbles or depictions, nameless blobs or specific representations, hen tracks or alphabetic characters, cursive or printed letters, upright or inverted forms, "good" forms or "bad" forms. All these variations and many others have been tried out. The results are disappointing. After hundreds of experiments, nothing decisive has emerged about visual perception, only perplexities. Wherein lies the meaning? Does a drawing have an intrinsic meaning or only an arbitrary meaning? Are there laws of organization that apply or only laws of association? Are there significant forms as such or only forms that represent objects? Can forms represent solid objects or only flat objects, and if the former, how?

Meanwhile, of course, modern artists of various schools have also been experimenting. Their drawings and paintings are said to be *nonrepresentative*, or *nonobjective*, or *nonfigurative*, or sometimes *abstract*; but the question is, what do we see? The artists, who do not have to worry about explicitness, have tried out a wider range of variations than the psychologists, and we now have a crowd of professional art critics trying to make them explicit. The critics, too, it seems to me, have not made any significant discoveries about visual perception. The old perplexities are unresolved.

The showing of drawings is thought to be a good way to begin the study of perception, because vision is supposed to be simplest when there is a form on the retina that is a *copy* of a form on a surface facing the retina. The retinal form is then in point-to-point correspondence with the drawn form, although inverted. But this is *not* the simplest case of vision, as the foregoing chapters have proved. Visual awareness of the surroundings cannot be explained on this supposition. Not even visual awareness of an object in space can be explained by it, because for any given form there exists an infinite set of possible objects in space and for any given solid object that moves there exists an infinite set of possible forms. A frozen form does not specify the solid shape of an object, *only some of the invariant features that a solid object must have,* as I explained in Chapter 9. And, in any case, we never see just a form; we see a sample of the ambient optic array. If I am right, most of the experiments by psychologists, including the gestalt psychologists, have been irrelevant.

As for the nonobjective painters, they scorn to represent domestic objects, animals, persons, gods, interiors, or landscapes in the old-fashioned way, but they claim that the forms and colors they put on canvas yield a direct experience of "space." What can be meant by that overworked term in this connection? The assertion that a still picture can yield an experience of "motion" is another paradox. Those terms are surely inappropriate in their physicomathematical meanings, but is there some truth in the claims?

Vision is simplest when it fulfills its function, not when it meets the criterion of one-to-one projective correspondence in geometry. Its function is to help the observer cope with the environment.

Figure 15.1
Projective correspondence. The correspondence of a geometrical form on one plane to a geometrical form on another.

The pencil of so-called rays that connect the two forms point-to-point is indicated only by four lines. In this diagram the common point of intersection of the rays in the pencil is between the planes, and one of the forms is therefore inverted relative to the other. One form is a congruent copy of the other when the two planes are parallel and equidistant from the point, or when they are parallel and the point is at infinity. In the latter case there is no inversion. Note that a pencil of geometrical rays as shown here, a sheaf or bundle of lines, is not the same as a focused pencil of radiating rays as shown in Figure 4.3. Geometrical optics and physical optics are not consistent in this respect.

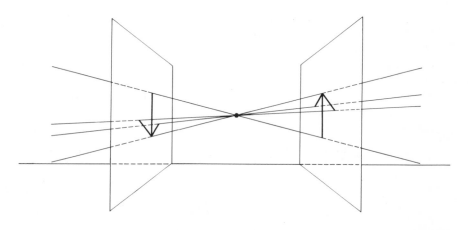

PICTURES AND VISUAL AWARENESS

WHAT IS A PICTURE?

The science of language is well established, but nothing even approximating a science of depiction exists. What artists, critics, and philosophers of art have to say about pictures has little in common with what photographers, opticists, and geometers have to say about them. They do not seem to be talking about the same topic. No one seems to know what a picture *is*.

Besides showing pictures to people, I have been trying to formulate a definition of a picture for years, but I have had to change it repeatedly as my optics shifted and my theory of perception developed. Perhaps the abandoned definitions will prove interesting as history. They can be found in four essays, only the last of which I would stand by (Gibson, 1954, 1960*b*, 1966*b* [Ch. 11], and 1971).

THE PICTURE AS AN ARRAY

All along I have maintained that a picture is a surface so treated that it makes available a limited optic array of some sort at a point of observation. But an array of what? That was the difficulty. My first answer was, *an array of pencils of light rays*. My second was, *an array of visual solid angles*, which become *nested solid angles* after a little thought. My third answer was, *an array considered as a structure*. And the final answer was, *an arrangement of invariants of structure*.

1. *An array of pencils of light coming to the pupil of an eye such that each corresponds in brightness (and hue, if any) to its radiating element of the picture surface.* This formula was my early attempt to apply classical optics to a picture. (A pencil of light rays to the pupil is illustrated in Chapter 4, Figure 4.3.) Because each pencil could be reduced to a single line from an element of the picture to the nodal point of the eye, I called the array a "sheaf of rays," as in projective geometry, which was confusing. (See the controversy about this in the *Handbook of Perception*, Boynton, 1974; Gibson, 1974.) There are many objections to this definition. For one thing, the supposed correspondence of brightness and color between elements of the array and elements of the picture is a great mystery. I was thinking of paintings and photographs that had what I called *fidelity* to the scene depicted, and the only kind of fidelity I could think of was of elements.

2. *An array of nested visual solid angles at the station point determined by steps or contrasts of intensity and spectral composition of the ambient light.* This definition is better, because it emphasizes the relations between genuine parts of an array instead of an abstract sheaf of lines intersecting at the eye, each with its point-sensation. The forms on the picture surface are unique and are included within larger forms. The solid

angles coming from a picture to its station point are analogous to the solid angles coming from the faces and facets of a layout to a point of observation.

3. *An array considered as a stationary structure.* This definition is still better, because structure includes gradients, discontinuities, and textures as well as simple contrasts. It begins to be information about an environment, not just stimulation. There are relations between relations, for which there are no names and no mathematical expressions. Gradual transitions in the array can specify shadows and curvatures in the world over and beyond the faces and facets of surfaces.

4. *An array of persisting invariants of structure that are nameless and formless.* This definition is the most general of all. It assumes that some of the invariants of an array can be separated from its perspective structure, not only when the perspective keeps changing, as in life, but also when it is arrested, as in a still picture. This says that formless invariants can be detected in a picture that seems to consist entirely of forms. Ordinarily, these invariants underlie the transformations and emerge most clearly when the persisting properties separate off from the changing properties, but they can also be distinguished in the limiting case of an unchanging structure.

The four essays on picture perception referred to above culminated in a fifth paper devoted to the concept of formless invariants (Gibson, 1973). Despite the argument that because a still picture presents no transformation it can display no invariants under transformation, I ventured to suggest that it did display invariants, even if weaker than those that emerged from a motion picture.

If it is true that the perception of a detached object is not compounded from a series of discrete forms of that object but depends instead on the invariant features of that family of forms over time, it follows that an arrested member of that unique family will have at least some of those invariants. If object perception depends on invariant detection instead of form perception, then form perception itself must entail some invariant detection.

This says that when the young child sees the family cat at play the front view, side view, rear view, top view, and so on are not seen, and what gets perceived is the *invariant* cat. The child does not notice the aspects of perspectives of the cat until he is much older; he just sees the cat rolling over. Hence, when the child first sees a picture of a cat he is prepared to pick up the invariants, and he pays no attention to the frozen perspective of the picture, drawing, photograph, or cartoon. It is not that he sees an abstract cat, or a conceptual cat, or the common features of the class of cats, as some philosophers would have us believe; what he gets is the information for the persistence of that peculiar, furry, mobile layout of surfaces.

When the young child sees the cat run away, he does not notice the small image but sees the far-off cat. Thus, when he sees two adjacent pictures of Felix in the comic book, a large Felix at the bottom of its picture and another small Felix higher up in its picture, he is prepared to perceive the latter as farther off. When he sees the cat half-hidden by the chair, he perceives a partly hidden cat, not a half-cat, and therefore he is prepared to see the same thing in a drawing.

The child never sees a man as a silhouette, or as a cutout like a paper doll, but probably sees a sort of head-body-arms-legs invariant. Consequently, any outline drawing with this invariant is recognized as a man, and the outlines tend to be seen as the occluding edges of a man with interchangeable near and far sides. Even when the outlines give way to line segments, as in so-called stick figures, the invariant may still be displayed and the man perceived.

The perceiving of the cat-on-the-mat contains invariants that are not explicit, as I pointed out in the last chapter. But they can be pictured. The gradient of size and the gradient of density of texture are invariants; the horizon considered as the line where sizes and textures diminish to zero is an invariant. There are many kinds of invariants.

To summarize, a picture is a surface so treated that it makes available an optic array of arrested structures with underlying invariants of structure. The cross-sections of the visual angles of the array are forms, but the invariants are formless. The array is delimited, not ambient. The array is arrested in time, except for the case of the motion picture, which will be considered in the next chapter. The surface can be treated in many ways so as to make the array available: by painting or drawing or depositing pigment on it so as to modify its reflectance or its transmittance; by engraving or indenting it so as to make shadows and give relief; or by casting light and shade on it so as to produce a temporary picture, in which case we call the surface a *screen* and the shadow caster a *projector*. These fundamental ways of creating an artificial array were discussed in Chapter 11 of my earlier book on perception (Gibson, 1966*b*). Whatever the artist may do, however, he cannot avoid showing his surface *in the midst of other surfaces of an environment. A picture can only be seen in a context of other nonpictorial surfaces.*

The enormously complex technologies of picture-making fall into two different types, the photographic methods that are only a hundred and fifty years old and what I like to call the *chirographic* methods (Gibson, 1954, p. 21) that have been practiced for at least twenty thousand years. The former involve a camera with accessory equipment for the hand-eye system of a human observer, and the latter involve a graphic tool of some sort for the hand-eye system. The invariants made available by these two ways of treating a surface have much in common but are not equivalent, as will be evident in the next section. The photographic picture has a unique, fixed station point in front of the surface. The chirographic picture may or may not have a unique station point, depending on whether or not it was drawn in so-called correct perspective. The actual point of observation will usually not coincide with the unique station point, however, since a rule for viewing a picture cannot be enforced in practice. (See the "prescriptions" of artificial perspective and the misunderstandings to which they have led, discussed later in this chapter.)

Note that treatment of a surface to display invariants excludes the case of treatment that modifies the surface as such. The surface can be ornamented, decorated, embellished; its reflectance can be altered; its texture can be changed—all *without causing it to specify something other than what it is, a surface.* No doubt there are true mixtures of decoration and description, especially in architecture and pottery, but the extremes are distinct. The painter who is a decorator and the painter who is a depictor are different people and should not be confused. Aesthetics, in my opinion, has nothing to do with it. We can distinguish between a surface as an aesthetic object and a surface as a display of information. The surface that displays information may *also* be an aesthetic object, but the cases are different. A *picture* is a surface that always specifies something other than what it is.

THE PICTURE AS A RECORD

The above definition is not sufficient. To say that a picture yields an array of optical information clears up a welter of confusion, I think, but it does not say enough. A

PICTURES FOR EDUCATION AND TRAINING

I became interested in pictures and films during the war as a psychologist concerned with training young men to fly airplanes. In 1940–1946 a million Americans were learning this quite unnatural skill. I was impressed by the possibilities of visual education, inadequately so-called. You cannot *tell* students how to fly; you cannot let them learn by trial and error. You can have them learn by imitation, but that is expensive; you should try to *show* them how to fly. If the stimulus situation could be *simulated,* they would learn without danger of crashing. But just how did a picture, still or moving, simulate the real situation that the student would later face? How did pictures in general prepare the young for life? The literature of visual education proved to be worthless. I wrote an essay entitled "Pictures as Substitutes for Visual Realities" (Gibson, 1947, Ch. 8), and then "A Theory of Pictorial Perception" (Gibson, 1954), abondoning one definition of a picture after another for twenty years, as noted above. A student of mine has written a book called *A Psychology of Picture Perception* (Kennedy, 1974) which makes a beginning but still does not get to the heart of the problem.

This is the problem of the picture as a provider of secondhand perception. It becomes even more difficult if extended to the picture as a source of secondhand fantasy, a provider of fictions, of creative imagination, of aesthetic enjoyment, or the picture as a way in which its maker can think without words (Arnheim, 1969).

picture is also a *record*. It enables the invariants that have been extracted by an observer—at least, some of them—to be stored, saved, put away and retrieved, or exchanged. Pictures are like writing inasmuch as they can be looked at again and again by the same observer and looked at by many observers. They allow the original observer to communicate in a fashion with unborn generations of other observers. Art museums, like libraries, are storehouses of knowledge, and they permit knowledge to accumulate. Pictures convey knowledge at second hand and thus are efficient methods of teaching the young. But the knowledge they convey is not explicit. It is not put into words. Most of the formless invariants in the array from a picture could not be put into words anyway. They can be captured by an artist but not described.

What exactly is a picture a record of? I used to think that it was a record of perception, of what the picture maker was seeing at the time she made the picture at the point of observation she then occupied. It *can* be a record of perception, to be sure, and a photographic picture is such a record, but the chirographic picture need not be. I tried to describe several kinds of nonperceptual experiences in the last chapter, and the artist can make a record of these just as well as she can of what she perceives. She can record imaginary things, from the probable and possible all the way to the most fantastic of her dreams and hallucinations. She can paint her recollection of something that no longer exists. She can paint fictions. And even when she is perceiving she is seeing into the past and the future to some extent, so that she captures more than the surfaces projected at the instantaneous present.

Even a photograph records a field of view, a sample of the ambient light, and is thus analogous to looking with the head. It is a record of what the photographer selected for attention. A chirograph is even more selective. Any picture, then, *preserves what its creator has noticed and considers worth noticing*. Even when she paints a fiction or a fantasy, she does it with invariants that have been noticed in the course of learning to perceive.

A THEORY OF DRAWING AND ITS DEVELOPMENT IN THE CHILD

Let us consider this remarkable business of preserving what one is aware of; let us try to understand it. Cro-Magnon man drew pictures of what interested him on the walls of caves, and people of all cultures have been drawing pictures ever since. All of us can draw, even those who never learned to write. Writing was not invented until our ancestors learned to record their *words* on a surface, and that is harder to learn than recording an awareness. Ideographs and syllabaries and alphabets would never have been devised if people had not already been drawing for thousands of years. But what *is* drawing?

The lore and literature of drawing masters and schools of art provide no help in answering this question. The manuals on how to draw are thoroughly confusing, for there has never been a coherent theory of the cooperation of the eye and the hand. Courses in mechanical or geometrical drawing using a ruler and compass do not answer the question. Neither do courses in architectural drawing. The courses in so-called graphics that I am familiar with are full of inexcusable contradictions, glossed over for the sake of covering up ignorance. The courses in so-called basic design are equally sloppy. Do we now have a coherent theory of the cooperation of eye and hand? Not yet, but perhaps the assumptions of Chapter 12 on the visual control of manipulation will give us at least a beginning.

THE FUNDAMENTAL GRAPHIC ACT

In the child, both drawing and writing develop from what I call the *fundamental graphic act*, the making of traces on a surface that constitute a progressive record of movement (Gibson, 1966b, Ch. 11). Presumably our primitive ancestors had also been making and observing traces long before the first artist discovered that by means of lines one could *delineate* something. The first man to make a mammoth appear on the wall of a cave was, I am confident, amazed by what he had done. The chimpanzee can make scribbles and do finger painting, but he cannot draw anything.

The words we have for this fundamental graphic act describe it badly and belittle it—scribbling, dabbling, doodling, daubing, scratching, and so on. But we should study it carefully and not belittle it. Of all the hand-held tools that have been invented, the sort that makes traces on a surface is especially noteworthy—the stylus, brush, pen, pencil, crayon, or marker. The movement of the tool over the surface is both felt and seen. The muscle-joint-skin kinesthesis is emphasized by orthodox sensory psychology, and the visual kinesthesis is emphasized by my perceptual psychology. But these are transient awarenesses. The seeing of a progressive record of the movement of the tool is lasting. There is a track or trail of the movement, like the afterimage of a firebrand whirled in the darkness, except that it is permanent—a stroke, a stripe, or a streak, in short a trace. This emphasizes lines and pointed tools, but the same principles hold for patches and brushlike tools.

The young child practices the fundamental graphic act in sand, mud, or a plate of food, to the dismay of his parents. When given a tracing tool, the child uses it on approved surfaces as soon as he can hold the tool, beginning at around sixteen months of age. The permanent trace is what interests the child. Gibson and Yonas (1968) found that one-and-a-half to three-year-olds who scribbled zealously with a pencil would stop when a nontracing pencil that provided everything but the trace was secretly substituted. Moreover, three-year-old scribblers in a nursery school refused to "draw a picture in the air" on request and asked for paper on which they could draw a "real picture."

Now consider what the child will begin to notice as he sees the accumulating traces on a surface, and if he sees them frequently. He has no words for what is there; in fact, there are no adequate terms for it.

The quality called *straight* looks different from that called *curved,* and there are opposite curves.
The trace can begin and end, or it can be continuous.
A continuous trace can change direction with a jerk, a zigzag (although terms such as *angle* and *apex* will not be learned for years).
A line can be made between existing marks to connect them, and marks can be *lined up.*
A continuous trace can come back to where it began, whereupon a peculiar feature emerges that we call *closure.*
A continuous trace is apt to produce an invariant called *intersection.* It makes *connections.*
Traces that do not intersect are very peculiar, and some have the quality of being *parallel.*
It will become evident that a new trace that exactly follows an old one adds nothing to the display (although the term *coincide* has yet to be learned).
It may be noticed that a trace on one sheet of paper can be *fitted over* a trace on another sheet, in the same way that a child's block can be fitted into an aperture (the template, or so-called form board). This is preparation for the axiom of *congruence* in Euclidean geometry.

All of these features in the scribbles of childhood are invariants. While they are being noticed in the child's own trace-making, they are surely also being noticed in the pictures that are shown him in the nursery, and eventually some of the natural invariants that appeared in the ambient array from the outset will begin to be identified with the graphic invariants.

REPLICATING OR COPYING

Copying is fundamentally the act of making traces on a surface that coincide with the traces on another surface, either one surface overlaid on another or one that could be overlaid on another. The child can "trace over" an existing trace, or he can "trace" an existing pattern on a transparent or semitransparent overlay so as to replicate it. He can thus perceive the congruence of the two patterns. He learns how to match traces and to see the match, or the mismatch, of separated traces. Eventually he will learn other methods of printing and template matching, but the graphic method, I suspect, comes first.

To copy by comparison is harder than to copy by coincidence-tracing. The ability to copy freehand a diamond-shaped form is not achieved by the average child until age seven, according to the Binet test norms. What we call *freehand trace-making* refers also to the fact that the movement of the tool is not constrained by a ruler, a compass, a scale, or any other drawing instrument. But it is controlled by something. I suggest that it is controlled by invariants of the sort listed.

Making a perspective drawing of a scene on a sheet of glass is a special case of coincidence-tracing. This was the method of artificial perspective discovered by the painters of the Renaissance and recommended by Leonardo da Vinci. It involves setting up the glass as if it were a window and then, with one eye exactly fixed in front of the window, drawing lines on the surface to coincide with the projections of the *occluding edges* of the layout, the *edges* and *corners* of the layout (the dihedrals), and the *fissures, sticks, fibers,* and *pigment borders* (Chapter 3). The penumbras of shadows or the shading of curved surfaces cannot be traced, however, and the method is not as easy as it is made to sound. Actually, it is not a practicable method but a sort of demonstration

Figure 15.2
The perspective projection on a picture plane of square units
of the ground out to the horizon.

This drawing shows the main invariants of artificial perspective as distinguished from those of natural perspective, which were shown in Figure 5.1. The parallel edges of a track or a pavement project to straight lines that converge to a point, the vanishing point. The squares of the track correspond to trapezoids on the picture plane, diminishing as a function of distance. No one who studies this drawing could fail to be impressed by the elegance of the principles of pictorial perspective.

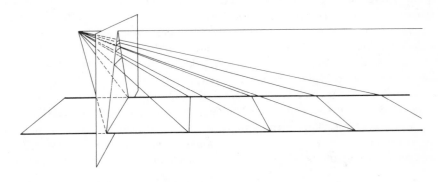

of how to visualize the surface of the canvas as if it were a transparent picture plane. The implication is that something like freehand copying is possible for a scene as well as for another drawing. But this, I believe, is false.

The terms *copy, replica, duplicate,* and *image,* however familiar, are vague and slippery. The ghostly copy of an ideal form on a transparent plane was illustrated in Figure 15.1, but the making of substantial copies on surfaces and sheets with ink or pigment is another matter entirely.

DRAWING PROPER

By gradual stages human children begin to draw in the full meaning of the term—to draw a man or a woman, a house, a flower, or the sun in the sky. The child is still making lines on a surface that record the movements of the tool in his hand, but he is now also recording an awareness in terms of the invariants he has picked up. He delineates for himself and others something he has apprehended or experienced. The traces he leaves on the paper are not just lines, or the outlines of forms, but the distinguishing features of the environment. While drawing, he may be looking at something real, or thinking about something real, or thinking about something wholly imaginary; in any case, the invariants of his visual system are resonating. The same is true of the artist as of the child. The invariants are not abstractions or concepts. They are not knowledge; they are simply invariants.

Let us contrast this theory of drawing with the traditional theory. The latter assumes that drawing is either from "life," from "memory," or from "imagination." Drawing is always copying. The copying of a perceptual image is drawing from life. The copying of a stored image in the mind is drawing from memory. The copying of an image constructed from other memory images is drawing from imagination. This theory of drawing is consistent with the mentalistic doctrine that assumes an optical image on the retina, a physiological image in the receptors, a transmitted image in the nerve, a cerebral image in the brain, and finally a mental image in the mind that is subject to all sorts of creative transformations.

How is the copying of an image supposed to occur? An ancient metaphor is often appealed to, the *projection* of an image outward from the eye. Many persons ignorant of vision find this easy to accept. The notion is lent a false plausibility by the fact that the aftersensation caused by overstimulating the retinal receptors with a strong light is called an afterimage and is visible on any surface looked at as long as the eye is fixed. If a physiological afterimage impressed on the retina can thus be thrown outward, why not a mental afterimage imposed on the brain? So the reasoning goes. Drawing from life would consist of looking at the model and getting an image, looking at the drawing pad, and then just tracing around the outline of the projected image. Drawing from memory or imagination would differ only in that the artist has to "consult" her memory and "summon" an image. If she cannot trace around the projected mental image, at least she can copy it freehand. Perhaps drawing is not exactly like this, they say, but *something* like this. Otherwise, what could it be? The projecting of a mental image outward upon an *existing* drawing is even supposed to explain one's perception of the drawing, as E. H. Gombrich (1960), for example, maintained at one time.

I insist that what the draftsman, beginner or expert, actually does is not to replicate, to print, or to copy in any sense of the term but to mark the surface in such a way as to display invariants and record an awareness. Drawing is never copying. It is impossible to copy a piece of the environment. Only another drawing can be copied. We have been misled for too long by the fallacy that a picture is *similar* to what it depicts, a *likeness*, or an *imitation* of it. A picture supplies some of the information for what it depicts, but that does not imply that it is in projective correspondence with what it depicts.

THE MUDDLE OF REPRESENTATION

If this new theory is correct, the term *representation* is misleading. There is no such thing as a literal re-presentation of an earlier optic array. The scene cannot be re-established; the array cannot be reconstituted. Some of its invariants can be preserved, but that is all. Even a photograph, a color photograph at its technological best, cannot preserve all the information at a point of observation in a natural environment, for that information is unlimited. As for re-presenting the stimulation in the sense of reimposing an old pattern of light energies on the retina, that is quite impossible. The full range

---

THE CONCEPT OF PROJECTION

Ever since it was first realized that an image of a solid object in the sense of its form or figure could be "thrown" upon a surface by a source of light such as the sun or a candle flame, the relation of the object to its shadow and the nature of this projection have provided food for thought. Art and geometry, philosophy, psychology, physiology, optics, and mathematics have borrowed the concept. Plato used it in the parable of the cave, whose dwellers could never perceive real objects but only their shadows cast upon the wall before them. The notion of projective correspondence in geometry came from this concept. The shadow plays came from it. The throwing of lantern slides on a screen by a projector came from it. The projecting outward of a mental image on a surface comes from it and I will have more to say about this later. But this is not consistent with the projecting *inward* of the form of an object onto the retinal surface and thence into the mind. Nevertheless, despite this contradiction, both kinds of projection, outward and inward, are accepted by those who believe that perception involves both a retinal image and a mental image.

---

of energies and wavelengths in light cannot be preserved on film. Some of the ratios, the contrasts or relations in the light, can be captured but not the sensations of brightness and color.

The efforts made by philosophers and psychologists to clarify what is meant by a *representation* have failed, it seems to me, because the concept is wrong. A picture is not an imitation of past seeing. It is not a substitute for going back and looking again. What it records, registers, or consolidates is information, not sense data.

WHAT ABOUT THE ILLUSION OF REALITY?
THE DUALITY OF PICTURE PERCEPTION

A picture is not like perceiving. Nevertheless, a picture is somehow *more* like perceiving an object, place, or person than is a verbal description. The illusion of reality is said to be possible. Painting can reach a degree of perfection, we are told, such that

Figure 15.3
Drawing by Alain. (© 1955 The New Yorker Magazine, Inc.)

viewers cannot tell whether what they see is a canvas treated with pigments or the real surfaces that the painter saw, viewed as if through a window. In his monumental study of pictorial representation, Gombrich (1960, p. 206) repeats the story of the Greek painter who had imitated grapes so perfectly that the birds came to peck at them, and the story of his rival who bested him by painting a curtain so deceptively that the painter himself tried to lift it from the panel. The tradition of "fooling the eye" is very ancient. The assumption that a false perception of real surfaces can be induced in the art gallery or the psychological laboratory is widely believed. If the artificial array is the same as the natural array, it will yield the same perception. There will arise an *illusion* of reality without a genuine reality. The perception of a solid cylindrical tunnel can be brought about by a mere display of light and dark rings, according to the experiment I described in Chapter 9. The eye is easily deceived, and our faith in the reality of what we see is therefore precarious. For two millenniums we have been told so.

The purveyors of this doctrine disregard certain facts. The deception is possible only for a single eye at a fixed point of observation with a constricted field of view, for what I called *aperture vision*. This is not genuine vision, not as conceived in this book. Only the eye considered as a fixed camera can be deceived. The actual binocular visual system cannot. A viewer can always tell whether he is looking at a picture or at a real scene through a window. I do not believe the stories about birds and painters being fooled, any more than I believe that Pygmalion really fell in love with his statue. The illusion of reality is a myth. The same automatic tests for reality that distinguish between a perception and a mental image, as described in the last chapter, will also distinguish between a perception and a physical image. We go on believing the myth only because it fits with what the authorities tell us about perception, with retinal image optics.

A picture, photographic or chirographic, is always a treated surface, and it is always seen in a context of other nonpictorial surfaces. Along with the invariants for the depicted layout of surfaces, there are invariants for the surface as such. It is a plaster wall, or a sheet of canvas, a panel, a screen, or a piece of paper. The glass, texture, edges, or frame of the picture surface are given in the array, and they are perceived. The information displayed is dual. The picture is both a scene and a surface, and the scene is paradoxically *behind* the surface. This duality of the information is the reason the observer is never quite sure how to answer the question, "What do you see?" For he can perfectly well answer that he sees a wall or a piece of paper. It is this duality in the optic array from a picture that makes the drawing a bad way to begin the study of perception.

I have in my time, like many perceptionists, arranged for a display of information to be seen through a peephole, that is, to be viewed through an aperture close to the eye. This is supposed to minimize the information for the surface as such and enhance the illusion of reality. I find, however, that, far from being a simple expedient, it complicates the act of perception. Keeping the observer from making tests for reality does not increase the impression of reality.

No painter and no photographer should ever strive to give viewers the feeling that they are looking at a real place, object, person, or event. There is no need to do so. In any case, the effort is bound to be a failure.

A picture is both a surface in its own right and a display of information about something else. The viewer cannot help but see both, yet this is a paradox, for the two kinds of awareness are discrepant. We distinguish between the surface *of* the picture and the surfaces *in* the picture. In such paintings as those of the impressionists, we can see the difference between the illumination *of* the picture and the illumination *in* the picture. The two sets of surfaces are not comparable, and the two kinds of illumination are not commensurable.

I once took a good, sharp photograph of a lawn with trees and a paved walk and had it enlarged about twenty times so that it could be mounted on a six-foot panel. The observer stood at a point where the visual angle of the picture at his eye was the same as the visual angle of the array admitted to the camera. He was told to estimate distances in terms of the number of paces needed. To the question, "How far away from you is the elm tree?" he would visualize himself walking up to it and reply, "Thirty paces." But to the question, "How far away from you is the picture?" he would pause and reply, "Oh, that's four paces." For the latter estimate he had to shift the operation of his visual system so as to pick up quite different invariants. The lawn in the picture was not *connected* with the floor of the room.

Consider next the kind of picture that stands at a far extreme from the photomural above. Psychologists have long been showing inkblots to their subjects and asking what they saw. A set of such random blobs on cards devised by Hermann Rorschach has now been standardized and is in use by clinical psychologists. Faced with a card, a sensible patient might very well say simply that she saw a blot, but she seldom does. She attends to the nameless squiggles, contours, textures, and colors and says, "A bleeding heart" or "A pair of dancing bears," allowing the psychologist to diagnose her fantasy life. I have argued that a Rorschach blot is a picture of sorts containing information not only for bleeding hearts and dancing bears but for dozens of other events (Gibson, 1956). It is different from a regular picture in that the invariants are all mixed up together and are mutually discrepant instead of being mutually consistent or redundant. It is rather like a mass of scribbles for a child in this respect.

The old mentalistic explanation of perceiving objects in clouds and inkblots, incidentally, is *projection*, the projecting outward of fantasy images from the unconscious mind as if by a mental magic lantern. Hence, the Rorschach is called a "projective" test. This is mischievous nonsense. But the dogma of two different contributions to perception, one objective and one subjective, one coming from the world and the other coming from the mind, is so strong that the notion of a picture being thrown outward to mix with a picture being thrown inward is widely believed.

What are we to call the tree in the photograph, or the bleeding heart in the inkblot? Neither is an object in my terminology. I am tempted to call them *virtual objects*. They are not perceived, and yet they are perceived. The duality of the information in the array is what causes the dual experience. We need to understand the apprehension of virtual objects and, of course, virtual places, events, and persons. We can only do so in connection with the perceiving of the real surfaces of the environment, including the picture surfaces. Note that our distinction between *virtual* and *real* will have to be independent of the distinction in classical optics between virtual and real *images*, which is swamped in epistemological confusion.

I conclude that a picture always requires two kinds of apprehension that go on at the same time, one direct and the other indirect. There is a direct perceiving of the picture surface along with an indirect awareness of virtual surface—a perceiving, knowing, or imagining, as the case may be.

THE POWER OF PERSPECTIVE IN PAINTING

If it is not true that a picture in perspective represents reality and a picture not in perspective fails to represent reality, what is true? My answer is that if a picture displays the perspective of a scene it puts the viewer into the scene, but that is all. It does not enhance the reality of the scene. The seeing of oneself is not negligible, but it is not the sole aim of depiction. The advocates of perspective representation are mistaken, but those who reject perspective as a mere convention are also mistaken. There is complete confusion on all sides. The terms in which that debate has proceeded are thoroughly misleading.

The dogma that linear perspective adds depth to a picture along with the other kinds of perspective that are "cues" for depth is a source of endless confusion. The term *perspective* is generally misunderstood. The theory of projection on a transparent picture plane to a stationpoint is a Renaissance discovery that is properly called *artificial perspective*. The theory of the ambient optic array from an environment to a point of observation should be called *natural perspective* and is not at all the same thing. Artificial perspective leads to a set of prescriptions for producing virtual streets, buildings, and interiors seen from a fixed position and a corollary requiring that the painting be viewed with one eye at a unique station point. Natural perspective leads to ecological optics and the concept of the invariant structure in a changing optic array. On the one hand, painters are inclined to reject the prescriptions of artificial perspective but are then tempted to disbelieve in any kind of perspective. On the other hand, scientists who are impressed with classical optics and the elegance of projective geometry are tempted to disbelieve in the efforts of modern painters. Each side is talking past the other.

What they need to understand in order to find a common ground, I think, is how it is possible for an observer to see something from no point of observation as well as from a given point of observation, that is, from a *path* of observation as well as a *position*. What modern painters are trying to do, if they only knew it, is paint invariants. What should interest them is not abstractions, not concepts, not space, not motion, but invariants.

The separation of invariant structure from perspective structure is the heart of the problem. The invariants display a world with nobody in it, and the perspective displays where the observer is in that world. One can depict without a fixed point of observation, just as one can visualize without a point of observation, although it is not easy to understand how. But depiction with a point of observation is the more natural sort, and the photographic picture is necessarily of this sort.

There are metaphors to describe the powerful experience aroused by the picture that locates the observer in a virtual environment: one is taken out of oneself; one is transported; one is set down in a far place. The place may be a distant part of the real environment or another world. Travel pictures take one to where the traveler has been. Battle pictures take one into the heart of the melee. Historical pictures take one to the forum of ancient Rome. Religious pictures take one straight to heaven, or hell. The viewer sees himself in the environment, for it extends out beyond the frame of the picture.

What is induced in these pictures is not an illusion of reality but an awareness of being in the world. This is no illusion. It is a legitimate goal of depiction, if not the only one.

IS DEPICTION A FORM OF DESCRIPTION?

It is troublesome for a painter to follow the prescriptions of artificial perspective, as any serious work on the subject clearly shows (e.g., Ware, 1900). Even when the prescriptions are followed it is impossible to enforce the rule for the beholder, for no viewer could be expected to maintain one eye at the proper station point in the air in front of the picture, even if the art gallery provided a bite-board or headrest to specify the viewpoint for each painting hung. But that is the only way to prevent distortions of the virtual layout, as students of perspective have long known and as the book by M. H. Pirenne (1970) has fully explained. The distortions themselves are not all that serious. Perspective was not worth the trouble, painters thought. The photographer could make an exact perspective picture automatically, so why bother to master all that geometry? It was a complicated and controversial business in any case. Visual scientists with all their theorizing know little about the actual art of painting. A fine art should not be subject to rules and regulations. This is the attitude of many modern painters and most schools of art.

The theory that artificial perspective is no more than a convention of Western art is a way of justifying this attitude. E. Panofsky (1924–1925) asserted that perspective is "symbolic." G. Kepes (1944) has written about the "language" of vision. R. Arnheim (1954) believes that we will learn to see what is represented by abstract painters even if we now cannot. And N. Goodman (1968) in *Languages of Art* assumes that depiction is fundamentally description, that we learn to read a picture as we learn a language, and that linear perspective could just as well be reversed from the way we have become accustomed to interpret it.

Now it is one thing to argue that the use of perspective is not necessary for a painting, but it is quite another to say that perspective is a language. That says that both the perspective and the invariants of a picture must be analogous to words and that, just as we can learn a new vocabulary, so we can learn a new mode of perception. If a language of words can be invented such as Esperanto, why not a language of art? But the essence of a picture is just that its information is *not* explicit. The invariants *cannot* be put into words or symbols. The depiction captures an awareness without describing it. The record has not been forced into predications and propositions. There is no way of describing the awareness of being in the environment at a certain place. Novelists attempt it, of course, but they cannot put you in the picture in anything like the way the painter can.

THE CONSCIOUSNESS OF THE
VISUAL FIELD

The doctrine of flat visual sensations together with the theories of sensation-based perception, of the cues for depth, and of how the cues get interpreted developed in close connection with the rise of perspective painting from the Renaissance to the nineteenth century. A picture was obviously a patchwork of pigments on a surface. By analogy the picture in the eye was a patchwork of colored light on the retinal surface. Hence, the deliverance of the eye to the mind was a corresponding patchwork of visual sensations. This was supposed to be what the infant saw at birth, and what a person born blind but given sight by the removal of a cataract saw when the bandage was first removed (Senden, 1960). The patchwork was the innate basis of visual perception, the product of untutored vision, unprejudiced by learning. The duty of a painter, said John

Ruskin, was to recover the *innocent eye* of infancy in depicting nature (Gombrich, 1960, p. 296). All psychologists accepted the doctrine of two-dimensional sensations; they disagreed only in that some believed the cues for depth to be wholly learned and others supposed that concepts of space were innate.

It has been generally believed that even adults can become conscious of their visual sensations if they try. You have to take an introspective attitude, or analyze your experience into its elements, or pay attention to the data of your perception, or stare at something persistently until the meaning fades away. I once believed it myself. I suggested that the "visual field" could be attended to, as distinguished from the "visual world," and that it was *almost* a flat patchwork of colors, like a painting on a plane surface facing the eye (Gibson, 1950*b*, Ch. 3). The awareness of depth in the scene could not be wholly eliminated, I thought, but it could be reduced. The similarity to a painting could be enhanced by not rotating the head and not displacing it, by closing one eye, and by avoiding any scene with motion. I recognized even then that the normal field of view of an ocular orbit is continually changing and that an arrested pattern is exceptional.

My comparison of the visual field to a perspective painting, although guarded, now seems to me a serious mistake. No one ever saw the world as a flat patchwork of colors—no infant, no cataract patient, and not even Bishop Berkeley or Baron von Helmholtz, who believed firmly that the cues for depth were learned. The notion of a patchwork of colors comes from the art of painting, not from any unbiased description of visual experience. What one becomes aware of by holding still, closing one eye, and observing a frozen scene are not visual sensations but only *the surfaces of the world that are viewed now from here.* They are not flat or depthless but simply unhidden. One's attention is called to the fact of occlusion, not to the pseudofact of the third dimension. I notice the surfaces that face me, and what I face, and thus where I am. The attitude might be called introspective or subjective, but it is actually a reciprocal, two-way attitude, not a looking inward. The surfaces viewed now from here were illustrated in Figure 11.1.

WHAT IS IT TO SEE IN PERSPECTIVE? PATCHWORK PERSPECTIVE VS. EDGE PERSPECTIVE

One can learn to view an object in perspective, or a whole vista, but that does not imply learning to see it as if it were a picture. One does not flatten out the object or the scene as if painting it on a picture plane; all one does is *separate* the hidden from the unhidden surfaces and observe the occluding edges. The natural perspective of visual solid angles is what counts here, not the artificial perspective of pigment patches.

Drawing in perspective does depend on viewing in perspective, it is true, but this only means that drawing requires the learner to notice the edges of the layout confronting him, especially the occluding edges. He must also notice other invariants, of course, but the edges are the fundamental basis for his picture. What we loosely call an outline in a picture refers to the outer edges of the face of an object. The surfaces need to be specified first in a picture; the colors, textures, shadows, and illumination can be rendered later. I am saying that edge perspective is a fact, whereas patchwork perspective is a myth. One can learn to view the former but not to see the latter.

The young child learning to draw has long interested both psychologists and artists. When he first draws a man or a truck or a table, I suggest, he depicts the invariants that he has learned to notice. He does not draw in patchwork perspective, for he never had the experience of a patchwork. He may not yet draw in edge perspective because he has not noticed it. Hence, he may draw a table with a rectangular top and four legs at the corners because those are the invariant features of the table he has noticed. This is a better explanation than saying he draws what he *knows* about the table, his concept, instead of what he *sees* of the table, his sensation. The fatal flaw of the latter explanation is that it ought to be the other way around. The child should begin by drawing sensations and progress to drawing concepts.

THE PRINCIPLES OF LINE DRAWING

To the extent that the natural optic array is composed of visual solid angles, and only to that extent, the information in the array can be captured by a line drawing. The envelopes of the solid angles, being discontinuous, must correspond to discontinuities in the environment instead of gradual transitions. More precisely, a line drawing can specify the following invariants of surface layout: a corner (the apex of a concave dihedral), an edge (the apex of a convex dihedral), an occluding edge (either apical or curved), a wire (fiber), a fissure (crack in a surface), and a skyline (division between earth and sky). A line drawing *cannot* specify the following invariants: the shading on a curved surface, the penumbra of a cast chadow, the texture of a surface, or the reflectance (color) of a surface, although it can specify an abrupt discontinuity of shading, of texture, and of color. The features of a terrestrial layout that can be shown by lines are illustrated in Figure 15.4.

The lines of a line drawing must *connect* with one another. They divide the picture into superordinate and subordinate areas in a lawful way. There must be visual solid angles at the station point of the picture analogous to visual solid angles at the point of observation of a natural optic array, those coming from the faces of surfaces, from the openings between surfaces, and from the patches of sky. The lines that separate areas on the picture plane should therefore not be called *outlines*, for this term implies detached objects in empty space and the fallacy that figure-on-ground is the prototype of perception. The term refers mainly to the occluding edge of a detached object but not to that of an aperture. A line in a line drawing can occlude either inward or outward depending on its connection with other lines. And a convex or concave dihedral, the junction of two planar surfaces, is given by a line, but this is not an "outline." The term *outline drawing* should be confined to the unusual and misleading case of a line with closure, one that returns upon itself, a form, and this kind of display contains only the weakest sort of information about anything, as I pointed out at the beginning of this chapter. It does not even specify the solid shape of a detached object.

The information in a line drawing is evidently carried by the *connections* of the lines, not by lines as such. To put it another way, the invariants are found in the ways that the areas are *nested,* not in the forms of these areas. These ways are difficult to describe in words. The connections, junctions, and intersections of lines remain invariant under a changing perspective of the surfaces.

Figure 15.4
Some of the possible meanings of a line: corner, edge, occluding edge,
wire, fissure, skyline, horizon, margin.
Can you find all these things in the picture?

A line segment in a drawing connected at one end in one way and at the other end in an incompatible way may specify a discrepancy in the layout of surfaces. This is the basis, I think, of the depictions of "impossible objects" that have recently gained popularity. The best known is perhaps the three-pronged tuning fork. At one end it is two rectangular bars, but at the other it is three cylindrical bars. How can this be?

In Figure 15.5, line 1 and line 6 are so connected at both ends that they specify occluding edges, although they are curved occluding edges on the left and apical occluding edges on the right. Line 2 is connected so as to specify a curved occluding edge on the left but a convex dihedral edge on the right. So is line 5. Line 3 produces a genuine shock to the visual system, for it occludes the background on its lower side at the left end but occludes the background on its upper side at the right end. Line 4 does the same, but inversely. The reversal of the direction in which the virtual edge hides or conceals is disconcerting. It involves what I will call an *ecological contradiction* as distinguished from a verbal contradiction. The transition from surface to air cannot possibly reverse in this way. The discrepancy of information is clearly to be found in the different connections of the line segment at its two ends, as is evident if one covers up one end and then the other.

These anomalies of depiction can be combined in very elaborate ways, as the drawings of the Dutch graphic artist Escher have demonstrated. Far from proving that the beholder creates the world he perceives in a picture, however, they suggest the existence of laws of optical information that are general and exact.

One thing at least should be clear: the "lines" of line drawings and the "lines" of

Figure 15.5
**Anomalies of pictorial occlusion. The incompatible connections of a line
segment at its two ends.**

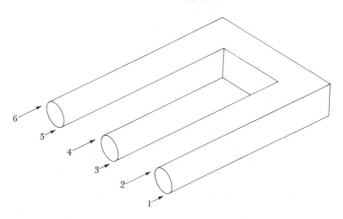

geometry are entirely different. The depicting of surfaces should not be confused with the ghosts of abstract geometry. We are taught in geometry that a line is derived from points, a plane from lines, and a space from planes. We learn the three axes of Descartes's coordinate geometry and the concept of space as a sort of boxlike container of points and lines that combine to make planes and solids, conceived for the benefit of abstract physics. Hence, the modern artist is constrained to assume what Paul Klee asserted, namely, that the graphic elements available to the painter are "points, lines, planes, and volumes." When the artist works to capture invariants, all that he knows to say about what he is doing is that he depicts "space." But this is misleading.

J. M. Kennedy (1974) has described many of the characteristics of line drawings in much the same spirit that has been adopted in this chapter. But his conception of optical information is imprecise, it seems to me, since it is not based on ecological optics.

The capturing of optical invariants by line drawings is a fascinating exercise. It has seemed to be both familiar and mysterious. It is not, however, fundamental. Much of the information in a natural optic array is lost in a drawing inasmuch as the array cannot be reduced to nested solid angles. The invariants under changing illumination and those under the changing *direction* of the prevailing illumination (Chapter 5) are lost. So are the invariant relations that specify the textures and colors of surfaces. Some of these are captured by painters who use a variety of tools other than the pen or pencil. But mostly what is lost in a picture, drawing, painting, or photograph is the information that can be extracted only from the changing perspective structure of the ambient optic array of a moving observer.

Figure 15.6
Four different types of occlusion as specified by different modes of intersection of the same line segments.

The connections of the lines in a drawing convey the information, not the lines as such. What differs in these drawings is the information for perceiving occlusion, not for perceiving depth. The information displayed in the third drawing is *contradictory*. The information displayed in the fourth is *ambiguous*, because either of two positions of the cube is possible, and the perception therefore fluctuates.

1. Opaque surfaces of a substantial body   2. Opaque sheets of a hollow body   3. Anomalous occlusion of opaque sheets   4. Either transparent sheets or wires

SUMMARY

The perplexities connected with the making and seeing of pictures are problems in their own right, independent of the problems of direct visual perception.

It is a fallacy to assume that perception is simplest when there is a form on the retina that is a copy of a form on a surface facing the retina, that is, in point-to-point correspondence with it.

The information in the optic array from a picture to a point of observation consists of invariants, not of forms and colors.

A picture requires two kinds of apprehension, a direct perceiving of the picture surface along with an indirect awareness of what it depicts. This dual apprehension is inescapable under normal conditions of observation. The "fooling of the eye," the illusion of reality, does not then occur.

When young children learn to draw, they certainly do not begin by drawing their sensations in patchwork perspective and then progress to the stage of drawing their concepts. But neither do they begin by drawing their concepts and then progress to the stage of drawing their sensations. They simply draw the invariants they have learned to notice.

A picture is a record of what its creator has seen or imagined, made available for others to see or imagine.

Depicting should be distinguished from the decorating, ornamenting, embellishing, or beautifying of a surface considered as such. The problems of aesthetics exist in their own right.

SIXTEEN

MOTION PICTURES
AND
VISUAL AWARENESS

I suggested in the last chapter that a picture is a surface so treated as to make available an arrested optic array, of limited scope, with information about other things than the surface itself. What, then, is a *motion picture*? There is a treated surface, but the treatment has to consist of throwing shadows on the surface by projection instead of depositing traces or pigments on it. An optic array of limited scope is delivered, and it contains information about other things than just the surface itself. The main difference is that the array is not arrested. Its structure undergoes change, disturbance, or transformation. It is not frozen in time. And that is what we need to understand about it.

This definition of the motion picture is broad enough to include not only the kind made with photographic film that uses the stroboscopic principle in the projector and camera but also the kind made with a modulated scanning beam as in television, and the kind made with shadows projected on a translucent screen as in a shadow play, and the various kinds made with the optical gadgets now being tried out experimentally by kinetic artists.

The technology of cinema and television has reached the very highest level of applied science. The psychology of the awareness provided by a motion picture, however, is nonexistent, apart from an essay by J. Hochberg and V. Brooks (1978), to whom I am indebted for much good talk about the problems of the film. There are no experts on this form of perception. Muddles and misconceptions prevail. We are led to conceive a sort of apparatus inside the head that is similar to the apparatus for making a picture show outside the head. We have been taught that a picture is sent from the eye up to the brain, and so we conclude that a *series* of pictures can be sent up to the brain. We all know what a snapshot is, and we know that a film is a series of snapshots. If we are told that a movie presents us with a sequence of *retinal* snapshots joined by what is called the "persistence of vision," we believe it. But we are misled. Nevertheless, this is what we are told by movie commentators who have read physiological optics and believed it.

The motion picture camera and projector do not comprise the only method that can be used to produce a changing optic array. Nor is the stroboscopic principle the only principle that can be applied. There are other ways of doing it, and the inventors of the nineteenth century tried out dozens of gadgets with names such as kinescopes and kinegraphs, vitascopes and vitagraphs, that have now been mostly forgotten. It is not even always true that the motion in a changing array is "apparent" and not "real." The important thing is not the apparatus devised for the motion picture but the information it provides for our vision.

THE CHANGING OPTIC ARRAY

Let us recall once again that the arrested optic array is an unusual case of the changing array; it is obtained in a frozen world by an observer who holds still and uses one eye. The eye continues to work, but it is not what the organ evolved for. Optical rest is a special case of optical motion, not the other way around. The eye *developed* to register change and transformation. The retinal image is seldom an arrested image in life. Accordingly, we ought to treat the motion picture as the basic form of depiction and the painting or photograph as a special form of it. What a strange idea! It goes counter to all we have been told about optics. But it follows directly from ecological optics. Moviemakers are closer to life than picture makers.

THE PROGRESSIVE PICTURE

Unfortunately, we have no adequate term to describe what I will call the *progressive picture* as contrasted with the *arrested picture*. The term *motion picture* implies that motion has been added to a still picture. *Cinematography,* or *cinema,* is no better. The term *photoplay* is not right. *Film* sounds neutral, but live television does not use film. What gets depicted is a flow of events. What gets displayed are disturbances of structure in the array, with underlying invariants of structure. These are what the visual system picks up.

The progressive picture displays transformations and magnifications and nullifications and substitutions of structure along with deletions and accretions and slippage of texture. These are the "motions" of the motion picture, as I put it in Chapter 6. They are thoroughly saturated with meaning. They are lawful, even if not described by geometry. They can show people, animals, objects, places, and events with the utmost precision and elaboration. They need to be studied by experimental psychologists on the one hand and by experimental moviemakers on the other. They cannot be usefully studied by taking the parameters of "motion" and plodding through the systematic variations of the traditional experiment. But on the other hand, neither can they be understood by playing around with aesthetic intuitions.

The progressive picture can also of course depict the movement of the observer himself in the environment as well as the motions of objects: it can arouse visual kinesthesis as well as visual event perception. This fact was pointed out in Chapter 10 and will be further discussed later in this chapter.

The progressive picture can turn into an arrested picture if a "stop-action" shot is inserted in the sequence. This is much used in film and television nowadays. The differences between the two kinds of depiction become clearly evident, along with the similarities between them.

THE ARRESTED PICTURE

If it is true that a drawing, painting, or photograph is actually an arrest of the normally changing array, we shall have to revise our thinking. The arrest has to be artificial, for no event can be stopped in midflight. It is an abrupt *non*continuation of the event, with a continuing *non*transformation of the array. The picture is not, as we have supposed, the optic array at an instant, a single moment of time, but an unnatural stopping of the flow. The painter of a quiet landscape, to be sure, arrests only the very slowest of the changes and emphasizes what is invariant in the scene but nevertheless stops action.

We can now understand, I think, why painters stubbornly continue to insist that they can portray "motion" in a still picture. This is one of the paradoxes mentioned in the last chapter. Painters cannot display or represent motion, but they can certainly specify an event. The stopped event may contain the information for perceiving it. The wind in the trees can be depicted if the painter selects the right form in the transformation. So can the smile of a sitter for a portrait. The act of dancing can be conveyed by a photographer because the invariants are different from those of standing or walking. There are event-invariants as well as formless object-invariants.

The arrested picture can specify a progressive event. What the progressive picture can do is to specify it more completely. As for the formless invariants, they are stronger in a changing picture than they are in a changeless picture, but they are still present.

WHAT CAN THE MOVIES MAKE AVAILABLE?

The film, like the photograph and the painting, makes possible not only perceptual awareness but also several kinds of nonperceptual awareness. I refer to the edited film made with a motion picture camera or its television equivalent. The perception or imagination is vicarious, an awareness at second hand. Consider the possibilities.

A film can depict situations and problems that you will have to face at a later time, we call this an *educational film*. It can depict vistas of distant scenic places to which you may never go and the connections between vistas, a *travel film*. It may show events that happened only yesterday, a *news film*. It may depict ways of life, histories, adventures, encounters with wondrous persons, prophetic events, fictions, and fantasies; we call these *documentary films, historical films, adventure films,* and *wish-fulfillment films*. They are usually full of what their producers call "action." We are addicted to them, all of us, children and adults. The beholder is apt to identify himself with a protagonist to whom he feels sympathy, and this means he puts himself at the point of observation of the protagonist in the way I have described. He thus gets perception, knowledge, imagination, and pleasure at second hand. He even gets rewarded or punished at second hand. A very intense empathy is aroused in the film viewer, an awareness of being in the place and situation depicted. But this awareness is dual. The beholder is helpless to intervene. He can find out nothing for himself. He feels himself moving and looking around in a certain fashion, attending now to this and now to that, but at the will of the film maker. He has visual kinesthesis and visual self-awareness, but it is passive, not active.

To behold a motion picture is thus similar in important ways to observing the ordinary happenings of life. But it is also radically dissimilar in other ways that are just as important. Both need to be understood. In the case of the film, one's movements of approaching to scrutinize or retreating to get a fuller view are controlled by the film maker. In the case of the real environment, one is free to move as one pleases, that is, as one "wills." But note that the scanning of fine details in the array sample is free and unconstrained in both cases. The film maker cannot interfere with your eye movements. He can control only your head movements and your locomotion.

WHAT DOES A VERBAL NARRATION
MAKE AVAILABLE?

A narration or description can also of course give one the kinds of awareness at second hand that the film can. And the reader is controlled by the writer as much as the film viewer is controlled by the film maker. Neither can look for herself, or visualize for herself, or imagine for herself. She is at the mercy of the artificer, the artist, the maker, the one-who-shows. But let us not confuse the kind of information that has been put into words with the kind that has been simply displayed. Film is not a language with

DEPICTION

a grammar, as some film makers like to believe. A graphic depiction is not an explicit description and, similarly, a motion picture is not a verbal narration.

A THEORY OF FILMING AND FILM-EDITING

The ecological theory of perceiving advanced in this book has implications for film-making. Film-viewing, I said, is both similar and dissimilar to natural observing. Let us follow up this suggestion.

THE COMPOSITION OF A FILM

A motion picture is composed of virtual events joined together. One kind of junction is obtained by turning the camera from one event to another during a continuous run of film (*panning*) or rolling the camera stand from one location to another during a run of film (*dollying*). But another kind of junction is obtained by splicing together strips of film, each being the result of a single run called a *take* or a *shot*. These junctions, the transitions between the events displayed, are crucial for film-making. Events have to be nested in a coherent way if the superordinate events are to be intelligible.

Note that the cameraman or motion picture photographer is the person who moves the camera and changes the lenses, whereas the editor or cutter is supposed to be the one who puts together the shots, using either splices called *cuts* or other optical transitions called *fades, wipes, dissolves*, and the like that are made by photographic special effects. But both functions ought to be performed by the same person, or at least under the direction of the same person for, if I am right, the cameraman and the editor are doing the same thing. Camera movement and film-splicing are not separate kinds of composition.

THE CAMERA AND THE HEAD OF THE VIEWER

The motion picture camera occupies a point of observation in a studio set or on a real location, just as the head of an observer does in an ambient environment. The camera can turn, look up or down, and undergo locomotion, more or less as the head does. The field of view of the camera is analogous to the combined field of view of the eyes in the head in the sense that both fields are bounded by occluding edges, although the visual solid angle sampled by the camera is much smaller than the visual solid angle sampled by the head, which is nearly a hemisphere. Note that the light entering an eye and forming a retinal image is emphatically *not* analogous to the light entering a camera, as photographers assume.

In this analogy, the camera, film, projector, and screen are all components of the same device, a way of providing information to a seated viewer. The field of view of the camera becomes the optic array to the viewer, even when he is not placed so as to get the same-sized angular field of view that the camera got. The screen picture functions as a mobile window hiding most of the environment being filmed, and the edges of the picture can sweep over the ambient array of the environment in the way described in Chapter 12, with gain and loss at the leading and trailing edges of the picture. The seated viewer never actually turns his head, of course, but he gets the essential optical information for doing so. And thus, he becomes aware of a whole new world behind the magic window.

The window can turn sideways quite naturally. This is called *panning*, on the intuitive belief that the awareness becomes "panoramic" during such a shot. It does in a way, but not because the picture is panoramic. The window can also look up or down. Theoretically it could also tilt, although this is seldom done in practice. The edges of the window can also go forward or backward, or travel sideways, when the camera is moved on a dolly, truck, or crane. The dolly shot is a well-known way of moving close up so that an item of interest fills the window or far back so that a whole array of items is included. The use of a zoom lens that alters the field of view from wide angle to narrow angle or the reverse is now common as a substitute for the dolly shot. It too gives the feeling of approach or retreat, but the dolly shot is preferable when it is possible, for the zoom shot cannot display the deletion or accretion that occurs at occluding edges.

The modes of camera movement that are analogous to the natural movements of the head-body system are, in this theory, a first-order guide to the composing of a film. The moving camera, not just the movement in the picture, is the reason for the empathy that grips us in the cinema. We are onlookers in the situation, to be sure, not participants, but we are in it, we are oriented to it, and we can adopt points of observation within its space. The illusion of participation can be enhanced by having the camera occupy the point of observation of one of the protagonists in the story. This has been done commercially only once to my knowledge, in *The Lady in the Lake*, a Hollywood murder mystery in which Robert Montgomery played the hero but was scarcely visible since his acts of locomotion and exploration, his adventures, and his encounters with the woman and the villain were carried out by the camera. It was the camera that was punched in the face and kissed by the woman. The so-called subjective camera does not deserve the neglect in which it is now held by film producers.

Films for training and education can profit by having the camera occupy the point of observation of the learner. A student can be shown what it is like to land an airplane or operate the controls of an earthmover or tie knots. But because a theory of visual kinesthesis and control has been lacking (Chapter 13), the method has not been exploited.

THE PSYCHOLOGY OF FILM-SPLICING

We have been talking about the filming of natural movements; what about the joining of shots? It seems plausible to me that the various kinds of cutting that a film editor can perform also have analogues in perception and that the insertion of fades, wipes, dissolves, and other special effects is at least an attempt to create transitions with psychological meaning. Composers of film are guided only by their feeling for what works. Some film theorists, as we shall note, try to take lessons from painters, but the lessons to be learned are not clear.

A *cut* represents a displacement of the camera *between* shots. The most intelligible cuts, I suggest, are those between shots that have some invariant structure in common. A displacement of the camera forward or backward yields a structure that is magnified or minified, and one sees the same layout afterward as before. Such a displacement is the same as a dolly shot or a zoom, except that it is discontinuous. The familiar sequence—long shot, medium shot, close-up—has a common structure at the center of the picture. A rotary displacement of the camera yields a shot that *overlaps* its predecessor unless the angle is greater than the camera's field of view. It is thus the same as a pan.

Next, there are cuts in which the viewer is displaced on a circular path around the event being filmed. He sees the lovers, say, from the north where the man's face is in sight and then from the south where the woman's face is in sight. Such differing vantage points, revealing different surfaces, seem to be called "camera angles," but it is not a good term. If underlying invariants are shared, the viewer will perceive the same two persons as before and be aware that he has been instantly transported to another viewpoint, not that the lovers are different persons or that they have been rotated.

Instant transportation of the onlooker can be attempted from one room to another in the same house or from one neighborhood to another in the same countryside—in short, from place to place. Intelligibility depends on whether the viewer has been previously oriented to the environment being portrayed, that is, whether the nesting of places has been established. This can be done with *establishing shots,* and it can also be done by connecting the major vistas of the environment with dolly shots. Orientation is crucial for comprehension.

Cutting back and forth between distant places, as in scenes of the heroine tied to the railroad tracks and the hero riding to the rescue, ought to suggest that the hero is getting closer, not farther away. The events are concurrent, but at what places? Chase sequences have a similar problem. There is no overlap of structure between such alternating shots, but there must be some common invariants. What are they?

The *split screen* provides a way of depicting concurrent events at widely separated places without cutting back and forth. Instant transportation of the onlooker is avoided, but the ecological paradox of being in two places at once is introduced.

Instant transportation in time is attempted by the so-called *flashback*. Characters who have already been depicted in later events are depicted as involved in earlier events, often in the same place. But the jump in sequence, like the jump from place to place, must be made intelligible. Aristotle had a psychological point when he argued that drama should maintain the "unities" of time and space.

The cut is abrupt. Gradual transitions are possible, such as the *fade-out*, the *fade-in*, and the combining of the two in a *dissolve* that superimposes the structures of the two shots so that a perception of transparency is induced and one layout of surfaces is gradually converted into another layout by way of becoming insubstantial, by passing into "thin air" and out again. Another gradual transition is the *wipe*, where a line something like an occluding edge (but not optically the same) passes across the screen, concealing one vista and revealing another. The psychological meaning of these transitions has never been studied experimentally by either film editors or perceptionists, but the ecological approach to vision suggests how they might do so. Cuts, fades, dissolves, and wipes are not pure conventions the meaning of which can be arbitrarily decided by film makers and taught to us. The practice of jump-cutting in films and television seems to me ill founded.

THE THEORY OF MONTAGE

A quite different theory of the nature of filmic transitions seems to be widely accepted by directors and critics. This theory is based on the assumption that *any* juxtaposition of shots, however disparate, will form a unified "image" with a new meaning. The combination is more than the sum of the parts. The doctrine is identified with a book translated as *The Film Sense* (Eisenstein, 1942). The author, a famous Russian director, is celebrated for the boldness with which he combined shots of events that did not ordinarily occur together.

Montage, in this sense of the term, is related to collage. The latter was invented by painters who tried composing a work of art by pasting items on the canvas instead of painting forms on it. The associating of scraps, pieces, pictures, or forms not previously associated was thought to yield a fresh insight, or an unexpected gestalt. The word *collage* means a paste-up. The creation could be photographed and displayed. Similarly, strips of film could be spliced together. "The juxtaposition of two separate shots resembles not so much a simple sum of one shot plus another shot as it does a *creation*" (Eisenstein, 1942, p. 7). The vague aesthetic optimism of this movement stands in contrast to the theory of natural underlying invariants of structure. But it had and has a considerable influence on both graphic artists and film artists.

The composing of a film, however, is not comparable to the composing of a painting. The film is composed of events and superordinate events, of episodes, happenings, and history. The linkages must be made with care, and the continuity must be preserved. At the end all the minor events should constitute a comprehensive major event.

I have said nothing in this treatment of the motion picture about the flow of sound that accompanies the flow of the optic array, the sound track that parallels the picture track. I have been discussing the silent film, for purposes of theoretical simplicity. The sequence of events in life is given by the acoustic flow of information as well as the optical flow, and accordingly, in film, the sound track is exactly synchronized with the picture track (with the exception of music). This helps to maintain the continuity of the viewer's awareness in the face of jump-cutting. But the theory of the invariants under auditory change and their relation to invariants under visual change is another matter entirely. They are not the same for the flow of environmental sounds as they are for the flow of speech sounds (Gibson, 1966*b*, Ch. 5).

DEPICTION BY FILM

If the foregoing approach is correct, there is such a thing as filmic depiction that is distinct from ordinary depiction. Its aim is to produce in the viewer the awareness of a train of events, and of the causal structure of these events. They are virtual instead of real events, to be sure, and no one is ever wholly deceived, as when having a hallucination, but the feeling of being present in the world behind the magic window is very strong.

This awareness of events is achieved by segmenting the flow of the pictorial optic array so that it specifies the same kinds of subordinate and superordinate happenings that are specified in a natural optic array. Persons, animals, places, objects, and substances are depicted along with the events. The *segments* of the optical flow are crucial, that is, the transients between parts as well as the parts themselves. Simply to call them "motions" is not to do justice to them.

Filmic depiction shares with verbal narration, storytelling, the capability of showing what happens if so-and-so happens, the predictable causal sequences of the world, along with the accidental happenings, the unpredictable sequences. But it shares with ordinary depiction, perspective pictures, the capability of putting the observer into the scene.

＊

SUMMARY

What we call the motion picture as distinguished from the still picture might better be called the *progressive picture* as distinguished from the arrested picture. It is not characterized by "motion" so much as by change of structure in the optic array. And the ordinary picture is not so much "still" as it is stopped.

The progressive picture yields something closer to natural visual perception than does the arrested picture. The nameless transformations that constitute it and that are so hard to describe are actually easier to perceive than the familiar frozen forms of the painting or photograph.

It provides a changing optic array of limited scope to a point of observation in front of the picture, an array that makes information available to a viewer at the point of observation. This delimited array is analogous to the temporary field of view of a human observer in a natural environment surrounding the observer.

The information in the display can specify the turning of one's head, the act of approaching or withdrawing, and the adopting of a new point of observation, although one is all the time aware of holding still and looking at a screen from a fixed position in a room. This is over and above the information in the display for an awareness of events and the places at which the events are happening, along with an awareness of the objects, persons, or creatures of the imagination to which the events are happening. The invariants to specify the places, objects, and persons emerge more clearly in the transforming array than they would in a frozen array.

The art of film-editing should be guided by knowledge of how events and the progress of events are naturally perceived. The composing of a film is not analogous to the composing of a painting. The sequential *nesting* of subordinate events into super-ordinate events is crucial. The transitions should be psychologically meaningful, and the sequential order of happenings should be intelligible. But the picture theory of vision and the stimulus sequence theory of perception are very poor guides to movie-making. The theory of ecological perception, of perception while moving around and looking around the environment, is better. The various kinds of filmic transition—zoom, dolly, pan, cut, fade, wipe, dissolve, and split-screen shot—could usefully be evaluated in the light of ecological optics instead of the snapshot optics that is currently accepted.

CONCLUSION

In the first pages of this book, I promised to give an account of natural vision, not just snapshot vision but vision that is ambient and ambulatory. *Ambient vision* is what you get from looking around at the scenery. *Ambulatory vision* is what you get from walking through the countryside.

The standard approach to vision begins with the eye fixed and exposed to a momentary pattern of stimuli. It then goes on to consider vision with the head fixed and the eye allowed to explore the pattern by scanning it, that is, by looking at parts in succession. Each fixation is a glimpse of the pattern comparable to a momentary exposure and is thus supposed to be analogous to a photographic snapshot taken by a camera with a shutter. Each successive snapshot is assumed to be transmitted to the brain. The result of all this is *aperture vision*, a sequence of snapshots.

The standard approach never gets around to ambient vision with head turning, and it does not even consider ambulatory vision. The process of perception is supposed to be localized in the head, not in the muscles, and it begins after the sensory input reaches the visual projection area of the cerebral cortex. The mind is in the brain.

The ecological approach to visual perception works from the opposite end. It begins with the flowing array of the observer who walks from one vista to another, moves around an object of interest, and can approach it for scrutiny, thus extracting the invariants that underlie the changing perspective structure and seeing the connections between hidden and unhidden surfaces. This approach next considers the fact of ambient awareness and explains it by the invariance of the sliding samples of the 360° array. Only then is the awareness of a single scene considered, the surfaces seen with the head fixed and the array frozen. The classical puzzles that arise with this kind of vision are resolved by recognizing that the invariants are weaker and the ambiguities stronger when the point of observation is motionless. Finally, the kind of visual awareness obtained with the eye fixed and the retina either briefly exposed or made to stay fixed is considered for what it is, a peculiar result of trying to make the eye work as if it were a camera at the end of a nerve cable. The visual system continues to operate at this photographic level, but the constraints imposed on it are so severe that very little information can be picked up. The level is that of cellular physiology, the photochemistry of retinal cells, the anatomy of the nerves and tracts, and the firing of nerve impulses.

The artificially produced *glimpse* is an abnormal kind of vision, not the simplest kind on which normal vision is based. It is a poor sort of awarenesss. But it has seemed to be fundamental for hitherto persuasive reasons: it results from an *image*; it comes from a *stimulus;* it is a *sensory input*; it is what the nerve *transmits*. But if this is so, how could the series of glimpses be integrated? How could the sequence, as I put it, be converted into a scene?

If perception of the environment is truly based on glimpses, it *has* to be a process of construction. If the data are insufficient, the observer must go beyond the data. How? Some of the greatest minds in history have undertaken to answer this question without success.

I suggested in Chapter 14 that explanations of perception based on sensory inputs fail because they all come down to this: In order to perceive the world, one must already have ideas about it. Knowledge of the world is explained by assuming that knowledge of the world exists. Whether the ideas are learned or innate makes no difference; the fallacy lies in the circular reasoning.

But if, on other hand, perception of the environment is not based on a sequence of snapshots but on invariant-extraction from a flux, one does not need to have ideas about the environment in order to perceive it. Another puzzle is resolved at the same time, the awareness of oneself in the environment. The young child does not need to have ideas of space in order to see the surfaces around him; he need pay no attention to the cues for depth if he can see the layout; he need not compensate for the small retinal image of a distant surface if he never notices the image but only extracts the invariant.

Such is the ecological approach to perception. It promises to simplify psychology by making old puzzles disappear. Especially do all the genuinely mischief-making puzzles connected with the concept of an image become irrelevant. How can one see an upright world with an inverted retinal image? Why doesn't the object change when its retinal image is transposed over the retina? Where is the little man who looks at the image? If the two eyes yield a double image of a single object under some conditions, why not under all?

The very notion of an image as a flattened-out object, a sort of pancake of a solid body, is shown to be misleading. It begins to appear that most of what has been written about pictures and images over the centuries is misleading, or hopelessly vague. We should forget it all and start fresh. The information for the perception of an object is not its image. The information in light to specify something does not have to resemble it, or copy it, or be a simulacrum or even an exact projection. *Nothing* is copied in the light to the eye of an observer, not the shape of a thing, not the surface of it, not its substance, not its color, and certainly not its motion. But all these things are specified in the light.

What is the future of this approach? It needs to be tested experimentally, it needs to be clarified further, and its implications need to be followed up. It already has adherents, and their work is beginning to appear. Robert Shaw has been thinking along the same lines for some time, and he is developing the theory of invariants (Shaw and McIntyre, 1974) and the implications for epistemology (Shaw and Bransford, 1977). William Mace has been expounding and elaborating the approach (Mace, 1974, 1977). Michael Turvey has been considering how to unify visual perception and action (Turvey, 1977). David Lee has been experimenting with visual kinesthesis (Lishman and Lee, 1973; Lee, 1974), and so has Rik Warren (1976). Above all, Eleanor Gibson has published a treatise on the development of perception from an ecological point of view (1969) and is carrying out experiments with infants on their discrimination of optical transformations (1978). Even the leading exponent of cognitive psychology, Ulric Neisser, has been sufficiently impressed with the advantages of this approach to describe it sympathetically in his new book (Neisser, 1976).

Nevertheless, as I pointed out in the Introduction, experimental studies that display optical information are not so easy to perform as the old-fashioned experiments that expose a stimulus to a fixed eye. The experimenter cannot simply apply a stimulus that he varies systematically, the "independent variable" of the scientific experiment. Instead, he must make available an optical invariant that he expects will specify something about the world on grounds of ecological optics. This takes ingenuity. Only a few experimenters have learned to do it as yet. But it can be done.

The experimenter should not hope, and does not need, to display *all* the information in an ambient optic array, let alone all the information in a transforming ambient optic array. He is not trying to simulate reality. He could not create the illusion of looking around and walking through the countryside in any case, for he would have to create the countryside. He should not want to deceive the observer. The observer who begins to be fooled should be allowed to make the standard tests for reality, such as getting up and looking behind the screen of the display. The information for a certain dimension of perception or proprioception can be displayed without interference from the accompanying information to specify the display. That is the lesson of research on pictures and motion pictures. What is required is only that the essential invariant be isolated and set forth.

The experimental psychologist should realize that he cannot truly *control* the perception of an observer, for the reason that it is not caused by stimuli. Only snapshot vision is triggered so that it can be touched off by imposing a stimulus on the receptor, and even then one has to have the agreement of the subject to look into the tachistoscope. Perception cannot be studied by the so-called psychophysical experiment if that refers to physical stimuli and corresponding mental sensations. The theory of psychophysical parallelism that assumes that the dimensions of consciousness are in correspondence with the dimensions of physics and that the equations of such correspondence can be established is an expression of Cartesian dualism. Perceivers are not aware of the dimensions of physics. They are aware of the dimensions of the information in the flowing array of stimulation that are relevant to their lives.

APPENDIX 1

THE PRINCIPAL TERMS USED IN ECOLOGICAL OPTICS

The *environment* of animals, as distinguished from the physical world, consists of a medium, substances, and the surfaces that separate the substances from the medium.

The *medium* for terrestrial animals is air. Air is insubstantial and thus permits locomotion. Locomotion is controlled by the information in the medium.

Information is provided by sound-fields, by odor-fields, and above all by illumination. Information, in this terminology, is not transmitted but is simply available.

Illumination is the steady state of reverberating radiant energy such that light is *ambient* at all points in the medium.

Substances are solids and liquids that vary in composition, and in resistance to change. Different substances have different affordances. Substances are generally opaque, that is, they reflect and absorb but do not transmit.

The *surface* of a substance has a characteristic texture, reflectance, and layout. The ambient light at any point in the medium is *structured* by the light reflected from surfaces so that these characteristics are specified.

Surfaces, substances, and the medium manifest both *persistence and change*, persisting in some respects and changing in others. The changes are *environmental events*. Animals need to perceive what persists and what changes. A surface *goes out of existence* when its substance evaporates or disintegrates; a surface *comes into existence* when its substance condenses or crystallizes.

Layout refers to the persisting arrangement of surfaces relative to one another and to the ground. Different layouts have different affordances for animals. The perception of layout takes the place of the perception of depth or space in traditional terminology.

The *ground* is the basic persisting surface of the environment. It is the surface of support, the terrain, the earth extending out to the horizon. It is normally cluttered.

Clutter of the environment refers to objects or surfaces that occlude parts of the ground and divide the habitat into semi-enclosures. Semi-enclosures provide *vistas*.

A *detached object* is a substance with a surface that is topologically closed and is capable of displacement. Animals are detached objects.

An *attached object* is a substance with a surface that is not wholly closed and is continuous with another surface, usually the ground. It cannot be displaced without breaking the surface.

An *edge* is the junction of two surfaces that make a convex dihedral angle.

A *corner* is the junction of two surfaces that make a concave dihedral angle.

An *occluding edge* is an edge taken with reference to a point of observation. It both separates and connects the hidden and the unhidden surface, both divides and unites them. The same can be said of the far side and the near side of an object. As the point of observation moves in the medium, or as the object moves, the hidden and the unhidden interchange, or the far side becomes the near side and the reverse. For curved surfaces and tangential occluding edges, instead of flat surfaces and apical occluding edges, the rule is the same.

A *point of observation* is a position in the medium that can be occupied by an animal. It is stationary only as a limit. A moving point of observation entails a *path of observation*. Different observers can perceive on the same path of observation. The point of observation in ecological optics should not be confused with the station point of a picture in discussions of artificial perspective.

Occlusion is one of the three main types of *going out of sight*. A surface can go out of sight at an occluding edge, at a great distance, or in the dark. In all three cases *coming into sight* is the reverse of going out of sight, and thus is unlike *coming into existence* which is not the reverse of *going out of existence*. All displacements and turns of an observer's body, or of an object, bring about a change of occlusion. There are two kinds, self-occlusion and superposition.

Going out of sight at an occluding edge is specified by progressive decrements of structure on one side of a contour in the optic array. *Coming into sight at an edge* is specified by progressive increments of structure on one side of the contour. Going out of sight in the distance is specified by optical minification of structure to the limit. Going out of sight in darkness is specified by reduction of illumination to the limit.

The optic array at a moving point of observation is disturbed by what we call changing "perspective" and changing "parallax," which have never been carefully analyzed. Nevertheless, there is reason to suppose that *invariants* of the array underlie these changes: ratios, gradients, discontinuities, and other relations in the ambient light that owe their existence to the persisting features of the environment. (The structure of the array is also disturbed by motions and deformations of parts of the environment and by movement of the sun in the sky, but invariants are presumed to underlie these changes also.)

An arrested optic array at a fixed point of observation has a kind of structure that is somewhat easier to understand. It can be described in terms of *visual solid angles* that are both densely packed and "nested" up to the hemispheric solid angle of the earth and the spherical angle of the whole ambient array. The envelope of each solid angle intercepts a face of the layout projected to that point, or a facet, or an aperture. Although this description of optical structure is superior to that in terms of rays and pencils of rays, it still cannot cope with shading and transparency, or surface color. But it does emphasize the fact that there is a unique optic array for every fixed point of observation in the environment; no two are identical.

Disturbance of structure is a general term that will encompass all kinds of change in the optic array. Different disturbances specify different happenings. The term *motion*, borrowed from mechanics, does not apply to an optic array, and the term *transformation*, taken from geometry, is not suitable either, because it does not cover a gain or loss of structure.

Successive overlapping samples of the ambient optic array are picked up by an observer during head movements. The field of view of the head is a *sliding sample* of the array as the head turns, gaining structure at the leading edge and losing structure at the trailing edge. The field of view of the head consists of the combined fields of view of the two eye-sockets. The amount of *simultaneous overlap* of the two fields of view differs, being large in the human and small in the horse, but successive overlap is common to all animals. Simultaneous disparity of the overlapping binocular fields has been overemphasized in physiological optics. Note that samples of the ambient array take the place of retinal images in physiological optics.

Scanning of the field of view is the successive foveating of details of its sample by each eye. The exploratory scanning of a field should not be confused with the exploratory sampling of the ambient array. Some animals do not have foveated eyes and do not scan.

The visual system is distinguished from the visual sense, from the modality of visual experience, and from the channel of visual inputs. It is a hierarchy of organs and functions, the retina and its neurons, the eye with its muscles and adjustments, the dual eyes that move in the head, the head that turns on the shoulders, and the body that moves around the habitat. The nerves, tracts, and centers of the brain that are necessary for vision are not thought of as the "seat" of vision.

APPENDIX 2

THE CONCEPT OF INVARIANTS
IN ECOLOGICAL OPTICS

The theory of the concurrent awareness of persistence and change requires the assumption of invariants that underlie change of the optic array. Four kinds of invariants have been postulated: those that underlie change of *illumination*, those that underlie change of the *point of observation*, those that underlie *overlapping samples*, and those that underlie a *local disturbance of structure*.

It would simplify matters if all these kinds of change in the optic array could be understood as transformations in the sense of *mappings*, borrowing the term from projective geometry and topology. The invariants under transformation have been worked out. Moreover it is easy to visualize a form being transposed, inverted, reversed, enlarged, reduced, or foreshortened by slant, and we can imagine it being deformed in various ways. But, unhappily, some of these changes *cannot* be understood as one-to-one mappings, either projective or topological (Chapter 6). Consider the four kinds.

1. *Invariants of optical structure under changing illumination.* Sunlight, moonlight, and lamplight can fluctuate in intensity, alter the direction from which they come to the layout, and differ in color. Hence the illumination can change in *amount*, in *direction*, and in *spectral composition*. Some features of any optic array in the medium will change accordingly. There must be *invariants* for perceiving the surfaces, their relative layout, and their relative reflectances. They are not yet known, but they almost certainly involve ratios of intensity and color among parts of the array (Chapter 5).

2. *Invariants of optical structure under change of the point of observation.* Note that a *different* point of observation is occupied by one eye of the human observer relative to the other, but that the invariants over this so-called *disparity* are the same as those under a change caused by a displacement of the head. A change and a difference are closely related. Some of the changes in the optic array are transformations of its nested forms, but the major changes are gain and loss of form, that is, increments and decrements of structure, as surfaces undergo occlusion. Proportions and cross-ratios underlie the transformations, however, and extrapolations, interpolations, gradients, and horizon-ratios underlie the increments and decrements. In short, the *flow* of the array does not destroy the structure beneath the flow (Chapters 5 and 13).

3. *Invariants across the sampling of the ambient optic array.* What I called *looking around* involves the reversible sweeping of the field of view over the whole array, back and forth, with continuous successive overlap. There is presumably a common structure in the sliding sample, and this may be thought of as invariant (Chapters 7 and 12).

4. *Local invariants of the ambient array under local disturbances of its structure.* Besides the motions of the sun, the observer, and the observer's head, there are local events. These include not only displacements and rotations of rigid detached objects, but also deformations of rubbery surfaces—in fact all sorts of events from a rolling ball to rippling water, and from a growing infant to a smiling face. Each produces a specific disturbance of optical structure. But the surface, the ball, the water, and the face are seen to be continuations of themselves by virtue of certain *non-disturbances* of optical structure (Chapter 6).

These four kinds of invariants are optical. There are also surely invariants in the flow of acoustic, mechanical, and perhaps chemical stimulation, and they may prove to be closely related to the optical, but I leave them for the reader's speculation. The study of invariants is just beginning.

The theory of the extracting of invariants by a visual system takes the place of theories of "constancy" in perception, that is, explanations of how an observer might perceive the true color, size, shape, motion, and direction-from-here of objects despite the wildly fluctuating sensory impressions on which the perceptions are based. With invariants there is no need for theories of constancy. The reader, however, may consult a recent survey (Epstein, 1977) for the view that invariance-detection is only one more theory of perceptual constancy.

These terms and concepts are subject to revision as the ecological approach to perception becomes clear. May they never shackle thought as the old terms and concepts have!

BIBLIOGRAPHY

Arnheim, R. 1954. *Art and visual perception*. Berkeley: University of California Press.

Arnheim, R. 1969. *Visual thinking*. Berkeley: University of California Press.

Avant, L. L. 1965. Vision in the Ganzfeld. *Psychological Bulletin, 64*, 246–258.

Barker, R. G. 1968. *Ecological psychology*. Stanford, Calif.: Stanford University Press.

Barrand, A. G. 1978. An ecological approach to binocular perception: The neglected facts of occlusion. Doctoral dissertation, Cornell University Library.

Beck, J. 1972. *Surface color perception*. Ithaca, N.Y.: Cornell University Press.

Beck, J., and Gibson, J. J. 1955. The relation of apparent shape to apparent slant in the perception of objects. *Journal of Experimental Psychology, 50*, 125–133.

Bergman, R., and Gibson, J. J. 1959. The negative aftereffect of the perception of a surface slanted in the third dimension. *American Journal of Psychology, 72*, 364–374.

Boring, E. G. 1942. *Sensation and perception in the history of experimental psychology*. New York: Appleton-Century-Crofts.

Bower, T. G. R. 1974. *Development in infancy*. San Francisco: W. H. Freeman.

Boynton, R. M. 1974. The visual system: Environmental information. In *Handbook of perception*, edited by E. C. Cartarette and M. P. Friedman, I, 285–307. New York: Academic Press.

Braunstein, M. L. 1962a. Rotation of dot patterns as stimuli for the perception of motion in three dimensions. *Journal of Experimental Psychology, 64*, 415–426.

Braunstein, M. L. 1962b. The perception of depth through motion. *Psychological Bulletin, 59*, 422–433.

Brunswik, E. 1956. *Perception and the representative design of psychological experiments*. Berkeley: University of California Press.

Cohen, W. 1957. Spatial and textural characteristics of the Ganzfeld. *American Journal of Psychology, 70*, 403–410.

Dodge, R. 1903. Five types of eye-movement. *American Journal of Physiology, 8*, 307–329.

Eisenstein, S. M. 1942. *The film sense*. Translated by J. Leyda. New York: Harcourt, Brace.

Epstein, W. 1977. *Stability and constancy in visual perception*. New York: Wiley.

Fieandt, K. von, and Gibson, J. J. 1959. The sensitivity of the eye to two kinds of continuous transformation of a shadow-pattern. *Journal of Experimental Psychology, 57*, 344–347.

Flock, H. R. 1964. Some conditions sufficient for accurate monocular perception of moving surface slant. *Journal of Experimental Psychology, 67,* 560–572.

Flock, H. R. 1965. Optical texture and linear perspective as stimuli for slant perception. *Psychological Review, 72,* 505–514.

Freeman, R. B. 1965. Ecological optics and slant. *Psychological Review, 72,* 501–504.

Garner, W. R. 1974. *The processing of information and structure.* Hillsdale, N.J.: Lawrence Erlbaum Associates.

Gibson, E. J. 1969. *Perceptual learning and development.* New York: Appleton-Century-Crofts.

Gibson, E. J. 1978. The ecological optics of infancy: The differentiation of invariants given by optical motion. (Presidential address, DRV 3, APA)

Gibson, E. J., and Bergman, R. 1954. The effect of training on absolute estimation of distance over the ground. *Journal of Experimental Psychology, 48,* 473–482.

Gibson, E. J.; Bergman, R.; and Purdy, J. 1955. The effect of prior training with a scale of distance on absolute and relative judgments of distance over ground. *Journal of Experimental Psychology, 50,* 97–105.

Gibson, E. J.; Gibson, J. J.; Smith, O. W.; and Flock, H. R. 1959. Motion parallax as a determinant of perceived depth. *Journal of Experimental Psychology, 58,* 40–51.

Gibson, E. J., and Walk, R. D. 1960. The visual cliff. *Scientific American, 202,* 64–71.

Gibson, J. J. 1929. The reproduction of visually perceived forms. *Journal of Experimental Psychology, 12,* 1–29.

Gibson, J. J. 1947. *Motion picture testing and research.* AAF Aviation Psychology Research Report No. 7. Washington, D.C.: Government Printing Office.

Gibson, J. J. 1950a. The perception of visual surfaces. *American Journal of Psychology, 63,* 367–384.

Gibson, J. J. 1950b. *The perception of the visual world.* Boston: Houghton Mifflin.

Gibson, J. J. 1951. What is a form? *Psychological Review, 58,* 403–412.

Gibson, J. J. 1952. The relation between visual and postural determinants of the phenomenal vertical. *Psychological Review, 59,* 370–375.

Gibson, J. J. 1954. A theory of pictorial perception. *Audio-Visual Communications Review, 1,* 3–23.

Gibson, J. J. 1956. The non-projective aspects of the Rorschach experiment: IV. The Rorschach blots considered as pictures. *Journal of Social Psychology, 44,* 203–206.

Gibson, J. J. 1957. Optical motions and transformations as stimuli for visual perception. *Psychological Review, 64,* 288–295.

Gibson, J. J. 1958. Visually controlled locomotion and visual orientation in animals. *British Journal of Psychology, 49,* 182–194.

Gibson, J. J. 1959. Perception as a function of stimulation. In *Psychology: A study of a science,* Vol. I, edited by S. Koch. New York: McGraw-Hill.

Gibson, J. J. 1960a. The concept of the stimulus in psychology. *American Psychologist, 15,* 694–703.

Gibson, J. J. 1960b. Pictures, perspective, and perception. *Daedalus, 89,* 216–227.

Gibson, J. J. 1961. Ecological optics. *Vision Research, 1,* 253–262.

Gibson, J. J. 1962. Observations on active touch. *Psychological Review, 69,* 477–491.

Gibson, J. J. 1966a. The problem of temporal order in stimulation and perception. *Journal of Psychology, 62,* 141–149.

Gibson, J. J. 1966b. *The senses considered as perceptual systems.* Boston: Houghton Mifflin.

Gibson, J. J. 1968a. *The change from visible to invisible: A study of optical transitions* (motion picture film). Psychological Cinema Register, State College, Pa.

Gibson, J. J. 1968b. What gives rise to the perception of motion? *Psychological Review, 75,* 335–346.

Gibson, J. J. 1970. On the relation between hallucination and perception. *Leonardo, 3,* 425–427.

Gibson, J. J. 1971. The information available in pictures. *Leonardo, 4,* 27–35.

Gibson, J. J. 1973. On the concept of formless invariants in visual perception. *Leonardo, 6,* 43–45.

Gibson, J. J. 1974. A note on ecological optics. In *Handbook of perception,* edited by E. C. Cartarette and M. P. Friedman, I, 309–312. New York: Academic Press.

Gibson, J. J. 1975. Events are perceivable but time is not. In *The study of time II,* edited by J. T. Fraser and N. Lawrence. New York: Springer-Verlag.

Gibson, J. J. 1976. Three kinds of distance that can be seen; or, How Bishop Berkeley went wrong in the first place. In *Studies in perception: Festschrift for Fabio Metelli,* edited by G. B. Flores D'Arcais. Milan: Aldo Martello-Giunti.

Gibson, J. J., and Cornsweet, J. 1952. The perceived slant of visual surfaces—optical and geographical. *Journal of Experimental Psychology, 44,* 11–15.

Gibson, J. J., and Dibble, F. N. 1952. Exploratory experiments on the stimulus conditions for the perception of a visual surface. *Journal of Experimental Psychology, 43,* 414–419.

Gibson, J. J., and Gibson, E. J. 1955. Perceptual learning: Differentiation or enrichment? *Psychological Review, 62,* 32–41.

Gibson, J. J., and Gibson, E. J. 1957. Continuous perspective transformations and the perception of rigid motion. *Journal of Experimental Psychology, 54,* 129–138.

Gibson, J. J.; Kaplan, G. A.; Reynolds, H. N.; and Wheeler, K. 1969. The change from visible to invisible: A study of optical transitions. *Perception and Psychophysics, 5,* 113–116.

Gibson, J. J., and Kaushall, P. 1973. *Reversible and irreversible events* (motion picture film). Psychological Cinema Register, State College, Pa.

Gibson, J. J., and Mowrer, O. H. 1938. Determinants of the perceived vertical and horizontal. *Psychological Review, 45,* 300–323.

Gibson, J. J.; Olum, P.; and Rosenblatt, F. 1955. Parallax and perspective during aircraft landings. *American Journal of Psychology, 68,* 372–385.

Gibson, J. J.; Purdy, J.; and Lawrence, L. 1955. A method of controlling stimulation for the study of space perception: The optical tunnel. *Journal of Experimental Psychology, 50,* 1–14.

Gibson, J. J., and Waddell, D. 1952. Homogeneous retinal stimulation and visual perception. *American Journal of Psychology, 65,* 263–270.

Gibson, J. J., and Yonas, P. M. 1968. A new theory of scribbling and drawing in children. In *The analysis of reading skill,* edited by H. Levin, E. J. Gibson, and J. J. Gibson. Washington, D.C.: U.S. Department of Health, Education, and Welfare, Office of Education. (Final report)

Gombrich, E. H. 1960. *Art and illusion: A study in the psychology of pictorial representation.* Princeton, N.J.: Princeton University Press.

Goodman, N. 1968. *Languages of art: An approach to a theory of symbols.* Indianapolis: Bobbs-Merrill.

Green, B. F. 1961. Figure coherence in kinetic depth effects. *Journal of Experimental Psychology, 62,* 272–282.

Held, R., and Bauer, J. A. 1974. Development of sensorially guided reaching in infant monkeys. *Brain Research, 71,* 265–271.

Helmholtz, J. Translated 1925. *Physiological Optics,* Vol. 3. Edited by J. P. C. Southall. Optical Society of America.

Hochberg, J. E., and Beck, J. 1954. Apparent spatial arrangement and perceived brightness. *Journal of Experimental Psychology, 47,* 263–266.

Hochberg, J., and Brooks, V. 1978. The perception of motion pictures. In *Handbook of perception,* Vol. X, edited by E. C. Cartarette and M. Friedman. New York: Academic Press, forthcoming.

Ittelson, W. H. 1952. *The Ames demonstrations in perception.* Princeton, N.J.: Princeton University Press.

James, W. 1890. *The principles of psychology,* Vol. I. New York: Henry Holt.

Johansson, G. 1950. *Configurations in event perception.* Uppsala: Almkvist and Wiksell.

Johansson, G. 1964. Perception of motion and changing form. *Scandinavian Journal of Psychology, 5,* 181–208.

Kaplan, G. A. 1969. Kinetic disruption of optical texture: The perception of depth at an edge. *Perception and Psychophysics, 6,* 193–198.

Kaufman, L. 1974. *Sight and mind: An introduction to visual perception.* Oxford: Oxford University Press.

Kennedy, J. M. 1974. *A psychology of picture perception.* San Francisco: Jossey-Bass.

Kepes, G. 1944. *The language of vision.* Chicago: Paul Theobald.

Koffka, K. 1935. *Principles of gestalt psychology.* New York: Harcourt, Brace.

Kohler, I. 1964. The formation and transformation of the perceptual world. *Psychological Issues, 3,* Monograph No. 12.

Köhler, W. 1925. *The mentality of apes.* New York: Harcourt, Brace.

Land, E. H. 1959. Experiments in color vision. *Scientific American, 52,* 247–264.

Lee, D. N. 1974. Visual information during locomotion. In *Perception: Essays in honor of James J. Gibson,* edited by R. B. Macleod and H. L. Pick. Ithaca, N.Y.: Cornell University Press.

Lishman, J. R., and Lee, D. N. 1973. The autonomy of visual kinesthesis. *Perception, 2,* 287–294.

Mace, W. M. 1974. Ecologically stimulating cognitive psychology: Gibsonian perspectives. In *Cognition and the symbolic process*, edited by W. B. Weimer and D. S. Palermo. Hillsdale, N.J.; Lawrence Erlbaum Associates.

Mace, W. M. 1977. Gibson's strategy for perceiving: Ask not what's inside your head but what your head's inside of. In *Perceiving, acting, and knowing*, edited by R. Shaw and J. Bransford. Hillsdale, N.J.: Lawrence Erlbaum Associates.

Marrow, A. J. 1969. *The practical theorist: The life and work of Kurt Lewin.* New York: Basic Books.

Metzger, W. 1930. Optische Untersuchungen im Ganzfeld II. *Psychologische Forschung, 13,* 6–29.

Metzger, W. 1934. Tiefenerscheinungen in optischen Bewegungsfelden. *Psychol Forsch, 20,* 195–260.

Metzger, W. 1953. *Gesetze des Sehens.* Frankfurt: Waldemar Kramer.

Michotte, A. 1963. *The perception of causality.* Translated by T. R. Miles and E. Miles. London: Methuen.

Michotte, A.; Thinès, G.; and Crabbé, G. 1964. Les compléments amodaux des structures perceptives. In *Studia Psychologica.* Louvain: Publications Université de Louvain.

Mill, J. 1869. *Analysis of the phenomena of the human mind.* London: Longmans, Green, Roeder, and Dyer.

Musatti, C. L. 1924. Sui fenomeni stereokinetici. *Archiv. Ital. di Psicologia, 3,* 105–120.

Neisser, U. 1976. *Cognition and reality.* San Francisco: W. H. Freeman.

Panofsky, E. 1924–1925. Die Perspective als Symbolische Form. *Vortrage der Bibliothek Warburg.*

Penfield, W. 1958. Some mechanisms of consciousness discovered during electrical stimulation of the brain. *Proceedings of the National Academy of Science, 44,* 51–66.

Perky, C. W. 1910. An experimental study of imagination. *American Journal of Psychology, 21,* 422–452.

Piaget, J. 1969. *The mechanisms of perception.* Translated by G. Seagrim. London: Routledge and Kegan Paul.

Pirenne, M. H. 1970. *Optics, painting, and photography.* London: Cambridge University Press.

Polanyi, M. 1966. *The tacit dimension.* Garden City, N.Y.: Doubleday.

Purdy, J., and Gibson, E. J. 1955. Distance judgment by the method of fractionation. *Journal of Experimental Psychology, 50,* 374–380.

Randall, J. H. 1960. *Aristotle.* New York: Columbia University Press.

Ronchi, V. 1957. *Optics: The science of vision.* Translated by E. Rosen. New York: New York University Press.

Runeson, S. 1977. On visual perception of dynamic events. Doctoral dissertation, University of Uppsala, Department of Psychology.

Schiff, W. 1965. Perception of impending collision. *Psychological Monographs, 79,* No. 604.

Schiff, W.; Caviness, J. A.; and Gibson, J. J. 1962. Persistent fear responses in rhesus monkeys to the optical stimulus of "looming." *Science, 136*, 982–983.

Sedgwick, H. A. 1973. *The visible horizon.* Doctoral dissertation, Cornell University Library.

Senden, M. von. 1960. *Space and sight.* Translated by D. Heath. London: Methuen.

Shannon, C. E., and Weaver, W. 1949. *The mathematical theory of communication.* Urbana: University of Illinois Press.

Shaw, R., and Bransford, J. 1977. Psychological approaches to the problem of knowledge. In *Perceiving, acting, and knowing,* edited by R. Shaw and J. Bransford. Hillsdale, N.J.: Lawrence Erlbaum Associates.

Shaw, R., and McIntyre, M. 1974. Algoristic foundations to cognitive psychology. In *Cognition and the symbolic process,* edited by W. B. Weimer and D. S. Palermo. Hillside, N.J.: Lawrence Erlbaum Associates.

Shaw, R., and Pittinger, J. 1977. Perceiving the face of change in changing faces: Implications for a theory of object perception. In *Perceiving, acting, and knowing,* edited by R. Shaw and J. Bransford. Hillsdale, N.J.: Lawrence Erlbaum Associates.

Smith, K. U., and Bojar, S. 1938. The nature of optokinetic reactions in animals. *Psychological Bulletin, 35*, 193–219.

Stratton, G. M. 1897. Vision without inversion of the retinal image. *Psychological Review, 41*, 341–360, 463–481.

Titchener, E. B. 1924. *A textbook of psychology.* New York: Macmillan.

Turvey, M. T. 1974. Constructive theory, perceptual systems, and tacit knowledge. In *Cognition and the symbolic process,* edited by W. B. Weimer and D. S. Palermo. Hillsdale, N.J.: Lawrence Erlbaum Associates.

Turvey, M. T. 1977. Preliminaries to a theory of action with reference to vision. In *Perceiving, acting, and knowing,* edited by R. Shaw and J. Bransford. Hillsdale, N.J.: Lawrence Erlbaum Associates.

Walk, R. D., and Gibson, E. J. 1961. A comparative and analytical study of visual depth perception. *Psychological Monographs, 75*, No. 519.

Wallach, H., and O'Connell, D. N. 1953. The kinetic depth effect. *Journal of Experimental Psychology, 45*, 205–217.

Walls, G. L. 1942. *The vertebrate eye and its adaptive radiation.* Cranbrook Institute of Science.

Ware, W. R. 1900. *Modern perspective.* New York: Macmillan.

Warren, R. 1976. The perception of ego motion. *Journal of Experimental Psychology, Human Perception and Performance, 2*, 448–456.

Witkin, H. 1949. Perception of body position and the position of the visual field. *Psychological Monographs, 63*, No. 302.

NAME INDEX

Adams, D. K., 138
Ames, A., 166
Aristotle, 99
Arnheim, R., 273, 285
Arno, P., 296
Attneave, F., 150
Avant, L. L., 151

Barker, R. G., 3
Barrand, A., 214
Bauer, J. A., 225
Beck, J., 31, 159, 165, 168
Bergman, R., 161, 162, 165
Berkeley, Bishop G., 117, 232, 257, 286
Bojar, S., 186
Boring, E. G., 160
Bower, T. G. R., 195
Boynton, R., 270
Bransford, J., 305
Braunstein, M., 173
Brooks, V. F., 292
Brown, J. F., 138
Brunswik, E., 2, 3, 252

Caviness, J. A., 175, 231
Cohen, W., 151
Copernicus, N., 85, 96, 132
Cornsweet, J., 165, 166
Crabbé, G., 82, 191

da Vinci, *see* Vinci, Leonardo da
Democritus, 14, 99
Descartes, R., 3, 225, 290
Dibble, F., 151
Dodge, R., 209, 210

Eisenstein, S., 300, 301
Epstein, W., 116
Escher, M. C., 289
Euclid, 69, 70, 80

Fieandt, K. von, 178
Flock, H., 153, 166, 181
Freeman, R. B., 166

Garner, W. R., 150
Gibson, E. J., 142, 152, 153, 156, 157, 158,
    161, 162, 177, 178, 179, 224, 230, 247,
    252, 275, 305
Gibson, J. J., 153, 165, 175, 178, 179, 231
    (1929), 268
    (1947), 149, 160, 182, 184, 273
    (1950a), 100, 165
    (1950b), 1, 59, 112, 114, 116, 124, 125,
        139, 148–150, 159, 160, 162, 195, 206,
        207, 215, 220, 221, 248, 286
    (1951), 178
    (1952), 164, 186
    (1954), 270, 272, 273
    (1956), 282
    (1957), 105, 173, 175, 176
    (1958), 36, 132, 231
    (1959), 150
    (1960a), 56
    (1960b), 270
    (1961), 48
    (1966a), 254
    (1966b), 1, 9, 42, 53, 54, 60, 61, 82, 86, 97,
        115, 122, 126, 133, 135, 176, 183, 198,
        205, 211, 218, 226, 233, 234, 243–245,
        257, 270, 272, 275, 301
    (1968a), 14, 80, 107, 190, 193
    (1968b), 94, 170, 171
    (1970), 257
    (1971), 270
    (1973), 271
    (1974), 270
    (1975), 100
    (1976), 152
    and Cornsweet (1952), 165, 166

Gibson, J. J. (*cont.*)
  and Dibble (1951), 151
  and E. J. Gibson (1955), 252
  and E. J. Gibson (1957), 177, 178, 247
  with Kaplan, Reynolds and Wheeler (1969),
    78, 80, 82, 190, 194
  and Kaushall (1973), 97, 100, 191
  and Mowrer (1938), 186
  with Olum and Rosenblatt (1955), 122, 182,
    184, 273
  with Purdy and Lawrence (1955), 153–155
  and Waddell (1952), 151
Gombrich, E. H., 279, 281, 286
Goodman, N., 285
Green, B. F., 173

Harris, S., 84
Held, R., 225
Helmholtz, H. von, 161, 183, 206, 209, 251,
  286
Hochberg, J., 150, 159, 292
Hume, D., 110, 181, 250

Ittelson, W. H., 168

James, W., 240
Johansson, G., 174, 179

Kant, I., 3, 251
Kaplan, G. A., 78, 80, 82, 189, 190, 194
Kaushall, W., 97, 100, 191
Kennedy, J. M., 273, 290
Kepes, G., 285
Kepler, J., 58, 59, 61, 217
Koffka, K., 138, 139, 143, 168, 206
Kohler, I., 216
Köhler, W., 235

Land, E. H., 91
Lawrence, L., 153–155
Lee, D. N., 185, 305
Lewin, K., 138, 234
Lishman, R., 185, 305
Locke, J., 31, 256

Mace, W., 305
Mach, E., 112
McIntyre, M., 305
Marrow, A. J., 138
Metzger, W., 150, 151, 174
Michotte, A., 82, 110, 171, 181, 191, 192
Mill, J., 90

Montgomery, R., 298
Mowrer, O. H., 186
Müller, J., 115, 246
Musatti, C. L., 173

Neisser, U., 305
Newton, I., 15, 93, 100, 110

O'Connell, D. N., 174
Olum, P., 122, 182, 227, 228

Panofsky, E., 285
Parmenides, 99
Penfield, W., 256
Perky, C. W., 256
Piaget, J., 13, 195, 235
Pirenne, M. H., 284
Plato, 279
Polanyi, M., 22
Ptolemy, C., 69, 70, 80
Purdy, J., 153–155, 161, 162

Randall, J., 99
Reynolds, H. N., 78, 80, 82, 190, 194
Ronchi, V., 48
Rorschach, H., 282
Rosenblatt, F., 122, 182, 227, 228
Rubin, E., 81, 191
Runeson, S., 110, 181, 182
Ruskin, J., 286

Scherer, J., 77
Schiff, W., 104, 132, 175, 231
Sedgwick, H. A., 164
Senden, W. von, 285
Shakespeare, W., 106
Shannon, C., 242, 243
Shaw, R., 305
Sherrington, C., 115, 240
Smith, K. U., 186
Smith, O. W., 153, 181
Stratton, G. M., 62

Ternus, J., 248
Thinès, G., 82, 191
Titchener, E. B., 252, 256
Turvey, M. T., 305

Vinci, Leonardo da, 277
von Fieandt, *see* Fieandt, K. von
von Helmholtz, *see* Helmholtz, H. von
von Senden, *see* Senden, W. von

Waddell, D., 151
Walk, R. D., 142, 156–158, 230
Wallach, H., 174
Walls, G. L., 58, 11, 203
Ware, W. R., 284
Warren, R., 123, 305

Weaver, W., 242
Wertheimer, M., 174
Wheeler, K., 78, 80, 82, 190, 194
Wittgenstein, L., 134

Yonas, P., 275

SUBJECT INDEX

Accommodation, 148, 217, 251
Accretion of texture, 107–108
  defined, 83
  and head turning, 118–120
  and minification, 103
  in motion pictures, 293, 297–300
  and occluding edge experiments, 189–190
  See also Deletion; Occlusion
Affordance, 127–143
  concept introduced, 36
  and ecological niches, 128–130
  as a fact of the environment, 129
  as invariant combination of variables, 134–135, 139–140
  and nature of environment, 130
  as opposed to experiences, 137–140
  recent history of concept, 138–140
Affordances
  of a cliff, 157–158
  of enclosures (shelter), 29, 37–38
  of events, 102
  during evolution, 18–19
  of fire, 38
  of ground for terrestrial locomotion, 16, 36–37, 95, 127–128, 225–227
  man-made, 129–130
  misinformation for, 142–143
  misperception of, 37, 243–244
  and niches, 128–129
  of objects in general, 133–135
  of other animals in general, 41–42, 135–136
  perception of, 133–135, 140–143
  positive and negative, 137–138
  relativity of, 127–128
  specification of, 140–142
  of substances, 97–98, 131–138
  of surfaces, 131–132
  of terrain, 36
  of tools, 40–41
  of water, 38, 224

Ambient light
  and accommodation, 217
  defined, 16–19, 65
  and events, 102–111
  homogeneous, 54
  and illumination, 53–54
  importance of, 203
  information in, *see* Ambient optic array
  and perception of surfaces, 23–26, 29–30
  vs. radiant light, 50–51, 58–59 (fig.), 64
  structuring of, 51–52, 57–58, 66–69, 86–88, 102–103, 148, 168. *See also* Ambient optic array; Information, stimulus
  unstructured, 151, 153
Ambient optic array
  binocular disparity in, 114, 120, 148, 159
  binocular overlap in, 203–205
  boundaries in, 203–207
  and changing perspectives, 75–76, 122, 159, 182–184
  contrasts in, 153–156
  and ecological optics, 65–71
  flow of, in a landing glide, 125 (fig.), 182
  flow of, in locomotion, 123 (fig.), 124 (fig.), 227–229
  importance of movement for, 72–76, 79–84
  vs. retinal image, 62
  scintillation in, 108
  sliding sample of, 118–119 (fig.), 309
  structure of, 66, 68, 69 (fig.), 71 (fig.), 72 (fig.), 73–75, 86–91, 102–103, 106, 168
  and successive sampling, 221–222, 246–250
  See also Ecological optics; Information, stimulus; Sampling, successive
Angles
  intercept, 68–71
  solid, 68–70, 91, 308
  solid visual, 112, 161–162, 193, 204, 206–207, 212, 270, 297–298. *See also* Field of view

Art, modern, 268–270, 284–285, 290
Aufforderungscharakter, 138

Binocular disparity, 114, 120, 148, 159, 173,
  203–205, 213–214
Binocular overlap, 111, 120, 203–205, 309
Blind region, 204–208
Borders, as distinguished from lines, 35
Boundaries, in ambient optic array, 203–207
Brinks, 37

Camera metaphor for vision, 1–3, 54, 61, 176,
  210, 298
  and accommodation, 217
  and eye movements, 209–210
  fallacies of, 219–220
  homunculus, 60
  role of images in, 58–60
Causation, 171–172
  and events, 109–110
  perception of, 171, 181–182
Chirographic methods, *see* Drawing; Graphic
  act
Classical optics, 2, 4, 69–71, 161–163
  and camera metaphor for vision, 54
  distinguished from ecological optics, 47–52
Cognitive maps, 198–200
Collision of objects, 181–182
Colors
  changes in, 97–98, 107
  under changing illumination, 91
  as hues, 29
  modes of appearances of, 31
  surface, 29–30, 87
Communication, and information, 62–63
Concavities, 78
  defined, 35
  illumination of, 89
  and objects, 39
  and shelters, 37
  and slant, 166
  and water surfaces, 92
Constancy, size, 160–164, 311
Convergence, 148, 210, 213–214
Convexities, 78
  defined, 35
  illumination of, 89
  and objects, 39
  and occluding edge, 80
  and slant, 166
  and water surface, 92
Corner, defined, 35, 308

Deletion of texture, 107–108
  defined, 83
  and head turning, 118–120
  and magnification, 103
  and occluding edge, 189–190
  See also Accretion; Occlusion
Depth perception, 150
  and binocular vision, 203–205
  cues for, 147–148, 244, 285–286
  fallacy of, 203
  in Metzger's experiments, 151
  separation of surfaces in, 179–181
  and visual cliff, 157–158
  See also Layout
Differentiation, 252–253
Dihedrals
  defined, 35, 308
  in line drawings, 287
  and occluding edges, 158
  in perspective drawings, 277
  used in shelters, 37–38
Diplopia, 208, 257
Direct perception
  of affordances, 133–135, 140–143
  compared with mediated, 10, 42, 54, 147,
    166–168, 238–262
  of motion in the world, 170–182
  of movement of the self, 182–188
  of surface layout, 147–169
  theory of, 238–262
Disappearance
  and occlusion, 79–80, 192, 194
  studies, 13
Disk-and-slot apparatus, 171–172
Disparity, *see* Binocular disparity
Displays
  of animals, 98
  defined, 42
  pictorial, *see* Pictures
  of stimulus information, 153, 171–
    190
Distance perception, 117
  along ground plane, 160–164
Distinctive features, 150
Disturbance of optical structure, 72–80, 83,
    102–103, 107–109, 247
  defined, 309
  and events, 170
  and going out of existence, 194–195
  importance of concept, 170
  in relation to occlusion, 80–83
  See also Ambient optic array; Information,
    stimulus; Invariants

Dolly shot, 185, 297–298
Drawing
  contrasted to copying, 276–279
  in perspective, 286–287
  theory of its development, 274–283
  See also Graphic act; Pictures
Drawings, *see* Pictures
Dualism, 141, 225, 306. *See also* Mentalism;
  Mutuality principle

Ecological events, 10, 38, 66, 93–110
  affordances of, 102
  causation of, 109–110
  cycles of, 98
  main varieties of, 94–100
  nesting of, 101–102
  recurrence and nonrecurrence of, 101
  reversibility of, 97–98, 100–101
  See also Persistence and change;
    Transformations
Ecological information
  about animals, 41–42, 98
  controlled display of, 3
  about events, 102–110
  about humans, 42
  in light, 62–63
  in moving pictures, 292–295
  in pictures, 282–286
  about surface colors, 29–31, 97–98
  See also Information, stimulus; Invariants;
    Specificity
Ecological laws
  of horizons, 162–163
  of light, 48–52
  of surfaces, 22–31
  See also Mutuality principle; Nesting
    principle; Occlusion; Persistence and
    change
Ecological optics
  and ambient optic array, 65–66, 308
  and arrested optic array, 308
  of binocular vision, 114, 120, 148, 173,
    203–205, 213–214
  central concepts of, 65, 75
  concept of invariants in, 310–311
  contrasted to physiological optics, 52–58,
    62, 149, 209–211, 217–219
  of egolocomotion, 122–126, 204–208
  and eye movements, 211–216
  and field of view, 114
  and functions of the visual system, 218–219
  invariance and variance in, 75, 86–88, 162,
    308

of moving pictures, 292–299
and natural perspective, 69–71, 161–163
and optical flow, 123–125, 182–188, 227–229
of pictures, 271, 286–296
and pupillary adjustments, 217–218
term introduced, 47–48
Ecology
  and affordance concept, 140
  and behavior, 44
  concept of, 13–14. *See also* Affordance;
    Niche
  contrasted to physics, 8–9, 13–14, 16, 33,
    127–128, 147–148, 161–162
  importance for psychology, 7–15, 44, 140
  importance for study of vision, 2
Edge
  dangerous, 157, 230
  defined, 308
  depth at an, 158–159
  in line drawings, 287
  See also Occluding edge; Occlusion
Egocentrism, 201
Egolocomotion
  information for, 182–188
  perception of, 122–126, 204–205, 207–208
Enclosure
  and concavities and convexities, 35
  defined, 34
  and hollow objects, 34
Encounters
  of animals with objects, 36, 233
  and control of locomotion, 231–234
  See also Looming
Environment, natural
  affordances of, 130–138
  changes in, 10, 38, 66, 93–110
  clutter of, defined, 307
  contrasted to artificial environment, 130
  contrasted to physical environment, 8–9,
    33, 140
  defined, 7, 307
  man-made alterations of, 129–130
  open, 33
  perception of, 195–196
  as a surround, 43
  terrestrial, 9, 20–22, 85. *See also* Layout
  See also Affordances; Ecological events;
    Substances; Surfaces
Equivalent configurations, argument from,
  166–168
Events
  chemical, 98, 105, 107
  in environment, 10, 38, 66, 93–110

Events (*cont.*)
information for perceiving, 102–109, 294
mechanical, 95–96, 103–105
and moving objects, 84
perception of, 11, 100, 102–110, 242
terrestrial, 94–102, 107
and time, 100
trains of, 96, 100
virtual, 297
Evolution
of locomotion, 223–224
of manipulation, 223–224
of visual system, 2, 218–219
Exterospecific information, 75, 111. *See also*
  Propriospecific information
Eye movements
compensatory, 210–211, 215–216
and ecological optics, 211–216
and physiological optics, 208–209
recognized types of, 209–211

Fibers
affordances of, 133
defined, 35
in line drawings, 287
in perspective drawings, 277
Field of view
binocular, 203–205, 204 (fig.)
contrasted to visual field, 114
defined, 111
of humans, 112, 113 (fig.)
Figure-ground
and occlusion, 191, 230
and structuring of ambient light, 66, 103
Film, *see* Motion pictures
Fissures
defined, 34–35
in line drawings, 287
in perspective drawings, 277
Fixation
ecological view, 211–212
traditional view, 209–210
Flow perspective
and imminent contact, 231–232
and locomotion, 227–229, 228 (fig.)
Foreshortening, 107–108, 176–177
and rigidity, 178
Form
and connectedness, 179
and formless invariants, 178, 247
frozen, 268–269
in optic array, 68
perception of, 83–84

and pictures, 268
and traditional theories of perception, 147–
  148, 150, 159–160
and transformation, 74, 83
Form perception, 147–150, 159–160
and object perception, 83–84
and pictures, 268, 271
psychophysics of, 149-150
Fovea, 209, 211–212, 220
Fusion, binocular, 213–214

Ganzfeld, 151
distinguished from ambient light, 51–52,
  54, 151, 215
Geometry
of natural perspective, 70
of planes vs. surfaces, 33, 44
of surface layout, 33–36
See also Invariance; Transformation
Gliding room, experiments with, 185
Gradients
defined, 116
of optical texture, 117, 149, 160–162
and slant perception, 164–165
Graphic act, fundamental, 275–276. *See also*
  Drawing
Gravity
and ecological events, 93–94, 96
and head-tilt, 116
and the vertical, 164
Ground surface
as background in experiments, 159–164
defined, 33, 307
importance of, 16, 66–68, 67 (fig.)
structure of, 10, 22–31
and the vertical, 96
See also Layout; Surfaces

Hallucinations
compared to fictions, 261
tactile, 257–258
visual, 257–258
Hierarchical organization, 9, 22–23, 101–102.
  See also Nesting principle
Horizon, 106, 162–164, 272
and binocular vision, 120
compared with occluding edge, 85
defined, 84
in line drawings, 287
ratio relation, 164
and size information, 160–161
and surfaces, 132
Horopter, 214

Illumination
and ambient light, 53–54
and dark adaptation, 218
defined, 307
dependence of vision on, 55
diurnal changes in, 29–30, 87–89, 91
homogeneous, 51–54, 65, 151–153
vs. luminosity, 47–48
vs. radiation, 48–50
and structure of ambient optic array, 68–70, 86–88
of surfaces, 29–30
Illusions
and information, 243–244
and pictures, 280–283
Image, *see* Retinal image
Imagining, contrasted with perceiving, 256–258
Imminence of collision, 231–232
Information, in communication, 62–63, 242–243. *See also* Ecological information; Information, stimulus
Information pick-up
contrasted to classical theories, 239–250
and memory, 253–255
resonating, 249
term introduced, 147
theory of explicated, 221–222, 238–263
See also Direct perception; Sampling, successive
Information, stimulus
for continuation of surfaces, 83–84
contrasted to classical stimulus, 56–57, 149
for controlling locomotion, 225, 227, 231–234
for controlling manipulation, 234–235
defined, 52–54, 242–243, 307
for distance, 117, 148–149, 160–162
distinguished from cues, 71, 160–161
for event perception, 102–110
for motion, 171–182
in motion pictures, 292–302
movement produced, 72–76, 121–126, 227–234
for occlusion, 189–202
optical, *see* Ambient optic array
for perceiving affordances, 140–141
for persistence, 208–209
pick-up of, *see* Information pick-up; Sampling, successive
in pictures, 267–288
for self-perception, 111–126, 182–188, 223–234

sequential, 76. *See also* Sampling, successive
See also Ambient optic array; Deformation of optical structure; Ecological optics; Invariants; Transformations
Invariance
and affordances, 18–19, 138–140
and disruptions of optical structure, 83, 73–75, 107–109
and persistence and change, 13–14, 73–75
resolves problem of integration, 221–222
Invariants
and affordances, 134–135, 139–142
under changing illumination, 88–91, 310
under changing point of observation, 73–75, 89, 122, 123, 128, 310
compound, 141
concept of, in ecological optics, 310–311
formless, 168, 178, 247, 272, 294
under local disturbances, 311
mathematical concept of, 13
in motion pictures, 292–295, 298–301
in pictures, 269, 272–273, 276–284, 286–291
of ratios of ground texture, 160–162
under reversible transitions, 208–209
stimulus, *see* Information, stimulus
of structure in optic array, 73–75, 86–88
in successive samples of optic array, 311. *See also* Sampling, successive
of surface deformation, 24–25
See also Vision, ambulatory; Egolocomotion; Persistence and change; Transformation

Kinesthesis, 123
relation to optical flow, 125
See also Visual kinesthesis
Kinetic depth effect, 173–174
Johansson's explanation, 174
Wallach's explanation, 174
Knowledge
ecological approach to, 258–262
innate, 252–253
traditional sources of, 253

Layout
affordances of, 157–158
changes in, 35, 95–96, 170–182
defined, 307
of environment, 7–8, 12–13, 161–166
experiments on perception of, 147–169
illumination of, 88–89
theory of, 33–43

Light
  radiant vs. ambient, 50–51, 58–59 (fig.), 64
  reverberating, 48–50, 49 (fig.). *See also*
    Ambient light
  structured, *see* Ambient optic array
Line drawings
  invariants discoverable in, 287
  principles of, 287–290
Locomotion
  affordances for, 16, 36–37, 129
  as cause of motion perspective, 73–75, 91,
    186
  in cluttered environment, 192–193
  control of, 225–227, 231–234
  evolution of, 223–224
  guidance of, 122–124
  information for, 122–124, 227–232
  obstacles to, 36, 229–231
  openings for, 229–231
  perception of environment during,
    197
  role in vision, 2, 72–76, 89. *See also*
    Egolocomotion
  and sequential information, 75–76
  along slopes, 37
  specifying of, 121–126
  symmetricalizing in, 122–123
  terrestrial, 16, 36
  varieties of, 129
Looming, 103–104, 132, 231–232
  experiments on, 175–176
  See also Encounters; Time-to-collision

Magic
  and disappearance, 194
  and nonreversible events, 101
Magnification, 103, 107, 175
  experiments with, 175–176
  in limb movements, 121
  of nested optical structure, 108, 230–234
  and outflow, 227
  and shadow projection, 173 (fig.)
  See also Minification
Manipulation, 29, 39
  control of, 225–227, 234–235
  evolution of, 223–224
  and grasping, 133–134
  information for, 120–121, 234
  and perceiving interior surfaces, 236
Margin of safety, 39, 234
Margins
  distinguished from lines, 35
  between land and water, 38

Meanings
  of the environment, 33, 127, 140
  in motion pictures, 292–293, 298–300
  traditional theories of, 238
  See also Affordances
Mediated knowledge
  concept introduced, 42
  by depictions, 284–285
  by descriptions, 260–261
Mediated perception
  compared with direct perception, 10, 42,
    54, 147, 166–168, 238–262
  and mediated knowledge, 260–261
  and optical instruments, 259–261
Medium
  air as a, 13
  and ambient light, 2, 16–19, 29–30, 48–52
  contrasted to space, 33, 130–131
  defined, 16–19, 307
  and information for control of movement,
    226
  modification of, by people, 129–130
  and paths of locomotion, 43
Memory
  applied to sensory inputs, 252–253
  and construction of events, 221–222, 247
  and present experience, 253–255
  relation to perception, 189
  role in drawing, 278–279
Mentalism, 2, 43, 114, 116, 180, 221, 257,
    278
  critique of, 137–138, 158, 161–162, 225,
    235, 238, 251–252
Metzger's experiment, 150–152
Minification, 103, 107
  due to locomotion, 231–234
  experiments with, 175–176
  and inflow, 227
  and limb movements, 121
  and shadow projector, 173 (fig.)
  See also Magnification
Mirrors, 28
Misperception, *see* Illusions
Molar analysis, 21
Montage, theory of, 300–301
Motion
  apparatus for study of, 170–174
  of bodies, 35
  and causation, 109–110
  in modern art, 269
  of objects, 93–96
  orbital, 171
  perception of, 94, 102–110, 170–179

Motion (*cont.*)
rigid and elastic, 178–179
in still pictures, 294
See also Ecological events; Movement;
Transformation
Motion parallax, vs. motion perspective, 182–
184
Motion perspective, 122, 159, 182–184
and locomotion, 227–229
vs. motion parallax, 182–184
Motion pictures
defined, 292
depiction in, 301–302
as a progressive picture, 293–294
psychology of splicing, 299–300
theory of, 292–302
theory of filming and editing, 297–301
theory of montage, 300–301
types of content, 294–295
Movement
of animals, 41–42
of eyes, 209–217
of head, 117–118
importance of, in vision, 72–76
of limbs, 120–121, 234–235
perception of self, 122–126, 204–208
Movies, *see* Motion pictures
Mutuality principle, 9, 15, 21
in affordance theory, 127–128, 135
in objective motion and subjective
movement, 183, 203–207, 211

Nesting principle, 9, 11, 22–23, 28, 66
and ambient optic array, 68, 70, 217, 231
and clutter, 33, 132
and ecological niches, 128–129
and events, 101–102
and eye movements, 212
and line drawings, 288
and places, 34, 240–241
Niches, ecological
and affordance concept, 128–130
vs. phenomenal environment, 129
as ways of life, 7, 128–129
Nystagmus, 211, 213

Object permanence, 208–209
Objects
affordances of, 127–129, 133–135
attached, 24–25, 34, 39, 43, 78, 93, 133,
241, 307
classifications of, 134
colors of, 30–31

denumerability of, 34
detached, 24–25, 34, 39, 78, 93, 133, 193–
194, 241, 288, 307
environmental, 29, 66
invisibly supported, 159
limbs as, 120–121
motions of, 35, 94–102
as obstacles, 36, 229–231
perception of, 82–84, 208–209, 241. *See
also* Occlusion
specification of, 56, 83
and structuring of ambient light, 66–68, 74
as tools, 40
virtual, 172, 179, 283
Occluding edge
defined, 308
discovery and importance of, 189–202
Kaplan's experiments on, 189–190
and openings and obstacles, 229–231
and perception of the self's surrounds, 206–
207
in perspective drawing, 277, 286–290
Occlusion, 78–86
and coming into sight, 79–80, 83, 308
defined, 308
and disappearance, 14, 192
in ego perception, 116–126
of far side of an object, 83–84
and going out of sight, 79–80, 83, 308
and head turning, 194
and invisibly-supported-object experiment,
159
and limb movements, 120
and orientation, 198–199
principle of reversible, 76–77, 136, 191–
195, 198–199, 243–244
and public vs. private knowledge, 200–202
of self, 81–82, 205–207
terminology concerning, 192
Optical flow, *see* Flow perspective
Optics, *see* Classical optics; Ecological optics;
Perspective, natural; Physiological
optics
Optokinetic drum, 186
Orientation
to the environment, 198–200
of eyes, 209–216
to gravity, 21

Panning shot, 185
Path of observation
contrasted with point of, 66
importance of, 43, 75

Path of observation (cont.)
  locomotion along, 36, 72
  and orientation, 198–200
  and perception over time, 197
  and route of locomotion, 75–76, 225–227,
    232–234
Perception
  as active attention, 149–150
  of affordances, 133–135, 140–143
  of causality, 171–172, 180–181
  of colors, 29–31, 91, 97–98, 107
  definition of, 239–240
  of depth, see Depth perception
  direct vs. indirect, 10, 42, 54, 147–150,
    166–168, 238–250
  of distance, see Distance perception
  evolution of, 7–10
  of form, see Form perception
  and hallucination, 257–258, 261
  and imagination, 256–258
  importance of movement for, 43, 203–237
  information for, see Ecological information;
    Information, stimulus
  and knowledge, 253, 258–260
  of layout, see Layout
  mediated, see Mediated perception
  and memory, 253, 254
  of motion, 170–182
  new theory of, 238–250
  of occlusion, see Occlusion
  of other animals, 7, 41–42
  of places, 240–241
  psychophysics of, 149–150
  related to other forms of awareness, 255–
    260
  of self, 182–188, 204–208
  of size, 160–164
  of slant, 164–166, 176–178, 196
  of space, see Layout
  theories of, see Theories of perception
  visual, see Vision, ambient; Vision,
    ambulatory; Vision, aperture; Vision,
    snapshot; Visual system
Perceptual system, 244–246, 256–259
  contrasted with senses, 52–62, 149–239
  as a hierarchy of organs, 53
  and knowing, 258–260
  and nonperceptual awareness, 256–258
  theory of, 238–250
Persistence
  information for, 208–209, 249
  of substances, 241–242
  of vision, 292

Persistence and change, 170, 208–209
  atomic theory of, 14
  with changing illumination, 73–75, 86–
    88
  in chemical events, 98
  defined, 12–15
  in the environment, 94–96
  of layout, 35–36, 147–169
  registering of, 246–249
  of substances, 21, 98
  of surfaces, 22–32, 99–100
  theory of, 14, 98
  See also Ambient optic array; Invariants;
    Transformation
Perspective
  aerial, 148
  and ancient optics, 70
  artificial (Renaissance), 70–71, 148, 160,
    196–197, 277, 283–285
  motion, 122, 182–184. See also Locomotion;
    Motion parallax
  natural, 69–71, 175, 196–197, 283–284. See
    also Ecological optics
  patchwork vs. edge, 286–287
  seeing in, 286–287
  structure (vs. invariant structure),
    73–75
Physiological optics, 4
  contrasted to ecological optics, 52–58, 68,
    116, 149, 209–211, 217–219
  and ocular adjustments, 216, 218
Pictures
  chirographic (vs. photographic) method of
    making, 272–273
  definitions of, 270–274
  duality of perception for, 280–283
  for education, 273
  information in, 63, 267–288
  origin of, 42
  and perspective, 70–71, 148, 160, 277, 283–
    287
  progressive vs. arrested, 293–294. See also
    Motion pictures
  as records, 273–274
  as stimuli in experiments, 172–182
  in study of vision, 267–270
  and superposition, 289–290
Places
  affordances of, 136–137
  defined, 34
  in environment, 43
  hiding, 136–137, 201–202
  locomotion among, 36, 199–200, 225–234

Places (cont.)
   perception of, 240–241
   and points of observation, 65
Point of observation, 65, 111
   and ambient optic array, 72–76
   contrasted with station point, 66
   defined, 308
   and disparity, 114
   and the field of view, 112
   and hiding, 136
   and looming, 103–104
   mobility of, 66, 72, 121–122. See also
      Vision, ambulatory; Path of observation
   and natural perspective, 70
   occupied and unoccupied, 207–208
   outflow and inflow, 182
   stationary vs. moving, 43, 72–73, 75. See
      also Vision, ambient; Vision, ambula-
      tory
Primary and secondary qualities
   of color and shape, 97
   rejection of distinction, 31
Projection
   different meanings of the term, 279
   and drawing, 278–279
   parallel and polar, 172
   on a picture plane, 277
   as projective correspondence, 269
Proprioception
   ecological view vs. classical view, 115
   visual information for, 182–188, 203–208.
      See also Egolocomotion; Visual
      kinesthesis
Propriospecific information, 75, 111, 182–188,
   203–208. See also Exterospecific
   information
Pseudotunnel, 153–156
Public knowledge, 200
Pupil, adjustments of, 217–218
Pursuit movements
   classical view, 210
   ecological view, 213

Radiation
   distinguished from illumination, 48–50, 49
      (fig.)
Reflectance, 30–31
Reflection
   scatter, 87
   scatter vs. mirror, 49
Representation, 279–280
Retinal images
   and classical eye movements, 209–211

disparity of, 114, 117
fallacy of, 1, 3, 62, 116, 174, 182–183, 210–
   212
fusion of, 214
not necessary for vision, 61–62
orthodox theory of, 58–61
as pictures of objects, 268, 285–286
and retinal stimulation, 52–54, 218
and the upright world, 116
Reversibility, see Occlusion; Transition,
   reversible
Rivalry, binocular, 214
Rorschach test, 282–283
Rotating disk apparatus, 171

Saccades, 209–210, 212–213
Sampling, successive
   of ambient optic array, 111–112, 117–120,
      219–222, 311
   defined, 309
   by head movements, 117–120, 205–206
   in motion pictures, 297–298
Scanning of field of view, 211–213, 309. See
   also Saccades
Self-perception
   and blind region, 207–208
   and exteroception, 116
   and field of view, 111–115, 204–209
   and head turning, 117–120
   information for, 111–126
   role of the nose in, 117, 203–205
Sensations
   insufficiency of the concept, 186, 238–250,
      285
   James Mill on, 60
   and specific nerve energies, 115, 246
   and stimulation of receptors, 52–53
Senses, contrasted with perceptual systems,
   52–62, 219–222, 244–246
Shadow projection, 172–173
Shadows, moving, 29–30, 88–89
Shearing of texture, 104, 107–108, 171
Sheets
   affordances of, 133
   defined, 34
   in occluding edge experiment, 190
Simultaneous overlap, see Binocular overlap
Size perception, 160–164
Slant perception, 196
   experiments on, 164–166
   optical vs. geographical, 166
Social interaction, affordances for, 42

Space
  contrasted to layout, 74, 93–96, 100, 147–148, 161–162
  contrasted to medium, 17
  geometrical, 3
  in modern art, 269
  perception of, 147–150
Specification
  of affordances, 140–142, 232
  of events, 102–103, 108–109
  and information, 242–243
  of layout, 147–169
  of limb movements, 120–121, 234–235
  of locomotion, 121–126, 182–188, 225–234
  of self, 114–115, 121–126, 182–188, 203–208
Specific nerve energies, 115, 246
Station point
  for chirographic and photographic pictures, 272–273
  contrasted to point of observation, 66
Stereokinesis, 173–174
Sticks
  affordances of, 39–40, 133
  defined, 35
Stimulation
  actual vs. potential, 52–53
  as ambient energy, 57–59
  obtaining of, 243
  persisting, 248
  of receptors, 52–54
  vs. stimulus information, 52–54, 149
Stimulus
  in ecological psychology, 57–59
  meanings of the term, 55–58
  in physiology, 55–57
Stroboscope, 170
Structure
  of ambient light, 65–92. See also Ambient optic array
  invariant structure vs. perspective structure, 73–75
Substances, 19–22
  affordances of, 131–138
  change of composition of, 97–98
  classification of, 99
  compositions of, 19–20
  defined, 307
  nondenumerability of, 34, 241
  persisting, 241–242
  properties of, 20
Substratum, 96
  experiments on, 156–159
  See also Ground; Surfaces, of support

Superposition, 82–83, 148, 191
Surfaces
  affordances of, 31–32, 127, 131–133
  contrasted to planes, 33
  defined, 307
  distant, 84–85
  distinguished perceptually from nothing, 150–156, 224
  ecological laws of, 22–32
  faces of, 28–29, 78–79, 81, 83
  going out of and coming into existence of, 99, 106–107
  hidden and unhidden, 76–78
  information for continuation of, 83–84
  projected and unprojected, 78–79, 81, 91
  of support, 127, 156–159
  viewed now from here, 195–197
  waxing and waning of, 99–100
Swinging room, 185

Tacit knowledge, 22, 260–261
Texture, of surface, 25–28, 86–88, 91
  change in, 97–98
  forms of, 26–28
  pigment and layout distinguished, 25, 86–88
  and structuring of ambient light, 51–58, 86–88
Texture, optical, 28
  amount in a solid visual angle, 161–162
  in egolocomotion, 122–124, 227–234
  gradient of density of, 164–166
  invariants of, 161–163
  kinetic disruption of, 179, 181, 189–190
  preservation of adjacent order of, 181
  See also Disturbance of optical structure; Flow perspective; Transformation
Theories of perception
  ancient, 69–70
  ecological, contrasted to others, 1–7, 237–260
  ground vs. air, 148
  homunculus in, 60
  and problem of direct perception, 147–149
  role of affordance concept in, 138–140
  sensation-based, 54, 57, 61, 83, 115, 147, 189, 201, 285
  stimulus-sequence, 221–222, 246–248
Time, contrasted to events, 100–101
Time-to-collision, experiments on, 175–176.
  See also Imminence of collision

Tools
    affordances of, 133–134
    as special kind of detached objects, 40
Topology, 25
Transformation
    in animal movement, 41–42, 73–75
    of the array during locomotion, 121–126
    compared to transition, 190
    concept of, 13
    experiments with progressive, 176–178
    and form, 74
    and invariants, 13
    rigid and nonrigid, 95, 178–179
    sequential, 150
    of surfaces (deformations), 23–25, 95
    topological, 108
    See also Persistence and change
Transition
    in occluding edge experiments, 190
    reversible, 190, 208–209
Tunnel effect, 82, 191

Unconscious inference, 251

Valences, 138–140, 234
Vanishing point, 163, 192, 277
Vectors, 138–140
Vertigo, 211
Vision, ambient, 2, 194, 203–222, 303
    and the ambient array, 116–120
    compared to aperture and snapshot vision,
        205–206, 219–220
    defined, 1
    and head movements, 203–205
    and motion pictures, 297–299
Vision, ambulatory, 2, 72–76, 121–126, 193–
    194, 197, 223–234, 303
    defined, 1
Vision, aperture, 3, 112, 114–115, 159, 166–
    168, 195–197, 303

compared to ambient vision, 205–206
    and pictures, 281, 286
Vision, snapshot, 3, 195–197, 219–220, 247
    compared to ambient vision, 205–206
    defined, 1
Vistas, 132–134, 195–196, 198–200, 230, 295
Visual cliff, 121, 142, 224, 230
    experiments, 156–158
Visual field
    compared to a picture, 285–286
    and cues for depth, 147–148
    vs. field of view, 114
    and surfaces viewed now from here, 196–
        197
    vs. visual world, 206
Visualizing, 10, 256, 260, 282
Visual kinesthesis, 125–126, 182–188, 203–
        208, 220
    and control of locomotion, 225–227, 231–
        234
    and control of manipulation, 225–227, 234–
        235
    vs. visual feedback, 184
    See also Propriocepton; Propriospecific
        information
Visual system
    adjustments of, 8–10, 205–219, 225–227
    binocular, 111, 114, 120, 203–205, 213–214
    contrasted to visual sense, 52–62, 115–120,
        237–250
    functions of, 7–10, 115–120, 203, 205, 218–
        219, 225–235
    and haptic system, 233
    role of locomotion in, 223–234
    role of manipulation in, 234–235
Visual world, 148
    and ambient vision, 195–196
    vs. visual field, 114, 206–209, 271–272

Water, affordance of, 38